THE OBJECT CONCEPT

THE PWS SERIES IN COMPUTER SCIENCE

THE OBJECT CONCEPT

An Introduction to Computer Programming Using C++

RICK DECKER
STUART HIRSHFIELD
Hamilton College

PWS Publishing Company

I⟨T⟩P   **International Thomson Publishing Company**

Boston • Albany • Bonn • Cincinnati • Detroit • London • Madrid
Melbourne • Mexico City • New York • Paris • San Francisco
Singapore • Tokyo • Toronto • Washington

PWS PUBLISHING COMPANY
20 Park Plaza, Boston, Massachusetts 02116-4324

I ⓉP™   International Thomson Publishing
         The trademark ITP is used under license.

For more information, contact:

PWS Publishing Co.
20 Park Plaza
Boston, MA 02116

Nelson Canada
1120 Birchmount Road
Scarborough, Ontario
Canada M1K 5G4

International Thomson Publishing GmbH
Königswinterer Strasse 418
53227 Bonn, Germany

International Thomson Publishing Europe
Berkshire House I68–I73
High Holborn
London WC1V 7AA   England

Thomas Nelson Australia
102 Dodds Street
South Melbourne, 3205
Victoria, Australia

International Thomson Publishing Asia
221 Henderson Road
#05–10 Henderson Building
Singapore 0315

International Thomson Publishing Japan
Hirakawacho Kyowa Building, 31
2-2-1 Hirakawacho
Chiyoda-ku, Tokyo 102
Japan

International Thomson Editores
Campos Eliseos 385, Piso 7
Col. Polanco
11560 Mexico D.F., Mexico

Library of Congress Cataloging-in-Publication Data
Decker, Rick.
   The object concept : an introduction to computer programming using C++/Rick Decker, Stuart Hirshfield
      p. cm.
   Includes index.
   ISBN 0-534-20496-1
   1. C++ (Computer program language)   2. Object-oriented program-ming (Computer science)   I. Hirshfield, Stuart.   II. Title.
QA76.73.C153D43   1995   94-41156
005.13'3—dc20   CIP

This book is printed on recycled, acid-free paper.

Sponsoring Editor: Michael J. Sugarman
Developmental Editor: Mary Thomas
Production Editor: Abigail M. Heim
Marketing Manager: Nathan Wilbur
Manufacturing Coordinator: Lisa Flanagan
Editorial Assistant: Benjamin Steinberg

Interior Designer: Catherine Hawkes Design
Cover Designer: Julia Gecha
Cover Artist: Angela Perkins
Typesetter and Interior Illustrator: Pure Imaging
Cover Printer: New England Book Components
Text Printer and Binder: Quebecor Printing/Martinsburg

Cover Image: The TINKERTOY® product © 1993 by Playskool, Inc., a division of Hasbro, Inc. All rights reserved. Used with permission.

Printed and bound in the United States of America.
95 96 97 98 99—10 9 8 7 6 5 4 3 2

For Barb and Joanne

CONTENTS

PREFACE

Motivation

Our dual goals in developing this text/lab package were (1) to render the concepts of object-oriented programming accessible and useful to novice programmers and (2) to do so in a manner that was coherent and meaningful to those of us who would be asked to teach these concepts. As such, the package can be viewed as representing a departure from traditional introduction to programming texts. We don't see it that way. Rather, it appears to us to be an evolutionary approach that applies common sense, established pedagogical techniques, and current software technology to the problems of teaching undergraduates to solve problems with computers. Further, it does so in a way that builds on all of our collective experience teaching programming.

Our own experience in recent years has been increasingly frustrating. Despite our best efforts (teaching Pascal; using highly interactive and supportive programming environments; incorporating hands-on laboratory experiences; providing students with interesting and complete sample programs to read, analyze, and experiment with; and so on), all but our very best students appeared to us to lack what are currently regarded as basic software engineering skills. That is, of those students who produce working programs, relatively few write programs that can be considered modular, readable, testable, and maintainable. Still fewer are capable—even after a typical CS1 course—of analyzing, specifying, designing, and managing even modest-sized programs of their own. Rhetoric and current programming texts notwithstanding, our students were not being trained as problem solvers and were not developing skills that we regarded as essential to both their subsequent course work and to their careers. Our frustration has led us to reconsider what and how we are teaching novice programmers.

Object-Oriented Programming in CS1

This package reflects the position that the object-oriented paradigm is the one best suited for teaching introductory programming. Philosophically, this approach is justified by our feeling that the real value of the paradigm (and its significance to computer science education) is that it effectively raises the level of abstraction for all programmers, novices included. Who, after all, stands to benefit more from a higher-level programming interface than do novices?

From the more practical standpoint of course content, the decision to teach object-oriented programming (OOP) in CS1 is justified on the grounds that it extends the familiar procedural paradigm to effectively address all of the aforementioned frustrations. Generally speaking, OOP emphasizes a strategic, problem-solving approach to programming. Such an approach, in which design decisions are not only paramount, but are also clearly reflected in the resulting code, brings us a step closer to the idealized program development life cycle that most of us have been advocating for some years now. Indeed, OOP supports directly many of the software engineering concepts that are among the most difficult to convey in procedural terms: code reuse, encapsulation, incremental development and testing, and, of course, program design.

Our Approach

Programming texts have for many years been organized around the fundamental syntactic and semantic constructs supported by the language being taught. In the most recent past, these constructs were primarily procedural. As subprograms, for example, came to be regarded as important to effective programming, they were increasingly emphasized and, in many cases, moved to earlier chapters in texts. Data types and data abstraction were introduced as needed to support the development of more ambitious algorithms. We have applied similar thinking to teaching object-oriented programming. We have identified the fundamental, empowering constructs of the paradigm—those that support most directly the identification, creation, and use of high-level classes—and pushed them to the fore, essentially reversing the order of presentation of what are otherwise conventional CS1 topics. Algorithmic constructs are introduced in this context as a means to support class implementations.

What is distinctive about this approach is the fact that we do more than acknowledge the object-oriented paradigm—we embrace it. We focus from the outset on the object-oriented features of C++; that is, how classes are declared, defined, used, and organized into coherent designs. In the first part of the course, we concentrate on using classes as the basis for program specification and design. Then, in the second part of the course, the predefined types of C++ are described in object-oriented terminology; that is, as related combinations of data, operators, and functions. The basic concepts of inheritance, construction, access control, and overloading are described in the third section. Thus, students are provided with both a framework and the building blocks with which they can define classes of their own, the primary activity of the final part of the course. Throughout the course, full-blown sample programs are used both to illustrate specific OOP and C++ features, and to allow students to interact with classes on a variety of levels.

The advantages of this approach to teaching novices are both numerous and tangible. First, introducing the object-oriented paradigm from the beginning allows us to exploit it as a design medium. Second, doing so puts the procedural paradigm (along with the ideas of top-down design and stepwise refinement) into a meaningful and useful problem-solving context. Third, it eliminates (at least, for the student!) the dreaded "paradigm shift" from procedural programming to object-oriented programming. Finally, and most important, it helps students to develop their problem-solving skills in conjunction with their programming skills.

Why C++?

A simplistic—and not totally irreverent—answer to the question of why we chose to write the book around C++ is "Why not?" If what we are hearing from industry and our students and what we are seeing at conferences is indicative, C is being replaced by its natural superset, C++, in the "real world." Truth be told, the pressure to teach C++ in the interest of better preparing our students for employment was, for us, a great reason *not* to use it as the language for this text. We succumbed—and have subsequently become converted—for a number of other reasons.

▶ First and foremost, C++ matches our interpretation of object-oriented programming. That is, just as the object-oriented paradigm extends the procedural one to incorporate user-defined classes, C++ is advertised as an extension of modern procedural languages with the features necessary to support classes.

▶ The fact that C++ is a hybrid language (not necessarily "purely" object-oriented) is also an advantage because it allows our (and some of our students') experience with algorithms and top-down design to come more directly into play than it might have had we chosen a "pure" OOP language.

▶ Most implementations of C++ support all of the modern software engineering concepts (for example, separately compilable files, incremental development and testing, and reusable code libraries) that we want students to take advantage of early in their programming experience.

▶ Although most of the reasons we had for adopting Pascal (over C) as the language for teaching CS1 some years ago still hold, C++ succeeds in overcoming most of what we regarded as the awkwardnesses of C (by, for example, providing reference parameters and loosening its dependence on the preprocessor). In short, we regard C++ as much more than "a better C." Based on its strengths as a design tool and its support of the entire software engineering life cycle, we consider it a better Pascal and thus an excellent choice for teaching CS1.

Pedagogy

Our approach to teaching CS1 has clearly changed, but the basic content and the goals of the course have not. It should not be surprising, then, that two of the pedagogical techniques that have proven most useful in teaching introductory programming have been adapted to the task of teaching object-oriented programming. First, our course is lab based. We provide students with detailed, directed, experimental laboratory exercises that help them explore firsthand the principles of OOP in a controlled fashion. Quoting from the preface of our (similarly lab-based) text, *Pascal's Triangle*, "These exercises are integrated precisely with the textual material and serve to bring the static text material to life. We've used a lab-based approach at our school for ten years for one main reason—it works."

In addition, each lab/chapter pair is based on a complete, working, motivating, and interesting sample program (a Program in Progress, or "PIP") written to illustrate particular language and OOP features and to provide a vehicle for experimentation in lab. Students are introduced to new concepts in the text. In the process of reading the text, students *read* the chapter's PIP, which is used to illustrate the new concepts. Then, in the laboratory they *use* the PIP they have read, *experiment* with it, and *extend* it using what they have learned from the text. With the exception of Chapter 1 (in which the students type in the PIP to gain practice with editing programs in their environment), all the PIPs are provided on the lab disk that accompanies the text.

The Details

Much about the organization of this package will look familiar to you. There are eleven chapters, each with a corresponding lab, roughly one for each week to fit a traditional semester once exams and review classes are figured in. We cover all of the traditional CS1 programming topics (admittedly, in an unconventional order) and wind up with presentations of algorithms and abstract data types—right where we want to be for CS2.

Conceptually, we have divided the text into four sections. The first section is devoted to providing students with the vocabulary and methodology needed to describe problems in object-oriented (or, more accurately, "class-oriented") terms. **Chapter 1**, "Designing with Classes," describes briefly the evolution of and motivation for the object-oriented paradigm and provides some real-world examples of hierarchical systems. Next, we introduce the topic of program design and demonstrate how classes can effectively serve as a means for high-level program description. Finally, we introduce a simple method and notation, which we have dubbed the "Declare-Define-Use" approach, for relating program descriptions and C++ code. This early concentration on "description" helps students to focus on problem analysis and design without worrying about the details of implementation (which is particularly easy since students haven't seen C++ yet!). To be sure, we don't expect them to appreciate the coding details of the PIP for Chapter 1. On the other hand, the program (a stop-watch simulation) is conceptually simple enough that it can be read and used as we intended: to illustrate the correspondence between an object-oriented description of a problem and its more formal representation in C++.

Chapters 2 through 6 comprise the second section of the text. Collectively, these chapters describe the basic data types of C++ in formal, class-oriented terms. The goals are to convince students that class description is the fundamental activity of C++ programming and to establish both a problem-solving framework and a C++ vocabulary with which they can come to define their own classes. "The Ingredients of Classes," that is, primitive data types, operators, and simple functions, are introduced in **Chapter 2**. The Chapter 2 PIP is a fraction package that references both a standard and a user-defined library to illustrate the basic structure and organization of a C++ program.

Chapters 3 and 4 describe the basic algorithm control structures of C++ in the context of defining member functions. The PIPs for these chapters combine to form a single program that simulates a soda machine. The design and implementation of the machine itself, along with the C++ repertoire of selection statements, are presented in **Chapter 3**. The classes that support a general, menu-based interface are developed with the help of C++ repetition statements in **Chapter 4**. In both chapters, we emphasize how control structures fit into an object-oriented paradigm. Rather than being used as a basis for making high-level design decisions, they serve to express algorithmic details in a top-down fashion within the context of an object-oriented design.

Chapter 5, entitled "Compound Data," presents the composite classes of C++, including arrays, structures, and enumerations. Again, these concepts are rendered somewhat less intimidating by virtue of the fact that students are already familiar with the C++ notation for describing classes, a natural extension of structures. The PIP for this chapter, a card-playing program, demonstrates both the access operators for the composite classes and the language control structures that facilitate their use.

We discuss the topics of pointers and references in **Chapter 6**, each being described as a derived class. The dereferencing and address operators are illustrated, as are the allocation and deallocation functions . Arrays and strings are also described in pointer-based terminology. In presenting these topics, we concentrate exclusively on the notions of indirection and notation, leaving for

Chapter 11 the more complex uses of pointers in abstract data types. The chapter's PIP is a simple phone directory that makes use of dynamic allocation.

The third major section of the text spans Chapters 7–9 and describes user-defined classes in much the same way as the built-in classes of C++ are described in section two. The obvious difference is that in this section we have the pre-defined classes to work with, thus enabling us to define higher-level classes that reflect the real-world applications they are intended to model. As you would expect, these chapters tend to emphasize the more purely "object-oriented" features of C++.

Chapter 7, for example, is entitled "Process I: Organizing and Controlling Classes," and its PIP is an elevator simulation. The C++ mechanisms for controlling access to member data and functions (private, public, and friends) are described, as is its means for enforcing type-safe linkage. The reference to "process" in the chapter's title is not to be taken lightly. This is the first of two chapters (the other being Chapter 9) that is devoted primarily to the process of programming. This chapter focuses on program design and develops more fully our DDU approach and its relation to C++.

Class inheritance is the topic of **Chapter 8**. We illustrate, through a payroll program PIP, how one derives classes from others. This, in turn, motivates a discussion of how to further control access to member functions and data via protected and static descriptors, as well as a more thorough treatment of class (in particular, base class) constructors. The topics of heterogeneous lists and polymorphism also are introduced, as our PIP prints paychecks for a variety of employee types.

Chapter 9, "Process II: Working with Classes," reconsiders the program development process in light of the C++ experience students have now had. As such, the chapter serves as a recap of the first three sections of the text and as a natural concluding point for many traditional CS1 syllabi. The intention is to show how the DDU approach can be used with C++ to not only design and code programs, but also to test, debug, and maintain programs. The program in this case is a simple word processor that uses the standard stream and string libraries along with our own extended string package.

The theme of the fourth and final section is defining general classes (for example, our string library from Chapter 9) that support the description and implementation of application-oriented classes. This leads to natural discussions of algorithm analysis (as illustrated by a collection of functions that implement searching and sorting techniques in **Chapter 10**) and finally to abstract data types in **Chapter 11**. The final PIP introduces the topic of generic types in the context of a linked list package.

As with most texts, this one can be used in a variety of ways to accommodate your goals for CS1 and your academic calendar. At Hamilton, with our 13-week semester, we cover Chapters 1 through 9 in order, using about one or two weeks per chapter. We spend slightly more time on Chapters 2 and 3 (to make sure that students are comfortable with the basic data types and algorithm control structures) and Chapter 9 (to emphasize solid program development skills), and devote whatever time remains to in-class exams and to covering either Chapter 10 or 11.

SUPPLEMENTARY MATERIAL   In addition to the data disk (IBM PC compatible) included with this book, and the accompanying *Lab Manual*, an *Instructor's Manual* is available from the publisher. A Macintosh version of the data disk is also available from the publisher.

Peroration

So there you are—you hold in your hands the makings of a one-semester introduction to programming course suitable for use in CS1. It applies established pedagogical techniques to the task of teaching high-level problem -solving skills to novice programmers. It illustrates clearly via meaningful examples the utility and power of the object-oriented paradigm and encourages students to work like professional programmers right from the start of their programming careers. Finally, it does so in a way that supports the way most of us have been teaching introductory programming for many years, and it fits naturally with a standard computer science curriculum.

While this project was in many ways our creation, it would not exist in its present form were it not for the contributions of many talented and dedicated people. Our thanks go out, in parallel, to the following people for their insightful reviews:

Owen Astrachan
Duke University

Frank Kelbe

Tom Bullock
University of Florida

Soheil Khajenoori
University of Central Florida

Mark Ciampa
*Volunteer State Community
College*

Stephen P. Leach
*Florida State
University*

George Converse
*Southern Oregon State
College*

John A. N. Lee
*Virginia Polytechnic Institute and
State University*

Charles Dierbach
Towson State University

Daniel Ling
Okanagan University College

Linda Elliott
La Salle University

Robert Lipton
*Pennsylvania State University,
Schuylkill*

Bruce Mabis
University of Southern Indiana

Nathaniel G. Martin
University of Rochester

Robert Noonan
College of William & Mary

Martin Osborne
Western Washington University

Frank Paiano
*Southwestern Community
College*

Rich Pattis
University of Washington

Jim Slack
Mankato State University

John Stoneback
Moravian College

David B. Teague
Western Carolina University

Christian Vogeli
Grand Valley State University

Raymond F. Wisman
*Indiana University,
Southeast*

Lynn R. Ziegler
St. John's University

Special thanks, also, to Mike Sugarman, Susan McCulley, Abby Heim, Frank Ruggirello, and Tammy Goldfeld, each of whom influenced the final product (and, in some cases, the authors) in some significant and positive way. Now, let's get on with it.

Rick Decker
Stuart Hirshfield

THE OBJECT CONCEPT

1

DESIGNING WITH CLASSES

The person with a reputation as an early riser can sleep late.

This chapter will put what we're about to do in a historical context and introduce you to the object-oriented way of thinking about programs. Object-oriented programming, the subject of this book, is a collection of ideas that form the basis of the design of an increasing number of programming languages. This collection of ideas—this paradigm, if you will—is by no means the only way to approach problem solving with computers. Indeed, you'll see that the object-oriented approach to programming and design is just the latest in an ongoing series of attempts to make the programming process easier, more reliable, and more efficient.

OBJECTIVES

In this chapter, we will

▶ Define computers as general-purpose information processors.

▶ Describe how computers store information and manipulate that information.

▶ Discuss the evolution and nature of object-oriented programming.

▶ Describe, through examples, our Declare-Define-Use approach to designing a program in C++.

1.1   COMPUTERS, PROGRAMS, AND PEOPLE

Generally speaking, anything we would regard as a machine—for example, a toaster, a bulldozer, or a radio—is designed to produce some sort of physical change. The toaster heats bread and bagels, drying them out and caramelizing the sugar they contain to produce the desired brown color and crispy texture we value so much in the morning. The bulldozer changes its own position and the position of pretty much anything in its path; and the radio's ultimate purpose is to vibrate the air in its immediate vicinity in such a way that we can hear the latest weather report, for instance.

Another common feature of these and most other machines is a certain singleness of purpose. One could use a toaster as a murder weapon, dropping it in a bathtub while the victim was bathing; one could use the bulldozer as a paperweight; and it's possible to use a radio as a hammer (though such a use would almost certainly void the radio's warranty). All of these uses, and many more, are possible, but we all would agree that they fall far outside the intended purposes of these machines.

We'd like to argue that the computer is different from almost all other machines in both of these respects. Although a computer does produce physical changes, these changes are in a sense incidental to its purpose. A computer also has a single function, but that function, as we'll see, is sufficiently abstract that it makes the computer fundamentally different from its mechanical cousins. We'll make our argument by taking the point of view that the computer is a *general-purpose information processing device*. In this view, a computer is capable of representing and storing a wide range of information and can apply a sequence of instructions in such a way as to accept new information from the user, modify and act on its stored information, and present its stored information to its user in some meaningful form.

In order to describe a computer in terms of these primitive functional capabilities, we must resort to a level of detail that is mostly hidden from programmers today. If and when you take a course devoted specifically to computer organization and hardware, these details will take on increased importance. In this book, which concentrates on software and programming, the following section constitutes background material that should provide you with both a perspective on and an appreciation of high-level programming languages such as C++.

Computers

To be sure, the information stored in a computer is represented physically. In modern computers, information is represented by electric potential — the presence or absence of a voltage across a transistor. At the level of abstraction that we're concerned with, the nature of a transistor is unimportant — all that really matters is that each piece of the hardware of the computer can be in one of two *states* — on or off, one or zero, black or white, or whatever other two-value terms you prefer.

A little thought should convince you that these two states are sufficient to represent many, if not most, of the information we would be interested in representing. For example, if we wanted our computer to represent character information, like the letters you're reading, all we would have to do is adopt a *binary* (two-value) code for characters. The ASCII code (American Standard Code for Information Interchange), in which the letter 'A' is coded as 01000001, 'B' is coded as 01000010, and other letters are given similar sequences of eight binary digits, is an example of such a character code.

Binary: having two possible values. For our purposes, we'll call the values 0 and 1, although we could equally use "white" and "black," or "false" and "true."

We could perform a similar binary encoding of integers if we wished: We could represent 0 as 0, 1 as 1, 2 as 10, 3 as 11, 4 as 100, and continue the pattern with the binary representations 101, 110, 111, 1000, 1001, 1010, 1011, 1100, 1101, 1110, 1111, and so on. This binary representation is very much like the decimal representation we are familiar with, except that each digit represents a power of two rather than ten. The first few powers of two are 1, 2, 4, 8, 16, 32, . . . , so the binary number 1101 would represent $1 \times 8 + 1 \times 4 + 0 \times 2 + 1 \times 1$, or the number we would represent in decimal as 13.

We don't have to limit ourselves to "simple" information such as integers or characters. If we want our computer to process pictorial information, we could decide to represent each black dot by 1 and each white dot by 0, so the picture in Figure 1.1 could be stored as a long string of bits representing its white and black dots.

Bit: binary digit; 0 or 1.

The point is that we can store all sorts of information in the computer. All the computer designers have to do is decide on a suitable binary code for the information we want to represent. Being able to represent information is a useful trick, but by itself representation of information in a machine is just a moderately amusing use of technology. We've had machines that store information for thousands of years. A book like this, after all, is just such a device, capable of storing characters, numbers, pictures, and so on in its patterns of ink and plain paper.

FIGURE 1.1
A picture is worth at least 187 bits.

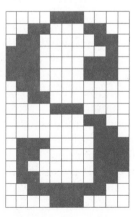

0000111000000011000110001100000110111000000010111
0000011011100001110011000000000001100000000000011
100000000000011000000000001100111000011101100001
11010000001110110000011000111111110000001110000

The real power of a computer comes from the fact that it also can store other kinds of information, namely a list of instructions that tell it how to manipulate its stored information. Each computer comes with a built-in collection of instructions it is capable of performing. These instructions can move information from one storage location to another, modify its information, and take action depending on the values of its information. A sequence of these commands is what we call a *program*. It is the ability of a computer to execute a stored program, thereby modifying and manipulating its information, that sets it apart from all other machines.

Programs

To get a computer to act as a general-purpose information processor, we must provide it with a list of instructions that it can execute to process its information. In short, we have to write a *program* for the computer to execute.

A program is a list of instructions for a computer to execute.

At the most fundamental level, any computer can act only on instructions of a very special form. These instructions make things easy for the computer that has to execute them and, at the same time, difficult for the people who have to write them. Much of the history of computer science can be viewed as a coming to terms with this fundamental dichotomy: The things that are easiest for computers are the same things that are hardest for people (and vice versa, for that matter). We'll see that the development of computer science has as one of its major themes the increasing elevation of abstraction, away from details dictated by the way the computer is designed and toward higher-level points of view that are more appropriate for human problem solvers. In particular, we'll see how computer languages were developed to make the programmer's job easier, by moving the focus of problem solving away from the computer and toward the problem itself.

In the early days of the development of the computer, the only way to write programs was in *machine language*, the language dictated by the nature of the computer's hardware. Machine language is, like the rest of the information the computer deals with, represented by a collection of binary codes. For example, a computer might have its storage arranged as a collection of locations, each of which is capable of storing 16 bits (binary digits). These locations — the *memory* of the computer — are each assigned a unique numeric address. In our hypothetical computer, illustrated in Figure 1.2, there might be 4096 such locations, with addresses from 0 to 4095,* along with another

---

* Computer scientists tend to count from zero, rather than 1. We chose 4096 locations because 4096 is a power of 2, so in binary the addresses would range from 000000000000 (binary 0) to 111111111111 (binary 4095).

FIGURE 1.2
A (highly simplified)
example computer

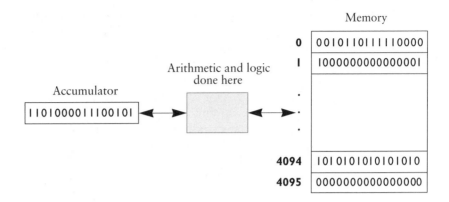

location, the *accumulator.* where 16 bits can be stored. We can think of the accumulator as a scratch pad for holding a temporary result. Some of the machine language instructions for our hypothetical computer might include

Load X, which makes a copy of whatever is in memory location X and loads that copy into the accumulator, replacing anything that was previously stored there.

Store X, which acts in the reverse direction from Load, copying whatever is in the accumulator into the memory cell with address X.

Add X, which acts like Load, except that it adds the contents of memory cell X to whatever is in the accumulator, again replacing the previous contents of the accumulator with the new sum.

These instructions would have binary codes, which for our computer might be four bits long.* For instance, Load might have code 0000, Store might have code 0001, and Add might have code 1000 (there's no magic in the choice of these codes — any distinct groups of four bits would suffice). If we then wanted to write a program that added the contents of memory locations 12 and 13 and placed the result in memory location 20, we would have to write the following code. In these machine language instructions each operation code is followed by the binary code for the location being acted on:

0000 000000001100   *Load the accumulator with whatever is in cell 12.*
                     (0000 is the code for Load, 000000001100 is 12 in binary.)
1000 000000001101   *Add the contents of cell 13 to the accumulator.*
                     (The accumulator now has the sum of the values of cells
                     12 and 13.)
0001 000000010100   *Store the result in cell 20.* (Now both the accumulator and
                     cell 20 have the sum.)

---

* With 4-bit *op codes* (short for "operation codes"), what is the largest number of different instructions our computer could have?

It doesn't take any imagination to see that programming in machine language would be a horribly tedious task. It's bad enough even in this simple example and would be truly daunting for a typical machine language program containing thousands of instructions. Programs must be written by people, and people are ill equipped to deal with problems like this, however efficient machine language is for computers.

On top of the difficulty of writing the program, there's the added problem that machine language practically invites errors that are exceedingly difficult to track down. If, for example, we made a simple typing mistake in the third line of our example and wrote 0000000000010010, the calculated sum would be stored in memory cell 18. Any subsequent reference to cell 20, where we expected the sum to reside, would refer to a completely erroneous (and probably unpredictable) value. Even if our program ran to completion it might produce nothing like the answer we expected. This could be far more than just an irritation if our program controlled the guidance system of an airplane and one pair of interchanged bits resulted in a landing sixteen feet under the runway.*

The way to avoid some of the problems inherent in machine language programming seems simple once you've been let in on the secret. Since machine language programs — the only kind of programs a computer can run directly — are stored in memory like any other information, they can be manipulated just like any other information. In particular, they can be the output of another program, one that writes machine language programs. Using this idea, we can design a language that is easier for people to use, and then write a program that acts like a translator from the *source code* program, written in the easy-to-use language, to an *object code* program, written in hard-to-use machine language. The virtue of this plan is that the computer is exceptionally well suited to handle the tedious details involved in the translation process.

In our example, for instance, we might decide that our *high-level* language should have an *assignment* operator, =, that evaluates whatever is on the right side and stores the result into whatever is on the left of the operator. We might also decide to have symbolic references to memory locations, using descriptive names like *wages, regular,* and *overtime.* We might even decide to have in our language ways of representing arithmetic expressions that look more familiar to us. Then, instead of having to write

```
0000000000001100
1000000000001101
0001000000010100
```

we could write the far more comprehensible

```
wages = regular + overtime;
```

---

* This not a frivolous example. A space shuttle launch a few years ago was aborted minutes before lift-off because of a single typing error in the program of one of the on-board computers.

and leave to the translator program* the tasks of deciding that *wages* will refer to memory cell 20, *regular* and *overtime* will refer to cells 12 and 13 respectively, + will produce the machine language instructions for Load and Add, = will generate a Store instruction, and the semicolon will indicate the end of the statement that is being translated (see Figure 1.3).

This is an example of the kind of abstraction we talked about before. We have effectively moved our description of a program away from the hardware level of the computer. We can define our high-level language to allow any operation that we think will make programming easier, as long as the language we define can be translated into machine language by a program. In effect, the programmer no longer has to be concerned with low-level machine details but rather can act as if he or she is programming directly on an imaginary *virtual computer* that can execute programs in a high-level language such as C++. The advent of high-level programming languages means that a programmer can remain (in theory at least) blissfully ignorant even about what kind of computer he or she is using. It also means that we can make our computer execute programs in any language we want: all we have to do is go out and purchase the appropriate compiler or interpreter.

We derive an unanticipated benefit here. Not only are high-level languages easier to use, but they are generally more concise and far more expressive than machine languages, as well. This fact is important in light of studies showing that programmers generally produce about the same number of lines of code per day, regardless of the language they're using. If, as in our example, a single line in our high-level language is equivalent to three lines of machine language, programs in our language will be three times shorter than their machine language equivalents and so will be completed three times faster (with far fewer nervous breakdowns on the part of the programmer, in the bargain).

FIGURE 1.3
How a computer recognizes programs in a high-level language

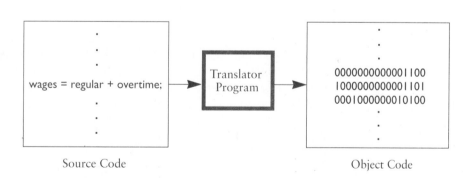

Source Code   Object Code

---

* Translators come in two forms: *Interpreters* translate each statement as it comes up during the execution of the program, and *compilers* translate the entire source code program first, before execution. Interpreters tend to be easier to write, but interpreted programs tend to run more slowly than compiled ones, since translation time is folded into run time. BASIC, LISP, and Smalltalk are usually interpreted; FORTRAN, Pascal, C, and C++ are usually compiled.

We don't want to give the impression that either designing a language or designing a translator for the language is an easy task; neither one is. Designing a language is still more of an art than a science, and writing a translator program can easily take a year or more. Both, however, are manageable tasks, as evidenced by the scores of high-level programming languages that exist today.

Any high-level programming language thus can be seen as the embodiment of a designer's philosophy of what should be done to make the programming process as efficient and painless as possible. Pascal, for instance, was developed by Nicholas Wirth in the early 1970s as a teaching language. Its expressed goal was to encourage the writing of clean, readable programs. Many design decisions led to the final form of Pascal, and all were made in the light of what was known at the time about the problems programmers had in writing, modifying, and maintaining programs. At about the same time that Wirth was designing Pascal, Dennis Ritchie at Bell Laboratories was developing the C language.* C was designed to program large systems, combining expressive power and simplicity with the ability to do the sorts of low-level, machine-oriented manipulations forbidden by Pascal. C++, as we shall see, is an *extension* of C. It contains C as a subset (so a C program can be translated, perhaps with some minor modifications, by a C++ compiler) and adds extra features not available in the older language. In particular, it adds features that make it an even higher level problem-solving tool.

People

What is it, then, that makes programming such a difficult task that people feel the need to invent new languages to make the task easier? We'll explain part of the problem by using a somewhat extended metaphor from the history of technology. Over the past few years, a number of researchers have observed that modern programming is very similar to pre-industrial technology. An eighteenth-century house carpenter, for example, might have shaped the framing timbers from trees, built the windows from other pieces of wood, and constructed each door from scratch. Such a house could take several months to produce and would have required the complete attention of a several skilled craftspeople for a considerable length of time. Even worse, if a window were later broken, it could be repaired or replaced only by another highly skilled carpenter.

Many programs today are constructed in the same way: They are built from scratch by highly skilled individuals and can be repaired and modified only by equally skilled workers. Parts of different programs are not interchangeable. They must be custom-fitted for each new job. As a result, building large programs is time consuming, expertise intensive, and prone to error. This

---

* Pascal was named for the seventeenth century mathematician Blaise Pascal who, among his many other accomplishments, designed a mechanical calculator. C, it's told, got its name by being the language that was designed after, and based on, Ken Thompson's language, B. C++ was designed in the early 1980s by Bjarne Stroustrup as an extension of C. You'll see later how it got its name.

explains, in part, why software is expensive and comes with disclaimers that translate from legalese into something like "If our software fails, and you lose a bundle because of the failure, you can't sue us." No toaster, bulldozer, or radio comes with a legal document like that. The reason has very much to do with the way motor vehicles and household appliances are built and the very different way programs are developed.

Home builders today can rely on a large stock of available parts, so, for example, they can simply order a set of windows, each of which is interchangeable with any other, rather than constructing each one from scratch. Furthermore, if the client's family dog gets excited over a cat outside and plunges through a window, it is easy enough to order a replacement (window, not cat), knowing that it will match the original exactly and perform in the same way that the original did. This organization into separate units has a design advantage, too. The house architect is thus freed from the need to concentrate on details of mullions, muntins, sashes, and the like, and can *encapsulate* the description of a window by specifying "Belview Windows Co. part #13359-50-34TP."

Object-oriented programming (which is abbreviated *OOP*) begins with this notion of encapsulation of structure and function and takes it several steps further. The development of object-oriented languages began with Simula67. This was followed by Smalltalk, which was developed at the Xerox Palo Alto Research Center at about the same time Nicholas Wirth was working on Pascal, in the early 1970s. Since then, as computer scientists have seen the potential of the object-oriented approach, a number of other object-oriented languages have been developed. Some, like Object Pascal, C++, and Objective-C, are extensions of traditional languages. Others, like Smalltalk, Trellis, and Eiffel, are more nearly attempts to develop an object-oriented language from the ground up.

1.2 OBJECTS AND CLASSES

We've said earlier that a program is a list of instructions for a computer to execute. That's true enough, but it's not the only way to describe programs. Thinking about programs as lists of instructions is the fundamental strategy of *imperative* languages like Pascal, C, or BASIC. Programming in these languages involves thinking in terms of *algorithms,* that is, the sequence of actions the computer will perform. Object-oriented languages, on the other hand, permit the programmer to take a broader view and think of a program as a collection of cooperating *objects.*

Objects

Each object has three aspects: what it is, what it does, and what it's called. We'll illustrate these aspects by considering a geometric object, a circle (see Figure 1.4). Now, C++ doesn't have circles built in as part of the language, so if we

FIGURE 1.4
The state of a circle
object

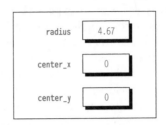

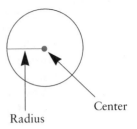

want to write a program that manipulates circles we have to extend C++ by writing our own descriptions of circle objects into a program. The descriptive information associated with an object, called its *state,* includes its properties and the values of these properties. For instance, a circle has a radius and a center and at a given time, these might have the values 4.67 and (0, 0).

For most objects, the state properties don't change, although the state values may be modified during the object's lifetime. In our example, the circle object will always have a radius and a center whose values will change if the circle's size or location does.

The collection of actions an object may perform on itself is called its *behavior.* In our example, we may want to use a circle as part of a program that draws on a computer screen, so we would need to be able to set the center and radius of the object and instruct the circle to draw itself on the screen. Notice that we said a circle would *draw itself* on the screen. This is an important feature of the object-oriented approach. In a language with an algorithmic approach, one could describe circles by radius and center, as we have, but the description of the actions to perform on a circle would not be as tightly associated with the state data as it is here. That is, the drawing command wouldn't be part of the circle object itself. Encapsulating data and actions together in an object helps us design and understand a program, since, for instance, all circle-related data and actions are collected in one place. If we had to modify a circle object's definition, we would know exactly where the modifications would go. Furthermore, we would know that we wouldn't have to modify any other part of the program.

Finally, each object has an *identity,* which serves to distinguish it from all others. In C++, as in most programming languages, we identify an object by giving it a name, so we might call our circle *theCircle.* As with other languages, C++ has rules for the form names must take. Figure 1.5 illustrates the three aspects of our circle object.

In C++, names of objects (and other things, as well) begin with a letter, which may then be followed by any collection of letters, digits, and underscores (the _ character, which counts as a letter). C++ is "case sensitive"; that is, it distinguishes upper- and lower-case letters and regards 'A' and 'a' as different.

FIGURE 1.5
An object has state, behavior, and identity.

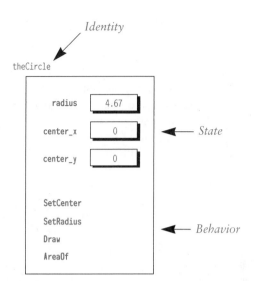

> An object has three aspects:
>
> 1. its state, called *member data* in C++;
> 2. its behavior, called *member functions;* and
> 3. its identity, the name we give it.

Classes

It's entirely reasonable to assume that a program that would use one circle object might use several. All of these circle objects would be similar; they would have the same collection of member data and functions. To describe each one separately would be a wasteful duplication of effort since they would differ only in their data values and names. Object-oriented languages allow us to describe a prototype, if you will, for an entire set of objects. Such a prototype is called a *class*.

Continuing our example, we could describe a class, *Circles,* by describing the states (but generally not the state values) and behaviors of all objects that belong to that class. Then we could describe as many circle objects as we needed merely by declaring that they are instances of the *Circles* class — that is, they are Circle objects.

> A class is a set of objects. Alternatively, an object is a single instance of a class.

An object can never exist in isolation; every object must be an instance of some class. This means that if we are going to use an object in a program, we must first describe the class to which the object belongs. Think again about what we need to describe a class: the *Circles* class must include a description of its member data, which we might name *radius, center_x,* and *center_y.* It must also include descriptions of its member functions *SetRadius, SetCenter,* and *Draw.* Notice, though, that a program that uses circles (which is to say, uses the *Circles* class) doesn't need to know how *SetRadius, SetCenter,* or *Draw* do what they do any more than you need to know the details of an internal combustion engine to drive a car.

With this in mind, we can separate a class description into two parts: the *interface* that we need to know in order to describe and make use of the class's objects and the *implementation,* which contains the details that are hidden from the outside world. This separation has two significant advantages. First, we can design a class without worrying about the details of how we will write its member functions. Second, we can change, improve, modify, or fix the member functions without ever having to change any part of the rest of the program.

A class description consists of two parts. The interface, called the class *declaration* in C++, contains descriptions of member data and functions, but no details about how the functions work. The implementation contains the detailed *definition* for each of the member functions.

Clearly, we can't talk in detail about the implementation part of a class yet, since we haven't told you anything about the C++ language itself. We can, though, talk briefly about the interface part, since declaring a class doesn't involve anything but simple descriptions. We have to include descriptions of member data and functions in a class declaration, but we might want to restrict access to some data and functions.

Consider, for instance, *StandardBoxes,* a class of rectangles that were twice as wide as they were tall. Objects of this class might have member data *height* and *width,* among others. A program that uses this class shouldn't be able to modify either *height* or *width,* since doing so might alter the assumed relation between them. We can restrict the access of member functions and data by declaring some or all of them to be *private* to the class. Doing so allows them to be accessed and modified by the object itself but by nothing else, including other objects of the same class.

In Chapter 8, we'll discover an intermediate level of access known as *protected*.

Member functions and data that are *public* can be referenced from outside an object. Member functions and data of an object that are *private* can be used only by the object itself.

In our example, the radius and center are accessed by member functions, so there's no compelling reason to allow outside access to *radius, center_x,* and *center_y* except through these functions. We'll make the member data private and the member functions, needed to access the data, public. Figure 1.6 illustrates the interface of the class *Circles* in the standard form that we will use throughout the rest of this text.

We'll explain the details of class declarations shortly, but even without explanation, the following C++ declaration can be seen to correspond to our graphical description of the *Circles* class.

```
class Circles
// Declaration of the class of Circle objects
{
public:       // This part can be used by objects that are not circles.
    void SetCenter(int x, int y);
    void SetRadius(int r);
    void Draw();
    double AreaOf();
private:      // This information is only accessible to a Circle object.
    double radius;
    double center_x;
    double center_y;
};
```

Inheritance

The class structure of C++ makes designing and programming easier by (1) encapsulating data and actions into objects, (2) hiding details in the implementation

FIGURE 1.6

The class declaration of the *Circles* class

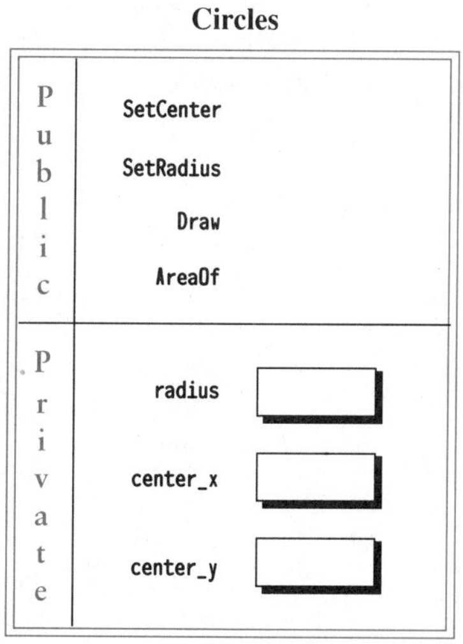

(or definition) part, and (3) restricting access to member data and functions where needed. These are all good programming practices, but they also can be used, to varying degrees, in languages that are not strictly object-oriented. Much of the power of object orientation comes from a feature that is nearly unique to this approach: Not only can we organize objects into classes, but we can also impose a hierarchical arrangement on classes so that some of the properties of one class can be *inherited* from another.

Going back to our geometric example, we don't have to restrict our objects to circles; we could equally well have objects that are rectangles, squares, triangles, ellipses, and so on. We could augment our program by including declarations and definitions for the classes *Rectangles, Squares, Triangles,* and *Ellipses,* just as we did when we built the *Circles* class. If we think about doing this, we notice that there are relations between some of the classes: a square is a kind of rectangle, and a circle is a kind of ellipse, and all of these are what we might call "geometric objects," as we illustrate in Figure 1.7.

C++ and other object-oriented languages allow a class like *Squares* to inherit the member functions and data from a parent class like *Rectangles.* In C++ the parent (more general) class is called a *base class* and the child (more specific) class is called a *derived class.* For example, both rectangles and squares have a top left corner, so we could include in the class *Rectangles* two member data items *top* and *left,* in such a way that every square object would also have these two member data items. Doing this, we would not need to re-declare these data items in *Squares* — they would be inherited from the base class *Rectangles.* In a similar way, every object in our hierarchy has an extent; that is, a bounding rectangle inside of which the object fits as closely as possible. We could thus declare the data *bounds_top, bounds_left, bounds_bottom, bounds_right,* and the member function *ReportBounds* within the class *GeometricObjects,* and these would apply to all the derived classes *Rectangles, Squares, Triangles, Ellipses,* and *Circles.*

There are times, though, when a base class action or state might not be appropriate for use by a derived class. All the classes in our hierarchy would have *Draw* functions, and *Squares* might inherit *Draw* from its base class *Rectan-*

FIGURE 1.7
A class hierarchy, showing "is–a" relations.

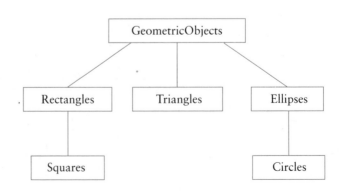

gles, but drawing an ellipse might involve different strategies than drawing a circle. C++ allows a derived class to redefine, or *override*, a member function inherited from a base class.

Another powerful feature of C++, one that doesn't exist in some other languages, illustrates the three-part process from design to a running program. We begin by designing and writing a program to solve a problem by decomposing it into cooperating classes. After we have written the program (or part of it), we compile it into object code. Finally, after all the parts have been compiled, we link them together (in a way we'll describe later) and cause the computer to execute the program. Some information, such as the names of all the objects and their member functions and data, is known at compile time, but other information cannot be known until the program is actually running. If, for example, we have an object called *theShape,* and we send it a message to draw itself (the message would look like *theShape.Draw()* in C++), how is the computer to know which *Draw* action to use? Other languages get around this problem at compile time, by disallowing duplicate function names. Doing this in C++, however, would defeat the power of inheritance.

C++ solves this problem at run time by looking up the class to which *theShape* belongs and working its way up the class hierarchy until it finds a reference to a *Draw* function it can use.* In our example, if *theShape* was a circle, ellipse, triangle, or rectangle, the computer would stop at the class itself. In the case of a square, which uses the definition in the base class *Rectangle,* the computer would go up one step in the hierarchy and would draw a square using the *Draw* function in *Rectangle.* This ability to use the same name for actions on objects of different classes is known as *polymorphism.*

1.3 PROGRAMMING WITH CLASSES

To see this object-oriented approach in action, consider the problem of designing a program to simulate a digital timer. We have in mind something that would look like Figure 1.8—a clock with two display panels, one for hours and one for minutes. Considered as a single entity, such a timer might be far too complex for us to make any headway in designing it. A cardinal rule in all problem solving, not just the design of programs, is, "Inside every big problem, there are one or more smaller problems waiting to get out, so start by breaking the big problem into smaller ones." One of the outstanding virtues of the object-oriented approach to program design (and, indeed, one of the compelling reasons we considered using OOP to teach novice programmers)

---

* In technical terms, this is known as *run-time binding*: The name of the object isn't associated (bound) with a class until the program is running.

FIGURE 1.8
A digital timer

hours   minutes

is that it provides us with a natural starting point for decomposing complex problems.

Deciding on the Classes to Use

A useful way to begin an object-oriented design is to give a narrative description of the problem. Once that is done, we make note of the nouns and verbs. The nouns give us hints about the classes and the member data we'll need, and the verbs give us an idea of what member functions the objects will require. Obviously, there won't be a complete correspondence between nouns and objects or between verbs and functions, but you'll see that this methodology will give you a good start.

> **Design Guideline 1:** Divide the problem into subproblems by identifying classes from a narrative description of the problem.

Let's give it a try. In the description below, we've underlined the nouns and italicized the verbs that seem to be important to the problem.

> A digital <u>timer</u> consists of two <u>display panes</u>, one for <u>hours</u> and one for <u>minutes</u>. Each display will hold a <u>value</u> between zero and some preset upper <u>limit</u>. The user of the program must be able to *initialize* the timer by *initializing* each display's value to zero. The user also must be able to *increment* the timer by *incrementing* the minutes display and sometimes *incrementing* the hours display as well. The user should be able to *set* the timer to a given value by *setting* the value of each of its displays. Finally, the user might ask the timer to *show* its value by *showing* the value of each display.

Based on this rather straightforward narrative description, it appears that we have seven important objects: the timer, which contains two display panes (hours and minutes), each of which contains two numbers (value and limit). Thinking of classes as collections of related state information and behavior, it looks like we'll need two classes: a *Timer*, which will contain two objects of type *Display*. Each display pane will in turn contain two integers, *value* and *limit.* The operations that each class will have are likewise easily identified from our narrative. We can make a first pass at our class descriptions, as follows:

Display
    Data
        value
        limit
    Functions
        Initialize(lim)
        Increment
        SetValue(val)
        Show

Timer
    Data
        hours: A **Display** with *limit* = 24.
        minutes: A **Display** with *limit* = 60.
    Functions
        Initialize
        Increment
        Set
        Show

Describing Communication Among Objects

Since a C++ program is a collection of interacting objects, we want to make sure that our class descriptions allow for and make explicit the necessary interactions. Again, our program narrative is the place to look for clues as to how our classes are to interact. In this case the key descriptive elements of the narrative are the verbs, as they (obviously) describe the actions to be performed on and by each object.

Having already identified which actions are performed by which classes of objects, we should now become explicit about how actions are invoked. While we still are not concerned about the details of how actions are performed, we want to know where actions are initiated. For example, it seems clear from our program narrative that a *Timer* object initializes itself by initializing its two displays. Similarly, a timer increments itself by incrementing its displays. In fact, it appears that all of the functions that we have described as member functions of class *Display* are invoked from within class *Timer*.

Who or what invokes a timer's member functions? You can think of the phrase "the user" in our program narrative as referring generically to the user of the class. This user will (according to the program development scheme we exploit throughout this text) most often take the form of a C++ main program. All that really matters for now is that the member functions we have identified as part of the class *Timer* are to be invoked from outside of the *Timer* class itself.

Describing the Classes

Now that we have a better idea of the organization of our program, we can begin to fill in the details. For both of the classes, we describe in more detail the member data, the member functions that act on this data, and the communication between other objects. Here's what we came up with:

> **Design Guideline 2:** The key to success in writing an object-oriented program is a complete and consistent description of all classes involved. Take the time to do this before you write any C++ code.

Display
Data
> *value:* The current value, integer in the range 0 . . . *limit* − 1.
> *limit:* The value at which the timer resets to 0.

Functions
> *Initialize(lim):* (from **Timer**) Set *value* to zero and *limit* to *lim*.
> *Increment:* (from **Timer**) Add 1 to *value,* turning it over to 0 if needed.
> *SetValue(val):* (from **Timer**) Set *value* to *val*.
> *Show:* (from **Timer**) Show the current *value* on the screen.

Timer
Data:
> *hours:* A **Display** with *limit* = 24.
> *minutes:* A **Display** with *limit* = 60.

Functions
> *Initialize:* (from main program, to each **Display**) Send an *Initialize* message to the *hours* and *minutes* **Display**s, setting their *limit*s to 24 and 60, respectively.
> *Increment:* (from main program) *Increment* the *minutes* **Display**, and *Increment* the *hours* **Display**, if incrementing has made the *minute* **Display**'s *value* become zero.
> *Set:* (from main program) Get new values from the keyboard and use those numbers to *SetValue* each of the two **Display**s.
> *Show:* (from main program) Show the time by sending a *Show* message to each **Display**.

Hiding Information Within Classes

We're almost done with our design. All that remains is to decide which data and functions should be publicly accessible and which can be hidden within the classes' objects. It's pretty clear that all the functions should be described as public, as they are all invoked from outside their respective classes. We don't want any outside routines to have access to the member data, though, as that would open us to the possibility that a program that uses these classes might increment *minutes* without checking whether that would require a modification of *hours*, for instance. So we make the member data of each class private . . . oops!

There's a subtle problem here, one that might not surface until we've written the classes and tried them out. Do you see it? Take a minute and look at what we've done before you go on. In particular, look at what *Timer's Increment* function has to do—but can't—because of the way we've restricted access.

*   *   *

The problem is that for *Timer* to increment itself correctly, it has to inspect the *value* of *minutes* in order to know whether to send an *Increment* message to *hours*. Unfortunately, we decided to make *value* private to *Display*, so no other object, not even its container *Timer*, can inspect it. Fortunately, that's easy to fix. All we need to do is add to *Display* a new public member function, *GetValue*, which will return the current *value* to whatever object wants to inspect it. Having done that, our two classes take the forms given in Figures 1.9 and 1.10.

> **Design Guideline 3:** If a member data item is accessed only from member functions, make it private. If a member function doesn't respond to any messages from outside the object, consider making it private, too.

That's it — in not much longer than it took you to read this section, we were able to provide the outline of what is really quite a complex process. The important lesson here is that we were able to do the design rapidly because object-oriented programming allowed us to think in broad terms. We could start by describing a system in natural, realistic terms. Having identified the major logical entities of our problem, we are then free to define them and to nail down their data, operations, and communications, without ever once having to get lost in considerations of *how* we would accomplish the nit-picky details.

An admission of complicity is in order here, we think. As instructors usually do when they're trying to make a point, we did select the example to suit our needs. A digital timer is obviously made up of fairly simple, distinct pieces, so it lends itself well to an object-oriented design approach. We'll freely admit that object-oriented design is not the answer to all programming problems. With some problems, such as sorting a list of numbers, the complexity lies not in the objects and their communication, but with the algorithm itself that would actually do the sorting. In designing a sorting algorithm, the object approach really

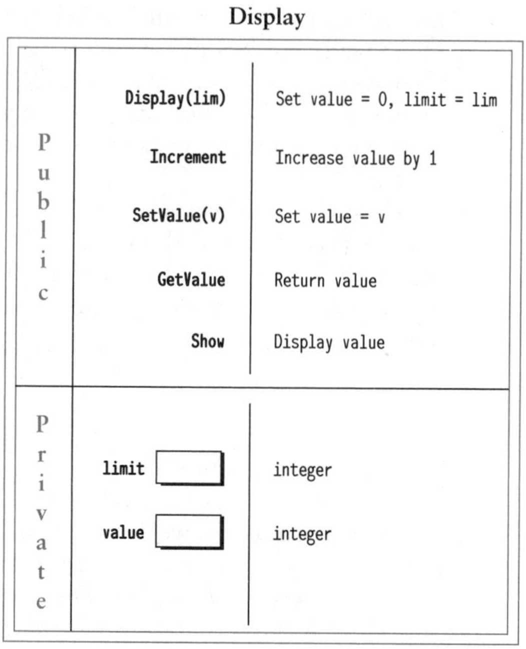

FIGURE 1.9
The *Display* class

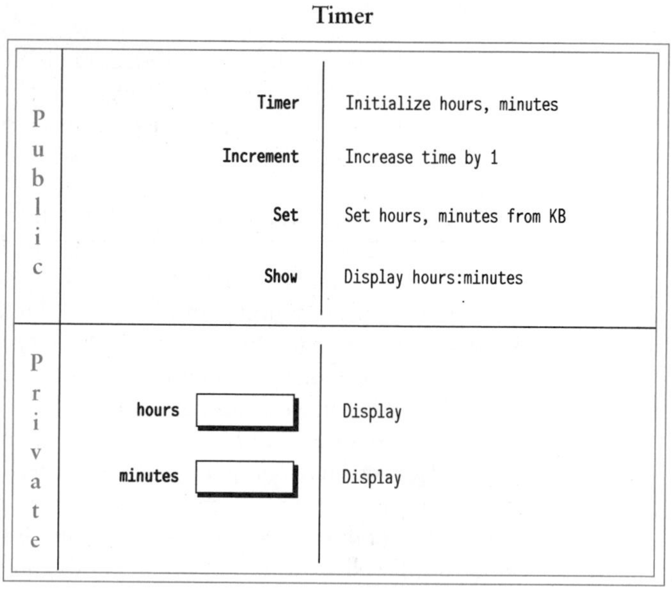

Display

Public	Display(lim)	Set value = 0, limit = lim
	Increment	Increase value by 1
	SetValue(v)	Set value = v
	GetValue	Return value
	Show	Display value
Private	limit ☐	integer
	value ☐	integer

FIGURE 1.10
The *Timer* class

Timer

Public	Timer	Initialize hours, minutes
	Increment	Increase time by 1
	Set	Set hours, minutes from KB
	Show	Display hours:minutes
Private	hours ☐	Display
	minutes ☐	Display

doesn't gain us much, so we may as well be using Pascal, C, or even FORTRAN or COBOL, or any other language.

Our justification for using an object-oriented paradigm here is twofold. First, there will be plenty of time in subsequent courses for you to gain the expertise in algorithms that comes in so handy at times (and even when it isn't directly useful, the study of algorithms is fascinating in its own right). Second, and more important, we believe most strongly that the overwhelming majority of programs that people write require the careful management of a large collection of objects in ways that are algorithmically simple. For those kinds of problems, the object approach is better than anything computer scientists have yet devised.

1.4 PROGRAM IN PROGRESS: A DIGITAL TIMER

Throughout this text, we'll include in each chapter a Program in Progress (or PIP) to illustrate the language and design features we'll be discussing. In the PIP for this chapter, we'll focus on the design and implementation of a class that implements the digital timer we designed in the previous section. We'll provide the entire program for your inspection; in the lab for this chapter you'll enter the program, run it, and explore some of its behavior.

Later PIPs will be designed to illustrate the features we introduce in the text, but you should consider this one a quick tour of the essential features of C++. A nice feature of C++ is how comprehensible it is: Even at this early stage, you should be able to get a pretty clear picture of how the program works because the C++ code reflects directly an object-oriented design. While you're reading the program, don't concern yourself overly with details; in the next few chapters, you'll see complete explanations of everything that goes on here.

Declaring, Defining, and Using Classes

As a general practice in this text, we will divide the programming process into three stages. First, we will identify and *declare* any classes we will use in our program. The declaration phase involves a careful description of the classes' member data and functions, but deliberately avoids any detailed description of how the member functions will accomplish what it is they are supposed to do. Once the program's classes have been designed to an extent equal to that of our digital timer, producing class declarations involves little more than translating the class descriptions into C++ terminology.

After we have declared our classes, the next step is to *define* them, describing in detail how the member functions work and how they are used to communicate between the objects that will comprise our program. Finally, having done what really amounts to most of the work, we will write the program that will *use* the classes we have declared and defined.

This separation of declaration, definition, and use is a powerful design aid that is built into C++. Separating declaration from definition frees us in the design stage from having to concentrate on details, so we can describe our classes and their interrelations without having to think about how to make them do what we want.

> A good way to write a C++ program is to *declare* the classes to be used, then to *define* the actions of those classes, and finally to *use* instances of the classes in a main program.

Declaration: The File "DIGITIME.H"

Unlike programs in many other languages, C++ is generally built from a collection of separately compilable *files*. A file is nothing more than a collection of information stored under a given name. A file is typically stored on a hard disk attached to a computer, so that we may instruct the computer to load it into memory, translate it into machine language, and execute the resulting object code.

In keeping with our practice of separating declarations and definitions, we'll put the *Timer* and *Display* class declarations in a file named "DIGITIME.H". Such a file is called a *header file*. The definitions of the functions we'll place in another file, which we call "DIGITIME.CPP". The parts of the file names after the periods are called *extensions*, and in this case they identify the nature of the code in the files. A header file will have a ".H" extension as part of its name, which serves to indicate to the C++ environment that this is a file that contains definitions and no (or very little) executable code. A file with a ".CPP" extension, on the other hand, generally contains C++ code that will be translated and run.

Finally, in order to test our classes, we'll write a simple *driver program* that will include calls (either directly or indirectly) to all the functions we've written. We'll call that file "PIP1.CPP". If we wanted to use the *Display* or *Timer* classes in another program, we could discard "PIP1.CPP" after making sure that our classes worked as we expected, and make the appropriate references to "DIGITIME.H" in our new program files, where appropriate.

Here's what the header file for the *Display* and *Timer* classes looks like:

> Your implementation of C++ may use different conventions, say, for example, a ".CP" extension for definition files.

```
//------------- DIGITIME.H -------------

// Declarations of classes Display and Timer

class Display
// A Display object stores and displays a single integer.
// That integer is always in the range 0 .. limit-1, where limit
// is also stored in the class.
{
public:
    Display(int lim);                    // Initialize a new Display object
```

```
    void Increment();              // Add 1 to value
    void SetValue(int val);        // Set the value


    int GetValue();                // Return the current value
    void Show();                   // Show the current value
    int GetLimit( );               // Return the Limit

private:
    int limit,                     // largest possible value
        value;                     // current value (0 .. limit - 1)
};


class Timer
// A Timer object consists of two Displays, one for hours
// and one for minutes.
// When the timer is incremented and minutes becomes 60, minutes is
// reset to 0 and hours is incremented.
{
public:
    Timer();                       // Initialize a new Timer object,
                                   // setting max hours to 24 and max
                                   // minutes to 60
    void Increment();              // Add 1 minute to timer
    void Set();                    // Set hours and minutes
    void Show();                   // Show hours and minutes

private:
    Display  hours,                // two displays, one for hours,
             minutes;              // and one for minutes
};
```

Let's look at this header file in order, from the first statement to the last. The first thing we see is the line

```
//-------------- DIGITIME.H --------------
```

This is nothing more than a reminder to us of the name of this particular file. A *comment* in C++ begins with the two characters //, and anything from there to the end of the line is simply ignored by the C++ compiler. Despite the fact that compilers ignore them, we cannot stress too strongly the need for comments. We write programs for computers, it is true; but equally important, we write programs for people. Programs have a life cycle: they are born, serve a useful term, and must be adapted to changing circumstances. In the real world of professional programmers, the person who must modify a program is almost never the person who wrote it. Even if the person who must modify a program happens to be the person who wrote it, it is highly likely that the modifier has completely forgotten his or her original intent in writing the program. At the very minimum, a program should include a comment block at the start of each file describing the contents of the file and explaining the action of each function and the interpretation of each data item. The listing should also contain individual comments on any part of the program the purpose or details of which are not completely transparent to a reader.

> Although it's possible to go overboard and smother the sense of a program with unnecessary comments, a good rule of thumb is that *it is better to err on the side of too many comments rather than too few.*

The remaining lines in "DIGITIME.H" contain the declaration of the *Display* and *Timer* classes. In skeletal form, a class declaration takes the following form:

```
class ClassName
{
public:
    // Public member data and functions are declared here.
private:
    // Private member data and functions are declared here.
};
```

The declaration begins with class ClassName, in which the *className* identifier follows the rules for other names in C++: any collection of letters, digits, and underscores that begins with a letter. The declaration itself is enclosed in braces { and } and ends with a semicolon punctuator, so that the compiler will be able to identify where the declaration starts and ends.

The public part of the declaration (the functions and data that will be accessible from other parts of the program) is indicated by the label public: and continues to the end of the declaration or to the first private: label, whichever comes first. The public part may be omitted entirely; if public: is not specified, all of the data and functions of the class are assumed to be private to the class and invisible to users of the class.

The public: label in the *Display* declaration is followed by six function declarations. The first is a *constructor* function, with the same name as the class itself, whose job is to set the initial member data values. The next two are the *manipulator* functions, *Increment* and *SetValue*, which modify some of the member data. The last three are the *access* functions, here named *GetValue*, *Show*, and *GetLimit*, which allow outside access to the member data.

```
Display(int lim);
void Increment();
void SetValue(int val);
int GetValue();
void Show();
int GetLimit();
```

C++ functions are designed to take information in through their *argument lists* — the parts within the parentheses — and return from their work with a single value, the type of which must be specified. If the function is intended only to do some processing, but not to return any value, we must also indicate that by using the void specification. In this example, the function *Show* is declared by writing void Show(), indicating that it receives no information (there are no arguments specified in the parentheses), does its job of displaying, and returns no information when it's done (since it has a void return type). The job of the constructor function, *Display,* (like that of all constructor functions) is to initialize a new object, in this case, a *Display* object. Its return type is implicit from the function's name, which must be the same as the class whose objects it is designed to construct.

Notice that these lines, and almost all the others in this file, end with a semicolon. This feature of C++ makes the translation process easier, since semicolons in C++ are statement terminators, indicating to the compiler that the end of a statement has been reached. Any class, variable, or function declaration in C++ must end with a semicolon, as most C++ compilers will readily remind you if you forget one.

The private part of the declaration consists of declarations of the two member data *limit* and *value.*

```
int limit, value;
```

Notice that we specified the type of information stored in *limit* and *value.* You'll see in the next chapter that int is a predefined type in C++ that describes integers.

Definition: The File "DIGITIME.CPP"

We can regard the declaration of a class as a prototype that tells the compiler the types of member data and the nature of the incoming and returned information of all member functions. As we mentioned, the implementation details of the member functions are specified in the class definition file, "DIGITIME.CPP".

```
//------------- DIGITIME.CPP --------------


#include <iostream.h>              // for cout, cin
#include "DIGITIME.H"              // for Display and Timer declarations


//------------- Definition of member functions for class Display


Display::Display(int lim)
// Initialize a new Display object.
{
    value = 0;
    limit = lim;
}
```

```
void Display::Increment()
// Add 1 to value. If incrementing makes value
// equal to limit, reset value to zero.
{
    value++;
    if (value == limit)
        value = 0;
}

void Display::SetValue(int val)
// Set the value. If the argument is negative, we make it positive.
// To make sure value is within the right range, we set the value
// to its remainder upon division by limit.
{
    if (val < 0)
        value = -val;
    value = (val % limit);
}

int Display::GetValue()
// Return the current value.
{
    return value;
}

void Display::Show()
// Show the value of a display.
{
    if (value < 10)                    // Pad with a leading zero, if needed,
        cout << '0';

    cout << value;                     // and in any case, display the value.
}

int Display::GetLimit()
// Return the limit for this display.
{
    return limit;                      // and in any case, display the value.
}

//------------- Definition of member functions for class Timer

Timer::Timer() : hours(24), minutes(60)
// Initialize a new Timer object,
// setting hours limit to 24 and minutes limit to 60.
```

```
{
    // All the work is done by the two constructor calls in the header.
}

void Timer::Increment()
// Add 1 minute to timer.
{
    minutes.Increment();

    if (minutes.GetValue() == 0)   // We've turned the minute counter over,
        hours.Increment();          // so we have to increment the hours counter.

}

void Timer::Set()
// Set hours and minutes from the keyboard.
{
    int setting;                    // user-input values for hours, minutes

    cout << "Set hours to what value?\n";
    cout << "Enter an integer between 0 and " << hours.GetLimit() <<":";
    cin >> setting;
    hours.SetValue(setting);        // Set hours.

    cout << "Set minutes to what value?\n";
    cout << "Enter an integer between 0 and " << minutes.GetLimit() << ":";
    cin >> setting;
    minutes.SetValue(setting);      // Set minutes.
}

void Timer::Show()
// Show the current timer's settings.
{
    hours.Show();
    cout << ':';
    minutes.Show();
}
```

Since this is a quick introductory look at a C++ program, we won't explain all of the definitions in detail; we'll cover most of what we need to understand from "DIGITIME.CPP" in Chapter 2. Some things, however, are worth mentioning here. First, near the beginning of the file we see the two lines

```
#include <iostream.h>
#include "DIGITIME.H"
```

A line beginning with #include is called a *preprocessor directive*. It causes the entire file whose name follows to be copied over the directive, just as if it had been typed there in the first place. We need this because of a very strict rule in C++:

> Before you can refer to any object, class, data, or function name in a C++ program it must be declared first.

In this program, for example, we couldn't define *Display*'s *Show* function without telling the compiler what we meant by the names *Display* and *value*:

```
void Display::Show()
// Show the value of a Display.
{
    if (value < 10)              // Pad with a leading zero, if needed,
        cout << '0';

    cout << value;               // and in any case, display the value.
}
```

We do so by using an `#include "DIGITIME.H"` directive. The file "DIGITIME.H" contains the declarations of all names the compiler needs to translate this definition into machine language. The definition of *Display*'s *Show* function illustrates the need for the other directive, as well. The statement

```
cout << value;
```

causes the contents of *value* to be displayed on the screen. The names we need to do output, cout and <<, are declared in a C++ *library file* named "iostream.h". In order to perform screen output, we must tell the compiler where these names are declared, which we do with the directive

```
#include <iostream.h>
```

The file name is enclosed in angle brackets < and >, rather than quotes, to distinguish it as a predefined C++ library file rather than one we wrote ourselves.

In the lab for this chapter, we'll explore the PIP in more detail, but for now take a look at some of the function definitions in "DIGITIME.CPP" and notice how easy it is to make sense of them, even without knowing the details of C++ syntax.

Use: The File "PIP1.CPP"

Now that we've declared and defined the classes *Timer* and *Display*, we're ready to use them. In fact, none of the code we have seen so far causes anything to happen. That is, we have declared and defined two classes and their associated member data and functions, but we have yet to create or manipulate any instances of these classes. This is the job of a program file, such as "PIP1.CPP".

```
//------------- PIP1.CPP --------------

#include <iostream.h>                  // for cout, cin
#include "DIGITIME.H"                  // for our Timer and Display classes

void main()
{
    Timer t;          // Create and initialize a Timer object, named "t."

    cout << "Here's the initial value of the timer: ";
    t.Show();
    cout << "\n\n";

    t.Set();          // Allow the user to set the timer's value.
    cout << "Here are the new settings: ";
    t.Show();
    cout << "\n\n";

    cout << "Now we run it for ten minutes . . .\n";

    for (int i = 0; i < 10; i++)
    {
        t.Increment();
        t.Show();
        cout << '\n';
    }

    // Freeze the screen until the user presses a key.
    cout << "\nPress 'x' followed by ENTER to exit the program...";
    char any;
    cin >> any;
    cout << "\nPROCESSING COMPLETED ... GOOD BYE";
}
```

The file "PIP1.CPP" begins with the same two include directives we saw before, and for the same reason. Since this file includes input and output routines (cin and cout), and references to the class *Timer* and its member functions (*t.Increment()*), we need to tell the compiler where these are declared.

Other than an initial comment and the directives, the file "PIP1.CPP" contains the definition of just one function, called main. This function is the heart of our program. C++ executes any program by executing a function named main, which you must provide. The main function in any C++ program, then, is where we use the classes we have declared and defined.

In main, we begin by invoking (or "calling") the constructor function for a *Timer* object, creating a new object named *t*.

```
Timer t;
```

> Any C++ program must include one and only one function named `main`. C++ executes a program by executing the `main` function.

We then continue by using `cout` to display a message on the screen, calling *t*'s *Show* function, and using `cout` again to skip down a line on the screen.

```
cout << "Here's the initial value of the timer: ";
t.Show();
cout << "\n\n";
```

Next, we test the *Set* and *Show* member functions of class *Timer*:

```
t.Set(); // Allow the user to set the timer's value.
cout << "Here are the new settings: ";
t.Show();
cout << "\n\n";
```

We then use a *loop* to test whether the *Increment* function works as it should by executing *t*'s *Increment* and *Show* functions ten times:

```
for (int i = 0; i < 10; i++)
    {
        t.Increment();
        t.Show();
        cout << '\n';
    }
```

Finally, we freeze the program by forcing it to wait for the user to type something. This allows the user to take a final look at the output before the `main` function, and hence the entire program, terminates.

```
cout << "\nPress an 'x' followed by ENTER to exit the program ...";
char any;
cin >> any;
cout << "\nPROCESSING COMPLETED ... GOOD BYE";
```

1.5 SUMMING UP

▶ A computer is a general-purpose information processor, capable of storing and manipulating information under the direction of a program.

▶ A program is a list of instructions for a computer to perform.

▶ Programming in binary machine language is a nasty process. To make the programming process simpler, we invent high-level languages whose statements are translated from an easy-to-use form into machine language.

▶ Object-oriented programming is a way to design and write programs using a language that supports classes, objects, inheritance, and polymorphism.

▶ A class is an encapsulation of data items and operations on those items. An object is an instance of a class.

▶ Using inheritance, a class may be defined as a subclass (also known as a derived class) of another, inheriting the data and operation templates from the parent class and overriding those operations that must be modified for the derived class.

▶ Polymorphism refers to the ability to use the same function name for functions that act on different classes of objects.

▶ A useful way to approach object-oriented programming is to declare the classes to be used, then to define the classes, and finally to write a program that uses the classes. We refer to this as the "Declare-Define-Use" approach to program design.

▶ A useful way to describe the classes to be used in a program is to write a narrative description of the problem to be solved. The nouns you use often suggest the classes you will need and their member data, while the verbs in the description often suggest member functions.

▶ Because C++ has a strict "declare before use" requirement, we will generally separate the class declaration from the definition part by placing declarations in header files and using include directives in the definition files to refer to the declaration parts. Usually, our programs will consist of an odd number of files: pairs of ".H" declarations and ".CPP" definitions, along with one ".CPP" file that contains the main function.

1.6 EXERCISES

1. At the start of the chapter, we talked about unusual uses for supposedly single-purpose machines. Here's a traditional exercise in creativity that explores this topic: How many ways can you think of to use a barometer to measure the height of a tall building? There are *lots* of possible answers, so we'll start by disallowing the most obvious: you could measure the barometric pressure at the top and the bottom of the building and then look up the weight of the atmosphere per foot to compute the height of the building. You can use other devices (like a reference book that tells the weight of air), but each solution must use the barometer in some significant way.

2. We saw that we can use two states, 0 and 1, to represent information of many different forms. Why is one state not sufficient? In other words, what are the problems inherent in representing information using only the digit 1 (known as *unary* notation)?

3. a. How would we represent the numbers 1, 2, 4, 8, 16, 32, 64 in binary?
   b. How would we represent the numbers 6, 23, and 2001 in binary?
   c. What numbers are represented by the binary strings 110, 1100, 101101, 1111111?

4. Take the bit pattern of Figure 1.1, pretend you haven't seen the picture, and reconstruct the picture, assuming it fits in a rectangle. That's not hard, so why would the reconstruction problem be harder if you were given a bit pattern of, say, 240 bits? Explain why a proposal to communicate with extraterrestrial civilizations suggested sending a pictorial message that was 1643 bits long.

5. Here's a bit pattern that represents a picture under our black = 1, white = 0 protocol. What's the picture? (By the way, we've collected the bits in groups of 8 only so the string will be easier to read — it has nothing whatever to do with the picture.)

```
00001111 10000001 10000011 00011000 00001100 10000000 00101000 10001000
11000000 00000110 00000000 00110000 11100001 10001000 10001010 00000000
10011000 00001100 01100000 11000000 11111000 0
```

6. Another way to store and communicate a picture is to make use of the fact that many pictures have long strings of black or white dots. *Run-length encoding* encodes a binary string by listing the lengths of each alternating run of color. For instance, the 187-bit string in Figure 1.1 starts with a run of four zeros, followed by three ones and six zeros, and so would have the following run-length encoding:

4/3/6/2/3/2/3/2/5/2/1/3/6/1/1/3/5/2/1/3/4/3/2/10/2/11/3/11/2/10/2/2/3/4/3/1/2/5/3/
1/1/6/3/1/2/5/2/3/6/6/3/4

This uses only 107 characters, but we're cheating here, since it takes fewer characters to write numbers in decimal form than in binary. If we write the numbers in binary, we have the following encoding:

100/11/110/10/11/10/11/10/101/10/1/11/110/1/1/11/101/10/1/11/100/11/10/1010/
10/1011/10/1010/10/10/11/100/11/1/10/101/11/1/1/110/11/1/10/101/10/11/110/
110/110/100

That's longer than the decimal version, but it's still better, at 162 characters, than the original. Unfortunately, we're still cheating, since our goal was to use a binary alphabet, and we still have the / delimiters.

   a. How would you solve this problem? Try a solution that uses *only* the digits 0 and 1 (no spaces, please — the space character isn't a 0 or 1) and see if it allows you to encode the bit pattern in less than 187 bits.
   b. Does your solution give better or worse results on the bit string of Exercise 5, which has longer runs than the string of Figure 1.1?

7. a. What is a high-level language? Why do we have them?
   b. Describe the process by which a C++ program is executed on a computer.

8. What is the difference between a class and an object?

9. Which of the following are illegal C++ object names, and why?
   a. *two*
   b. 2
   c. *class*
   d. *the object*
   e. *O.K.*
   f. *supercallifragillisticexpialidocious*
   g. *output_temperature3*

10. Explain the difference between a declaration and a definition.

11. Modify the example in the text by describing a class hierarchy for polygons (plane figures with straight-edge boundaries, such as triangles, squares, rectangles, and so on), including the data and operations each class would contain. Notice that we have the possibility of *multiple inheritance* here, since a square "is a kind of" (i.e., could be a subclass of) both rectangles (four-sided parallelograms with right angles but perhaps unequal sides) and rhombuses (four-sided parallelograms with perhaps non-right angles but equal sides).

12. Write a class hierarchy for motor vehicles. Do you see any possible multiple inheritances, as we defined in Exercise 11?

13. a. Why do we separate most of our programs into distinct files?
    b. What is the purpose of a header file?

14. What changes would you have to make to our digital timer to have it work as the timer does on a microwave oven, where we set the timer and it counts down to zero?

15. What changes would you have to make to our digital timer to have it include hours, minutes, and seconds?

16. What changes would you have to make to our digital timer to turn it into an odometer, like the ones that measure mileage in a car?

17. Since comments are ignored in C++ and semicolons terminate declarations, could we have a line that looked like this? (Notice we've moved the semicolon.) Explain why or why not.

```
int position    // the position that is visible;
```

In Exercises 18–24, provide descriptions of the classes you would use in programs that must perform the indicated tasks. These descriptions are very much like those you might get at the start of a programming job — vague and open-ended — so feel free to make any reasonable assumptions you want.

18. Implement a calculator program that would display a calculator on a computer screen. The user would "click" the buttons with the mouse or arrow keys.

19. Keep an electronic gradebook for this course (read your syllabus, if you haven't already, to find the number and weight of assignments and exams).

20. Keep track of a checking account.

21. Operate a traffic light that was attached to traffic sensors that could tell whether a car was waiting at the light.

22. Control the action of a bank of elevators.

23. Manage the inventory of a fast food restaurant

24. Manage the payroll of a fast food restaurant.

2

THE INGREDIENTS
OF CLASSES

You can't make an omelette without having eggs.

We can't begin to write programs in C++, or any other language, without having some idea of the ingredients that allow us to build programs. In the next three chapters, we'll cover the building blocks of C++, the built-in data types, functions, and control structures we can use to manipulate these types of information. We've already said that a class consists of data, along with functions that are used to manipulate the class's data. In this chapter we'll cover the simple data types: whole numbers, real numbers, and characters. Then we'll talk about the functions, operators, and expressions that C++ provides for us to manipulate these types of information. In other words, we'll describe the built-in classes of C++.

OBJECTIVES

In this chapter, we will

► Explore the basic data types that come built in as part of C++.

► Describe the operators that may be used to manipulate simple data.

► Discuss simple input and output.

► Describe functions in C++ and explain how they work.

► Explore the use of libraries, both predefined and user-defined.

2.1 ATOMIC DATA TYPES

Atomic types are the simple, indivisible data types that are defined as part of C++. Obviously, we wouldn't be able to do much in any program without the ability to store and manipulate numbers and characters. Fortunately for us, these types are already prepared for our use. Here, we'll talk about these types and the operations we have available to manipulate these kinds of information. Although they aren't strictly classes, at least not in the high-level sense that we've been using the term, they are classes in a practical sense. After all, any information consists of the data itself, along with a collection of operations that we can perform on the information. Although the details of how the primitive data types of C++ are implemented are decidedly private, they are public in the sense that they are available for our use. Let's see now what we have to work with.

The Integral Types

The first types we'll consider are those that represent *integers;* that is, whole numbers such as 0, –34, and 762442344550052. There are four basic integer types, distinguished by the amount of space in memory allocated for them. From shortest to longest, the integer types are char, short, int, and long. The char type is the fundamental dimension for storage of C++ entities; it is typically one *byte* of 8 binary digits, but it can be of any size that is sufficient to store the character set used by the implementation. Eight bits would provide $2^8 = 256$ possible values, which is generally sufficient for representing characters, but would certainly be too small to represent the ranges of integers seen in most programs.

> Although **char** is represented internally by an integer, **char** types are almost never used to represent numbers, as we'll see shortly.

For this reason, C++ provides the larger types, short, int, and long. The C++ standard stipulates that short never be bigger than int and, similarly, that int never be bigger than long. The details, however, are left to the implementation. The only things you can count on beyond that ordering are (1) char types must be at least 8 bits long, (2) short types must be at least 16 bits long (so you can count on at least $2^{16} = 65,536$ different short integers), and (3) long types must be at least 32 bits long (giving you at least 4,294,976,296 different long integers).* This wealth of types can provide more efficient storage in cases where you know that the numbers your program will represent lie within a certain range. Modern computers, though, generally have enough memory available so that we won't worry about storage efficiency and will use int and long to represent integers almost exclusively.

Integer types come in two varieties, signed and unsigned. A signed type represents both positive and negative values, usually about the same number of

---

* C++ provides an operator, *sizeof,* that takes a type or variable name as argument and returns the storage size of the type in multiples of the size of char. Thus, sizeof(char) is always 1 and sizeof(long) may be 4 or more, depending on the actual size of long types in your implementation.

each, and an unsigned type represents numbers from 0 to some upper limit.*
Depending on the system, the char type might be signed or unsigned while the
other types, unless specified otherwise, are always assumed to be signed.

Representing integer *literals,* specific values, is easy. Integers are written as
a collection of digits, optionally preceded by a sign. The only thing to be aware
of is that C++ integers are never written with commas and may not begin with
a zero, so 90, –233, and 40000000 are all integer literals we could use, but 061
and 32,767 are not.[†]

The Floating Types

The other class of numeric values are the *floating-point numbers,* used to represent numbers with a fractional part; for example, 3.1415926536 and –.00001.
As with the integer types, C++ provides different sizes for floating-point numbers. From shortest to longest, they are float, double, and long double. We will use
double almost exclusively. Floating-point literals may begin with an optional sign
and must have either a decimal point or an exponent, represented by e or E, or
both a decimal point and an exponent. If a floating-point literal has an exponent,
it represents the number of positions right or left to shift the decimal point, so
3.01e3 would represent 3.01×10^3, or 3010. If a decimal point is not present, it
is assumed to be immediately to the left of the exponent, so 2e–3 would be the
same as 2.0e–3, which is the same as 0.002 (or 20E–4, or .0002e+1).

The Character Type

Aside from numbers, we often need to represent and manipulate other types of
information. The first non-numeric C++ type we'll introduce has already been
mentioned briefly—the char type, which is used to represent characters, such as
'G', 'g', or '%'. Although characters are represented internally by integer codes
(assigning 'A' the number 65, for instance), declaring an entity as char will ensure that the numeric codes will be treated as ordinary characters for purposes
such as input and output. Character literals are letters enclosed by single
quotes: 'A', '$', 'a' (C++ treats upper- and lower-case characters as distinct if
the machine's character set supports both forms). Some characters don't have
a nice visible form, so they are represented in C++ by *escape sequences,* such as
'\n' for the *newline* character, which forces output to continue on the next line;
'\t' for the *tab* character, which moves output to the next tab stop; and '\" (what
character do you suppose this represents?).

Although not an atomic type, we should mention that C++ also supports
character strings, which consist of a sequence of characters enclosed by double

---

* For example, on a system with 16-bit ints, signed int would be capable of representing integers in
the range –32,768 . . . 32,767, and unsigned int would represent the range 0 . . . 65,536.
[†] Actually, 063 is a legal integer, but the 0 prefix identifies it as a base-8 or *octal* number, in this
case the number $6 \times 8 + 3 \times 1 = 51$.

quotes. These are often used with the << operator to display a message on the screen; for example,

```
cout << "This is a message.\n";
```

which would display the character string within the quotes, followed by a new-line character, on the screen (so further output would begin on the line below).

Declaring and Defining Objects: Variables and Constants

In C++, as in most other languages, we may use *variables* to represent informa-tion whose values may not even be known at the time we're writing a program and whose value may change during the course of execution. A variable is noth-ing but a name for an object. Because the size and the nature of storage differ for objects of different types, we must tell the system the type of information that any variable will represent before we use the object. Such a *declaration* in C++ takes the form

typeName variableName1, variableName2, ...;

A declaration sets aside a storage location of the appropriate size for the indi-cated type and associates that storage with the indicated names. For example, to declare three integers *larry*, *moe*, and *curly*, and two doubles *clipper* and *sparky*, we would write the two declaration statements

We described the rules for C++ names in Chapter 1.

```
int larry, moe, curly;
double clipper, sparky;
```

▼

All variables must be declared before they are used.

It's important to note that neither of these statements defines any initial values for their variables. We can do that, though, if we wish by using the assignment operator = in the context of a declaration, as below.

```
int larry = 3, moe, curly = 2;
double clipper = 93e2, sparky = -5.004;
```

In this example, we've declared five variables and we have defined initial values for all but *moe*. You can avoid a frequent source of programming error if you're careful about initializing all variables. Unlike some other languages, you shouldn't assume that C++ variables begin their lives with any predictable val-ues; unless you give them values, they may start out with any random values that happened to be left in their assigned memory locations.

Actually, C++ will set uninitialized global variables (which we'll define shortly) to zero, but it's still a good idea to initialize everything explicitly.

▼

Make sure you initialize your variables in a definition before you use them.

A variable is a named object whose value may change while a program is running. There are times, though, when we want to fix the value of some object and guarantee that it will not change during its lifetime. To do that, we declare a *constant* object by placing the keyword const in front of its declaration. This can be handy for two reasons. First, declaring

```
const double PI = 3.1415926536;
```

makes a program easier to read, since PI / 4.0 is far more expressive to a human reader than is the number .7853981634. Second, suppose we had a program that did a variety of manipulations on arrays of 100 numbers. If we wanted to modify that program to manipulate lists of 200 numbers, we'd have to search through the program to find all instances of the number 100 and change them to 200. You might respond that most programming environments have a global search-and-replace feature that would make the process simple, but the rub is that there might be other instances of the number 100, like the number of cents in a dollar, that you certainly wouldn't want to change. Alternatively, defining

```
const int ARRAYSIZE = 100;
```

and then using *ARRAYSIZE* where needed would mean that you could modify the program by changing one declaration, rather than having to find and modify perhaps twenty other statements throughout several files. (Notice that we conform to the convention of using all uppercase letters in naming constant objects.)

2.2 SIMPLE OPERATORS

Now that we know how to call a variable into existence, we need to know how to manipulate the value a variable represents. C++ provides a wealth of operators that we can use to manipulate atomic information.

Numeric Operators

C++ has five basic numeric operators: +, −, *, /, and %. The first three are exactly what you would expect: addition, subtraction, and multiplication. These apply to both integer and floating-point values. Division, though, acts differently depending on whether the numbers being divided are integers or floats. Division of floating-point numbers is accomplished by using the / operator, so 19.0 / 5.0 evaluates to the float 3.8. If the numbers are integers, the / operator gives the quotient and % gives the remainder of the division, so 19 / 5 would yield 3 and 19 % 5 would yield the remainder, 4. Notice that % is not defined for floats.

C++ has *precedence* rules that determine the order in which expressions are evaluated. We do this in the real world when we evaluate 3 + 4 * 5 as 23, rather than 35 (which we would get if we did the addition before the multiplication).

The precedence of the numeric operators is, from highest to lowest:

unary +, unary − (as in −13, for example)
*, /, and %
+ and −

We are free to use parentheses to group terms in an expression, just as we are accustomed to doing when writing arithmetic expressions: (31 + 8) * (5 − 7) would cause the two parenthesized subexpressions to be evaluated first and then multiplied. The binary operators +, −, * , /, and % group from left to right if we have a string of several operators of the same precedence, so 3 − 4 + 5 would be evaluated in the order ((3 − 4) + 5), rather than the somewhat less conventional (3 − (4 + 5)).* The *unary* minus operator, like the − in −5, groups from right to left and has a higher precedence than the binary operators. Thus, the expression −5 + 3 would be evaluated in the order we would expect: (−5) + 3. C++ has complicated precedence rules covering all of its operators, so we've put a summary table in Appendix B.

Whenever the slightest doubt exists about how to evaluate an expression, parenthesize.

Since incrementing (increasing a value by 1) and decrementing (decreasing a value by 1) are so often used in programs, C++ provides operators that perform these operations directly. The operator ++, when placed after a variable, increases the value of what it is operating on by 1. If *counter* is a numeric variable, the expression *counter*++ first returns the value of *counter* and then increases *counter* by 1. Note the order that things happen here, since it takes a bit of getting used to: (1) *counter* is used in whatever expression, if any, it is in and then (2) the value of *counter* is incremented.

If, for example, *counter* had the value 3 and *sum* had the value 10, the expression

```
sum * counter++
```

would evaluate to 30, and as a *side effect* the value of *counter* would then be changed to 4. On the other hand, if ++ is used before a variable, the value is incremented first, before it is used in an expression. Thus, if we had modified the example above to read

```
sum * ++counter
```

---

* This grouping property is called *associativity*, so we could as well say that the binary operators (except for the assignment operators, which we'll see soon) are left associative.

the expression would evaluate to 40, since *counter* would be incremented before its value was used in the expression.

The decrement operator – – (two adjacent minus signs) behaves similarly to ++, and they both have the same precedence as the other unary operators. It is important to note that the objects on which ++ and – – operate must be modifiable: These two operations cannot be used on constants, literals, or expressions.*

> Order matters with the increment and decrement operators: The *preincrement* operator is written *before* a variable and increments first, then returns a value; the *postincrement* operator is written *after* a variable and increments after returning the value of the variable. The same rules hold for decrementing.

Assignment Operators

The assignment operator = sets the value of whatever is on its left to be whatever the result is of evaluating what's on its right. This operator applies to all of the types we've seen so far and acts somewhat differently than any of the other operators we've seen so far. For one thing, it is not symmetric: the part on the left must represent a storage location (so for our purposes at this time there must be a variable on the left), and the right side must be some expression that returns a value. For example, the first three assignments below are legal, while the last three are not.

```
// These three are legal
a = 3 * (b + a);        // sets the value of a
double x = y;           // declares x and sets it to y's value
a = b = 5;              // sets both a and b to 5

// These three are illegal
a + 2 = b;              // a + 2 isn't a storage location
PI = 3;                 // constants can't be modified
x++ = y;                // x++ isn't a storage location
                        // x = y++ would be legal, though
```

The last of the legal assignments above, *a* = *b* = 5, is worth examining more closely, as it illustrates the functional nature of C++. C++ differs from many other languages in that there is no separate assignment *statement*. Assignment is an operator, such as / or ++, and like other operators, its primary effect is to return a value to the program. Assignment groups from right to left (unlike all

---

* This makes sense, since 3++ should never be allowed to modify the value of the constant. Similarly, there's no unique storage location for (*a* + *b*)++ to increment. In technical terms, the argument of ++ and –– must be a modifiable *lvalue*, a value that specifies a storage location, and can be used on the *left* side of an assignment operator.

other binary operators), so the expression $a = b = 5$ is evaluated in the order $a = (b = 5)$. The first subexpression, $b = 5$, not only sets b to 5, but also returns the value b was set to, in this case 5. That value then is returned to the program where it serves as the right side of the second assignment, which sets a to 5. Figure 2.1 illustrates the two-part action of each of the assignments in our example. Assignment has the lowest precedence we've seen so far, so we can be sure it will be performed only after all other involved operators.

> All the operators we've seen return values to the program for use in subsequent evaluations. Some, like =, ++, and − −, have additional actions (called "side effects").

There are a number of other assignment operators, as illustrated in the following box. They are not absolutely necessary, since they could be defined in terms of other operators, but they do serve as useful abbreviations for common operations. Note that assignment operators have the same precedence, and all group from right to left. Notice too that the precedence of the assignment operators is lower than that of any arithmetic operator. This implies that in an expression like $a \mathrel{*=} b+5$, the addition operation will be performed before the multiplication and assignment..

Operator	Equivalent Expression
$v \mathrel{+=} e;$	$v = v + e;$
$v \mathrel{-=} e;$	$v = v - e;$
$v \mathrel{*=} e;$	$v = v * e;$
$v \mathrel{/=} e;$	$v = v / e;$
$v \mathrel{\%=} e;$	$v = v \% e;$

FIGURE 2.1
How the assignment
operator works

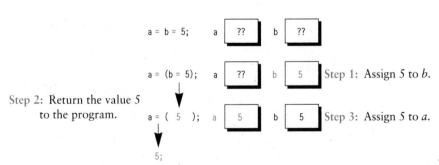

$a = b = 5;$ a [??]   b [??]

$a = (b = 5);$ a [??]   b [5]   Step 1: Assign 5 to b.

Step 2: Return the value 5
to the program. $a = (\; 5 \;);$ a [5]   b [5]   Step 3: Assign 5 to a.

5;

Step 4: Return 5 to the program
(where it's ignored, since
there's nothing more to do).

In general, C++ provides us with a number of ways of accomplishing what we want. For instance, all four of the following expression statements accomplish the same thing, namely increasing the value of *n* by 1.

We'll define *expression statements* in the next section.

```
n = n + 1;
n += 1;
n++;
++n;
```

By the way, a common mistake for beginners is to mistake the assignment operator for something it's not. The assignment operator is *not* the equals sign from high school algebra.* The expression *n = n + 1* does not assert that *n* is equal to one more than itself. Instead, the expression first evaluates *n + 1* (since + has higher precedence than =), returns the calculated value, and then sets *n* to this new value. The equality operator in C++ is ==.

2.3 STATEMENTS

A *statement* is the smallest complete, executable unit of a program. A program in C++ consists of a sequence of statements. There are several kinds of statements in C++. We'll describe three kinds here that are most closely related to the atomic types.

Declaration Statements

You've already seen declaration statements. They are used to establish the existence and, optionally, the initial values of objects identified by name. While there are a variety of forms for declaration statements, the three that are of interest to us here are

> *typeName identifier*, ... ;
> *typeName identifier* = *expression*, ... ;
> const *typeName identifier* = *expression*, ... ;

Note that each declaration statement ends with a semicolon. In the descriptions above, the ellipses (. . .) indicate an optional comma-separated list of identifiers or *identifier = expression* terms. The examples below are all legitimate C++ declaration statements.

```
char c1;
int p, q = 3, r = a + b;        // (assuming a and b have been
                                // declared and initialized before)

const double RATE = 0.075;
```

---

* Some languages address this source of confusion explicitly by using special symbols like := for assignment. C++ addresses this problem by using = for assignment and == for equality.

Expression Statements

Expression statements cause the expression to be evaluated and any side effects (like increment or assignment) to be performed. These statements take the general form

> *expression;*

Again, notice that an expression statement ends with a semicolon. The statements below show some of the forms expression statements can take, assuming that all identifiers have been previously declared.

```
n++;                        // we're using only the side effect here
5;                          // legal but silly, since it does nothing
interest = principal * interest_rate;
a += b = 3;                 // tricky: sets b to 3 and increments a by 3
x = double((3 + n) / (4.8e-2 * (1 - a / b)));
```

Compound Statements

As you'll see in the next chapter, there are times when we want to be able to treat a collection of statements as a single unit. We do this by enclosing a list of statements between the braces { and }, forming what is known as a *compound statement*. Compound statements take these general forms:

```
{                                          {   statement
    statement                                  statement
        statement                              .
        .                                      .
        .                                      .
        .                                  statement }
    statement
}
```

C++ is a free-format language: Spaces, tabs, and carriage returns may be used at your discretion, so you are free to format a program in any way that makes it easy for you to read.

The enclosed statements may be any we wish: declarations, expressions, compound statements, and others we'll learn about shortly. We might, for example, make a compound statement like this:

```
{
    int i = 3;
    double x = 2.01, y = -3.89;
    int j = 2 - i;
    x = 2.4 * (x - y);
}
```

Notice in the example above that individual expressions and declaration statements are punctuated by semicolons, as required. Compound statements do not require semicolon terminators, as the closing brace acts as a punctuator.

Scope

Every identifier that you use in a program has a *scope*, a portion of the program in which it is defined and may be used. An identifier's scope is determined by where it is declared and by the organization of the program surrounding the declaration. In the preceding compound statement example, the variable *i* has a scope that begins at its declaration and ends at the closing brace of the compound statement. This means that we may refer to *i* anywhere in the *block* of code. The variable *j*, on the other hand, has as its scope only the last two statements in the block defined by the braces. It would be an error to refer to *j* before its declaration. The identifiers *i, j, x,* and *y* are declared within the block and so have no meaning outside it; any reference to them outside their scope is an error.

This is a very useful feature of C++ (and one that is missing in many other languages), since it means that we can declare identifiers right where they are used, eliminating the need to hunt through a program asking, "Now, what the heck kind of object is *x* and what value does it have?" Since identifiers have meaning only in their scope, we can reuse the same identifiers in different blocks of a program to refer to entirely different objects, like this:

```
{... int i = 0; ...}
{... const double i = 1.045; ...}
```

> A variable that is declared within a block (a part enclosed by { and } braces) has meaning only from its point of declaration to the end of that block.

If an identifier is declared outside of any block (for example, in a file, but not enclosed within braces), its scope is *global;* that is, it can be referred to and retains its meaning anywhere in the file.

As we'll see later, blocks — and, hence, scopes — can be nested within one another. As a result, it is quite common for a name to be used in two different but coexisting blocks, as follows:

```
{... int i = 0; ... { double i; ... } ... }
```

In this case, all references to variable *i* from within the inner braces refer to the double *i*, since it is the "closest" declaration. The double version of *i*, of course, does not exist outside of that inner block and so references to *i* from the outer block refer to the integer version.

2.4 FUNCTIONS

We have described an object as having associated behaviors — actions that an object can perform on itself. Every action that takes place in a C++ program happens in the context of a function. Indeed, every C++ program is itself a function, called main(), whose job is to declare objects and to call upon other

FIGURE 2.2
Illustration of a
function

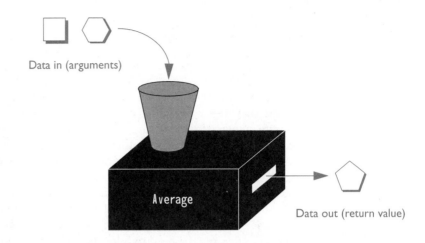

Data in (arguments)

Average

Data out (return value)

functions, which may call other functions that themselves call other functions, and so on, all for the purpose of acting on objects.

A *function* in C++ is very similar to the mathematical functions we've seen in school. If mention of mathematics makes you nervous, think instead of a function as a black box, like that in Figure 2.2. The black box takes information in, does something with it, and returns a single value. That's all there is to a function.

Every function has four components: (1) its name, (2) the type of value it returns when it has done its task, (3) the information it takes in to perform its task, and (4) the (compound) statement it uses to perform its task. To use (or *call*) a function, we write the function's name, followed by a parenthesized list of the information we want it to process. For example, if *Average* is a function that takes two doubles as inputs and returns as its value a double, we would call it like *Average(x, y)*. The C++ rule that requires each name to be declared before it is used applies to function as well. That is, before we can call a function, we must first specify three of its components (all but its compound statement) in a function declaration.

Declaring Functions

Declaring a function, like declaring a variable, is a way of telling the compiler what form it will take so that there will be no confusion about its name, its return type, and the number and types of its *arguments* (the incoming information). At the time of declaration, the compiler doesn't need to know the details of how the function works. All it needs is enough information to ensure that the function is called correctly. In other words, to declare a function, all we need to do is provide a *prototype* for the function that describes its name and associated types.

We declare a function by writing a *function declaration* that takes the following form (note the required semicolon for a declaration statement):

typeName identifier (*argumentList*);

The identifier that forms the function name follows the same rules as all other identifiers like variable, class, and constant names. The *argumentList* in parentheses is a possibly empty list of type names and (optionally) names of the arguments, separated by commas. We can't, however, use the shorthand form of declaration, following a typename by a list of variable names: The declaration

```
double Average(double x, y); // incorrect
```

is incorrect because argument *y* has no associated type. All of the following, on the other hand, are valid function declarations:

```
double Average(double x, double y);
double Average(double, double);
char GetACharacter();
void PrintValues(int count, double amount);
```

The first two examples are alternate ways of saying the same thing. The compiler—and, for that matter, a user of the function—doesn't need to know what names you will give to the function's arguments (though we prefer giving the names, since it makes it easier to match the declaration against the later definition, where argument names *must* be specified). The third example probably gets a character from the keyboard and returns it to the calling location. It takes no arguments (as indicated by the empty argument list) and returns a single character. The last example is, in a sense, the opposite of the third one. The function *PrintValues* might display the values of *count* and *amount* on the screen. It needs to be given those variables, but it doesn't need to return anything. We indicate that by using the special type void as the return type.

We can declare the same function as many times as we like; If we use a function in six different files, we can declare it in each. In fact we *must* declare it in each. This is why we generally put function declarations in header files and put a #include directive in each of the files that use the function. If our header file contains a dozen functions, we save a lot of typing by just using #include.

Most of the function declarations you will see occur within the context of a class declaration. That is, you will be declaring *member functions* of a particular class. Member functions, as we'll see when we examine this chapter's PIP, have direct access to all of the state data associated with a class and so do not require formal arguments to access the class member data. Functions like those above, which are not declared as part of a class declaration, are called *free functions*. Free functions have access only to globally declared data and to information passed to them as arguments. We'll discuss other important differences between member and free functions after we see how functions are defined.

Defining Functions

Sooner or later, we have to tell the compiler what it is that a function actually does. In other words, we have to define the function. In contrast to declarations, which may be duplicated as often as we need, a function may be defined only once. A function definition begins very much like its declaration and is followed by a compound statement that is executed when the function is called. The only difference between a function declaration and its definition, beyond the addition of the compound statement that forms the *function body,* is that function definitions are not punctuated by a terminal semicolon. We could define the functions that we declared earlier by writing

```
double Average(double x, double y)
// Returns the average of x and y.
{
    return (x + y) / 2.0;
}


char GetACharacter();
// Returns a character from standard input.
{
    char c;
    cin >> c;
    return c;
}


void PrintValues(int count, double amount);
// Displays on standard output the values of
// the two arguments, along with some window dressing.
{
    cout << "Here are the two values:\n";
    cout << "----------------------------------------\n";
    cout << '\t' << count << '\t' << amount << '\n';
}
```

Most of this should appear familiar. The blocks that form the function body are ordinary compound statements (they must be, even if there is only one statement, as in *Average*), and the headings look just like the declarations we've seen already, except that they don't end in semicolons (the braces from the compound statements serve the purpose). The variable *c* in *GetACharacter* is known as a *local variable*: Its scope is within the function block and has no meaning outside the block. Similarly, the argument names have scope only within the function.

There is one surprise, though. The first two functions have a statement we haven't seen yet:

```
return expression;
```

You can probably guess that the purpose of this statement is to set explicitly the value that is to be returned by the function. What might not be so obvious is that return also forces immediate exit from the function, skipping any statements that might follow. A function that has a non-void return type must have an explicit return statement for every possible exit, including "falling out of the bottom." You can use a return to force exit from a void function, but in that case, the return may not contain an expression.

> We can have as many return statements as we need in a function. A non-void function must return some value, no matter what happens within the function body.

Using Functions

Once a function has been declared and defined, it can finally be used from within a program. To use a function, we merely call it by referring to the function's name and providing it with a list of arguments to operate on. The specific form a function call takes depends on how the function was declared. In particular, we must take into account the number and types of the function's arguments as well as its return type.

We could, for example, call the functions defined above in statements like these:

```
double theAnswer = Average(x, y);
cout << "Do you want to print the average?";
char ch = GetACharacter( );
if ((ch == "y") || (ch == "Y")) // got an affirmative answer
PrintValues (2, theAnswer);
```

There are a few things here that deserve a special mention. First, observe that *Average* has return type double, so it is appropriate to use the returned value in an expression that assigns it to the double variable *theAnswer*. In a similar way, *GetACharacter* returns a char, so it is appropriate to use the returned value to initialize variable *ch*. Second, notice that *PrintValues*, having a void return type, is completely at home in an expression statement of its own but would be inappropriate as part of an assignment or comparison statement.

Finally, notice that *PrintValues* is called with the arguments 2 and *theAnswer*, although it is declared with the arguments *count* and *amount*. Hmm. It would appear that the names of the *formal arguments* (those used in the declaration) and the *actual arguments* (those used in the call) don't have to match. The types do, but the names don't. This makes perfect sense when you consider that a function might be called a number of times with different arguments from different parts of a program, and we couldn't possibly guarantee a name match every time.

> A formal argument and its corresponding actual argument don't have to have the same names, but they must have the same types (or at least, the type of an actual argument must permit it to be converted to its corresponding formal argument).

What actually happens when a function is called is that the actual arguments are used as definition values for the formal arguments. For example, if we have declared *PrintValues* as above,

```
void PrintValues (int count, double amount);
```

and then call it by writing

```
PrintValues (2, theAnswer);
```

it is as if the function was invoked like this:

```
{
    count = 2;
    amount = theAnswer;
    // The rest of the function definition
}
```

This has an important consequence. Since the actual arguments are used simply to initialize the formal arguments, it means that any change we make to *count* and *amount* in the function will not be reflected in changes to the actual arguments.

We'll see in Chapter 6, however, that it is possible to work around this restriction and make a function modify its actual arguments.

> Although there is a correspondence between formal and actual arguments, information flow in a function's arguments is one way. A function cannot modify the values of its actual arguments.

The numbers of formal and actual arguments don't have to match if we declare a function to have *default arguments,* or arguments whose values are initialized in the function's formal argument list, like this:

```
void PrintValues(int count, double amount = 0.0);
```

Since values for default arguments are provided in the formal argument list, a default argument need not appear as an actual argument. Given the declaration above, we could call *PrintValues* in two different ways:

```
PrintValues (n, a);
PrintValues (n); // equivalent to PrintValues (n, 0.0)
```

We can define default arguments in either the function declaration or its definition, but not in both places. We use the common convention of always defining default arguments in the declaration part. The only other caution about default arguments is that they all must appear at the tail of the argument list:

```
double f(int n, int m, int p = 0);
                                           // LEGAL
double f(int n, int m = 1, int p = 0);     // LEGAL
double f(int n = 2, int m = 1, int p = 0); // LEGAL
double f(int n, int m = 1, int p);         // ILLEGAL
double f(int n = 2, int m, int p = 0);     // ILLEGAL
```

A little thought should make the reasons for this requirement clear.

Below are some additional examples of function calls to the functions we defined above, along with the necessary variable declarations. See if you can determine why each is described as either LEGAL or ILLEGAL.

```
char c1, c2;
double d1, d2, d3;
int i1,i2;


Average(d1, d2);        // ILLEGAL
c1 = Average(d1, d2);   // ILLEGAL
d1 = Average(d2, d3);   // LEGAL
d3 = Average(d2, i2);   // LEGAL
c1 = GetACharacter;     // ILLEGAL
c2 = GetACharacter();   // LEGAL
i1 = GetACharacter();   // LEGAL
PrintValues(int, double); // ILLEGAL
i2 = PrintValues(i1, d1); // ILLEGAL
PrintValues(i2, d2);    // LEGAL
```

2.5 FILES AND LIBRARIES

A *file*, recall, is merely a collection of information stored on, for example, a floppy or hard disk under a given name. Historically, the code for a program (say, in FORTRAN, COBOL, or Pascal) was stored in a single (often very large), monolithic file. It was a challenge to get a program to access a separate data file, much less to communicate with another program. As our collective software experience has grown, and as the machines and the languages that we have available for expressing our programs have rapidly evolved, two essential ideas about the file structure of a program have emerged and evolved to the point of being regarded today as common programming wisdom.

The first idea stemmed from the recognition that many programs perform common processing tasks on common types of data. As a result, many programmers have spent a great deal of time writing, testing, and debugging programs that have been written, tested, and debugged before. This constant reinventing of the programming wheel was regarded as a significant hindrance to software productivity, and with good reason. The C programming language, the natural ancestor of C++, was among the first to provide programmers with *libraries* of precompiled code to implement common processing tasks. A C program that needed, for example, to communicate with certain types of input/output devices, or to calculate certain mathematical functions, or to perform a certain sorting algorithm could simply "check out" the appropriate collection of code from a C library and use it directly. Each library is itself a distinct file containing code related to a particular type of processing or data. As we have already seen, to make use of a particular library in a program, the programmer need only place an #include directive in the program, referring to the name of the file to be used.

The second innovation in program file structure extended this code library notion in a somewhat subtle way. As we became more experienced with defining and using program libraries, it became clear that the user of a library file did not need to know the details of how that piece of code was written. That, after all, was the primary intention of the library — to save each programmer from having to reimplement the same code. As a programmer, one wanted to *use* the library code without having to understand it in full detail or even to see it. This recognition led the developers of C to distinguish between a code library's *interface* — how it can be described to someone who wants to use it — and its *implementation* — how it is programmed.

Thus, the interface to a portion of the C library (containing the names of the routines and data types included) was stored in a separate file from the program that actually implemented the library. The C++ language was defined to build on these insights. Every implementation of C++ comes with a collection of predefined code libraries for describing and implementing a wide range of processing tasks and data types. Further, each portion of the library is accessible by means of a *header file* that describes, in essence, the contents of each of the libraries' "books" and how to use it.

The real power, of C++, however, derives from the facility with which C++ programmers can augment the built-in code libraries with header and implementation files of their own to build powerful and useful software systems. This is the activity toward which most of this text is directed. We want to encourage you to think of C++ programs as being organized as pictured in Figure 2.3, which reflects our Declare-Define-Use approach to C++ program development.

We have as our starting point an extensive collection of C++ libraries of predefined classes and associated operations. Any of the other files in our system can access any of these libraries. We extend this collection by using it to declare (in header files of our own devising) a collection of higher-level classes that reflect as nearly as possible the problem domain our program intends to model. We provide implementation files that contain detailed descriptions of the algorithms and data described in each of our header files. Finally, we write what, in the more tradition-

FIGURE 2.3
A C++ program with built-in and programmer-defined libraries

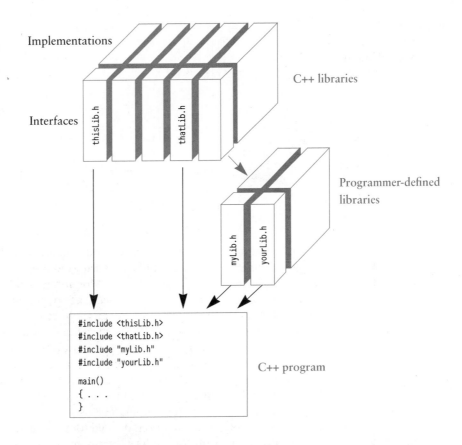

al algorithmic sense, would be regarded as the real C++ "program." Because of the energy devoted to declaring and defining the classes in the problem domain, the program has little to do except to use the predefined classes to perform its intended processing. You will see this organization reflected in all of our PIPs.

Simple Input and Output: The *iostream* Library

As we mentioned in Chapter 1, a fundamental fact of life when dealing with computers is that they don't speak the same language we do, in several respects. Not only is the language of the machine completely unlike any natural language used by people, but computers don't even represent information in the same way that people do. If you interact with a computer, you usually do so by typing characters on a keyboard and reading characters that appear on a screen. Input and output are difficult to implement precisely because we use characters to represent information and the computer does not.*

---

* Of course, people represent information in other ways. The problems with sound and graphics input and output are even worse than those of character I/O, so much so that we won't even attempt to address those issues.

FIGURE 2.4
The use of streams
for input and output

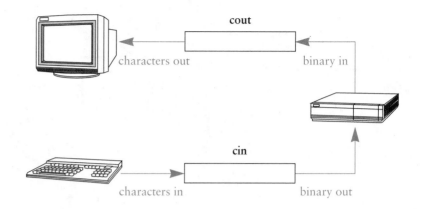

Unlike many languages, C++ has no built-in facilities for handling input or output (frequently abbreviated I/O). Instead, input and output are handled by library routines.* The classes C++ uses for input and output are known as *streams*. In simple terms, a stream is a sequence of characters, along with a collection of routines for inserting characters into streams (for eventual display) and extracting characters from a stream (for eventual input). The member functions of these streams handle the translation from characters to, say, integers, and from integers back to human-readable characters (see Figure 2.4).

If you look at the C++ header file *"iostream.h"* in the standard libraries that came with your compiler, you'll find the declaration of the class *ostream*. This is the class that C++ uses for output. The *ostream* object we will use for all of our screen output has already been defined for us — it's called cout. Suppose we wish to display the value of the int object named *i*. We'd write the statement

```
cout << i;
```

What actually goes on here is that C++ uses the << operator (which we call "insert") to convert the internal representation of *i* to characters and sends those characters to the ostream cout. The operator << is designed in such a way that it sends values to the stream cout from left to right, so if we wanted to display the value of *i* and then skip down to the next line on the screen, we could insert a newline character into the stream after *i,* as below:

We'll see more about
the way << works in
Chapter 5.

```
cout << i << '\n';
```

Input is handled by the class *istream*. As with *ostreams*, there is a standard, predefined *istream* object, called cin, that refers to the standard input device (the keyboard, for our purpose). The operator we use to get a value from the

---

* This is a language design issue: Do you complicate the compiler designer's job by putting the burden of generating code for input and output devices in the language, or do you keep the language simple and put the I/O burden on the people who have to write libraries? Pascal, FORTRAN, and BASIC place the burden on the compiler (or interpreter), and C and C++ make the libraries handle the work.

keyboard is the *extraction* operator >>. For instance, if *i* was an int object, we could write

```
cin >> i;
```

to get a number from the keyboard and store that number in the location associated with variable *i*. Roughly speaking, the statement above "extracts" a collection of characters from the *istream* cin, up to the first character that couldn't possibly be part of an integer. It then converts the characters to an integer, and stores the result as the value of *i*.

2.6   PROGRAM IN PROGRESS: A FRACTION PACKAGE

Several times so far, we've mentioned that a particularly nice feature of C++ is that it is extensible, in the sense that we may define types of our own to augment the predefined types of objects that are built in to the language. In this chapter's PIP, we give a simple example of just such an extension and use this example to illustrate some of the C++ concepts we've discussed so far.

The atomic numeric types char, short, int, long, float, double, and long double are adequate for many programs we might want to write, but they certainly don't cover all possible kinds of numbers. In particular, we might want to have a type that represents rational numbers, such as 1/3 or 22/7. We could, of course, use a floating-point type like double to represent fractions, but doing this would force us to approximate fractions like 1/3 by 0.3333333. No matter how many places of accuracy were available, we'd never be able to completely represent a fraction. What we'd like to have is a class that we could use to represent fractions exactly.

Designing the PIP

As you know, a class encapsulates both the *member data* that would be part of every object of the class, along with a collection of *member functions* and other operations that we can use to manipulate objects of the class. In the case of fractions, the member data are easy to describe: A fraction can be represented by two integers, the *numerator,* or top part, and the *denominator,* which represents the bottom number in the fraction.

The operations that will be part of the *Fraction* class are not much more difficult to invent. All you have to do is answer the question "What does one do with fractions?" Obvious answers include:

1. Construct and initialize a new fraction object.
2. Display a fraction on standard output, in the form "*numerator/denominator*".
3. Get a fraction from standard input, in the same form.
4. Perform the arithmetic operation + on two fractions, yielding a fraction as a result.

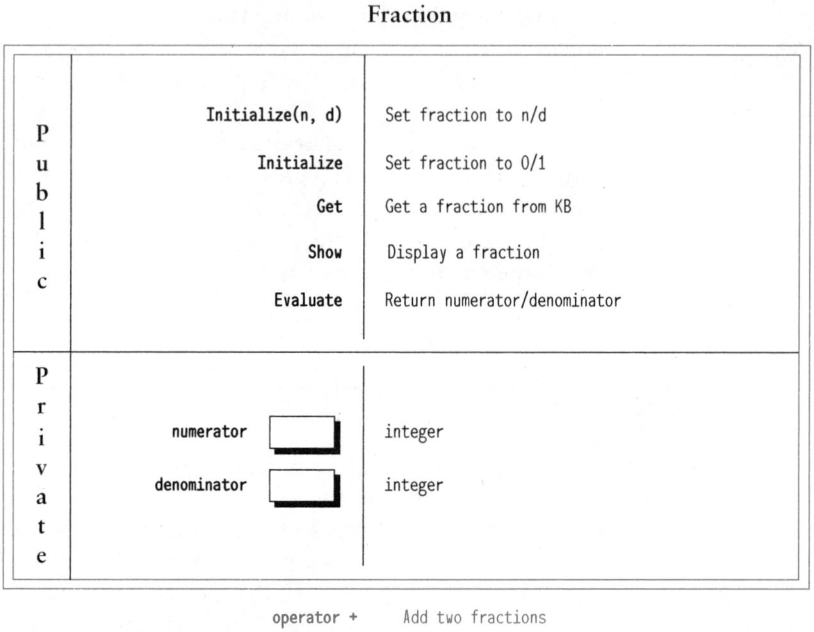

FIGURE 2.5
The *Fraction* class

Fraction

P u b l i c	Initialize(n, d)	Set fraction to n/d
	Initialize	Set fraction to 0/1
	Get	Get a fraction from KB
	Show	Display a fraction
	Evaluate	Return numerator/denominator
P r i v a t e	numerator [ ]	integer
	denominator [ ]	integer

operator +   Add two fractions

We may come up with some more operations later (as we'll see in the lab), but for the time being, our class definition can take the following form:

Fraction
> Data (private):
>> *numerator, denominator:* Integers representing the top and bottom parts of a fraction
>
> Operations (public):
>> *Initialize*(*n, d*): Set *numerator* = *n, denominator* = *d.*
>> *Initialize:* Set *numerator* = 0, *denominator* = 1.
>> *Get:* Set *numerator* and *denominator* to user-entered values.
>> *Show:* Display a fraction.
>> *Evaluate:* Calculate and return *numerator/denominator.*
>> The operator +, redefined for fractions

Figure 2.5 shows what the *Fraction* class looks like. Notice that the operator + is not illustrated as part of the class. You'll see the reason for this shortly.

2.7   EXPLORING THE PIP

In keeping with our practice of separating declarations and definitions, we'll put the class declarations in a header file, "FRACTION.H". The definitions of the functions we'll place in another file, "FRACTION.CPP". Finally, in order to test our class, we'll write a simple *driver program* that will include calls to all the functions we've written. This third file is where the main( ) function will go—we'll call the file "PIP2.CPP". If we were planning to use the *Fraction* class in another program, we could discard "PIP2.CPP" (after making sure that *Fraction* worked as we expected), and add #include references to "FRACTION.H" in our new program files, where appropriate.

Declaration: The File "FRACTION.H"

The declaration part of the *Fraction* class is, as it should be, relatively simple to understand. Notice that we use a default argument in the first constructor. Doing so allows a programmer using this class to specify a fraction by giving just the numerator. In fact, this form of the *Fraction* constructor acts like a type converter, since the definition

```
Fraction f(3);
```

would convert the integer 3 to the fraction *f* with value 3/1.

The second constructor is an example of a *default constructor*, since it takes no arguments. These two constructors allow us to initialize a fraction in three different ways: specifying both numerator and denominator, specifying just the numerator, and specifying neither. In the main function, all three forms are used in the declaration

```
Fraction f1(3, 2), f2(4), f3();
```

Notice, too, that the C++ compiler will not get confused over the fact that we seem to have defined the constructor function for class *Fraction* twice. C++ treats functions as different unless they match exactly in name, argument list, and return type. In this case, the names and return types (none explicit, since they're constructors) match, but each has a different argument list.

```
//-------------- FRACTION.H --------------

// The class declaration for fractions. A fraction is represented
// by a pair of integers: the numerator (top part) and denominator
// (bottom part).
// Note: this class definition includes more than the rational
// numbers, since we allow the number "infinity," i.e., any
// fraction with a zero denominator (except 0/0, which can never
// be defined to make sense).

class Fraction
{
    // operator overload, so we can do fractional arithmetic
    // using a familiar operator

    friend Fraction operator+ (Fraction f1, Fraction f2);
```

```
public:
     Fraction(int n, int d = 1);
     // Set numerator to n, denominator to d
     // if no second argument, default to 1
     Fraction();
     // Set numerator to 0, denominator to 1

     void Get();                    // Get a fraction from keyboard
     void Show();                   // Display a fraction on screen

     double Evaluate();             // Return the decimal value of a fraction

private:
     int numerator;                 // top part
     int denominator;               // bottom part
};
```

The only unusual part of the declaration file is at the very beginning, where we have the declaration

```
friend Fraction operator+ (Fraction f1, Fraction f2);
```

This is an *override* (or *overload*) of the operator +. In other words, we are declaring a new operator, named +, which takes two fractions as operands and returns a fraction as a result. It is often handy to use the same name for functions that do similar things, but to different kinds of objects. We saw that in the PIP for Chapter 1, in which we had member functions named *Show* declared in two different classes, *Display* and *Timer*. C++ provides a similar feature for operators, as well.

> This feature of using the same name for different things is called *polymorphism,* you may recall.

We may override almost all of the predefined operators such as +, =, &&, ==, and even ( ). We do so by a declaration of the form

   ReturnType operator *OperatorName* (*operand list*);

An overloaded operator has the same precedence, number of operands (called *arity,* a nifty piece of jargon), and grouping direction as the predefined operator that is being overridden.

> The only operators we cannot redefine are ., .*, ::, ?:, and **sizeof**.

In the *Fraction* class, for instance, we realized that it would be useful to do arithmetic on fraction objects. In many other languages, we would have to define functions like *Fraction Add(Fraction f1, Fraction f2)*, and then perform addition with calls like *f4 = Add(f1, f2)*. We could adopt this approach in C++, of course, but doing so would be far more verbose and less clear than overloading the + operator and writing addition of fractions in the natural way:

$$f4 = f1 + f2;$$

The overload of the operator + is *not* a member function of the *Fraction* class. Strictly speaking, it isn't part of the *Fraction* class at all: It is an auxiliary operation that happens to apply to fractions. It may appear at first to be part of the *Fraction* class because its declaration appears in the class declaration, but in fact its mention in *Fraction* serves another purpose entirely:

> A class may declare functions or other classes to be friends. A *friend* of a class has access to all the private member data and functions of the class, but is not itself a member of the class.

In our example, the *Fraction* class includes the friend declaration in order to allow our version of the + operator to access member functions and data that would otherwise be denied to it. There would be no way to do arithmetic on two fractions without access to their (private) numerators and denominators, so the + operator must be designated as a friend of the class *Fraction*. Friend declarations are independent of the public/private division in a class and so may appear anywhere in the class declaration. We follow the common convention of declaring friends at the beginning, before the public part.

Definition: The File "FRACTION.CPP"

The file "FRACTION.CPP" contains the implementation part of our *Fraction* class; that is, the definitions of all the member functions and the friend addition operator. Notice first the #include directives. We need iostream.h because we use input and output operations in our function definitions. We need "FRACTION.H" because that's where all the names for *Fraction* data and functions are declared, and the C++ compiler needs that information to understand these definitions.

```cpp
//-------------- FRACTION.CPP ---------------

// The class definition for fractions.

#include <iostream.h>
#include "FRACTION.H"

Fraction operator+ (Fraction f1, Fraction f2)
// Override of operator "+" for fraction addition
{
    Fraction r;                                     // the return value of f1 + f2
    r.numerator = (f1.numerator * f2.denominator) +
                  (f2.numerator * f1.denominator);  // compute numerator
    r.denominator = f1.denominator * f2.denominator; // compute denominator
    return r;                                       // return the result
}
```

```
Fraction::Fraction(int n, int d)
// A Fraction constructor which allows the numerator and
// denominator to be specified.
{
    numerator = n;
    denominator = d;
}


Fraction::Fraction()
// Another constructor. If no arguments specified, default to 0/1.
{
    numerator = 0;
    denominator = 1;
}


void Fraction::Get()
// Get a fraction from standard input, in the form "numerator/denominator."
{
    char divSign;                          // to consume the '/' character during input
    cin >> numerator >> divSign >> denominator;
}


void Fraction::Show()
// Display a fraction, in the form "numerator/denominator."
{
    cout << numerator << '/' << denominator;
}


double Fraction::Evaluate()
// Calculates and returns the decimal value of a fraction
{
  double n = numerator;            // convert numerator to float
  double d = denominator;          // convert denominator to float
  return (n / d);                  // compute and return float representation
}
```

The *Fraction* class contains five member functions: *Show, Get, Evaluate,* and the two constructors, both named (as they must be) *Fraction.* All of these act on the object that is named in the function call, and each has access to all member data, both public and private. The syntax of member function definitions and calls is a bit different from that of free functions and requires a bit of explanation.

First, notice that member functions are called by placing the name of the object on which they act in front of the function name, like the calls in "PIP2.CPP":

```
f3.Get();
    . . .
f3.Show();
```

Since each fraction object has its own copies of *Fraction*'s member functions, you may think of these as saying "Call *f3*'s *Get* function," and "Call *f3*'s *Show* function." Since the fraction object to which the message (i.e., function call) is sent is specified in the call, it isn't necessary to mention the fraction object by name in the definition of the function. Instead, we can refer to the member data of the object directly by name, as we do in *Get*:

```
void Fraction::Get
{
    char divSign;
    cin >> numerator >> divSign >> denominator;
}
```

Notice that we refer directly to the member data *numerator* and *denominator*. Both are assumed to refer to the numerator and denominator of the fraction object, *f3*, whose member function we're calling.

> In the definition of a member function, any reference to member data and member functions is assumed to be to the object to which the function call is made, unless specific mention is made to a different object.

The first line of this definition uses the *scope resolution operator* ::, where we write *void Fraction::Get(void)*. This operator is used to specify that the definition of *Get* is that of the member function of the class *Fraction*. We need this because there may be several different functions in several classes named *Get*. We have to tell the compiler that we are defining the function named *Get* to be the one in the context of the *Fraction* class, and not some other function with the same name.[*] Notice that we don't include the scope resolution operator in the override of the addition operator. That makes sense because the operator +, as we mentioned, is not a member of the *Fraction* class; it's just a friend.

It's worth taking a closer look at the definition of our override of +. We know that the sum of two fractions may be defined as follows:

$$\frac{n1}{d1} + \frac{n2}{d2} = \frac{n1\ d2 + n2\ d1}{d1\ d2}$$

Our addition operator takes two operands, fractions *f1* and *f2*, and returns another fraction whose numerator and denominator are defined as indicated above:

```
Fraction operator+ (Fraction f1, Fraction f2)
{
    Fraction r;                              // the return value
    r.numerator = (f1.numerator * f2.denominator) +
                  (f2.numerator * f1.denominator);
```

---

[*] Now you can understand why we considered making the subtitle of this text "C++ :: CS1."

```
    // compute numerator
    r.denominator = f1.denominator * f2.denominator;
    // compute denominator
    return r;                                        // return the result
}
```

Note first that we declare a local *Fraction* object, *r*. We need it because the operator must have a *Fraction* object to return. Also, observe that since the + operator is not a member of *Fraction,* we must explicitly refer to the *Fraction* objects *r, f1,* and *f2* when accessing their member data, as we do when we set *r*'s denominator:

```
r.denominator = f1.denominator * f2.denominator;
```

Finally, recall that the only reason that we are allowed to access the private member data of the fractions involved is that we declared our override of + to be a friend of the *Fraction* class.

Use: The File "PIP2.CPP"

As is often the case when doing object-oriented programming, almost all of our work is done by the time it comes to using our classes in a main program. The purpose of our program in this case is to exercise all the functions we invented in order to ensure that they work as they should. Having done that, the main program becomes superfluous, since we'd keep the files "FRACTION.H" and "FRACTION.CPP" and use them in some "real" program that dealt with fractions.

```
//-------------- PIP2.CPP ---------------


// Driver routine to test the Fraction class

#include <iostream.h>            // for cout
#include "UTILITY.H"             // for Terminate
#include "FRACTION.H"            // for Fraction declarations


void main()
{
    // Try all three possible fraction constructors
    // and the input/output routines.

    Fraction f1(3, 2), f2(4), f3;
    cout << "\n The fraction f1 is ";
    f1.Show();
```

```
cout << "\nThe fraction f2 is ";
f2.Show();

cout << "\nThe fraction f3 is ";
f3.Show();

cout << "\nNow enter a fraction of your own: ";
f3.Get();
cout << "\nYou entered ";
f3.Show();

// Now try the overloaded operator.

Fraction f4 = f1 + f3;
cout << "\n\nThe sum of ";
f1.Show();
cout << " and ";
f3.Show();
cout << " is ";
f4.Show();

// Finally, find the floating-point value of f4

cout << "\nThe value of this fraction is " << f4.Evaluate() << '\n';

Terminate();          // Freeze the screen so the user can review the output.
}
```

To run our suite of tests, we begin by calling the three versions of the *Fraction* constructor

```
Fraction f1(3, 2), f2(4), f3;
```

and then use the *Show* function to make sure the fractions were initialized correctly, like this:

```
cout << "The fraction f1 is ";
f1.Show();
```

Having verified that the constructors work as they should, we then test to make sure the overridden operator works as it should on fractions, and, finally, we test the *Evaluate* function.

The final statement is a call to the function *Terminate*. The purpose of this function is to freeze the screen so that the user can take a look at the output before it scrolls out of view. This is a library function, but it does not come from a built-in C++ library. Rather, it is part of a library that we've written, named

UTILITY. You can inspect the definition file, "UTILITY.CPP", but — and this is one of the virtues of C++ — you don't have to unless your curiosity compels you. As with other libraries, all a programmer needs to know are the declarations in the header file "UTILITY.H":

```
// ---------- UTILITY.H----------

// This file contains the definitions for
// a few functions that are useful for controlling the
// running of C++ programs.

#ifndef _UTILITY_H
#define _UTILITY_H

void Terminate();
// Freeze the screen until the user types a character,
// then print a concluding message.

int ReadyToQuit();
// Ask if the user is ready to quit the program.
// Return 1 if and only if the user enters 'y' or 'Y'.

void WaitForUser();
// Freeze the screen until the user types a character.

void SetNumeric(void);
// Set C++ format flags for numeric output.

void Swap(int &, int &);
// Exchanges the values of two integers.

#endif
```

We've talked about the value of being able to reuse code, and this is a good example. In a very real sense, what we've done here is augment C++ by providing a library of functions that we can write and test once and be done with. Forever after, we can use these functions by including them in our programs and never have to worry about inventing fractions anew for each new program.

2.8 SUMMING UP

▶ The integral types in C++ are, from shortest to longest, char, short, int, and long. Each of these may be either signed or unsigned. Integer literals consist of a string of digits, optionally preceded by a sign.

▶ C++ recognizes three floating-point types: `float`, `double`, and `long double`. Floating-point literals begin with an optional sign, followed by a string of digits and either a decimal point, an exponent (e or E), or both. If a floating-point literal has an exponent, it represents the number of positions right or left to shift the decimal point.

▶ Character literals consist of a single character or an escape sequence (like '\n' or '\t') enclosed by single quotes. A string literal consists of a collection of characters and escape sequences enclosed by double quotes (not two single quotes).

▶ Every variable and function in a C++ program must be declared before it is used. A variable declaration takes the form *typeName variableName, ...*

▶ A variable may be defined at the point of declaration by following the variable name with an assignment expression, = *expression.*

▶ A constant declaration looks like a variable definition, preceded by the word `const`. The value of a constant may not be changed by any other statement.

▶ Every operator returns a value to the program. Some operators, like = and ++ also have side effects, meaning that they modify something in addition to returning a value.

▶ Although C++ ignores spaces, tabs, and carriage returns within a program, there are some places where you are not free to add space. The operators that consist of two characters, such as ++, +=, and so on, may not be broken with spaces, nor may identifiers like function and variable names.

▶ Almost nobody memorizes all of C++'s seventeen precedence levels. When in doubt, parenthesize complex expressions.

▶ We've talked about the following statements:

  • declaration statement:
      typeName identifier;
      typeName identifier = *expression*;
      `const` *typeName* = *expression*;

  • expression statement:
      expression;

  • compound:
      { *simpleStatement simpleStatement . . .* }

  • function return:
      `return` *expression*;

▶ Note the semicolon punctuator: compound statements do not require a semicolon; declaration, expression, and `return` statements do.

▶ A variable has meaning only within its scope. A block is any collection of statements enclosed in {} braces. A variable that is declared within a block has a scope that begins where it is declared and ends at the end of a block. A variable that is not declared within a block is said to have file (or global) scope and has meaning from its point of declaration to the end of the file.

▶ To declare a function, we must declare (1) the function's name, (2) the type of value it returns when it has done its task, and (3) the information it takes in to perform its task. A function declaration is a declaration statement and must be punctuated by a semicolon.

▶ Functions and variables may be declared as many times as you wish, but they may be defined only once.

▶ To indicate that a function that does not return a value, use void for its return type.

▶ To define a function, we follow its declaration by the compound statement it uses to perform its task. A function definition is not punctuated by a semicolon.

▶ Every non-void function must have one or more return statements that define the value to be returned and force immediate exit from the function.

▶ It's good practice to make sure that formal and actual arguments have the same types, although they don't have to have the same names.

▶ If a formal argument specifies a value, it is known as a default argument and doesn't need to appear as an actual argument in a function call. Default arguments all must be placed at the tail of the argument list.

▶ C++ considers functions with the same name but different argument lists to be different, so no name conflicts will occur.

▶ It's a good idea to place declarations in a header (.H) file and the corresponding definitions in a different executable (.CPP) file.

▶ The operator >>, when used with cin, gets input from the standard input device. Similarly, the operator <<, when used with cout, sends output to the standard output device. In most (but not all) systems, these are declared in the library file "iostream.h".

▶ Member functions — those that are declared within a class — are called by using the dot operator: *objectName.functionName(argumentList)*. The statement body of member functions assumes that member data and functions refer to the object on which the function was called, unless specified otherwise by the dot operator.

▶ We may overload almost any operator by redefining it to suit our needs. When doing this, be kind to the reader and don't overload – to perform addition, for instance.

▶ A class may declare any function (or another class) to be a friend. Doing so gives the friend function (or class) access to all the member data and functions of the class.

▶ A constructor is a member function that is used to create and initialize objects of a class. A constructor must be given the name of its class. Unlike other member function calls, a call to a constructor must be written in the form *ClassName objectName(argumentList)*.

2.9 EXERCISES

1. Suppose that the int type was represented by 24-bit numbers. What ranges of numbers would be represented by int and unsigned int?

2. Which of the following literals are correctly written? For those that are incorrect, tell why.
   a. –3
   b. 1,000,000
   c. 0.33
   d. .33
   e. .9 e 4
   f. 3E–3
   g. 'F'
   h. "Gee!"
   i. 'F\n'

3. What is the output of the following program segment? Be careful.
```
double p = 2.5, q, r;
q = 1 + 2 * p;
r = p - q;
cout << "2 * p + r";
```

In Exercises 4 and 5, parenthesize the expression to indicate the order of evaluation as dictated by the precedence rules of C++.

4. a. p - 4 % p + x - y / 2
   b. p = ++y - 4

5. a. 1 - 2 * 3 + 4 % 5
   b. --x * p --(y + 3)

For each of the expressions in Exercises 6 and 7, tell the type of the expression, along with its value. Throughout, assume the declarations

```
int p = 1, q = 0;
double x = 2.0, y = 0.0;
```

6. a.   x - p + 2 / p
   b.   p + () (2 * x - 1)
   c.   p = y = 1
   d.   p = x = 3.2

7. a.   q % p + q * 3
   b.   p += 2
   c.   y = p /= 1
   d.   --x * p --(y + 3)

8. This section of code swaps the values of *x* and *y*. Or does it? Trace the following statements as we did in Figure 2.1 and describe in concise terms the action of this segment.

   ```
   y = x;
   x = y;
   ```

9. How would you test whether an integer variable *n* was evenly divisible by 17?

10. Write the definition for a function double C_to_F(double c) that converts Celsius temperatures to Fahrenheit. If *c* is Celsius temperature, the equivalent Fahrenheit temperature, *f*, is given by $f = (9 / 5) c + 32$.

11. Are the two expressions below equivalent for all values of *x* and *y*?

    ```
    (x * x - y * y) / (x - y)
    x + y
    ```

12. Explain the inside joke behind the name "C++."

13. Give the C++ equivalents for the following algebraic expressions:

    a. $(3p + q)(p - 2q)$

    b. $\dfrac{1}{x + y} + \dfrac{1}{x - y}$

    c. $x^4 - x^3 + x^2 - x + 1$

    d. $1 + \dfrac{1}{1 + \dfrac{1}{1 + x}}$

In Exercises 14 and 15, tell which expression is correctly formed. For the incorrect expressions, explain what's wrong with them.

14. a.   x = y;
    b.   ++x = y
    c.   a + b(c + d)
    d.   3

15. a. (p + q * [1 - y])
    b. x + y = z
    c. x =/ y
    d. p = p = p

In Exercises 16 and 17, tell which statement is correctly formed. For the incorrect statements, explain what's wrong with them.

16. a. {{return i++;};};
    b. cin >> int n;
    c. const MIN;
    d. 0 / 1;

17. a. return i++
    b. x =+ y;
    c. n := 2;
    d. { int x = 1; {int x = 2} cout << x;}

In Exercises 18 and 19, tell which function declaration is correctly formed. For the incorrect declarations, explain what's wrong with them.

18. a. real Findint);
    b. char Convert(x, y, z);
    c. int Increase();
    d. int return(double n);
    e. function F(int x): int;

19. a. double F(int i; int j);
    b. int G(double, double)
    c. void H(int i = 0, char);
    d. float(char c = 'A');
    e. int Build(int, double);

20. Who wrote this mess? The function definition below is riddled with errors. Identify as many as you can. *Hint:* Depending on how you count, there are about a dozen errors.

```
int Bad Function(i, j);
{   int i = 1, j, sum;
    const int temporary;
    sum = i + j
    temporary = i;
    j = temporary;
    i++ = temporary - sum
    cout >> j - i;
```

21. Except for the operators && and ||, C++ makes no stipulation about the order in which subexpressions are evaluated, so in $(a + 1) * (b - 2)$, we cannot guarantee that the left subexpression will be evaluated before or after the right. Show that this can cause problems by showing that there are two

different values the expression $i * (2 + i{++})$ might take. Assume that i initially has the value 3.

22. Why does C++ require that default arguments appear at the tail of the argument list?

23. In what ways do the declaration and call of a constructor differ from those of other member functions?

24. The output operator << is actually an override of the built-in *bit shift* operator, which we haven't talked about. The designers of C++ could have chosen to overload another of the predefined operators, like = or <, yielding possible forms for output statements like this:

    ```
    cout < numerator < '/' < denominator;
    ```

    or

    ```
    cout = numerator = '/' = denominator;
    ```

    Discuss the problems with both of these choices. *Hint*: An overloaded operator keeps its original precedence and associativity (grouping direction).

25. What would happen in our PIP if in response to *Get*( ), you had entered the characters "3@4"?

26. One of the purposes of "PIP2.CPP" was to test whether the *Fraction* class was defined correctly. It's not really an adequate test, however. If you had to design a driver program to test "FRACTION.CPP", what would you have to do to be confident that the class definitions were correct?

27. Write a class definition for maintaining and manipulating coin change. In the U.S., a collection of change consists of a certain number of pennies, nickels, dimes, quarters, and half dollars. Consider, as you would for any class definition, both the data and the operations to manipulate the data.

28. A handy feature of U.S. coinage is that a *greedy* strategy of making change—using the coins in value from highest to lowest—always uses the fewest coins. For example, to make 37 cents, we can use a quarter, a dime, and two pennies—a total of four coins—as opposed to a dime and 27 pennies, which requires 28 coins.

    a. Find a coinage system for which the greedy strategy doesn't use the fewest coins.
    b. For a real challenge, discover the rule that determines the coinage systems for which the greedy strategy always yields the fewest coins.

29. a. Write a class declaration that manages a bank account. An *Account* object contains the current balance and is capable of accepting deposits (both ordinary deposits and the deposit used to start the account), handling withdrawals (if there are sufficient funds to cover the withdrawal amount), computing interest, and displaying the current balance.
    b. Write definitions for the member functions of *Account*.

3

CLASS ACTIONS I: SELECTION STATEMENTS

 At this point, the only functions we can write are straight-line collections of statements to be executed one after the other:

```
do this;
next do this;
. . .
then do this;
finally do this;
```

In a sense, such functions are the computer equivalent of predestination: The order of execution is strictly set when we write the function, and that order can never be altered while the function is running. In this chapter and the next, we explore statements that give our programs the computer equivalent of free will. With these statements, the order of execution may depend on information that exists at run time—information that may not be known at the time we write the function and that may change each time we run it. All of these statements *transfer control* to another statement, based on the state of the program's information at the time, breaking us out of the straight-line lockstep of execution we've seen so far.

Chapters 3 and 4 are further linked by the fact that their PIPs combine to form a single program that simulates a soda machine. We'll tackle the part of the program that models the soda machine itself in this chapter, and we'll need selection statements to do it.

OBJECTIVES

In this chapter, we will

▶ Demonstrate the need for selection in programming.

▶ Introduce the logical operators of C++ and show how they are used in writing logical expressions.

▶ Describe C++'s selection statements, if and switch.

▶ Describe the common sources of error in control statements and how to avoid them.

▶ Describe the design and C++ implementation of this chapter's PIP, a soda machine simulation.

3.1 SELECTION STATEMENTS

Frequently, we want a program to take different actions, depending on the values of variables at run time, as we illustrate in Figure 3.1. C++ provides us with a few different means for describing this sort of selection.

FIGURE 3.1
Conditional
execution

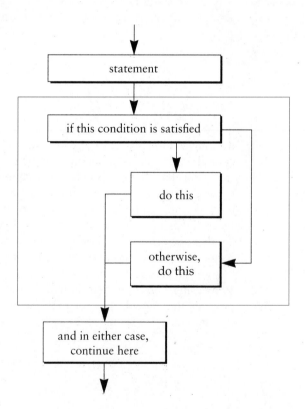

Logical Operators and Expressions

All of the C++ *control statements*—those that have the potential for changing the order in which statements are executed—operate by checking the value of some condition while the program is running. The form of selection enclosed in the box of Figure 3.1 illustrates this. As programmers we want to be able to have the program follow different courses of action based on the state of the program at some point in time. In order to express the conditions that describe the state of the program, we must make use of the C++ operators that express logical expressions; that is, expressions that evaluate to either *true* or *false*. In contrast to some other languages, C++ does not have a separate type for the boolean values *true* and *false*. Like characters, booleans are represented as integer types, with 0 representing *false* and any nonzero value used to represent *true*.

The comparison operators take two expressions as operands and return *true* or *false*, depending on the result of the comparison. The == operator is used to test for equality, so we might write $a == 3$ to test if the numeric variable a was 3. There are five more comparison operators, for a total of six, which we list in the following box. The comparison operators have lower precedence than (and, hence, would be evaluated after) any of the arithmetic operators.

Operator	True (returns 1) When
$a == b$	a is equal to b
$a\ != b$	a is not equal to b
$a < b$	a is less than b
$a <= b$	a is less than or equal to b
$a > b$	a is greater than b
$a >= b$	a is greater than or equal to b

All these return 0 for false and 1 for true.

Just as we can combine arithmetic expressions to make more complicated ones, we can combine boolean expressions, using the boolean operators && for logical AND, || for logical OR, and ! for logical NOT. The actions of the logical operators are summarized in the next box.

Operator	True When
a && b	Both a and b are *true*.
a || b	Either a or b or both are *true*
!a	a is *false*

All these return 0 for *false* and 1 for *true*.

These operators have the lowest precedence we've seen so far—even lower than the comparison operators. So, $a == 1$ && $b < 0$ would be evaluated in the order $(a == 1)$ && $(b < 0)$ and would be true only when a is equal to 1 and b is negative.* The operators && and || group from left to right. The negation operator ! has a high precedence—the same as unary − and ++.

The operators && and || have a very useful property, known as *short-circuit evaluation*. Although there's no guarantee across different implementations of C++ about the order in which arithmetic expressions are evaluated—in the expression $(a + 1)$ * $(b + 2)$, either subexpression might be evaluated first—logical expressions using && or || are uniformly evaluated from left to right, stopping as soon as enough information is available to evaluate the expression. This is valuable, since && is *false* when either of its operands is, and || is *true* whenever either of its operands is. This means, for example, that in computing an average, we can check whether there are no numbers to average before we do the division, so can write a grade assignment like this:

```
if ((items > 0) && (sum / items > 90))
grade = 'A';
```

We'll discuss the if statement in the next section.

Without short-circuit evaluation, if *items* were zero, the computer might be forced to divide by zero (the *sum/items* part) while evaluating the entire boolean expression. With short-circuit evaluation, the expression *items* > 0 *guards* the division part of the expression, since evaluation of the && expression stops as soon as any part evaluates to *false*.

To Do or Not to Do: The if Statement

The most common use in C++ of logical expressions is as expressions that control how selection and iteration statements are evaluated. We'll discuss iterative statements in the next chapter. For now, let's focus on C++'s variety of selection statements.

The first, and most common, selection statement is the if statement. Syntactically, the if statement takes the following form:

```
if (expression)
    statement
else                         // This part, and the statement following
    statement                // are optional.
```

The components of the if statement should look familiar to you. Expressions were first introduced in Chapter 2, as were some C++ statements. In particular, the *statement* parts of the if statement can be any statements: expression, compound, or even other if statements. Notice, too, that the if statement itself does not take a semicolon punctuator (although its last statement might require one of its own).

---

* Pascal speakers take note: This fixes one of the glaring inconsistencies of Pascal, in which logical AND has the same precedence as * and /, leading to $a > 1$ **and** $b < 3$ being evaluated in the nonsensical order $(a > (1$ **and** $b)) < 3$.

When an if statement is encountered, several things happen in sequence:

1. The expression is evaluated.
2. If the expression evaluates to *true* (which, recall, means any nonzero integer), the first statement is executed.
3. If the expression evaluates to *false* (i.e., zero), the second statement (the one following else, if any) is executed.
4. No matter which branch was taken, execution then proceeds to whatever comes after the if statement.

Example 1

```
if (a < 0)
    negatives++;
```

This is an example of a simple if statement; that is, one that does not have an else clause. The intent is pretty clear: if the variable *a* is negative, we increment the variable *negatives*. Notice that although the if statement itself does not require a semicolon punctuator, the statement it contains still must end with one. ◁

Example 2

```
if (numScores == 0)
    cout << "No scores to average";
else
    average = total / numScores;
```

Example 2 illustrates a very common use of the if statement: as a *guard* against a possible error (division by zero, in this case). The possibility of disaster always lurks in any program. As responsible programmers, we want to anticipate errors and write our programs to handle errors gracefully. If error handling is left to the computer, errors are often "fatal" to the program (but not, we hope, to the programmer).

In this case, if *numScores* is zero, we clearly don't want to perform the division *total / numScores* to compute the average, so we first check that *numScores* is not zero. If it is zero, we display an error message; otherwise, we go ahead and perform the (now legal) average calculation. ◁

> Program defensively. Expect the worst to happen (it will, take our word for it), and write your program to be *robust* enough not to fail when it does.

Example 3

```
if ((n < 0) && (d < 0))
{
    n = -n;
    d = -d;
}
```

If you had any doubts about why we have compound statements (other than for use in function definitions), they should be resolved here. In this example, we have *two* things to do if the condition is satisfied. The if statement, however, formally requires only one statement as part of its if and else clauses. We get around this restriction by using a compound statement. Syntactically, everything within paired braces is considered a single statement by the C++ compiler, so it is satisfied that this is still a legal if statement. Notice, again, the punctuation: The expression statements require semicolons, but the compound statement and, of course, the if statement itself do not.*

The clauses of an if statement can be any statements at all, including other if statements. For example, the following is a perfectly legal if statement:

```
if (a > 100)
    if (b <= 0)
        bigAndNeg = 1;          // done if a > 100 and b <= 0
    else
        bigAndPos = 1;          // done if a > 100 and b > 0
else
    small = 1;                  // done if a <= 100, regardless of b
```

We've indented this statement to make it easier to understand. Some systems will do this indenting ("prettyprinting," as it's called) automatically, but many do not. If your system doesn't indent for you, we urge you to do it yourself.

Here's an example that illustrates how the logical sense of the statement is obscured when we don't provide any indentation. It also illustrates a possible ambiguity in C++:

```
if (a > 100)
if (b <= 0)
x = 1;                  // done if a > 100 and b <= 0
else
y = 1;                  // when would this be done?
```

Do you see the problem here? It's not clear whether the else clause should be part of the outer or inner if statement. If it is part of the outer statement, $y = 1$ would be done only when $a <= 100$. If the else is part of the inner statement, $y = 1$ would be done only when $a > 100$ and $b > 0$. What do we do? Indentation doesn't help. It makes programs easier to read for us, but the compiler doesn't pay attention to spaces or tabs. What the designers of C++ did was what often happens in cases of ambiguity. They simply legislated the ambiguity out of existence by settling on one choice as the one that would be considered correct:

▼

else clauses are always paired with the nearest unpaired if statement above.

Our example, then, would have the following interpretation (as indicated by our indentation):

---

* It wouldn't hurt to put a semicolon after the closing } brace. C++ would interpret }; as a closing punctuator followed by an *empty* (or *null*) statement—one that does nothing at all. In other words, C++ would consider { . . . }; as meaning { . . . } *null*; . As a general rule, it's safer to err on the side of too many semicolons than too few.

```
if (a > 100)
    if (b <= 0)
        x = 1;                  // done if a > 100 and b <= 0
    else
        y = 1;                  // done if a > 100 and b > 0
```

To force the alternate interpretation, we would close off the inner if with braces:

```
if (a > 100)
{
    if (b <= 0)
        x = 1;                  // done if a > 100 and b <= 0
}
else
    y = 1;                      // done if a <= 100
```

It's quite common to have a "waterfall" of nested if statements, each of which controls whether the subsequent ones will be executed. Here's an example that might be used to compute letter grades:

```
if (score >= 90)
    grade = 'A';
else                                // below here, we know score < 90
    if (score >= 80)
        grade = 'B';                // 80 <= score < 90, so grade = 'B'
    else                            // now we know score < 80
        if (score >= 70)
            grade = 'C';
        else                        // now we know score < 70
            if (score >= 60)
                grade = 'D';
            else                    // oh dear, score < 60
                grade = 'F';
```

Notice how this works. As soon as any of the expressions evaluates to *true*, the following assignment statement is executed and control passes out of the if statement, and hence out of all the subordinate ones that follow. Incidentally, all this indentation gives some people the screaming meemies. If you're one of those people, the indentation format below is conventionally used and easier to read.

```
if (score >= 90)
    grade = 'A';
else if (score >= 80)
    grade = 'B';
else if (score >= 70)
    grade = 'C';
else if (score >= 60)
    grade = 'D';
else
    grade = 'F';
```

Designing for Comprehensibility

Consider the problem of defining a function, int Max(int x, int y, int z) that takes three integer arguments and returns the value of the largest. As Figure 3.2 shows, we can decide on the largest element by three comparisons.

Having done this, it's easy enough to write the function, using a collection of nested if statements:

```
int Max(int x, int y, int z)
{
    if (x < y)
        if (y < z)
            return z;
        else
            return y;
    else
        if (x < z)
            return z;
        else
            return x;
}
```

The problem is that this is close to the limit of what we can expect any reader to understand at first glance. We might be able to make the function definition clearer if we use boolean expressions to combine the three if statements into two:

```
int Max(int x, int y, int z)
{
```

FIGURE 3.2

Using comparisons to find the largest of three elements

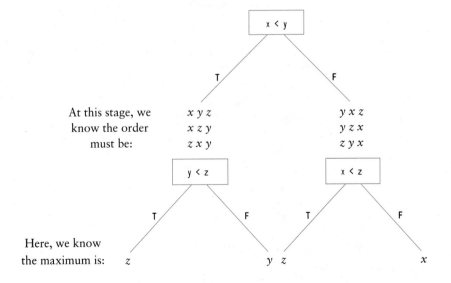

```
        if ((x < y) && (z < y))
            return y;
        else if ((y < x) && (z < x))
            return x;
        else
            return z;
    }
```

Finally, we can make use of the fact that the return statement forces an immediate exit from the function and eliminate the else parts entirely:

```
int Max(int x, int y, int z)
{
    if ((x < y) && (z < y))
        return y;
    if ((y < x) && (z < x))
        return x;
    return z;
}
```

Which of these three should we use? Good question. The first is too complex for our taste, and the third is too telegraphic, but we'll admit it's a close call. One of the unfortunate properties that C++ inherits from C is the more comfortable you become with the language, the better able you are at writing code that is overly compressed and, consequently, incomprehensible to others. In fact, none of the three examples above is a real winner in terms of ease of reading.

Let's take another tack. One of the design guidelines we've mentioned before is that if a function seems unclear to you, it almost certainly will be unclear to someone reading it, so you should consider breaking the function into smaller pieces. With this in mind, we submit the last sample, one that makes use of an auxiliary two-argument maximum function (which in C++ is considered different from the three-argument version, so we don't get into any trouble using the same name for both):

```
int Max(int x, int y)
// Returns the maximum of x and y.
{
    if (x < y)
        return y;
    else     // We don't need this, but it's clearer this way.
        return x;
}

int Max(int x, int y, int z)
// Returns the maximum of x, y, and z.
{
    return Max(Max(x, y), z);
}
```

Not only is this the most transparent of our examples, but it has the significant advantage of being extensible, as well. Using the two-argument maximum function, we can easily define a four-argument maximum function by making a simple change to the function body, writing it as

```
return Max(Max(x, y), Max(z, w));
```

The moral is clear, we hope: Because C++ allows you to perform a task in a number of different ways, it is well worth the effort trying to come up with the clearest way you can of expressing your intent. In crafting prose, the fundamental rule is "Writing is rewriting"; this rule is no less important when programming.

Selecting Among Many Choices: The switch Statement

The switch statement works in a way that's somewhat similar to the cascade of nested if statements we've just discussed. Like those statements, it provides a multiway branch. Formally, the switch statement looks like this:

```
switch (expression)
{
    case constant:
        statements
    case constant:
        statements

            .

            .

            .

    case constant:
        statements
    default:          // optional
        statements
}
```

The case and default (there can be at most one default) parts are *labels* within a compound statement. This helps explain how switch works. The expression is evaluated (it must evaluate to an integral type). If the value matches any of the constants (each of which must be an integral const identifier or a literal) in one of the case labels, control passes to the statement below that label and *continues to the end* of the compound statement. If the evaluated expression doesn't match any of the labels and a default label appears, control passes there and continues to the end of the switch.

Notice that we said that control passes to the indicated label and runs to the end of the compound statement. This means that *all* of the subsequent statements are executed—not just the ones down to the next label. In other words, we couldn't make our grade-setting if statement into a switch statement by writing it this way:

```
// This is syntactically correct but logically wrong
switch (score / 10)
{
    case 10:                    // score is 100 .. 109
        grade = 'A';
    case 9:                     // score is 90 .. 99
        grade = 'A';
    case 8:                     // score is 80 .. 89
        grade = 'B';
    case 7:                     // score is 70 .. 79
        grade = 'C';
    case 6:                     // score is 60 .. 69
        grade = 'D';
    default:                    // anything below 60 (or over 109) flunks
        grade = 'F';
}
```

This looks perfectly fine at first glance, but unfortunately it wouldn't make the students very happy (nor would it look too good for the instructor's effectiveness rating). According to this code every student gets an 'F', no matter what the score is! Suppose, for instance, that *score* was 85. The expression 85/10 yields the integer quotient 8, so control would pass to the statement below case 8: and the assigned grade would be 'B'. That's what we (and the student) expected, but now execution continues down the line and the student's grade gets changed in a few microseconds to a 'C', then to a 'D', and finally to the dreaded flunkaroo.*

This somewhat bizarre feature of rolling execution over all the statements below the one selected is more an historical accident (derived from the C language) than anything else, and fortunately for us there's a way out (quite literally, in fact). The break statement may be used within a switch and causes an immediate exit out of the switch to the statement, if any, that occurs after the switch statement. Using break, we can correct our example so that it works as it should.

break also may be used within **while, do,** and **for** statements, which we'll describe in the next chapter.

```
// This is the correct version.
switch (score / 10)
{
    case 10:
        grade = 'A';
        break;                  // Notice that break requires a semicolon
    case 9:
        grade = 'A';
        break;
```

---

* Pascal speakers: This is not at all like the **case** statement. C speakers: You've seen this already.

```
        case 8:
            grade = 'B';
            break;
        case 7:
            grade = 'C';
            break;
        case 6:
            grade = 'D';
            break;
        default:
            grade = 'F';                   // No need for break here: we're done
    }
```

3.2 PROGRAM IN PROGRESS: SODA MACHINE

Now that we know a bit more about C++ and object-oriented programming, we can tackle a somewhat more formidable design problem. Let's consider the problem of designing a program to simulate a soda machine. As you'll see, the problem is interesting from a design standpoint, and the resulting program will make liberal use of C++'s selection statements.

Designing the PIP

Considered as an entire entity, a soda machine is pretty complex for us to make any headway in designing it. We'll follow our own design guideline and try to decompose the problem domain into simpler pieces. Since a soda machine is a familiar physical entity, we can begin by identifying the physical component parts.

One possible division (and there are many, depending on the degree of detail one wants to describe) would be

1. a coin counter that accepts coins and returns change
2. several buttons for the drink selection
3. a can dispenser

We might go on from here, but if we think about the problem a bit more carefully we notice that our description is inaccurate. If you've ever seen the innards of a soda machine, or if you were given better specifications for the problem, you'd recognize that the can dispenser actually consists of several columns of cans, each column containing one variety of soda and each being associated with a single button. It appears that a more accurate decomposition of the problem (and therefore one that is more likely to lead to a workable program) would be something like this:

1. the coin counter
2. several identical columns of cans, each associated with a button

Let's see how far this pass at design will carry us.

The coin counter seems simple enough, so let's start by describing it as an object. We might describe it by saying something like, "The coin counter object gets coins from the customer and keeps track of the total amount received so far. It communicates this amount to . . . hmmm. Which object gets the amount? Probably the drink dispensers. Keep that in mind; we'll use it when we get to the drink dispensers. The counter needs to be able to reset itself, making the total amount zero. It will do that in response to a message from one of the drink dispensers when that dispenser has released a can." Figure 3.3 illustrates the communication needed between our objects.

Oh, dear. We haven't even finished describing our first class, and already the communication between the objects in our design is getting unwieldy. The coin counter needs to have references to all the can dispenser columns so it can communicate to them the amount it has received. This means that if we add another dispenser column to our soda machine, we would have to modify the coin counter. Something's not right here—our system already looks too "loose."

What we need is a manager to handle the communication between objects. We'll invent a *SodaMachine* class to help us out. This class will do things such as get the new amount from the coin counter, send the new amount to all the dispensers, get messages from them saying that they've dispensed a drink, and send the amount of change back to the coin counter.

> **Design Guideline 4:** An object should communicate as simply as possible with as few other objects as possible. When interfaces are large or complex, consider introducing a manager class.

FIGURE 3.3
A first pass at designing a soda machine

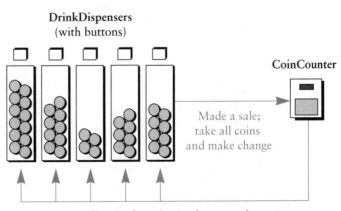

DrinkDispensers
(with buttons)

CoinCounter

Made a sale;
take all coins
and make change

Received a coin; send new total

It appears that our design requires yet another start. Now our classes look like this, as illustrated in Figure 3.4:

1. a coin counter
2. several identical columns of cans, each associated with a button
3. the soda machine itself, containing the coin counter and the dispensers

We were lucky because we spotted a problem before we had gone too far. Even if we hadn't noticed the design problem until much later, we still would have been better off making the change then, rather than trying to limp along with what we had.

> **Design Guideline 5:** Never be afraid to chuck it all and start over, especially at the design stage. If your organization is a mess, patching it generally will produce a patched-up mess, at best.

We were lucky because we spotted a problem before we had gone too far. Even if we hadn't nticed the desing problem until much later, we still would have been better off making the change then, rather than trying to limp along with what we had.

Now that we have a rough idea of the organization of our program, we can begin to fill in the details. For each of the three classes, we describe the member data, the member functions that act on this data, and the communication between other objects. Here's what we came up with:

Coin Counter
Data
> *amount:* The amount deposited so far.
> *available:* The total amount of money available for making change.

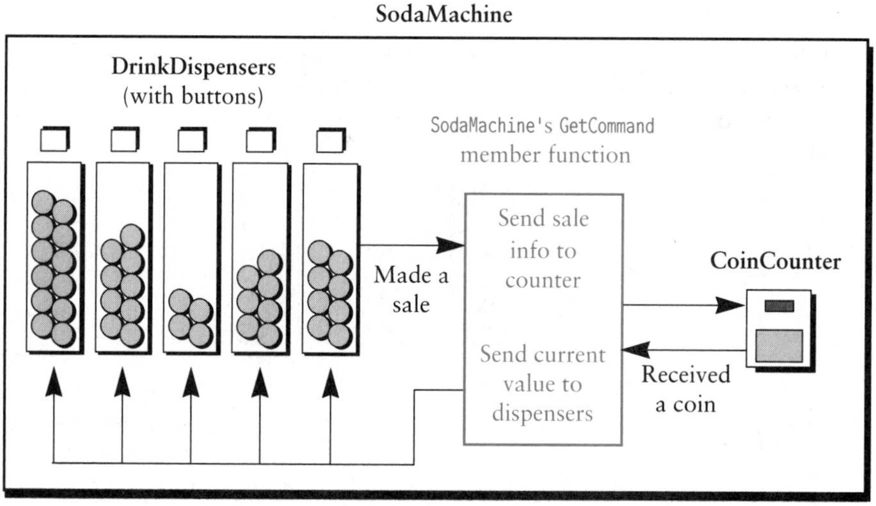

FIGURE 3.4
Designing the soda machine using a manager for communication

Functions

Initialize (value): (from **SodaMachine**) Set *amount* to zero and set *available* to the specified *value.*

CurrentAmount: (from **SodaMachine**, to **Soda Machine**) Return the value of *amount.*

AcceptCoin(value): (from **SodaMachine**) Add *value* to *amount.*

TakeAll: (from **SodaMachine**) **Add *amount*** into *available* and set *amount* back to zero.

DispenseChange (value): (from **SodaMachine**) If *available* is at least as large as *value*, dispense the amount of change indicated. If not, turn on the "Exact change only" light.

Dispenser

Data:

numCans: The number of cans left in the dispenser.

Functions:

Initialize(number): (from **SodaMachine**) Set *numCans* to the specified *number.*

HandleButton: (from **SodaMachine**, to **SodaMachine**) Respond to a pushed button by attempting to make a sale. If *numCans* is nonzero, make a sale and return a code indicating success. If *numCans* is zero, turn on the "Make another selection" light and return a code indicating that no sale was made.

SodaMachine

Data:

theCounter: The machine's **CoinCounter**.

cola, lite, root, orange, free: Five **Dispensers**.

price: The price of a can of soda.

Functions:

Initialize: (from main program, to all data objects) Send an *Initialize* message to *theCounter* and all five **Dispensers**, and set *price* to 75.

DoCommand (cmd): (from main program, to all data objects) Depending on what *cmd* is, take one of two actions. If the command is to take in a coin or return all coins, either send an *AcceptCoin* message to *theCounter* or send messages to *theCounter* to (1) get the *CurrentAmount*, (2) *TakeAll* coins, and (3) *DispenseChange* in the amount so far received. If the command is to make a sale, send a *CurrentAmount* message to *theCounter* to get the amount inserted. If that amount is enough, send a *HandleButton* message to the indicated **Dispenser**. If the dispenser object returns the code for success, compute the amount of change to be dispensed and, if needed, send a *DispenseChange* message to *theCounter.*

Notice, by the way, that in designing the *SodaMachine* class we made some concessions to the fact that this is a *simulation* of a soda machine. In a real machine, the *Initialize* function would be invoked by the service technician (perhaps by pressing an internal button) and the *DoCommand* function would be invoked by the customer by pressing the appropriate controls or by inserting a coin.

We've almost completed our design. All that remains is to decide which data and functions should be publicly accessible and which can be hidden within the classes' objects. The functions of a *CoinCounter* all need to be public: Our description shows that they are all invoked from outside, by the *SodaMachine*. On the other hand, there is no outside access to any of the member data: Any inspection and modification of *amount* and *available* is performed by *CoinCounter*'s member functions, so we can make the member data private to the object. Figure 3.5 illustrates our final version of the *CoinCounter* class.

The *Dispenser* class is also easy to divide into private and public sections. The two member functions are invoked from outside the class and so must be public. The datum *numCans*, though, is used only within the object itself and so should be private, as we indicate in Figure 3.6.

Finally, we need to decide which parts of the *SodaMachine* class should be public. This is a slightly more interesting problem to solve. Our program will construct a single instance of a *SodaMachine* and will do nothing but send commands to the machine for it to respond to. That means that both *Initialize* and *DoCommand* must be public. Then the member data can be private, since it's never seen or used directly by the main program except through the member functions. That's simple enough, but if we delve a little more deeply into the problem, we might notice that *DoCommand* is somewhat complicated. *DoCommand* breaks naturally into two distinct logical units: handling coin

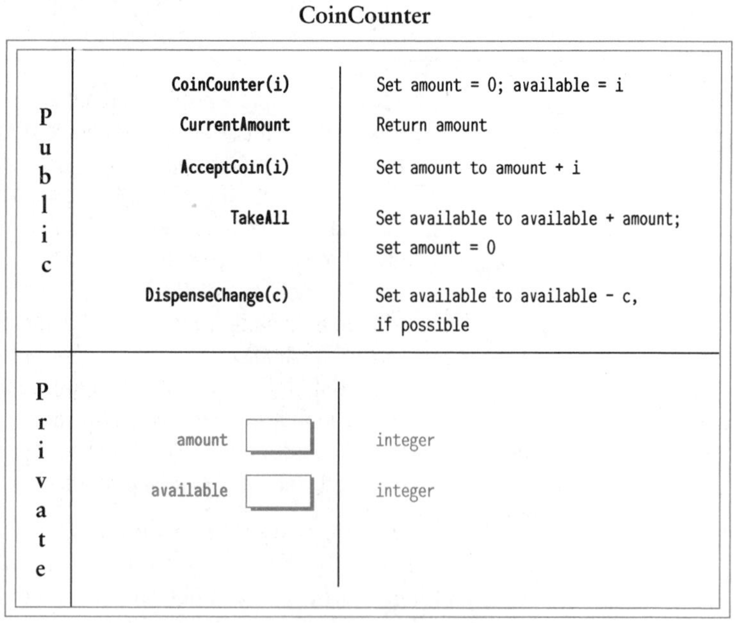

FIGURE 3.5
The *CoinCounter*
class

CoinCounter

P **u** **b** **l** **i** **c**	CoinCounter(i)	Set amount = 0; available = i
	CurrentAmount	Return amount
	AcceptCoin(i)	Set amount to amount + i
	TakeAll	Set available to available + amount; set amount = 0
	DispenseChange(c)	Set available to available - c, if possible
P **r** **i** **v** **a** **t** **e**	amount ☐	integer
	available ☐	integer

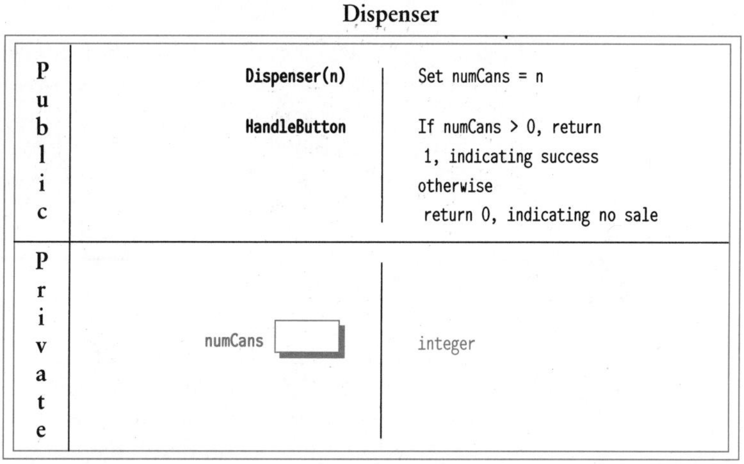

FIGURE 3.6
The *Dispenser* class

Dispenser

P u b l i c	**Dispenser(n)**	Set numCans = n
	HandleButton	If numCans > 0, return 1, indicating success otherwise return 0, indicating no sale
P r i v a t e	numCans	integer

events (like insertion of a coin and requests to return all coins) and responding to button presses to make a sale. It would make good sense to make this separation explicit by defining two new *private* member functions, *DoCoin* and *DoSelection*, as we do in Figure 3.7.

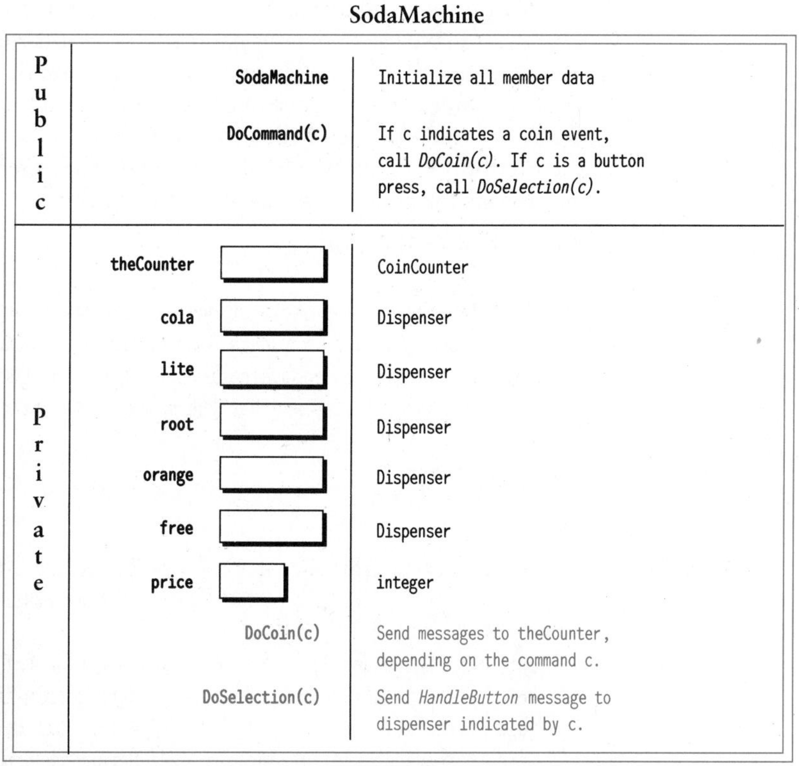

FIGURE 3.7
The *SodaMachine*
class

SodaMachine

P u b l i c	**SodaMachine**	Initialize all member data
	DoCommand(c)	If c indicates a coin event, call *DoCoin(c)*. If c is a button press, call *DoSelection(c)*.
P r i v a t e	theCounter	CoinCounter
	cola	Dispenser
	lite	Dispenser
	root	Dispenser
	orange	Dispenser
	free	Dispenser
	price	integer
	DoCoin(c)	Send messages to theCounter, depending on the command c.
	DoSelection(c)	Send *HandleButton* message to dispenser indicated by c.

▼

> **Design Guideline 6:** Keep your functions simple. If a function divides naturally into logically related units, consider dividing the function so that it sends messages for action to separate subsidiary functions. These subsidiary functions usually can be described as private member functions.

3.3 EXPLORING THE PIP

Since the three classes we have designed to describe our soda machine are all so intimately related (that is, it doesn't make much sense to describe a can dispenser independently of a soda machine), we will take some liberty with our Declare-Define-Use approach in developing this chapter's PIP. We will declare classes *CoinCounter*, *Dispenser*, and *SodaMachine* in a single file and will do the same for their definitions. We will describe how a program might use these classes in full detail in the next chapter, wherein we develop a PIP that simulates the user of a soda machine.

Declaration: The File "MACHINE.H"

The declarations of our soda machine classes are derived almost directly from the design we've discussed. Notice that the constructors for *CoinCounter* and *Dispenser* make use of default parameters to set the initial values for the available change and the number of cans. Notice, too, that the *DoCommand* function of *SodaMachine* accepts a character as its argument. Since our computer does not come equipped with a coin slot and dispenser buttons, we decided that the user of this program would enter single-character codes for the operations as a means for interacting with our soda machine.

```
//------------------ MACHINE.H ------------------

// This file contains the declarations of the classes having to do
// with the soda machine. A SodaMachine object is a manager that
// contains (and handles communications among) a ChangeCounter,
// five Dispenser objects, and has the member data price (of a can).

class CoinCounter
{
public:
    CoinCounter(int initial = 100);    // Initialize a counter,
                                       // setting available change.

    int   CurrentAmount();             // Report amount tendered so far.
    void  AcceptCoin(int amt);         // Handle coin insertion.
    void  TakeAll();                   // Accept all coins in response to a sale.
    void  DispenseChange(int amt);     // Return change, if possible.
```

```
private:
    int amount;                        // the amount tendered so far
    int available;                     // the amount available for making change
};

class Dispenser
{
public:
    Dispenser(int num = 24);    // Initialize a dispenser with default number of cans.

    int HandleButton();         // Try to make a sale

private:
    int numCans;                // the number of cans available
};

class SodaMachine
{
public:
    SodaMachine();              // Initialize a machine.
    void DoCommand(char cmd);   // Respond to a command from a User object.

private:
    CoinCounter  counter;       // A soda machine contains a coin counter,
    Dispenser    cola,          // five can dispensers,
                 lite,
                 root,
                 orange,
                 free;
    int price;                  // and the price of a can of soda.

    void DoCoin(char cmd);      // Handle a coin event.
    void DoSelection(char cmd);// Handle a drink button press.

};
```

Definition: The File "MACHINE.CPP"

It's no accident that the definitions of the member functions for the classes *CoinCounter*, *Dispenser*, and *SodaMachine* make extensive use of the selection statements we've discussed in this chapter. Of course, we selected a problem that would provide appropriate examples for this chapter, but it would have been difficult to avoid doing so, since selection is such a fundamental action that it's quite hard to write an interesting program that doesn't use it.

```
//------------------ MACHINE.CPP ------------------


// This file contains definitions of member functions for the classes
// CoinCounter, Dispenser, and SodaMachine
```

```cpp
#include <iostream.h>
#include "MACHINE.H"


//------------------- CoinCounter Definitions


CoinCounter::CoinCounter(int initial)
// Initialize a counter, setting available change.
{
    amount = 0;
    available = initial;
}


int CoinCounter::CurrentAmount()
// Report amount tendered so far.
{
    return amount;
}


void CoinCounter::AcceptCoin(int amt)
// Handle coin insertion.
{
    amount += amt;
}


void CoinCounter::TakeAll()
// Respond to a sale by taking in all coins so far tendered.
{
    available += amount;
    amount = 0;
}


void CoinCounter::DispenseChange(int amt)
// Return change, if possible.
{
    if (available >= amt)
    {
        cout << "\n*** Change returned: " << amt;
        available -= amt;
    }
    else
        cout << "\n*** EXACT CHANGE ONLY from now on";
}


//------------------- Dispenser Definitions

Dispenser::Dispenser(int num)
// Initialize a dispenser, with num cans.
```

```
{
    numCans = num;
}


int Dispenser::HandleButton()
// Respond to a button push. Return 0 if no cans left, return 1 if successful sale.
{
    if (numCans == 0)      // no cans left
    {
        cout << "\n*** MAKE ANOTHER SELECTION for this from now on";
        return 0;
    }
    else                        // success, make sale and decrement numCans
    {
        numCans--;
        cout << "\n*** Sale complete";
        return 1;
    }
}


//------------------- SodaMachine Definitions

SodaMachine::SodaMachine()
// Initialize a SodaMachine object, by initializing the coin counter
// and all can dispensers (implicitly, since they all have default constructors)
// and setting the price of all cans.
{
    price = 75;
}


void SodaMachine::DoCommand(char cmd)
// Get a legal character (Q, D, N, R, C, L, B, O, F) and send
// the appropriate message to either the coin counter or a dispenser.
{
    if ((cmd == 'Q') || (cmd == 'D') || (cmd == 'N') || (cmd == 'R'))
        DoCoin(cmd);
    else
        DoSelection(cmd);
}


void SodaMachine::DoCoin(char cmd)
// Respond to a coin insertion or a request to return all coins tendered.
{
    int amt;
    switch(cmd)
    {
        case 'R' :   amt = counter.CurrentAmount();
                     // Return all coins tendered
                     counter.TakeAll();
```

```
                         counter.DispenseChange(amt);
                         break;
              case 'Q' :  counter.AcceptCoin(25);   break;
              case 'D' :  counter.AcceptCoin(10);   break;
              case 'N' :  counter.AcceptCoin(5);    break;
       }
}


void SodaMachine::DoSelection(char cmd)
// Respond to a dispenser button push by determining if there's enough
// money inserted to make a sale. If not, do nothing, else send a
// request to make a sale.
{
     int tendered = counter.CurrentAmount(); // amount inserted so far
     int success;                            // 1, if a successful sale, 0 otherwise

     if (tendered < price)
          cout << "\n*** Insert more money";
     else
     {
          switch(cmd)                        // Send sale message to a dispenser.
          {
              case 'C' : success = cola.HandleButton();   break;
              case 'L' : success = lite.HandleButton();   break;
              case 'B' : success = root.HandleButton();   break;
              case 'O' : success = orange.HandleButton(); break;
              case 'F' : success = free.HandleButton();   break;
          }

          if (success)                       // Dispenser signaled a successful sale
          {
              counter.TakeAll();             // so eat the money
              if (tendered > price)          // and make change if needed.
                  counter.DispenseChange(tendered - price);
          }
     }
}
```

Take a look at *Dispenser*'s *HandleButton* function. This function is invoked by the *SodaMachine* object in response to a command from the user indicating that a dispenser's button was pressed. This function tests the value of
the dispenser's *numCans* datum, and if it is zero, the function displays a message and returns 0. On the other hand, if *numCans* is nonzero, the function dec-
rements the number of cans remaining, displays a message, and returns 1,

indicating a successful sale. Since there are two courses of possible action, an if statement is the obvious choice.

```
int Dispenser::HandleButton()
{
    if (numCans == 0)            // no cans left
    {
        cout << "\n*** MAKE ANOTHER SELECTION for this from now on";
        return 0;
    }
    else                         // success, make sale and decrement numCans
    {
        numCans--;
        cout << "\n*** Sale complete";
        return 1;
    }
}
```

The *DoCoin* function in the class *SodaMachine* is a simple example of the switch statement. This function takes as its argument the command 'R', 'Q', 'D', or 'N', and does different things depending on the command. We could have used a cascade of nested if statements, but the switch makes the action of the function clearer.

```
void SodaMachine::DoCoin(char cmd)
{
    switch(cmd)
    {
        int Amt;
        case 'R' :       // Return all coins
                    amt = counter.CurrentAmount();
                    counter.TakeAll();
                    counter.DispenseChange(amt);
                    break;
        case 'Q' :  counter.AcceptCoin(25);   break;
        case 'D' :  counter.AcceptCoin(10);   break;
        case 'N' :  counter.AcceptCoin(5);    break;
    }
}
```

It's worth noting, by the way, that since the function consists of just one switch statement, we could have forced exit from the switch by using return statements instead of break. Notice as well that since this is a void function we don't need to return from the function explicitly; the return from the function happens when execution comes to the end of the function body.

We can, as we mentioned, use any statement within an if statement, including switch and if statements. This is just what we do within *SodaMachine*'s *DoSelection* function. In skeletal form, the function body looks like this:

```
if (tendered < price)
    Not enough money yet.
else
    Enough money for a sale, so send a message to a dispenser.
{   switch(cmd)
    Use the switch to send the message to the right dispenser.
    {   case 'C' : success = cola.HandleButton(); break;
        . . .
    }


    if (success)
        The dispenser signaled a successful sale,
        so take all money tendered.
    {   counter.TakeAll();
        if (tendered > price)
            More money was tendered than needed, so make change.
            counter.DispenseChange(tendered - price);
    }
}
```

We'll admit that the logic here is fairly complicated. In fact, this function is close to the upper limit of what any reader can comprehend in a glance. If the action was any more complicated, we would have been tempted to break the function into one or more calls to functions each of which handled part of the action. This is exactly what we did, for example, when we broke *Soda-Machine*'s *DoCommand* function into calls to *DoCoin* and *DoSelection*.

3.4   SUMMING UP

▶   The boolean values of *true* and *false* are represented as integers in C++ (0 representing *false*, and any nonzero value representing *true*).

▶   C++ comparison operators (including ==, !=, <, <=, >, and >=) take two expressions as operands and return a boolean (integer) value.

▶   We've talked about the following statements:

•   conditional-if:
      if (*expression*)
          statement

- conditional-if-else:

   if (*expression*)
      statement
   else
      statement

- switch:

   switch (*expression*)
      statement (compound, with case labels)

▶ if and switch statements do not require a terminating semicolon (although their subordinate statements may); the break statement does.

3.5 EXERCISES

Selection statements are controlled by boolean expressions. It takes a bit of practice before one becomes comfortable with the process of taking a condition and translating it into a C++ boolean expression. In Exercises 1 and 2, you are asked to give boolean expressions that represent the given sentences.

1. a. *x* is greater than 10.
   b. *temp* is strictly between 3.7 and 3.8.
   c. At least one of *j, k,* or *l* is odd.
   d. *j, k,* and *l* are all odd.
   e. *newChar* is not a digit character (i.e., is not '0' . . . '9').
   f. *found* is at least twice *given,* or *found* is zero and *given* is negative.

2. a. *theChar* is an upper-case vowel.
   b. Exactly one of *index* and *count* is positive.
   c. At least one of *j, k,* or *l* is even.
   d. −*limit* ≤ *sum* < *limit*.
   e. *shot* is no more than 1.5 away from *target*.
   f. *sign* is positive, or both *x* and *y* are negative.

3. Fill in the blanks. We haven't indented the statements so as not to give you extra clues.

```
if (a > 1)
if (m <= 0)
```
This is executed when _____.
```
else
```
This is executed when _____.
```
else
```
This is executed when _____.

4. Is the following a legal statement? Whether it's legal or not, what does the compiler do with it?

```
if (b * b < 4 * a * c)
    ;
else
    cout << "Negative discriminant. Can't compute roots\n";
```

5. In the following statements, there are a number of boxes. Into which boxes could we put semicolons without causing syntax errors? Of the "legal" boxes, which are most likely to receive semicolons in normal programs, and which *must* have semicolons?

   a. if ☐ (x != 0 ☐) ☐

         a = a / x ☐

   b. if ☐ (n % 2) ☐

         n = 3 * n + 1 ☐

      else ☐

         n = n / 2 ☐

6. Suppose *E1* and *E2* are integer-valued expressions and that *S* is a statement. What is the difference between these two expressions, if any?

   ```
   if ((E1) && (E2))          if (E1)
                                  if (E2)
           S                          S
   ```

7. Write the definition of a function *int Ordered(int p, int q, int r)* that returns 1 if and only if *p*, *q*, and *r* are in order, i.e., if $p \leq q \leq r$, and returns 0 if they are not.

8. Write the definition of a function *int IsSum(int p, int q, int r)* that returns 1 if and only if any of the arguments is the sum of the other two (if, for example, we had *a + c == b*), and returns 0 otherwise.

9. Write a function that determines eligibility for student financial aid. The rules for eligibility are

   1. Count the number of children in the family below the age of 21.
   2. If the family income minus $2,500 for each child under 21 is less than $30,000, then the family is eligible for aid.

   The function should check for potential errors in its arguments by using a boolean flag *error*. In particular, *error* should be set to 1 if the income is negative or larger than $10 million, or the number of children is negative or greater than twenty. The function will return −1 if *error* is true, 0 if there are no errors and the family isn't eligible for aid, and 1 if there are no errors and the family is eligible for aid. The function declaration looks like this:

   ```
   int TestEligibility(double income, int minorChildren);
   ```

10. Write the definition of a function int *Min(int n, int m)* that returns the smaller of its arguments *n* and *m*.

11. a. Write the definition of a function int `Divides(int n, int m)` that takes two integer arguments *n* and *m* > 0 and returns 1 if *m* evenly divides *n* and that returns 0 otherwise.
    b. The *precondition* of this function—the condition that is assumed to be true when the function is called—is that *m* is not zero. Rewrite the function so that it first tests whether the precondition is true. If it is, the function should go ahead and test whether *m* divides *n*, returning 1 or 0 as required. If, on the other hand, the precondition is not satisfied, the function should display an appropriate error message and return 0.

12. Write the definition of a function *int Min(int p, int q, int r)* that returns the minimum of *p*, *q*, and *r*.

    a. Do this using the two-argument *Min* function we declared in Exercise 10.
    b. Do this without using the two-element *Min* function.

13. This is a somewhat peculiar but perfectly legal statement:

```
switch (height > 75)
{
        case 0:
            break;
        default:
            cout << "This is a tall person.\n";
}
```

What is the simplest equivalent that doesn't use a switch statement?

14. The tax rate schedules for the 1990 U.S. federal income taxes contain, in part, the following directions for a person filing with single status:

If your taxable income is over—	But not over—	Enter on 1040, line 38	of the amount over—
$0	$19,450	................15%	$0
19,450	47,050	$2,917.50 + 28%	19,450
47,050	97,620	10,645.50 + 33%	47,050

    a. Write a function that will take as its argument the amount of taxable income (double) between 0.0 and 97620.0 and will return the tax payment to be entered on line 38 of form 1040. If the amount of taxable income is not in the required range, the function should display an appropriate error message and return –1.0.
    b. Is the tax rate schedule *continuous;* that is, does the tax that must be paid make a smooth transition between 19,450.00 and 19,450.01 and between 47,050.00 and 47,050.01?

15. In a quadratic equation, such as $ax^2 + bx + c = 0$, we are given three double coefficients *a, b,* and *c,* and are to find the values of x that make the equation true. The nature of the solution depends on the coefficients as follows:

    If $a = 0$ and $b \neq 0$, there is one solution.
    If $a = 0$ and $b = 0$, then there are no solutions if $c \neq 0$, and all x values are solutions if $c = 0$.
    If $a \neq 0$, let d denote $(b^2 - 4ac)$. If $d < 0$, then there are two complex solutions. If $d = 0$, then there are two equal real solutions, and if $d > 0$, then there are two unequal real solutions.

    a. Write a function `void Quadratic(double a, double b, double c)` that will take three coefficients and display the nature of the solutions of the quadratic equation having these coefficients.

    b. Extend part (a) so that your function will display the solution(s), where appropriate.

4

CLASS ACTIONS II: REPETITION STATEMENTS

In Chapter 3 we were introduced to two of C++'s control statements. In programming terms, the if and switch statements allow the functions we write to make simple comparisons while a program is running and to choose which statements to execute based on the results of these comparisons. In higher-level problem-solving terms, these abilities—to compare values and to alter the order of execution as the program is running—allow functions to make informed decisions and to direct their processing accordingly.

These same abilities help us to write functions that accomplish a second useful form of program control called *repetition* (or iteration). With the statements we will introduce in the chapter—the while, do, and for statements—we can write functions that repeat groups of statements over and over again.

Knowing how to use repetition statements extends our ability to write interesting functions (and, hence, classes) dramatically. Indeed, by the end of this chapter you will have seen most of what you need to describe any kind of action your classes will ever have to perform, including those described by this chapter's PIP. The Chapter 4 PIP describes a class that implements a general menu-based user interface; that is, a way to communicate effectively with a running program. This, not too coincidentally, is exactly what our soda machine PIP from Chapter 3 lacked. We'll integrate these classes to produce a fully functional (but still simulated!) soda machine. Then, in subsequent chapters, we'll turn our attention back to the more strictly object-oriented aspects of describing classes.

OBJECTIVES

In this chapter we will

▶ Demonstrate the need for iteration in programming.

▶ Discuss the C++ loop statements while, do, and for.

▶ Offer some design guidelines that will help you make effective use of loops.

▶ Provide a brief history of how users interact with programs, and describe some general models for a user interface.

▶ Explore in this chapter's PIP a class that implements a menu-based user interface, and demonstrate how it can be used to run our soda machine PIP from Chapter 3.

4.1 REPETITION STATEMENTS

Suppose we wished to write a function that would compute the average of three integers entered by the user. One way to do it would be as follows:

```
int n, sum = 0;
cout << "When asked, type an integer and press ENTER\n";

cout << "Entry? ";          // Prompt the user,
cin >> n;                   // get the number,
sum += n;                   // and add it to the sum.
cout << "Entry? ";
cin >> n;
sum += n;
cout << "Entry? ";
cin >> n;
sum += n;

cout << "The average is " << double(sum / 3);
```

This certainly would accomplish what we want, but it's rather verbose. Imagine what the corresponding code would look like if we had to find the average of 100 numbers—the extended code would be 303 statements long! Even worse, imagine that we did not know ahead of time how many numbers our function was to average, but we wanted it to work for any number of entries.

Clearly, C++ must provide some better way to do this. If we step back from the problem details and think like language designers, one solution might present itself. Given the computer's demonstrated abilities for making comparisons and for altering the order of statement execution, it seems reasonable to expect that we could not only express something like the following, but do so more or less directly.

```
Execute as many times as is necessary everything from here . . .
    cout << "Entry? ";
    cin >> n;
    sum += n;
    counter ++;
down to here, in order

cout << "The average is " << double(sum / counter);
```

Well, it's our pleasure to inform you that C++ provides not one, but *three* different ways to repeat a collection of statements until or as long as some condition is satisfied. In computer science terms, each of the three statements is known as a *loop*, since execution loops back over the statements we wish to repeat.

The while and do Statements

The while statement looks like this:

```
while (expression)
    statement              // note: no terminating semicolon needed,
                           // except for any required by statement
```

The semantics of the while statement mirror its syntax, as pictured in Figure 4.1. First, the value of *expression* is determined; as long as the expression is

FIGURE 4.1
The flow of control
in a while statement

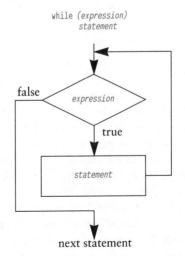

true (meaning that it evaluates to some nonzero value), the *statement* is repeatedly executed. Once *expression* becomes false (i.e., evaluates to zero), execution passes to the statement after the *loop body* statement, if any. This implies that something that happens as a result of executing the while loop's statement body must have the potential for changing the loop's controlling expression. Otherwise, the loop will be an *infinite* one in the sense that its body will be executed repeatedly with no hope of passing on to the next statement in the program.

We could use a while loop to solve our problem of averaging 100 numbers. We begin by setting the index variable *i* equal to 1. Then, we want to prompt the user, get a number, and add it to the running sum repeatedly, with *i* taking the values 1, 2, . . . , 100. We want to do the assignment as long as *i* is less than or equal to 100, so our loop will take the form

```
int n, sum = 0;
int i = 1;
cout << "When asked, type an integer and press ENTER\n";
while (i <= 100)
{
    cout << "Entry? ";
    cin >> n;
    sum += n;
    i++;
}
cout << "The average is " << double(sum) / 100.0;
```

When designing a loop, we need to answer three questions:

1. What *initial conditions* must be satisfied before execution of the loop?
2. What is the *precondition* that must be true before each loop iteration?
3. What *actions* do we want to perform during each loop iteration?

In our example, the initial condition is that the index variable, *i*, must be 1. The precondition for each loop iteration is that the index be in the range we want, namely that *i* must be less than or equal to 100. Finally, the obvious actions are the prompt, the input, and the addition; and the other, less obvious, action is to increment *i*, to prepare for the next iteration (to give us a way out of the loop when we're done). This last step is critical, since, again, something must happen within the loop that has the potential for changing the value of the loop's controlling expression.

The following code provides another example of a while loop. In it, a loop is used to repeatedly read temperature values (from a sensor, for example) and check if any three consecutive values are over 200. If and when this happens, control passes out of the while loop and a function is invoked to sound an alarm.

```
int temp, consecutiveHighs = 0;
cin >> temp;
while (consecutiveHighs < 3)
{
    if (temp > 200)
        consecutiveHighs++;
    else
        consecutiveHighs = 0;
    cin >> temp;
}
SoundAlarm;
```

Notice in this case that, unlike in the averaging example above, we don't know ahead of time how many times this loop is to be iterated. That is, our problem is not described as "do something this many times." Rather, it is described as "do something as long as some condition holds" (the condition here being three consecutive high readings). Both of these types of iteration can be modeled using a while loop.

The do statement looks and acts very much like the while statement. The only real difference is that the evaluation and test of the loop's exit expression is made *after* the loop body is executed, rather than before. The do statement is written as follows and is evaluated as pictured in Figure 4.2.

```
do
    statement
while (expression);                    // note the terminating semicolon
```

FIGURE 4.2
The flow of control
in a do statement

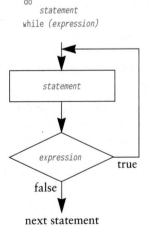

```
do
    statement
while (expression)
```

We could have performed our averaging calculation using a do statement. It would have taken the following form:

```
int n, sum = 0;
int i = 1;
cout << "When asked, type an integer and press ENTER\n";
do
{
    cout << "Entry? ";
    cin >> n;
    sum += n;
    i++;
} while (i <= 100);
cout << "The average is " << double(sum) / 100.0;
```

One can't help but notice the similarity between the while and do versions of this problem. In fact, the two segments are so similar that you might be tempted to ask why C++ provides two ways of doing what seems to be the same thing. The difference lies in where the test for the exit case is done. Notice that the do statement will always execute its body at least once; the while statement body, on the other hand, may not be done at all, depending on the exit condition. The difference in when the controlling expression gets evaluated allows our temperature checking code to be rewritten as follows. Notice here that the statement that accomplishes the reading of the temperature value occurs at the beginning of the do loop's body.

```
int temp, consecutiveHighs = 0;
do
{
    cin >> temp;
    if (temp > 200)
        consecutiveHighs++;
    else
        consecutiveHighs = 0;
}
while (consecutiveHighs < 3)
SoundAlarm;
```

Consider now the problem of adding a list of positive integers. We'll assume that the number of entries isn't fixed and that the user will indicate that the list is complete by entering the *sentinel* value −1. What we want to do is to keep reading numbers and adding them to a running sum until we encounter the sentinel. The while loop version of the code would look like this:

```
int n, sum = 0;
cout << "Entry? ";              // "Prime the pump"
```

```
cin >> n;                     // by getting the first number.

while (n != -1)               // As long as we haven't seen the sentinel,
{
    sum += n;                 // add the number to the running sum,
    cout << "Entry? ";        // prompt the user,
    cin >> n;                 // and get another number.
}
cout << "The sum is " << sum;
```

Think for a moment about how you would write this with a do loop. The code below would *not* do what we need:

```
int n, sum = 0;
do
{
    cout << "Entry? ";
    cin >> n;
    sum += n;
} while (n != -1);
cout << "The sum is " << sum;
```

The problem here is that by the time the computer gets to the point of evaluating the control expression, it already would have added the sentinel to the sum, making it one smaller than it should be. We could have forced the segment to work correctly with a do loop, but if you think about it (as we ask you to do in the Exercises), you'll see that any way we try to solve this problem with a do statement would lead to less comprehensible code.

Before we leave while and do loops, we should alert you to two common sources of error that bedevil even experienced programmers. Take a look at this loop:

```
while (n != -1);
{
    cout << "Entry? ";
    cin >> n;
    sum += n;
}
```

This appears at first glance to be exactly what we had written in our earlier example. However, unless the first number entered was the sentinel –1, program execution would never continue past the while loop! The program would appear to work normally up to the loop, but would suddenly "hang up" and never continue any further. Take a minute and see if you can figure out what's causing the problem. We'll wait.

*   *   *

Got it? It's all because of the semicolon after the test expression! If we indented the segment to reflect the way it would actually work, our loop would look like this:

```
while (n != -1)
    ;           // There's a null statement body here,
                // so the loop continues to do nothing, repeatedly!

{               // This is not part of the loop any more.
    cout << "Entry? ";
    cin >> n;
    sum += n;
}
```

By improperly placing one semicolon, we have completely altered the way the loop works. If the first *n* weren't –1, the test expression would evaluate to *true* and stay that way forever, since *n* is never changed. There are two morals to this story. The first is that C++, like all other programming languages, requires much more precision of expression than a natural language like English. The second moral is not to assume more than is actually true about your program.

> A semicolon in the wrong place won't always lead to an error that the compiler will catch. It's often the case that a superfluous semicolon punctuator will add a null statement to your program, so if things go awry, check your semicolons.

The for Statement

The while and do forms of loops are very useful when we don't know ahead of time how many times a loop will iterate. Many times, though, we know at the time of writing a function precisely how many iterations we want a loop to make. For such instances, C++ provides a statement that permits us to write a loop in a condensed form. The for statement is slightly more complicated to write than the while or do statements because it allows you to specify (1) an initialization, which will be performed before iteration begins; (2) a loop test, which controls exit from the loop; and (3) an iteration expression, which is done after each iteration of the loop body. A for statement takes the following form:

```
for (initStatement; testExpression; iterationExpression)
    loopBodyStatement
```

Its effect, described graphically in Figure 4.3, is identical to

```
initStatement                    // do any initialization here
while (testExpression)           // controls exit from the loop
```

FIGURE 4.3
The flow of control
in a for statement

```
for (initStatement; testExpression; iterExpression)
    bodyStatement
```

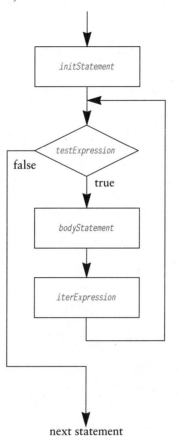

```
{
    loopBodyStatement             // the loop body
    iterationExpression;          // Note: the iteration expression
                                  // becomes a statement here.
}
```

In English, the initialization is performed and the loop's test expression is evaluated. If the expression evaluates to true, the loop's body is performed once, the iteration expression is evaluated, and the loop test is performed again. Whenever the loop test evaluates to false, control passes out of the loop to the next statement.

If the syntax and the semantics of the for loop seem overly complex, take heart. The primary use of for loops is simply to perform the loop body some fixed number of times, and this can be accomplished pretty easily, as illustrated in the following examples.

Example 1

To find the sum of 100 numbers, we could use a for loop as follows. This simple form of the for loop is the most common one you will see and use.

```
int n, sum = 0;
for (int i = 0; i < 100; i++)
{
    cout << "Entry? ";
    cin >> n;
    sum += n;
}
```

This is equivalent to and clearer than the more verbose while loop version:

```
int n, sum = 0, i = 0;
while (i < 100)
{
    cout << "Entry? ";
    cin >> n;
    sum += n;
    i++;
}
```

We intentionally make *i* range from 0 to *N* - 1, rather than from 1 to *N*, for reasons that we'll make clear in the next chapter.

> To perform some statement *N* times, with an index variable *i* that successively takes the values 0, 1, . . . , *N* – 1, you can write
>
> ```
> for (int i = 0; i < N; i++)
>     statement to be iterated
> ```

Example 2

Let's write a function that computes and returns the amount of interest that would be earned on an account over a period of time given an initial deposit, an annual interest rate, and the number of months over which interest should be compounded. From this description, we derive the function header below. From our understanding of the problem (knowing that interest is to be computed on a monthly basis), we can expect the function definition to make use of a for loop.

```
double ComputeInterest (double deposit, double rate, int numberMonths)
{
    double balance = deposit;           // start with the initial deposit
    double monthlyRate = rate / 12.0;   // convert annual rate to monthly rate
    for (int i=0; i < numberMonths; i++)   // for each month
        balance += (balance * monthlyRate); //update balance by adding
                                            //interest earned

    return balance;
}
```

As described above, we use the standard for loop form to perform the balance calculation *numberMonths* times. Notice, too, that since the body of the loop has been written as a single statement, we don't need to include the braces that would have been required had we chosen to write the loop as:

```
float interestEarned;
for (int i = 0; i < numberMonths; i++)        //for each month
{
    interestEarned = balance * monthlyRate;
    balance += interestEarned;
}
```

Designing for Comprehensibility

The second example points to a series of design questions that become pertinent as soon as we introduce loops into our programming repertoire. The relatively complex semantics of all of the loop forms—that is, what the computer must do in order to evaluate them—dictate that we exercise considerable care in how we use loops in writing functions. The simplest misuse of a loop can result in a function that either performs inefficiently or, worse still, doesn't perform at all. The following design guidelines address some of the more common difficulties that come part and parcel with repetition statements. A good way to start is by looking back at some of the advice we gave you earlier in this chapter.

First, we mentioned that in designing a loop you must identify the precondition that must be true before each loop iteration. This condition becomes the test expression that controls when the loop will be exited and when control will pass to the statement after the loop. Remember, though, that it is the relationship between the loop body and the test expression that controls whether the loop will even be exited at all. That is, there must be at least one statement within the loop body that has the potential for changing the value of the test expression.

If, for example, the test expression of a while loop is

```
(inputVal != 0)
```

there had better be a statement within the loop's body that changes the value of *inputVal*; for example:

```
cin >> inputVal, or
inputVal--
```

Notice, too, that if the loop's body contains a selection statement, as was the case in our temperature reading example earlier, you may have to provide a statement that affects the test expression for each logical path through the body.

▼

Whenever you design a loop, make very sure that the test expression will eventually become *false*, no matter what happens. Test your loop by hand, simulating what the computer will do, and make sure you look at the special cases, such as the first and last iterations. If your program appears to get stuck in the midst of its processing, there's an excellent chance that it's hung in what programmers call an "infinite loop."

We also mentioned earlier that you must identify which actions you want performed during each iteration. Given that the whole point of loops is to execute statements repeatedly, this hardly seems worth mentioning. What we didn't say, though, was to make sure that *only* the actions that you want repeated get included in the loop body. Since the statements in the body are executed with each pass through the loop, including an extra statement or two—a variable declaration, for example—can cause your program to do a lot of extra work.

▼

Make sure a loop's body contains only those statements that are to be executed with each iteration. In general, it's a bad idea to include declaration statements in a loop body.

Even if you are careful to include only the essential statements in a loop's body, you still may have a lot of statements. Because loops, by their very nature, are tougher to understand than are most other C++ statements, it doesn't take much to make them totally confusing. Perhaps the quickest way to do so is to include excessive detail in the loop's body statement. Remember that any compound statement—even one like that below, which itself contains other logically complex control statements—can serve as the body of a loop.

```
// compute the first 100 partial sums
int partialSum;
for (int limit = 1; limit <= 100; limit++)
{
    partialSum = 0;
    for (int counter = 1; counter < limit; counter++)
        partialSum += counter;
    cout << "The sum of the integers from 1 to " << limit
        << " is " << partialSum;
}
```

▼

If a loop's body statement becomes complex to the point that it obscures the processing being performed by the loop, consider defining additional functions to perform the detailed processing, and then call these functions from the loop's body.

Remember that every statement in a loop's body is executed completely for each iteration of the loop. Thus if we have a loop within the body of another loop, as in the previous statement, the inner loop (the one controlled by *counter*) gets executed completely with each pass through the outer loop (the one controlled by *limit*).

On a stylistic note, how you write a loop can affect how easy the loop is to work with as you analyze and debug your program. For example, look at the following two loops, both of which count the number of positive values being read in.

```
Version #1:
    int numInputs = 0;
    int thisValue;
    cin >> thisValue;
    while (thisValue > 0)
    {
        numInputs ++;
        cin >> thisValue;
    }
Version #2:
    int numInputs = 0;
    int thisValue;
    cin >> thisValue;
    while (1)
    {
        if (thisValue <= 0)
            return numInputs;
        numInputs++;
        cin >> thisValue;
    }
```

Version #1 of the loop uses its test expression to make its exit condition perfectly clear. Looking at the loop one sees immediately how the loop is being controlled. Version #2 obscures this information by burying the statement that controls exit from the loop within the loop's body.

In general, the test expression of a loop should control the exit from the loop. In certain situations, this guideline can be violated, in the interests of efficiency or due to some particular condition of the problem—but such situations are relatively few and far between (we'll discuss one in this chapter's PIP). In the interest of readability, the condition that controls how many iterations are to be performed should be evident by looking at the loop's test expression.

Along these same lines, the choice of which loop form to use can influence dramatically the readability of a function. The fact is that C++ provides us with three loop statements, and most loops can be expressed (with varying degrees of clarity) using all three statements. We saw earlier how the loop to sum up 100 numbers could be written as both a for loop and a while loop. It could just as easily be expressed as a do loop, as below.

```
int n, sum = 0, i = 0;
do
{
    cout << "Entry? ";
    cin >> n;
    sum += n;
    i++;
} while (i < 100)
```

The computer doesn't care which form we use in our program. All three accomplish the identical purpose, and all three make sense to the machine. But which one makes the most sense to a human reader? We offer the following as a basic guideline.

Loops that are controlled by counting (that is, performing a loop statement for some prescribed number of times) are best written as for loops. Loops whose exits are controlled by logical conditions (until some condition arises) should be written as while or do loops. If there is the possibility that the loop's body will never be executed, use a while loop. If a logically controlled loop's body must be executed at least once before exiting, use a do loop.

Finally, the fact that we have three forms of repetition statement, each of which can be combined with another and with any of the other C++ statements we have seen, should give you a feeling for how expressive and powerful C++ is as a programming language. And, believe us, we've only scratched the surface. Not only are there still more C++ statements that we will cover in detail in subsequent chapters, but there are numerous other features of the language that we have intentionally avoided discussing (because they are either less useful to our purpose or too complicated to worry about). Suffice it to say, C++ will permit you to be clever to the point of incomprehensibility. So, as your programming expertise continues to develop, take this final guideline to heart. We think it's important enough to devote two upcoming chapters to it.

Your responsibility as a programmer is to do more than produce working programs. Your programs should also be "workable" in the sense that they can be understood and manipulated effectively by you and by any other C++ programmer. Take every precaution possible to make your programs clear and concise.

4.2   USER INTERFACE

We mentioned in Chapter 1 that object-oriented programming reflects the state of the art in programming methodologies because it allows a programmer to communicate at the highest, most human-like level with the computer. It took many years of experimentation, development, and insight for the programmer:machine interface to evolve to the point that we have languages like C++ to support these interactions directly.

A similar evolution has taken place in how the *users* of programs—the student using a word processor, the accountant using a spreadsheet, the shopper using the ATM machine at the mall, and the astronaut training in a flight simulator—interact with computers. This latter evolution is equally important to us as programmers because it describes what users expect from our programs and dictates to a certain extent how we write them. It is no longer enough, as it was in the not-too-distant past, to write programs that merely work correctly. Programs today must also interact in a supportive and "friendly" manner with their users.

The notion of a "user" (as opposed to a "programmer") interface to the computer is relevant to our PIP for this chapter, in which we describe a simple class that can serve to control how a user communicates with any interactive program. First, however, let's consider briefly how the notion of a *user interface* was born and the extent to which it has evolved.

We will begin by talking about the good old days, which, as your authors can attest, weren't so long ago and weren't always good. In the very early days of computers, the only users were the specialists—the programmers who had written the programs and were intimately acquainted with their quirks and foibles. The first user interface was wires and plugs. To change the programs on the first electronic computers, an operator literally had to rebuild the computer by reconnecting the components.

It didn't take long for the programmers/designers/engineers of computers (often the same person held all three titles) to realize that rebuilding the computer for each new task took entirely too much time. Indeed, many computers soon came equipped with a device (switches or a keyboard) to control the connections between the functional units of the computer. A user turned on the machine, set the right switches or pushed the right keys, and "let it rip." Even the first hobby computers of the 1970s, some thirty or more years after the pioneer computers, still had to be programmed by setting switches on their front panels.

When the user of a computer was its builder, designer, or programmer, the user interface wasn't too important. Although many of the earliest programs were computationally complex, the demands they placed on the user were very simple, requiring little more than a mass of numeric input along with a command to run the program on that input. As computers made their way into commercial applications, it became clear that their hunger for data could not be appeased by having the operators set switches. To speed input, data was stored on paper tape or punched cards, prepared on a machine much like a typewriter, and read mechanically. The user was in effect being separated from the machine. A typical session consisted of entering a program and its input on cards and then carrying the completed deck of cards to the operator, who would place the cards in a mechanical card reader, wait for the computer to run the program, and, five minutes to several hours later, return the cards and the printed output to the user.

This batch mode operation was slow, at best. The computer operator controlled scheduling of jobs, running job 1 until completion, then running job 2, then job 3, and so on. In effect, the user interface was the counter at the operator's window, with an in-basket for the user to place his or her cards, and an out-basket, where the user would find the results. Not only was this process slow, it was anything but user-friendly. In addition to the program and the data, the user had to include in the deck cards that told the computer how to handle the job. The full deck of cards for a job might look like the following.

```
//CPSCI241          JOB 136767, RICK.STU,MSGLEVEL = 1
//                  EXEC ASMFLAG
//ASM.SYSIN         DD *
(Some of your program cards would go here)
/*
//LKED.SYSLIB       DD DSNAME=USERLIB,DISP=OLD
//LKED.SYSIN        DD *
(Some of your program cards would go here)
/*
//GO.SYSPRINT       DD SYSOUT=A,DCB=(BLKSIZE=133)
//GO.MYDATA         DD DISP=OLD,UNIT=TAPE3,DSNAME=INDATA13,
                    VOLUME=SER=131310
//GO.SYSIN          DD *
(Your data cards would go here)
/*
```

With the advent of time-sharing in the late 1960s, some control (or at least the illusion of it) was returned to the user. In such an arrangement, a computer would be connected to several terminals, each of which looked like an electric typewriter with a roll of paper attached (called TTY, in the jargon, for "teletype"). Unlike batch mode, the computer would divide its attention among the terminals, running each job for a fraction of a second in turn. Since the computer could perform its operations vastly faster than either the user could type or the TTY could print, each user could act as if he or she had complete control of the computer. Time-sharing was a considerable improvement in the user interface. The user could see what he or she had typed without having to leaf through a deck of punched cards, and the interaction with the machine was in "real time," so that the interval between making an error and being informed of the error could be measured in seconds, rather than hours. One could run a program, find an error, edit the program to fix the error and try again, all in the space of a few minutes.

Of course, editing a program—or any text, for that matter—was still somewhat cumbersome. Text editors of the time were generally line oriented, meaning the basic unit of text was a single line. Lines were identified by number, and a typical session might consist of typing the following editing commands:

p 125:450	print lines 125 through 450
i 220	insert a new line before line 220
d 245:350	delete lines 245 through 350
stotalsum340:#	substitute 'sum' for every instance of 'total' in all lines from 340 to the end

This line orientation reflected the punch-card technology from which it was derived. The video display terminal (VDT for short, or "glass TTY," to insiders) soon replaced the teletype's roll of paper with a video screen and ushered in a new era of user interface. This form of interface should be familiar to you if you ever looked behind the scenes at an airline ticket counter or the Department of Motor Vehicles. With such an arrangement, the user can move to any location on the screen by pressing the right combination of keys (the up arrow might move the cursor up one line, for instance) and modify the text at the location by typing. For example, in a simple system to handle airline reservations, the screen might contain several lines of text. To make a reservation, the clerk would begin by typing a code for the departure airport, press the tab key and type the code for the destination airport, tab once more to move to the flight number field, and enter the flight number. At that time, the screen would display the available seats on the flight, and the clerk could enter the chosen seat number. The rest of the process, such as payment method and so on, would be handled similarly.

This process is a smoother version of what would happen with a typewriter terminal, but it is still text oriented and essentially line based. It took a few years to realize that the VDT was not inherently constrained to presenting only lines of text. When we think in terms of any modern computer that supports graphics and has a mouse attached, we can imagine what the reservation system could look like. A simple addition, for instance, would be to display a picture of the aircraft for the selected flight, with available seats highlighted, perhaps in a different color. Instead of requiring the reservation clerk to memorize the seating arrangement of each plane the airline used, the picture would provide instant verification that there was a forward aisle seat available on the starboard side of the aircraft. Then, a move of the mouse and a click on that seat would instantly reserve seat 8D for the customer.

The modern version of the reservation process would likely be no faster for this addition, but it would probably make the system easier for the clerk to use, and ease of use is what we have been aiming for throughout the evolution of the user interface. We should make the point here that there is a considerable chronological overlap among the varieties of user interface we have described. All the types we have mentioned, with the possible exception of rewiring, are in use today and will almost certainly continue into the future. After all, the horse wasn't replaced overnight by the automobile, and for a variety of reasons will never be completely eliminated.

4.3 PROGRAM IN PROGRESS: A MENU-BASED INTERFACE

You will recall that we provided you with a class that allowed you to run the soda machine simulation in Chapter 3. We didn't look into that class at that point for a few reasons. First, the details of how that class was implemented were not pertinent to our discussion of selection statements. Second, C++ provides—even encourages—us to use classes without worrying about their implementations. So long as we are careful to include in our programs the files containing the classes we need to access, and to use the classes as they were intended to be used (that is, refer to the member data and functions consistent with their declarations), our programs can use any classes defined within our C++ environment. Finally, you might not have understood the code for the user interface to the soda machine because it makes extensive use of C++'s repetition statements—and therefore is a perfectly suited PIP for this chapter.

Designing the PIP

As you saw when you ran the Chapter 3 PIP, the interface that our *User* class describes is text based. It presents a menu of choices for the user of a program to consider and accepts single-character codes as input indicating the user's choice, as described below.

Command	Intended Action
'Q'	Insert a quarter
'D'	Insert a dime
'N'	Insert a nickel
'R'	Press the coin return button
'C'	Press the "Cola" button
'L'	Press the "Lite Cola" button
'B'	Press the "Root Beer" button
'O'	Press the "Orange" button
'F'	Press the "Caffeine Free Cola" button
'M'	Show the menu of available commands
'X'	Exit the simulation

Since this type of program interaction won't be unique to the last chapter's PIP, we will design a *User* class whose primary job will be to get character input from the keyboard. The only other job the *User* class will have is to display a *menu* of available choices at the start of the program and whenever the user requests it.

It will be left to a main program to determine what processing should be associated with each input character and to invoke the appropriate functions. We will, as part of this PIP, review a main function that applies our *User* class to the task of controlling a soda machine. In Figure 4.4 we illustrate class *User* and its members.

A function that returns either *true* or *false* is often called a *predicate*.

FIGURE 4.4

The *User* class

User

P u b l i c	Initialize	Call ShowMenu
	GetCommand	Return a legal character gotten from KB
P r i v a t e	ShowMenu	Show the menu
	IsLegal(c)	Return 1 if c is a legal command character

The constructor function for class *User* and the *GetCommand* function both must be declared as public, since each will be invoked from a main program. Function *IsLegal*, which returns a boolean (int) value that indicates whether or not a particular character is a legal input for our program, can be private since it will be used internally by the class as it gets commands, and not directly by another program. Function *ShowMenu* could be described as either public or private. Since its purpose is to display a menu for the user of the program, it might be invoked directly from, say, a main program. We have chosen to describe it as a private member of class *User* and to have the public member functions call it for the main program.

4.4 EXPLORING THE PIP

The code we need to declare, define, and use our menu-based interface is spread over five files, each of which we'll examine here. The class *User*, as you have come to expect, is declared and defined in two files, "USER.H" and "USER.CPP", respectively. The third and fourth files, which we have named "UTILITY.H" and "UTILITY.CPP", contain the declarations and definitions for some generally useful functions (hence, the name "Utility") that are not associated with any particular class. The main program that we need to run our soda machine, which makes use of both the *User* class and some of the utility functions, is described in file "PIP4.CPP".

Declaration: The Files "USER.H" and "UTILITY.H"

We created a separate file for the functions declared in "UTILITY.H" because, even though these functions didn't fit our notion of a class, they were seen to be useful to many programs. By declaring them in a header file of their own we make them easy to access from any program. The same is true to a lesser extent of our *User* class. Whereas the declaration of class *User* is completely generic, its definition (at least, the definition we'll consider) is specific to its intended role as the interface to a soda machine. You will see, however, that with minor modifications class *User* can be made to serve as a menu-based interface for any interactive program.

The declaration part of the *User* class is reasonably straightforward since it consists of only two public functions, a constructor and a function for accepting an input command from the keyboard. Function *GetCommand* reads a command from the user, checks that it is legal, and returns the legal command character as its value. *User* also has two private functions, one to display the menu and a second to test whether a character is among the ones we have defined as legal for this program.

```
//
//-------------------USER.H-------------------

// Declaration of the class User. This is a simple class whose
// only responsibilities are to get a legal command character from
// the keyboard and to display a menu of choices when requested.

class User
{
public:
    User();                     // Initialize a User object by
                                // showing the menu.
    char GetCommand();          // Return a legal char from KB.

private:
    void ShowMenu();            // Show the available choices
    int IsLegal (char cmd);     // Return true (1) if cmd is one we recognize.
};
```

File "UTILITY.H" is equally straightforward. It contains declarations for three functions that are generally useful for controlling the user interface to a C++ program. Indeed, we have already made use of two of them in previous PIPs. Function *WaitForUser,* as we have seen, simply freezes the screen so that a user can review a program's output. Once the user hits the *Enter* key, control returns to the program and processing continues. Similarly, function *Terminate* waits for the user to hit the *Enter* key before terminating a program's processing and returning control to the C++ environment.

The function that is of most interest to us here is *ReadyToQuit.* It is intended to return a boolean flag indicating whether or not the user of the program wants to quit the program. If the user responds "no," processing will continue. Used in combination with a repetition statement, *ReadyToQuit* can be used to run a program repeatedly until the user indicates that it should stop.

Remember that these functions are "free" in the sense that none is a member of any class. The lack of any reference to a class in the function declarations (they are not declared using the "::" operator) makes this clear.

```
//------------------USER.H------------------

// This file contains the definitions for
// a few functions that are useful for controlling the
// running of C++ programs.

#ifndef _UTILITY_H
#define _UTILITY_H

void Terminate();
// Freeze the screen until the user types a character,
// then print a concluding message.

int ReadyToQuit();
// Ask if the user is ready to quit the program.
// Return 1 if and only if the user enters 'y' or 'Y'.

void WaitForUser(void);
// Freeze the screen until the user types a character.

void SetNumeric(void);
// Set C++ format flags for numeric output.

void Swap(int &, int &);
// Exchanges the values of two integers.

#endif
```

Definition: The Files "USER.CPP" and "UTILITY.CPP"

When you look at the definition of class *User*, and that of function *ReadyToQuit* from file "UTILITY.CPP", you will see why they were used in this chapter's PIP. They exploit C++'s repetition statements to define a user interface that is not only adaptable to a wide range of programs, but also "friendly." A friendly interface provides its user with multiple opportunities to respond to prompts and handles improper responses deftly, without damaging the program (our soda machine, in this case).

```cpp
//------------------ USER.CPP -------------------

// Definitions of the member functions for the User class.

#include <iostream.h>              // for cin, cout
#include <ctype.h>                 // for toupper
#include "USER.H"

User::User()
// Initialize by displaying the menu.
{
    ShowMenu();
}

char User::GetCommand()
// Get a char from KB and send the char back to main.
// NOTE: if the command was 'M', just show the menu without
// returning.
{
    char cmd;          // the command character entered by the user

    while (1)          // Keep trying until we get a legal command.
                       // (peculiar loop: we never leave it the usual way)
    {
        cout << "\n> ";                // Prompt the user,
        cin >> cmd;                    // get a new command,
        cmd = toupper(cmd);            // and convert it to upper-case

        if (IsLegal(cmd))              // We got a legal command
        {
            if (cmd == 'M')
                // If it's 'M', show the menu and stay in the loop,
                ShowMenu();
            else                       // otherwise just send it back
                return cmd;            // and break out of the loop
                                       // (this is the only way out).
        }
        else                           // Illegal command, so notify operator.
        {
            cout << "\n*** Unrecognized command.";
            cout << " Type M to see menu.";
        }
    }
}
```

```
int User::IsLegal(char cmd)
// Return 1 if cmd is one that we can handle, else return 0.
{
    return(  (cmd == 'Q') || (cmd == 'D') || (cmd == 'N') ||
             (cmd == 'R') || (cmd == 'C') || (cmd == 'L') ||
             (cmd == 'B') || (cmd == 'O') || (cmd == 'F') ||
             (cmd == 'X') || (cmd == 'M'));
}


void User::ShowMenu()
{
    cout << "Please select one of the following options\n";
    cout << "by pressing the indicated key:\n";
    cout << "\n\tMoney-handling\n";
    cout << "\t\tQ: Quarter\n";
    cout << "\t\tD: Dime\n";
    cout << "\t\tN: Nickel\n";
    cout << "\t\tR: Return all coins\n";
    cout << "\n\tDrink selection ($0.75 each)\n";
    cout << "\t\tC: Cola\n";
    cout << "\t\tL: Lite cola\n";
    cout << "\t\tB: root Beer\n";
    cout << "\t\tO: Orange\n";
    cout << "\t\tF: caffeine-Free, diet, clear, new-age cola\n";
    cout << "\n\tSimulation control\n";
    cout << "\t\tM: show this Menu\n";
    cout << "\t\tX: eXit the program\n";
}
```

Three of the four member functions of the class *User* are defined simply and directly from their descriptions. All that is involved in constructing a *User* object is displaying the interface menu. To display the menu (in function *ShowMenu*), we use a series of output statements to display it on the screen, making liberal use of tabs and newlines to do so in a readable format. Determining whether a character is one of the legal menu inputs (in function *IsLegal*) is just a matter of checking whether or not the character provided matches one of the characters prescribed by the menu.

Most interesting by far is the definition of function *GetCommand*. It not only uses a while loop; it uses a while loop of a somewhat peculiar form. This function prompts the user for a character, gets a character from the keyboard, and keeps prompting and getting characters until the user enters a legal character. Since we want to keep repeating an action until some condition (legality of input) is satisfied, a loop is a natural choice. Under most circumstances, we'd prefer the exit from the loop to be controlled by the loop's test expression, like this:

```
Get a command, cmd;
while (cmd isn't a legal command)
    Display a warning and get another command
```

As a matter of fact, that's exactly what we do in the function *ReadyToQuit* in the file "UTILITY.CPP":

```
int ReadyToQuit()
{
    char ans;
    cout << "\nDo you wish to run the program again ";
    cout << "(Y for yes, N for no)? ";
    cin >> ans;
    ans = toupper(ans);              // convert the answer to upper case
    while ((ans !='Y') && (ans!='N'))
    {
        cout << "\nPlease answer again with Y or N";
        cout << "\n\tRun the program again? ";
        cin >> ans;
        ans = toupper(ans);
    }
    return (ans =='N');  // returns 1 when ready to quit; else 0
}
```

The situation in *GetCommand*, however, is complicated by the fact that we want to keep getting a command in *two* cases: when the command is illegal and when the command is the legal 'M,' to display the menu. In the Exercises we ask you rewrite this function so that the test expression controls the exit from the loop. What we did, though, was to bend the rules slightly in the interest of illustrating for you an alternative approach. We wrote an intentionally infinite loop with a test expression that was always *true* (1, in this case). Then we use a return statement to break out of the loop, as we indicate in skeletal form below.

```
while (1)
{   Get a command
    if (IsLegal(cmd))
    {   if (cmd == 'M')
            Legal command, but it's 'M' so we stay in the loop
            ShowMenu();
        else
            Legal command, not 'M' so we leave the loop
            return cmd;
    }
    else
```

```
    {
        Illegal command, so we stay in the loop
        cout << "\n*** Unrecognized command. ";
        cout << "Type M to see the menu.";
    }
}
```

The decision we made here involved a tradeoff: We ran the risk of reducing readability for simplicity in programming. It was a close call, we admit, one that points out the fact that programming involves esthetic as well as logical decisions.

Use: The File PIP4.CPP

As we have seen, with the Declare-Define-Use approach most of the programming work is done in declaring and defining the classes used to build a program. By the time we are using our classes, writing a main function tends to be pretty simple. In this case, our main program is going to use and coordinate the actions of two somewhat independent classes, our *Machine* class from PIP 3 and the *User* class we just described. As a result, the main program here consists of two initializations, for the soda machine object and for the user object, along with a main processing loop that is typical of most interactive programs. This loop repeatedly gets a command from *theUser* and passes the command to *theMachine* to be handled. We use a do loop here, since we know that the user must enter at least one command, which we execute if it's not 'X,' and then test the command to see whether the user is ready to exit the program.

```
///------------------- PIP4.CPP -------------------

// Main routine for our soda machine simulation.

#include <iostream.h>
#include "UTILITY.H"                          // for Terminate
#include "MACHINE.H"
#include "USER.H"

void main()
{
    SodaMachine     theMachine;               // Initialize the machine.
    User            theUser;                  // Initialize a user.

    char theCommand;
    do
    {
        // Get a command from the user,
        theCommand = theUser.GetCommand();
```

```
      // and if it's not the exit command,
      if (theCommand != 'X')
      // pass it on to the machine.
         theMachine.DoCommand(theCommand);
   } while (theCommand != 'X');
   // Quit when the user enters 'X'.

   Terminate();
}
```

4.5 SUMMING UP

▶ We've talked about the following statements:

- while-loop:
  ```
  while (expression)
      statement
  ```

- do-loop:
  ```
  do
      statement
  while (expression);
  ```

- for-loop:
  ```
  for (initStatement; testExpression; iterationExpression)
      loopBodyStatement
  ```

▶ A while loop repeatedly executes its statement as long as the expression evaluates to a non-zero value. This statement tests for loop exit before executing the loop body, so the loop body may not be executed at all if the expression has value zero (*false*) at the start.

▶ A do loop also repeatedly executes its statement as long as its expression evaluates to a non-zero value. This statement tests for loop execution after executing the loop body, and so will always execute the loop body at least once.

▶ The for statement has the same action as

```
initStatement
while (testExpression)
{
    loopBodyStatement
    iterationExpression;
}
```

▶ The most common form of the for statement is used to execute a loop with an index, i, varying from 0 to $n - 1$. In this case, the loop leader looks like this:

```
for (int i = 0; i < n; i++)
```

4.6 EXERCISES

For Exercises 1 and 2, identify and correct the syntax errors, if any. Don't worry about whether these loops do anything useful—you're interested only in whether they'll compile. You may assume that all undeclared variables have been declared earlier.

1. a.
```
do
     g++
while (g > g);
```

   b.
```
cin >> limit;
for (int i = 0, sum = 0; i < limit; k = 2 * i + 1, i++)
   sum += k * k;
```

   c.
```
cin >> n;
while (n != -1)
{   int sum = 0;
   sum += n;
   cin >> n;}
```

2. a.
```
cin >> n;
while (n = -1)
   sum += n;
   cin >> n;
```

   b.
```
do
{ cin >> n;
   sum += n; }
while (n != -1)
```

   c.
```
for (int i = 1, i < n, i *= -2)
   sum += i;
```

Exercises 3 and 4 refer to Exercises 1 and 2, respectively.

3. For the corrected segments in Exercise 1, try to guess the programmer's intention and then point out the likely semantic problems that would keep the segments from doing what they should or would lead to a run-time error.

4. For the corrected segments in Exercise 2, do the same thing.

5. Write a function int GetNumber () that asks the user for an integer in the range 0 to 100 and returns the number the user entered, if it is in the correct range. If the number is not in the correct range, the function should display an appropriate error message and try again, repeating this process until the user enters a legal number.

6. Assume that *S* is a statement and *E* is an expression.

a. Using a do statement, write the equivalent of

```
while (E)
    S
```

b. Using a while statement, write the equivalent of

```
do
    S
while (E);
```

7. In the following statements, how many times is statement S executed?

a.
```
for (int i = 0; i < 5; i++)
    for (int j = 0; j < 5; j++)
        S
```

b.
```
for (int i = 0; i < 5; i++)
    for (int j = i; j < 5; j++)
        S
```

c.
```
for (int i = 0; i < 5; i++)
    for (int j = i; j < 5 - i; j++)
        S
```

8. There are times when we want the index variable in a for loop to increment or decrement by values other than 1.

a. What would the header of a for loop look like if the variable i had to take the values 3, 7, 11, 15, 19, 23, 27?

b. What would the header look like if i had to take the values 1, 2, 4, 8, 16, 32?

9. The following segment is supposed to investigate the numbers from 2 to 1000. For each number, the sum of its proper divisors is computed and displayed. For example, 8 has proper divisors 1, 2, and 4 (since we're looking at *proper* divisors, we don't include the value 8), so the sum of the proper divisors is 1 + 2 + 4 = 7. The number 28 is an example of a rare *perfect number*, one that is equal to the sum of its proper divisors, since 1 + 2 + 4 + 7 + 14 = 28. The organization of this segment is simple enough:

```
For all numbers, n, from 2 to 1000,
    Test all trial divisors from 2 to n - 1 to see if they divide n evenly.
    If a divisor is found, add it to the sum of divisors.
    Display the number and the sum of divisors.
```

The segment below fails to work as we intended. Describe the first three lines of output and fix the code so that it works correctly.

```
int trialDivisor = 1;
for (int n = 2; n <= 1000; n++)
{
    while (trialDivisor < n)
```

```
    {
        int sumOfDivisors = 0;
        if (n % trialDivisor == 0)
            sumOfDivisors += trialDivisor;
    }
    cout << "\nn = " << n << "\tsum = " << sumOfDivisors
}
```

10. (This requires a bit of math background.) The *harmonic series*,

$$1 + \frac{1}{2} + \frac{1}{3} + \frac{1}{4} + \cdots + \frac{1}{n}$$

increases without limit as n increases. We might want to know how fast the series increases, in the sense of asking how big n has to be to make the sum have a value greater than, say, 20. This seems a simple enough programming task; all we have do is write a routine like this:

```
double sum = 0.0;
int denominator = 0;
do
{
    denominator++;
    sum = sum + 1.0 / denominator;
} while (sum <= 20.0);
cout << "It took " << denominator;
cout << " terms to get above 20";
```

This may not work, however. Why? *Hint*: This sum is close to *ln(n)*.

11. The following function takes a number n in binary (so n consists solely of the digits zero and one) and returns the decimal equivalent of n. For example, if n were 1101, the function would return 13.

   a. Fill in the boolean expression that controls the loop.

```
int BinaryToDecimal(int n)
{
    int sum = 0;
    int power = 1;
    while (_____)
    {
        int digit = (n % 10);      // Get the rightmost digit.
        sum += power * digit;      // Update the sum.
        power *= 2;                // Double the power.
        n /= 10;                   // Remove the rightmost digit.
    }
    return sum;
}
```

b. Show the values of the variables when this function is called with $n = 1101$.

12. Write the definition of the function int Digits(int n) that counts the number of digits in *n*. *Hint:* Look at Exercise 11.

13. a. Write the definition of the function int Reverse (int n) that reverses the digits of *n* so that *Reverse*(4723) returns 3274. This is a tricky problem. It involves extracting the digits from the right of *n* and building the reverse using these digits as they come in. You might want to refer to Exercise 11 for help.

    b. Use *Reverse* to write a function int Palindrome (int n) that returns 1 if and only if *n* is a *palindrome*, which is to say *n* is the same as its reverse, like 454 and 3333.

    c. An interesting problem that appeared on *Square One* (a Public Broadcasting System kid's show about mathematics) is the following: Take a number, *n*, add it to its reverse, and continue the process until the result is a palindrome. For example, starting with 95, we add it to its reverse to get $95 + 59 = 154$. Add this to its reverse and we get $154 + 451 = 605$. Add this to its reverse and we get $605 + 506 = 1111$, which is a palindrome after three iterations. Write a program to count the number of iterations it takes for this process to produce a palindrome. Since the numbers get pretty big, you might want to make the numbers long integers. Even that won't help for the starting value 98, which takes only 24 iterations but results in the palindrome 8,813,200,023,188. Don't even consider trying this on 295—if 295 ever produces a palindrome, the result is at least 3,200 digits long!

    d. Prove that the process outlined in (c) eventually terminates (produces a palindrome) for any starting value.

14. Discover the next term in the sequence 24, 20, 4, 16, 37, . . . and write a program to generate such a sequence from any starting value (which in itself is a hint). We were humbled to discover that a ten-year-old in our local school system got the answer before we did, so congratulate yourself if you get it quickly and don't feel bad if you don't.

15. Design a program that displays a tree, like this:

Write your program so that it is general enough to be able to draw other figures with little modification (for instance, you might want to break the program into several functions such as one that prints a centered line consisting of an odd number of stars).

16. If *a* and *b* are positive integers, the *greatest common divisor (gcd)* of *a* and *b* is the largest number that divides both *a* and *b* evenly. For example, the *gcd* of 15 and 24—which we would write as *gcd* (15, 24)—is 3, whereas *gcd* (15, 16) = 1, since 1 is the largest number that divides both 15 and 16. The following function computes the *gcd* of two positive integers.

```
int GCD (int a, int b)
{ do
     { a %= b;
         int swap = a;
         a = b;
         b = swap;
     } while (b > 0);
     return a;
}
```

It's tricky to prove that this function is correct. In fact, it's not even trivial to prove that the loop terminates. It is, and it does; the nice part is that this function is *fast*.

   a. Try it with *a* = 1377 and *b* = 1088, showing the values of the variables at the start of each iteration of the loop.
   b. Use *GCD* to modify the *Fraction* class from Chapter 2 so that fractions are always represented in lowest terms. For example, the fraction 15/24 would be stored as 5/8.

17. A *prime number* is an integer (generally assumed to be greater than 1) that has no proper divisors except for itself and 1. We see that 7 is prime, but 6 is not, since 6 can be divided evenly by 2 and 3, as well as by 1 and 6. The first few primes are 2, 3, 5, 7, 11, 13, 17, 19, 23, 29, 31, 37, 41, and 43.

   a. Write the function int IsPrime (int n) that returns 1 if *n* is prime and returns 0 otherwise. Remember that you can test whether *b* divides *a* by using the expression (*a* % *b* == 0).
   b. *Wilson's theorem* states that *n* is prime if and only if the expression $((n - 1)! + 1)$ % *n* is zero. (See Exercise 20 for a definition of !—this is not the C++ logical *not* operator.) Use this expression to produce a new prime-testing function. *Hint*: Since the numbers get pretty big, you should follow each multiplication by the reduction %, since all quantities will eventually be reduced by % *n* anyway.

18. It's not always easy to prove that a loop will terminate eventually. Consider the following:

```
while (n > 1)
    if (n % 2 == 1)
        n = 3 * n + 1;
    else
        n /= 2;
```

a. This is known as *Ulam's functions.* It's not known whether this loop terminates for all initial values of *n.* Try it for $n = 160$, $n = 15$, and $n = 1920$. *Hint*: $1920 = 128 \times 15$.

b. Write a program that counts how long this loop takes to terminate for starting values $n = 1, 2, 3, \ldots, 100$.

c. Prove that the loop terminates for all positive starting values. Write to us and let us see your proof. We promise we'll share the credit with you for your discovery.

19. We can find the square root of a nonnegative number N without using the C++ function *sqrt* that is declared in the library header `<math.h>`. To do this, we use the following code:

```
double a = N;
do
    a = a - (a * a - N) / (2.0 * a);
while (abs (a * a - N) < 1e-8);
```

(The function *abs* is also declared in `<math.h>`, and returns the absolute value of its argument.) In this segment, we do the loop until the answer *a* has a square that is within 0.00000001 of N. This technique is known as *Newton's method,* and the nice part about it is how fast it works. Get out your calculator and try it by hand, writing down successive values that *a* takes to find the square root of 100 to within 8 places. Try it again, this time to find the square root of 10,000.

20. A *recursive* function is one that includes a call to itself in its definition. We could, for instance, define the *factorial* function of a positive integer n, written $n!$, by the recursive definition

$$1! = 1$$

$$n! = n \times (n - 1)!, \qquad \text{for } n > 1$$

or by the nonrecursive definition

$$n! = 1 \times 2 \times \cdots \times (n - 2) \times (n - 1) \times n$$

We can verify that $3! = 6$, $5! = 120$, and $7! = 5040$ (that's why the factorial function is written as an exclamation mark—it grows surprisingly! fast). Any recursive function may be written without recursion. Using informal arguments, show that the following two functions both compute $n!$.

```
long RecursiveFactorial(long n)
// Recursive factorial function
{ if (n <= 1)
     return 1;
   else
     return (n * RecursiveFactorial(n - 1)); }
```

```
long IterativeFactorial (long n)
// Iterative factorial function
{ for (int product = 1, term = 1; term <= n; term ++)
    product *= term;
  return product; }
```

21. In recent years, college tuition has risen at a national average annual rate of 6%.

   a. Write a function

```
double Tuition(double current, int thisYear, int targetYear);
```

       that will take as its arguments the current tuition, the date of this year, and the target year we are interested in and will return the tuition in the target year by repeatedly multiplying the starting tuition by 1.06.

   b. Write a program that will repeatedly get the current tuition, current year, and target year and display the resulting tuition, until the user enters zero for any of the three values.

   c. For some depressing news, you might want to enter and run your program with reasonable values, to find out what it will cost for your children to go to college.

5

COMPOUND
DATA

One of the main virtues of C++—and one of the main reasons we chose it for use in this text—is that it helps us describe our world more directly than do many other programming languages. A natural and common way of describing our world is to organize collections of related things into groups. A timer can be described as a collection of displays. A deck is a collection of 52 playing cards. We can even describe collections of collections: For example, a sentence is a collection of words. A collection of sentences about a topic may be grouped into a paragraph, and we may organize a collection of paragraphs into an essay or a chapter in a book. We've seen this same kind of organization in the world of programming: A collection of logically related statements may be grouped into a function, and a collection of related functions and data may be grouped into a class. Describing our world in terms of collections of related information—that is, as compound data— allows us to concentrate our attention on a higher level of abstraction, freeing us, at least temporarily, from having to devote our energies to the details.

We've already seen one of the two main forms of *compound* data in C++: the class. In this chapter, we'll discuss the other, arrays. Arrays allow us to group data of a particular type together into a single conceptual unit. Having done that, we'll see how repetition statements are particularly well suited for manipulating arrays and how together with classes they can be used to model a complex, real-world problem.

OBJECTIVES

In this chapter, we will

▶ Describe the array compound type and give examples of how arrays may be used.

▶ Discuss the natural correspondence between arrays and for loops.

▶ Review how we declare, define, and use classes as compound data.

▶ Illustrate how arrays and classes can be used together in this chapter's PIP to model a card game.

5.1 ARRAYS

Like classes, arrays allow us to describe collections of information. Arrays, however, differ from classes in three fundamental ways. First, the elements that make up an array must all be of the same type. Second, the elements in an array are *indexed* from 0 to some upper limit, so that an individual element is accessed by its index rather than by a distinct member name. Finally, and most importantly, an array only encapsulates data, and it may not contain any user-defined member functions.

An *array* is an indexed collection of data elements of the same type.

Arrays generally seem to cause more confusion than classes, but they're nothing more than the kind of itemized list we use daily to describe collections of things of the same type. A list of dogs, for instance, is nothing but an indexed collection of elements of the same type:

0. Clipper
1. Sparky
2. Bear
3. Luke
4. Tessa
5. Bailey
6. Luca
7. Zannie
8. Pete

The only peculiar aspect in this "array of dogs"—and of all C++ arrays—is that the index numbers we use to label the list's elements begin with zero.

Declaring Arrays

We declare an array by describing the type and number of its elements. The following are all legal array declarations. We've presented each in pictorial form in Figure 5.1.

```
int numList[2];          // two integers
char charArray[10];      // ten characters
Dog kennel[9];           // nine dogs (assuming the Dog type
                         // had been declared earlier)
```

An array declaration takes the following form:

```
typeName variableName[n];
```

This declares *variableName* to be an array of *n* elements of type *typeName,* indexed from 0 to $n - 1$. These elements are named *variableName*[0] through *variableName*[$n - 1$].

In Figure 5.1, notice that all indices begin with zero, as we mentioned earlier, and that the elements are not filled in with values. This makes sense, since we have declared the arrays, but have not defined them by specifying what the element values should be.

Notice, too, that an array may be composed of elements of *any* type, including user-defined types such as *Dog.* In fact, we can even have arrays of arrays, or *multidimensional arrays,* as they are called. To declare an array of arrays, we read levels of grouping from left to right, so the declaration

```
int table[2][3];
```

would be interpreted as declaring a *table* to be a two-element array, each element of which is a three-element array of integers, as shown in Figure 5.2.* We

FIGURE 5.1

Three arrays

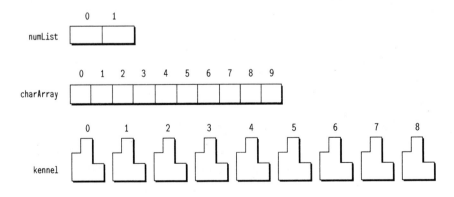

---

* Pascal speakers will have to unlearn old habits here. In Pascal, there's a shorthand way of writing declarations of multidimensional arrays, using [2, 3] to represent what we call [2] [3]. This comma notation is allowed in C++, as we've seen, but has an entirely different meaning.

FIGURE 5.2
A multidimensional
array int table[2][3]

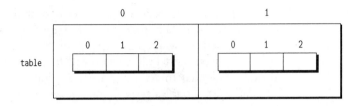

This is the way the array is stored, but you can think of it like this, too:

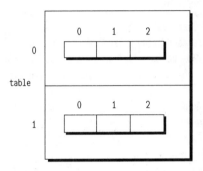

Or, once you get comfortable with arrays, like this:

table   0   1   2

can declare arrays of dimension as high as we need, although the pictures get pretty tricky once we get beyond two dimensions.

There is another significant difference between array declarations and those of classes. You may have noticed that the array declarations we've made describe an object, such as *numArray, kennel,* or *table,* but don't give a name to the type of object described. This could be a problem, and certainly would be an inconvenience, if we wanted to have several arrays of the same type in several parts of our program. Consider the following example:

```
char response[20];              // used to get some response from user
struct Employee
{
    char name[20];              // the employee's name
    char address[3][20];        // a 3-line address
    . . .
};
```

In three separate instances—in declaring response, name, and address—we've made use of arrays of twenty characters, defining each on the fly, as it were. We have the same kind of inconveniences here that motivated us to use const declarations. First, it's a bother to type the same code three times. More important, if we decided we wanted to expand all the arrays to 25 characters, we would have to search the whole program to find and change 20 to 25, all the while making sure that the changes were appropriate. Finally, it's not immediately obvious that variables *response* and *name* are of the same type.

C++ allows us to overcome these confusions by choosing a name to serve as a synonym for any type we wish. The typedef specification permits us to give a name to any type. We could simplify and clarify the declarations using a typedef by writing

```
typedef char CharString[20];
// Here, we've made "CharString" a synonym for
// "array of 20 characters," so we can use "CharString"
// in exactly the same way we would any other type name.

CharString response;
struct Employee
{
    CharString name;
    CharString address[3];
    . . .
};
```

> A type may be given a name by using a typedef declaration. A typedef is written exactly as if we were making a variable declaration, except that (1) the declaration begins with the specifier typedef and (2) the type name synonym is used where the variable name would be.

The advantage of naming a type is that typedefs save typing and make a program easier to understand and modify. The disadvantage is that we're forcing the reader to look up or to remember the typedef declaration to find the meaning of the user-defined type name. As with many such programming problems, you have to weigh the advantages and disadvantages. Your authors typically try to localize typedefs, placing them near where they are used, if possible, and commenting clearly where we can't.

Defining Arrays

Since arrays have no member functions, and since the elements of arrays are always public, we can initialize arrays using a shorthand like this:

```
int a[3] = {5, 10, 15};
char st[5] = {'a', 'b', 'c', 'd', 'e'};
int table[2][3] = {{1, 2, 3} {3, 4, 5}};
```

The resulting arrays *a, st,* and *table* would then be defined to look like those in Figure 5.3.

In a similar way, we can use a string to initialize an array of characters, but we have to be a bit more careful. C++ strings are *zero terminated,* which means that they can be of any length as long as they end with the char with code zero.* In other words, the string "hello" actually consists of six characters, 'h', 'e', 'l', 'l', 'o', and '\0', the terminating character. With this in mind, we can initialize an array of characters with a string, like

Remember, the escape mark, \, is used to specify nonprinting characters like '\t' for tab and '\n' for newline.

```
char greeting[6] = "hello";
```

or

```
char greeting[] = "hello";
```

Both of these definitions are exactly equivalent to

```
char greeting[6] = {'h', 'e', 'l', 'l', 'o', '\0'};
```

and all produce an array like that illustrated in Figure 5.4.

When using a string to initialize an array of characters, don't forget the terminating '\0' character. It's there, even if you can't see it, so there must be room in the array for it.

If we had specified the array size to be larger than the string length (including the terminating *null* character), the definition would work perfectly well, but any array elements after the null character would not be explicitly

FIGURE 5.3
Three arrays after initialization

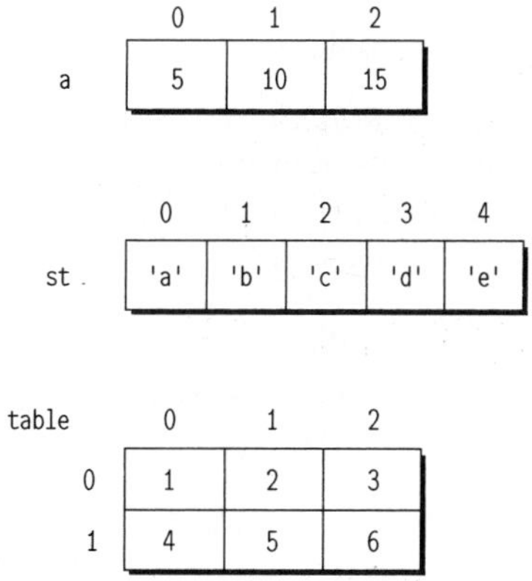

* There are two common ways for languages to deal with character strings. Some languages (like Pascal) use the first numeric code in a string to represent the length of the string; others, like C and C++, do not specify the length of the string but instead use a special terminating character, like zero, to indicate the end of a string.

FIGURE 5.4

Using a string to initialize an array of characters

The definition

```
char greeting[6] = "hello";
```

produces the array

	0	1	2	3	4	5
greeting	'h'	'e'	'l'	'l'	'o'	'\0'

initialized.* It would be an error to initialize an array of characters with a string that was longer than the number of available array elements (just as it would be to have an initialization list longer than the array, for arrays of any type).

We said earlier that an array may have elements of any type, including user-defined types. User-defined types often have constructors, and we may want to use those constructors when constructing arrays. As usual, C++ is designed to anticipate our needs as well as possible by filling in any gaps it can with defaults. To illustrate how this works, suppose we have declared the class *Fraction* as we did in Chapter 2:

```
class Fraction
{   . . .
public:
    Fraction();          // the default constructor
    Fraction(int n, int d = 1);          // another constructor
    . . .
};
```

And suppose that we wanted to define an array, *rationals,* of three fractions. We could declare the array in the usual way

```
Fraction rationals[3];
```

Because *Fraction* is a class (as opposed to another kind of user-defined type) and has its own constructors, by making this declaration we would actually be instructing the compiler to initialize the array, using the default (i.e., no-argument) constructor for the *Fraction* class. The statement is equivalent to

```
Fraction rationals[3] = {Fraction(), Fraction(), Fraction()};
```

We could also combine declaration with definition by invoking the constructors for the *Fraction* elements explicitly:

```
Fraction rationals[3] = { Fraction(),          // default constructor
                          Fraction(2, 3),      // other constructor
                          Fraction(4)          // other constructor
                        };
```

---

* On most systems, uninitialized array elements would be filled with zeros of the appropriate type.

This would use the two constructors to generate the array {0 / 1, 2 / 3, 4 / 1} (although, of course, we couldn't write the array in this form in a program).

▼

> If a user-defined type has default constructors (with no arguments), then any definition of an array of elements of that type will use the default constructors, unless you specify otherwise.

Using Arrays

Now that we know how to declare and define arrays, we can talk about how they may be used in programs. The array is a powerful and useful construction, so much so that we'll devote this subsection and much of the PIP to describing how to use arrays.

First, to make good use of an array we need to be able to get to its elements just as we needed access to the member data of structures and classes. We do this by mirroring the way they are declared. In the declarations

```
int numList[2];
int table[2][3];
```

for instance, the two elements of *numList* would be referred to as *numList*[0] and *numList*[1]; and the six elements of *table* would be *table*[0][0], *table*[0][1], *table*[0][2], *table*[1][0], *table*[1][1], and *table*[1][2].* Figure 5.5 shows how to select array elements.

▼

> If an array is declared as *typeName variableName*[*size*], then the element of the array with index *i* is referred to as *variableName*[*i*].

In our first example, the two objects *numList*[0] and *numList*[1] are *assignable lvalues*, which is a fancy way of saying that they can be used in an expression anywhere a variable may be. For example, all of the statements below are valid, given our declarations:

```
numList[0] = 73;
numList[1] = 12 * (numList[0] % 11 - 1);
if (numList[0] <= numList[1])
    cout << "The elements are in order\n";
numList[0] = numList[1]++;
cin >> numList[0] >> numList[1];
numList[1] = 1 + SomeFunction(numList[0], numList[1]);
```

---

* Again, Pascal speakers will have to unlearn old habits: It is not correct to refer to *table*[1][2] as *table*[1, 2].

FIGURE 5.5
Selecting array elements by indices

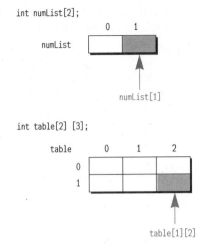

Remember, array indices in C++ always start with zero.

One of the handiest features of arrays—as you'll quickly come to appreciate—is that we can use any integer expression as an array index. For example, since *numList* is a two-element array, any expression that yields the integers 0 or 1 can appear within the array selector brackets for *numList,* like this:

```
int j = 0;
numList[j] = numList[1 - j];
// same as numList[0] = numList[1];
cout << numList[j+1];
// same as cout << numList[1]
```

Unfortunately, the compiler can't always check that the index expression is within the proper bounds. For example, there's no way to know at compile time that the following segment will result in *i* having the value 0 or 1:

```
cout << "What entry do you want to see? ";
cin >> i;
cout << "That element has value " << numList[i] << '\n';
```

Some C++ systems will provide run-time warnings if array indices stray beyond their bounds, but you should always guard access to arrays by doing your own checking, like this:

```
cout << "What entry do you want to see? ";
cin >> i;
if ((0 <= i) && (i <= 1))
    cout << "That element has value " << numList[i] << '\n';
else
    cout << "There is no array element with that index\n";
```

Be careful to ensure that array indices stay within their proper ranges. Don't count on the C++ system to do range-checking for you.

We now know how to access and manipulate the elements of an array, but what about performing operations on arrays as entire objects? The answer to this question derives from the fact that C++ treats arrays in a way that is fundamentally different from the way it treats other compound objects. Without delving into the details here, we'll simply state what you can and cannot do with arrays:

As we'll see in Chapter 6, an array name refers to a constant pointer to the first of the array elements, and not to the array itself.

1. Arrays may be passed as arguments to functions.
2. Arrays may *not* be returned from functions.
3. Assignment between arrays is *not* allowed. To assign one array to another, you must write the code to perform the assignments on an element-by-element basis.

Note, however, that functions may return array *elements,* and that assignment between array *elements* is allowed (except, in both cases, when the elements are themselves arrays).

The following program illustrates the things one can and cannot do with arrays.

```
#include <iostream.h>          // so we can use cout

typedef int Nums[4];           // "Nums" now means "array of 4 ints"

void Show(Nums x)
// OK: we can use an array as a function argument
{
    cout << x[0] << '\t' << x[1] << '\t';
    cout << x[2] << '\t' << x[3];
}

Nums SetToZero()
// NO: functions cannot return arrays
{
    Nums r;                    // this is the array we'll try to return
    r[0] = r[1] = r[2] = r[3] = 0;   // OK to assign elements
    return r;                  // ERROR
}
```

```
void main()
{
    int a[5] = {34, -8, 0, 16, -3};
    int b[5];
    b = a;              // ERROR: we can't assign arrays
    Show(a)             // OK: we can use arrays as arguments
}
```

Arrays and loops are natural companions. A salient feature of arrays is that their elements may be accessed by using the array name and an index, which is an integral type, from zero to some upper limit. A salient feature of loops is that they may be used to repeat a collection of statements, with an index variable that varies from a starting value to an ending value. By using the same variable to control a loop and to access an array, we can easily write code to perform similar processing to all elements of an array.

Suppose, for example, that a and b were both arrays of four integers, as in the example above. Since C++ doesn't allow array assignments, how would we perform the equivalent of the assignment $b = a$? The most direct solution is to use a for loop, which accomplishes the element-by-element assignment, as follows:

```
b[0] = a[0];
b[1] = a[1];
b[2] = a[2];
b[3] = a[3];

for (int i = 0; i < 4; i++)
    b[i] = a[i];
```

The key notion here is that the integer serving as the control variable in the loop is being used as the index variable to reference array elements within the loop. In this case, as the value of i varies from 0 to 3 (the iteration will stop when i reaches 4), successive elements of arrays a and b will be accessed.

Example | Consider the problem of searching for the first zero element in an array, a, of ten integers. What we want to do is to keep incrementing the array index until we find an array element whose value is zero and jump out of the loop either when we find a zero element or when we run out of elements to inspect. This is an example of a common process known as *bounded linear search*. In C++ terms, we want to increment the array index, i, as long as $(i < 10)$ && $(a[i] != 0)$. The code for such a search would look like this:

```
int i = 0;                          // set the starting index value
while ((i < 10) && (a[i] != 0))
// as long as there are elements to inspect
// and we haven't found a zero yet,
    i++;                            // look at the next array element
```

```
if (i == 10)                             // we went past the end of the array
    cout << "There are no zero values in the array";
else                                     // we found a zero
    cout << "The first zero element has index " << i;
```

◁

5.2   CLASSES, REVISITED

There is, as we mentioned, another form of compound information in C++, one with which you are already familiar—the class. Like an array, a class describes a collection of related information. We can access both the entire collection as a whole (as we do when we declare an object) and its individual constituents (when we invoke one of its member functions), as we can with arrays. Classes are, of course, decidedly more complex than arrays, since classes can describe both functions and data, and even the data members of a class can be of differing types. Still, the notion of a compound data type applies perfectly well to classes.

At this point it is worth reconsidering what we already know about classes, paying particular attention to how classes fit the mold of a compound data type. We'll do so by reviewing the features of C++ that allow us to declare, define, and use classes.

Declaring Classes

In this section we declare two classes using the declaration format we have adopted throughout this text. The first, class *Card,* describes a single playing card. It, like all class declarations, provides a template for any object declared to be an instance of this class. The template tells us that any *Card* object comprises five functions and two data members. The data members, in this case describing the card's suit and value, are declared as are any variables. Each is given a type and a name, and each member declaration is terminated with a semicolon. A class can describe any number of data items of any type (even a user-defined type, like *Suit,* in our example). We tend to describe the data members of a class as being private to the class (again, meaning that they are accessible only to the member functions of the class, or to those of friend classes). This protects the information in the class from unwarranted use by other types of objects.

```
//----------------------CARDDECK.H----------------------

// These are the declarations of classes Card
// and Deck, to be used by card-playing programs.

enum Suit (clubs, diamonds, hearts, spades);
```

```
class Card
// This class describes a single card
{
public
      void Display ();       // for displaying a card in a readable fashion
      int GetVal ();         // retrieves the card's value
      void SetVal (int);     // sets the card's value to the value provided
      Suit GetSuit ();       // retrieves the card's suit
      void SetSuit (Suit);   // sets the card's suit to the suit provided

private:                     // we keep these private so that only authorized
                             // users of the class can access them directly
      Suit s;                // each card has a suit
      int val;               // and a value (2 ... 14, representing 2 ... Q, K, A)
};

class Deck
// This class describes a collection of 52 cards
{
friend class Dealer;         // since a Dealer has complete control over a deck

public
      Deck();                // the constructor opens a new deck of cards

private:
      int topCard;           // points to position of current top card of deck
      Card cards [52];       // a deck is 52 cards
};
```

The functions declared as part of class *Card* are also quite typical of member functions. First, each function is described in terms of a return type, a name, and an argument list (which may be empty, but it must be there to identify *GetVal,* for example, as a function instead of an integer value). In those cases in which the argument list is not empty (for *SetVal* and *SetSuit*), the number and type of each argument are provided. Again, each function declaration ends with a semicolon.

Whereas we tend to describe a class's member data as private in order to protect it, if a class object is to be useful to a program or other objects at all, at least some of its member functions must be declared as public. There can, as we have seen, be member functions that are of use only to the class and are declared as private. In this case, though, we have five public member functions that serve very general purposes.

The first, function *Display,* displays a card (its suits and value) in some readable form and falls into the category of an access function. Similarly, *GetVal* and *GetSuit* are used to provide public access to the card's private data. Functions *SetVal* and *SetSuit* are examples of manipulator functions, which actually change the values of the private data.

Function *Deck,* the only member function of class *Deck,* is an example of a constructor function. We provide constructor functions for classes to control the creation and initialization of objects of the class. We can provide any number of constructor functions for a class, as long as they differ in their argument lists. This difference is essential, because all constructors must have the same name (which matches precisely that of the containing class) and all will have the same associated return type, which is implicitly that of the class itself. That is, a constructor function for class *Deck* can be thought of as returning an object of type *Deck.* Notice that no return type is specified for a constructor function.

The lone constructor function for class *Deck* is referred to as a default constructor since its argument list is empty. It is the constructor that will be invoked when we declare a *Deck* object without providing any additional information. Note, too, that constructor functions will of necessity be declared as public so that objects of the class can be created and initialized from outside of the class.

The member data items of our class *Deck* are interesting as well because they illustrate two important features of how classes can be organized and related to one another. First, remember that data members can be almost any type at all. We say "almost" because we can't have, for example, a data member of type *Deck* in the *Deck* class declaration. Think for a moment why this would be illegal. This recursive declaration would lead to an infinite regress in which one would say, "A *Deck* object contains as one of its members a *Deck* object, which would have to have as one of its members a *Deck* object, which would have to have as one of its members a *Deck* object, . . . " You see the problem.

It *is* legal for a class to have a member that is a *reference* to an object of the same class, as you'll see when we talk about the pointer and reference operators in the next chapter.

In this case, *Deck* has a data item that itself is an array of 52 objects, each of which is an instance of class *Card.* That is, we have defined one class (*Deck*) as containing another (*Card*). This makes pretty good sense when we think in terms of what it is we are trying to model. A deck, after all, is a collection of cards. C++ allows us to declare increasingly complex classes from existing ones.

As we have seen, C++ also allows classes that are not explicitly related through containment to be related as "friends." In our example, class *Dealer* is declared to be a friend of class *Deck.* This means that any instance of class *Dealer* has full and complete access to the private and public members of *Deck* objects. This makes sense both intuitively (since the dealer in a card game certainly has access to and control of the cards) and from a programming standpoint (since this allows us to declare the data members of class *Deck* as private, thus limiting access only to *Dealer* objects). We'll see more clearly the implications of the friend declaration when we look at the definition of class *Dealer* in this chapter's PIP.

Finally, notice the file format we have adopted for writing class declarations. From a syntactic standpoint, we have considerable leeway in how we write class declarations. That is, we can declare things in almost any order, we can indent items however we please, we can name classes and members to suit our whims, and we can include as many or as few comments as we feel like typing. The fact is that all of these features of a declaration file mean little to the computer itself. Rather, they are features that help us humans read and make effective use of classes.

Most of our conventions are probably clear to you by now. As you have seen, we tend to use separate files for declaring each class, except, as in the case here, where the classes are so intimately related that it's hard to imagine using one class (*Card*) without the other (*Deck*). Second, each file begins with a comment describing its contents and purpose. Each class declaration also begins with a comment, and comments are provided to describe in English the role of each class member. Public members are declared together, before the private members. We do so on the grounds that if you want to use a class, the public members are the ones that should be easy to find as you read the declaration. Friend declarations are listed before declaring the public members. The entire body of each class declaration is enclosed in braces and terminated with a semicolon. All of these conventions are illustrated in Figure 5.6.

Defining Classes

The file format we use for defining classes, as illustrated in the following file "CARDDECK.CPP", is similar to that for declaring classes. Our definition files begin with descriptive comments, followed by the required include directives (one of which will refer to the header file in which the class being defined is declared). We try to define the member functions in the order that they appear in the corresponding declaration. Each definition begins with a comment and con-

FIGURE 5.6
Stylistic conventions for declaring classes

```
// File name
// Describe the contents of this file
 . . .
    # include directives              // members accessed in this file
 . . .
user-defined types specific to this file
 . . .
class className
// describe the class
{
friend declarations, if any
 . . .
public:
    member declaration              // role of member
      . . .
private:
    member declaration              // role of member
      . . .
}
```

tains comments for individual statements. The compound statement that constitutes each function body is, of course, surrounded by braces.

```cpp
//--------------------CARDDECK.CPP--------------------------

// This file contains the definition for the
// classes Card and Deck.
    #include <iostream.h>          // for cout
    #include "CARDDECK.H"

void Card::Display()
// display the suit and value of an individual card
{
    int v = GetVal();           // get the card's value
    if ((2 <= v) && (v <= 10))  // for number cards, show value
        cout << v;
    else                        // for face cards, use abbreviation
    {
        switch (v)
        {
            case 11: cout << 'J'; break;
            case 12: cout << 'Q'; break;
            case 13: cout << 'K'; break;
            case 14: cout << 'A'; break;
        }
    }

    switch (GetSuit())                      // display suit
    {
        case clubs:     cout << " of clubs"; break;
        case diamonds:  cout << " of diamonds"; break;
        case hearts:    cout << " of hearts"; break;
        case spades:    cout << " of spades"; break;
    };
    cout << '\n';
}

int Card::GetVal()
// return the numeric value of a card
{
    return (val);
}

void Card::SetVal(int v)
// set the numeric value of a card
{
    val = v;
}
```

```
Suit Card::GetSuit()
// return the suit value of a card
{
    return (s);
}

void Card::SetSuit (Suit st)
// set the suit of a card
{
    s = st;
}

Deck::Deck()
// constructor for initializing a new deck of 52 cards
{
    topCard = 0;                        // we haven't dealt any cards yet
    for (int i = 0; i < 52; i++)        // for each card in the deck;
{
        cards[i].SetVal((i % 13) + 2);  // assign it a numeric value (2 - 14)
        switch (i / 13)                 // and a suit.
        {
            case 0: cards[i].SetSuit(clubs);        break;
            case 1: cards[i].SetSuit(diamonds);     break;
            case 2: cards[i].SetSuit(hearts);       break;
            case 3: cards[i].SetSuit(spades);       break;
        }
    }
}
```

Definitions are necessarily more complex than declarations since it is here that we provide the implementation details for each member function declared as part of our classes. The definition headers for each function convey this additional complexity. They look similar to the corresponding function declarations in that they use the same member function names and return types. They differ, though, from the declarations in two important ways.

First, the scope resolution operator (::) is used in each definition header to associate the function being defined with a particular class. Remember, there may be more than one function in a given program with the name, say, *Display*. Our definition, then, must make clear which function *Display* we are defining. We do so by referring to the function in the definition header as *Card::Display*. Indeed, every member function that we define uses the :: operator to express this relationship and has a header of the general form:

returnType *className::memberFunctionName (argumentList)*

The other difference between a function declaration and its header in the definition file is in the argument list. When declaring a function, we must indicate the number and type of each argument, as we do in declaring member function *SetVal* of class *Card,* for example. We need not provide a name for each argument (although we can if we wish). Names, though, are essential to a function definition because we will always refer to them from the function body (why else have them as arguments?). So the definition of function *Card::SetVal* includes a name (*v*) for its integer argument and correctly refers to *v* within its body.

Notice how class members, both data and functions, are referenced from within our member function definitions. For example, when we refer to data item *val* from the definition of *Card::GetVal,* we simply use the name *val.* Because this definition is for a member function of class *Card,* the name *val* refers unambiguously to the integer data item *val* associated with class *Card.* Similarly, we refer directly and unambiguously to data member *s* of class *Card* from within the definition of function *Card::GetSuit,* and to member functions *GetVal* and *GetSuit* from within the definition of *Card::Display.*

Things get a bit more complex in the definition of function *Deck::Deck.* In this constructor function we initialize a deck by assigning values and suits to each of the 52 card objects in a deck. Since the value and suit of a card are declared as private to class *Card,* we cannot access these data members directly from the definition of one of class *Deck*'s member functions. We must in this case use the public manipulator functions provided by class *Card* (*SetVal* and *SetSuit*) to set the data members of the individual cards. Since these functions are members of class *Card*—and not of class *Deck*—we must also use the dot (or member selection) operator to indicate which instance of these functions we intend to access.

Remember the critical difference between the scope resolution (::) and the member selection (.) operators: The scope resolution operator describes an identifier as being associated with a particular class (as in *Card::GetVal*), and the member selector associates an identifier with a particular instance of a class—that is, an object (as in *cards.v*).

The format we have adopted for defining a class is illustrated in Figure 5.7.

FIGURE 5.7
Stylistic conventions for defining classes

```
// File name
// Describe the classes that are being defined
local declarations
. . .
#include directives          // members accessed in this file
. . .
// define members in same order as their declarations
returnType className::memberFunctionName (argType arg, . . .)
// describe role of this function
{
      function body           // describe specific statements
}
. . .
```

Using Classes

Even after fully declaring and defining a class, all we have done is describe for the computer the form and meaning of a class. We still have not created any useful C++ objects. Objects, as we have seen, are created by declaring an object to be an instance of a class, as follows:

```
Card c;
```

This declaration, as the result of our efforts in declaring and defining class *Card*, creates a single object of type *Card* and names it *c*. We can then use the dot operator to access *c*'s public member functions to set its private data member and to display its value:

```
c.SetVal(4);
c.SetSuit(diamonds);
c.Display();
```

More realistically, we would probably want to create and make use of an entire deck. We could then create a *Deck* object, as

```
Deck d;
```

Since we have provided a constructor function for class *Deck*, whenever a *Deck* object is created the constructor automatically will be invoked. We have defined *Deck*'s lone constructor to initialize its 52 cards to form a standard deck.

The process actually is slightly more complex than that because a *Deck* as we have declared it comprises in part 52 card objects. What really happens when we declare a *Deck* object is that 52 instances of class *Card* are created and associated with *Deck*'s member data array, named *cards*. This is tantamount to declaring 52 objects of type *Card*, and indeed, if we had defined a constructor function for class *Card*, it would be invoked 52 times prior to invoking *Deck*'s constructor function. Since we didn't define a *Card* constructor, however, C++ handles the construction process automatically, allocating, but not initializing, the necessary storage for each card.

If a class contains member data that are themselves objects of other classes, and if those classes have default constructors (i.e., constructors with no arguments), then those constructors are called at the start of the constructor for the class that contains them.

Once a *Deck* object and its 52 *Card* objects have been created, we can use the deck as we do any object. We use the dot operator to access member data and functions, as in these examples.

```
Deck d;                  // create a Deck object with 52 cards
d.card[17].GetVal();     // get the value of the 17th card
```

```
d.card[5].SetSuit(clubs);        //set the suit of the 5th card
for (i=0; i<52, i++)
    d.cards[i].Display();        //display all 52 cards in deck d
```

Note a couple of important features that are illustrated by these examples. Since C++ allows us to declare and define classes that include other compound types (like arrays and classes) as members, we must be careful about how we refer to objects. In our examples, all references to individual cards use the dot operator twice—once to choose a card member from the deck and once to choose the member function (*GetVal*, *SetSuit*, or *Display*) for the particular card—and the array selection operator once. Furthermore, they are used in the order (reading left to right) from the highest conceptual level to the lowest. That is, if we want to invoke a function for a particular *Card* from a *Deck*, we refer first to the deck (*d*), then to the desired individual card (*card[i]*), and finally to the desired member function for that card.

> ▼
>
> To access elements in a compound object, always work from the top conceptual level down (in our example, from deck to card to the card's *Display* function), following each component by its selector.

This is a good place to mention a common source of error with classes. Names of types and names of objects of a given type serve very different purposes. Whereas it makes sense to refer to *d.topCard* or *card[i].val*, it would be an error to refer to *Card.s*, since the dot operator may have only an object name on its left. *Card* is a type, not an object of a given type, so *Card* has no member *s*. This error would be similar to referring to "human being's eldest daughter," rather than "Leslie J. Smith's eldest daughter," or to "adding 1 to int," as opposed to adding 1 to an integer object named *n*.

> ▼
>
> You can use the dot operator to access a member of a class *object*. It makes no sense to access a member of a class *type*.

5.3 PROGRAM IN PROGRESS: BLACKJACK

Let's use our description of a card deck to build a more complete and realistic program. What we have in mind is an interactive program to play a game of blackjack (or "21"). In it, the computer will serve as the dealer and will play against the user of the program, as in a casino.

Briefly, the object of the game is to get your cards to total as close to 21 as you can without going over 21. Face cards count as 10, and aces in our simplified version of the program always count as 11. A hand begins with the player and the dealer each being dealt two cards—both face up for the player, one up and one down for the dealer. The player then accepts up to three more cards, one at a time, until either she wants to stop doing so or the total value of the hand exceeds 21. The dealer then draws up to three more cards, one at a time, while the total value of the hand is less than 17. Once the dealer's total hand value reaches 17 (or higher) no further cards are dealt. If the dealer's and the player's hands have the same total value, or if both exceed 21, the hand is declared a draw. Otherwise, the hand closest to 21 wins. Hands are dealt repeatedly until there are not enough cards in the deck to deal a complete hand.

Designing the PIP

One big advantage of an object-oriented approach is that by describing our game in even these simple, natural, and realistic terms, we already have enough information at hand to design the classes our program will require. Here is a first crack at the classes we will need:

1. **Card**: described by a value and a suit, with the ability to display itself.
2. **Deck**: consisting of an ordered collection of cards, along with a marker to the topmost remaining card (which we advance through the collection as cards are "dealt out"). A deck must be able to initialize itself in order, just as a real deck comes from the factory.
3. **Player**: containing the hand the player is currently holding and the player's winnings so far. The player must be initialized, be able to show the current hand, and be able to evaluate its hand.
4. **Dealer**: controls the action of the game. The *Dealer* class is a manager (like our *SodaMachine* class was in the Chapter 3 PIP) as well as an active participant in the game. It keeps track of the play of the game and so will need for its data the player and the deck that it is managing. It must also keep track of its own hand, much as a player does. The responsibilities of the dealer are those we would assign to a human blackjack dealer: shuffle the deck, deal a hand to each player, determine the winner of each hand (and update the player's pot), keep track of the end of the deck, play a complete game, and determine the winner at the end.

That's it. By describing the problem in these familiar terms, we've taken a big step toward designing the program. What remains is to fill in the details and to translate this game description into a collection of C++ header files. This, in fact, is what object-oriented design (and the Declare-Define-Use approach, in particular) is all about. We concentrate from the start of the program development process on describing the classes involved. We make no mention at this early stage of how any of our classes will be defined in C++, nor do we concern ourselves explicitly with how our classes will be used. These considerations are deferred, respectively, to the "definition" and "use" phases of our programming life cycle. Notice, too, a powerful side benefit we gain from this approach to design: Our class description makes no mention whatsoever of what card game we're playing! We could use this same description, with different details, to play almost any card game we want.

We'll take you through the rest of this section in the same order we used when we developed the PIP—from the class declaration to class definitions to class use—pausing from time to time to point out items that pertain particularly to C++ classes, arrays, and loops.

Cards and Decks: The Files "CARDDECK.H" and "CARDDECK.CPP"

Clearly our *Card* and *Deck* classes from the previous section will serve us well in this PIP. Let's look at them in more detail as we begin to develop and analyze our blackjack program. In Figure 5.8 we illustrate the declarations of cards and decks.

Here again is the single-header file we wrote for these classes.

```
//-----------------------CARDDECK.H----------------------

// These are the declarations of classes Card
// and Deck, to be used by card-playing programs.

enum Suit {clubs, diamonds, hearts, spades};

class Card
// this class describes a single card
{
public:

        void Display();       // for displaying a card in a readable fashion
        int GetVal();         // retrieves the card's value
        void SetVal(int);     // sets the card's value to the value provided
        Suit GetSuit();       // retrieves the card's suit
        void SetSuit(Suit);   // sets the card's suit to the suit provided

private:                      // we keep these private so that only authorized
                              // users of the class can access them directly
        Suit s;               // each card has a suit
        int val;              // and a value (2 ... 14, representing 2 ... Q, K , A)
};

class Deck
// This class describes a collection of 52 cards
{
friend class Dealer;          // since a Dealer has complete control over a deck
```

FIGURE 5.8
The *Card* and *Deck*
classes

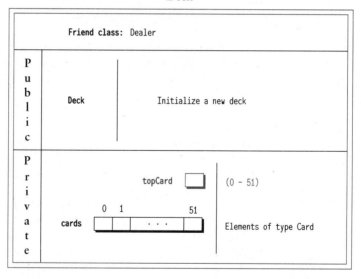

Card

Public	Display	Show a card
	GetVal	Return val
	SetVal(v)	Set val to v
	GetSuit	Return s
	SetSuit(st)	Set s to st

Private	s ☐	{clubs, diamonds, hearts, spades}
	val ☐	(2 - 14)

Deck

Friend class: Dealer

Public	Deck	Initialize a new deck

Private	topCard ☐	(0 - 51)
	cards	Elements of type Card

```
public:
      Deck();                    // the constructor opens a new deck of cards.

private:
      int topCard;               // points to position of current top card of deck
      Card cards[52];            // a deck is 52 cards.
};
```

A few features of this file that were mentioned briefly earlier are worth mentioning again in the broader context of designing the PIP. We chose, for example, to represent a card as a pair of data members: an integer indicating its numeric value and a suit. We use the numbers 2 to 14 to represent the value (2 to 10 representing the value of the corresponding nonface cards and 11 for jack, 12 for queen, 13 for king, and 14 for ace). Even though these values don't reflect the values used in playing blackjack, we adopt them in the interest of making the *Card* class generally useful. You'll see shortly how we use these codes to calculate the value of a blackjack hand.

There is one new language feature here, as well: the declaration

```
enum Suit {clubs, diamonds, hearts, spades};
```

This establishes a new type, named *Suit*, with four values, called *clubs, hearts, diamonds,* and *spades*. The declaration of an *enumeration* like this is analogous to a collection of constant declarations:

```
const int clubs = 0, diamonds = 1, hearts = 2, spades = 3;
```

We could have simply used numeric codes for the suits, but you must agree that the identifier *hearts* is far more expressive than would be the number 2, with no explanation.*

Given the declaration for *Card*, the class declaration for *Deck* is reasonably straightforward: We use an integer, *topCard,* to mark the index in the array *cards* where the next available card resides, and we have one constructor that initializes the deck. Again, these data members are declared as private to class *Deck* on the grounds that only designated *Dealer* objects should be able to access the details of a deck. We afford this access by making class *Dealer* a friend of class *Deck*.

The definitions of *Card* and *Deck* are included in the file "CARDDECK.CPP". Of course, since we're using names defined in the header file, we need to make reference to that file, through the directive #include "CARDDECK.H." Also, since the *Display* function of *Card* performs output, we need to include a reference to the I/O library "iostream.h". The rest of the file consists of definitions of the five member functions of class *Card* and the constructor for class *Deck*.

```
//----------------------CARDDECK.CPP--------------------


// This file contains the definition for the
// classes Card and Deck.
#include <iostream.h>              // for cout
#include "CARDDECK.H"
```

---

* We generally use enumerations as if they were constants, but we can use some numeric operators on enumerations, too. We cannot, however, use the I/O operators << and >> to read or write enumerations.

```
void Card::Display()
// display the suit and value of an individual card
{
    int v = GetVal();                   // get the card's value
    if ((2 <= v) && (v <= 10))          // for number cards, show value
        cout <<v;
    else                                // for face cards, use abbreviations
    {
        switch (v)
        {
            case 11: cout << 'J'; break;
            case 12: cout << 'Q'; break;
            case 13: cout << 'K'; break;
            case 14: cout << 'A'; break;
        }
    }

    switch (GetSuit())                          // display suit
    {
        case clubs:      cout << " of clubs"; break;
        case diamonds:   cout << " of diamonds"; break;
        case hearts:     cout << " of hearts"; break;
        case spades:     cout << " of spades"; break;
    };
    cout << 'n/';
}

int Card::GetVal()
// return the numeric value of a card
{
    return (val);
}

void Card::SetVal(int v)
// set the numeric value of a card
{
    val = v;
}

Suit Card::GetSuit()
// return the suit value of a card
{
    return (s);
}
```

```
void Card::SetSuit(Suit st)
// set the suit of a card
{
    s = st;
}


Deck::Deck()
// constructor for initializing a new deck of 52 cards
{
    topCard = 0;                          // we haven't dealt any cards yet
    for (int i = 0; i < 52; i++)          // for each card in the deck:
    {
        cards[i].SetVal((i % 13) + 2);    // assign it a numeric value (2 - 14)
        switch (i / 13)                   // and a suit.
        {
            case 0: cards[i].SetSuit(clubs);    break;
            case 1: cards[i].SetSuit(diamonds); break;
            case 2: cards[i].SetSuit(hearts);   break;
            case 3: cards[i].SetSuit(spades);   break;
        }
    }
};
```

The function *Card::Display* does nothing more than display the member data of a card object in a readable form. If the value is between 2 and 10, the number is displayed, and if the value is 11 or more, we use a switch to show the abbreviation 'J', 'Q', 'K', or 'A'. The second switch statement displays the suit, in a similar way. Notice, too, the virtue of having a distinct member function for displaying a card. If we wanted to "upgrade" this program so that it displayed its cards in graphical form, all we would have to do is change this function; that is, the required change to our program would be properly localized.

The *Deck* constructor loops through the index values $i = 0, \ldots, 51$ and assigns initial values and suits to each element of *cards[i]*. For each index i, the value is set to the remainder of i divided by 13, plus 2. Using the remainder allows us to cycle through card values: as i takes the values $0, 1, 2, 3, \ldots, 51$, the expression $(i \% 13) + 2$ takes the values $2, 3, \ldots, 14, 2, 3, \ldots$, and so on. In a similar way, we use the quotient $i / 13$ in a switch statement to set the suit of the first 13 cards to clubs, the next 13 to diamonds, and so on.

Note again how we access each card from within *Deck's* constructor function by working down from the top conceptual level (array *cards*), to an individual card (*cards[i]*), to a card's suit (*card[i].SetSuit*).

After having designed these classes, we tested them by writing a small "driver program" that used them. To see that cards could be displayed correctly and that a deck could be initialized, we added (temporarily) another member function to *Deck,* called *ShowDeck*, which looped through the entire deck using *Card:: Display* to show each card. Our driver program looked like this:

```
void main()
{
    Deck d;
    d.ShowDeck();
}
```

This process of testing each new class as it is written is known as *incremental testing,* and it is a Very Good Idea. We know how tempting it is to build an entire program first and then test it. Incremental testing appears to slow the rush to a complete program, but in fact it actually speeds the process substantially. It goes without saying that you will make mistakes when designing and coding a program —everybody does. Incremental testing, when done properly, allows you to isolate your errors. For example, after testing *Card* and *Deck,* we can go on to the rest of the program with the confidence that when the inevitable errors arise they will probably not be in the two classes we've already tested and debugged.

> Include testing as part of the programming process. As soon as you've finished writing a new class, test it before going on.

Players: The Files "PLAYER.H" and "PLAYER.CPP"

The *Player* class is also fairly realistic. What information, after all, is associated with a player in our card game? Member data consist of a five-card hand and two integers: one keeping track of the player's pot of money (one unit of which is wagered on each hand) and another indicating the number of cards currently being held. There are three member functions: a constructor that sets the pot to 10 and the number of cards to zero, a function that displays the contents of a hand, and one that computes the value of the player's hand. All data and functions except the constructor are private. This allows us to control which classes can access them, which we do explicitly by making *Dealer* a friend class. This, again, is a design decision that reflects the reality our program is intended to model. In a real card game, the dealer certainly would have access to the player's cards. Figure 5.9 illustrates the *Player* class. Since *Player* uses definitions from *Card,* we need to include a reference to the file "CARDDECK.H".

```
//----------------------PLAYER.H-----------------------

// Declarations for a player in our simple card game.
// These could be modified to accommodate a variety
// of different card games.
```

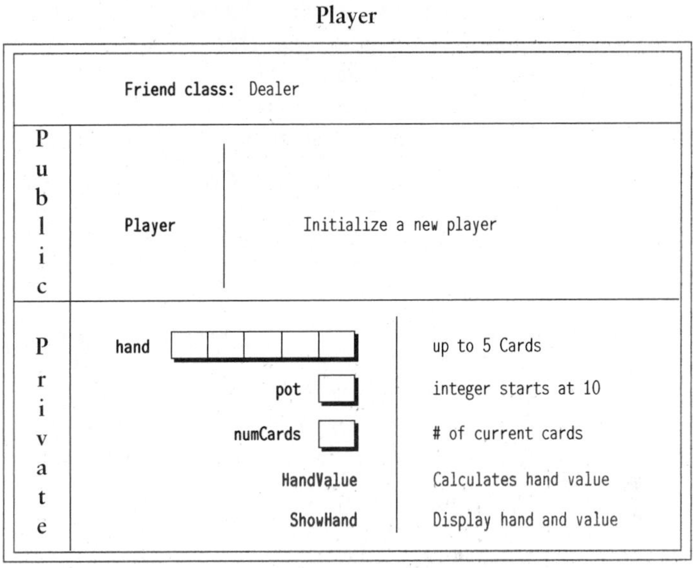

FIGURE 5.9

The class *Player*

Player

```
#include "CARDDECK.H"          // for class Card

class Player
// we make class dealer a friend since a player can't play
// without a dealer, and dealer (in this game) has complete
// access to all player information
{
friend class Dealer;

public:
      Player();                // initializes a new player

private:
      Card hand[5];            // for this game, a hand is at most 5 cards
      int pot;                 // one point for a win, lose one for a loss
      int numCards;            // the number of cards currently in the hand
      int HandValue();         // calculates the numeric value of the hand
      void ShowHand();         // displays a player's hand and value
};
```

There's little that is new about the definition file "PLAYER.CPP". We include the library file "iostream.h" so that we can refer to cin and cout, and, as usual, we include the header file that contains the declarations for the class we are defining, *Player*.

The default constructor for class *Player* initializes the player's pot (arbitrarily to 10) and hand (to hold no cards). Function *HandValue* uses a for loop-array combination to calculate the numeric value of the entire hand. It does so by adding up (in variable *total*) the individual values for each card held, according to the rules of the game (remember, in our version aces always count as 14). Another for loop is used in function *ShowHand* to invoke each card's *Display* function to display the entire hand and its value.

```
//----------------------PLAYER.CPP----------------------

// Definition file for class Player

#include <iostream.h>      // for cin, cout
#include "PLAYER.H"        // for class Player

Player::Player()
// this constructor for class Player defines a player's initial
// pot to be 10 and gives the player an empty hand
{
    pot = 10;
    numCards = 0;
}

int Player::HandValue()
// determine the numeric value of the player's hand
{
    int v;
    int total = 0;
    for (int i = 0; i < numCards; i++)
    {
        v = hand.GetVal();
        if (v <= 10)
            total += v;
        else if (v <= 13)              // it's a face card
            total += 10;
        else                           // it's an ace
            total += 11;
    }
    return (total);
}

void Player::ShowHand()
// use the Display function of class Card to show the hand
{
    cout << "\nPLAYER #1's hand: \n";
    for (in i = 0; i < numCards; i++)
        hand[i].Display();
    cout << "*** Total value: " << HandValue() << '\n';
}
```

Dealers: The Files "DEALER.H" and "DEALER.CPP"

As we said at the beginning of this section, the class *Dealer* is part manager and part player and is really where all the useful work of the program takes place. *Dealer* has no public data and only three public member functions. The main function that makes use of *Dealer* will first call *Dealer*'s constructor to create a new dealer to play the game. It will then send a message to the newly constructed dealer object to play a complete game, and finally it will ask the dealer object to determine the results, as a good dealer should.

The rest of the class is private, since the main program has no need to access *Dealer*'s player, deck, or hand member data. Similarly, the dealer object will need to be able to keep track of its own hand (including its cards, the number of cards, and the hand's value), shuffle the deck, deal hands, find the winning hand, and test for the end of the deck. These are all activities involved in playing a game, however, and there is no need for the main program to call any of these functions directly. Figure 5.10 illustrates the *Dealer* class.

FIGURE 5.10

The class *Dealer*

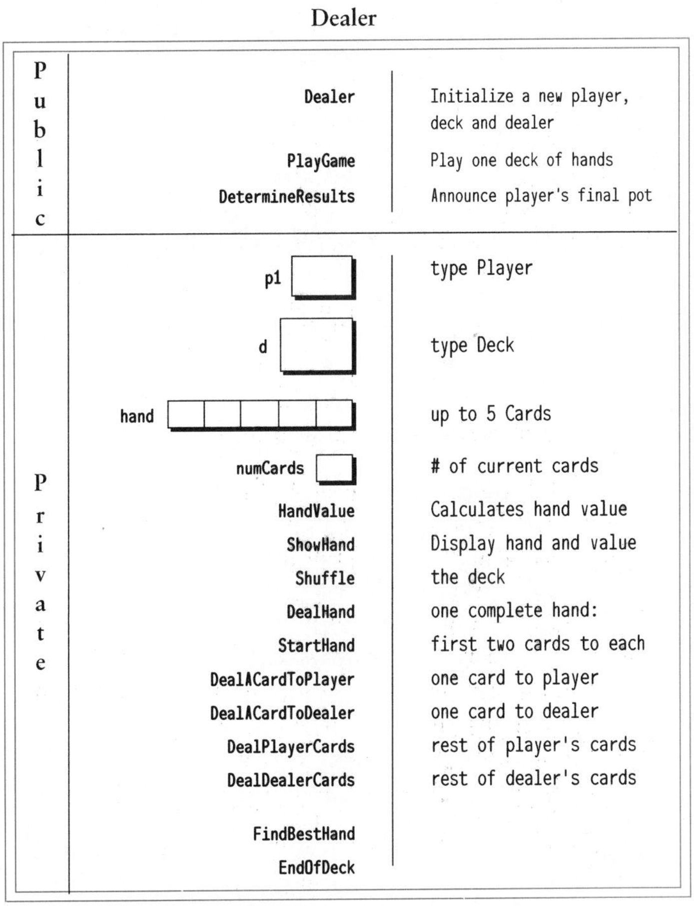

Dealer

P u b l i c	**Dealer**	Initialize a new player, deck and dealer
	PlayGame	Play one deck of hands
	DetermineResults	Announce player's final pot
P r i v a t e	**p1** ☐	type Player
	d ☐	type Deck
	hand ☐☐☐☐☐	up to 5 Cards
	numCards ☐	# of current cards
	HandValue	Calculates hand value
	ShowHand	Display hand and value
	Shuffle	the deck
	DealHand	one complete hand:
	StartHand	first two cards to each
	DealACardToPlayer	one card to player
	DealACardToDealer	one card to dealer
	DealPlayerCards	rest of player's cards
	DealDealerCards	rest of dealer's cards
	FindBestHand	
	EndOfDeck	

The header file "DEALER.H" contains the declarations of the *Dealer* class. The first feature worth noting is that we have a #include reference to "PLAYER.H," but not to "CARDDECK.H." Remember, such a reference is an instruction to copy the file at the place where the directive is written. Since "PLAYER.H" begins with a directive to include "CARDDECK.H", the card deck header declarations also will be copied into "DEALER.H", eliminating the need for any separate mention.

The second point is that function *Dealer::HandValue* is slightly different from its counterpart in class *Player*. Since the dealer's hand in blackjack is dealt with its first card face down, we don't always want to report the total value of the hand to the player. Sometimes we just want to indicate what the value of the cards showing is. By declaring functions *Dealer::HandValue* to have an integer parameter, we let it control how many card values it adds up, as you'll see in the function definition.

Finally, notice that there are five additional private functions declared as part of class *Dealer* and that their declarations are indented beneath that of function *DealHand*. These are functions that help decompose the rather complex process of dealing a complete hand. We recognized the need for them as we struggled to define function *DealHand*. Their utility will become clearer to you when you examine the class definition.

```
//----------------------DEALER.H------------------------

// This embodies the activities of a dealer as well as the rules
// of a particular game. The numbers of players and decks used,
// and the DealHand and FindBestHand functions, can be redefined
// to describe any card game.

#include "PLAYER.H"              // for class Player
// Note that since file "PLAYER.H" includes the file "CARDDECK.H,"
// we need not include the latter here, even though we refer
// to declarations from it (Deck).

class Dealer
{
public:
    Dealer();                   // prepare a dealer to play
    void PlayGame();            // play one complete game
    void DetermineResults();    // announce the final tally

private:
    Player p;                   // this game has one player,
    Deck d;                     // and one deck

    Card hand[5];               // a dealer has a hand of at most 5 cards
    int numCards;               // the current number of cards in the hand
```

```
    int HandValue(int)            // determines the hand's numeric value
    void ShowHand(int);           // display the hand starting with specified card

    void Shuffle();               // shuffle the deck
    void DealHand();              // deal one hand, which involves . . .
        void StartHand();         // deal the first 2 cards to each player
        void DealACardToPlayer(); // deal a single card to the player
        void DealACardToDealer(); // deal a single card to the dealer
        void DealPlayerCards();   // deal remaining cards to the player
        void DealDealerCards();   // deal remaining cards to the dealer

    void FindBestHand();          // find the winner of a hand
    int EndOfDeck();              // check whether there are enough cards left
};
```

The definition file for the *Dealer* class begins with six include directives. The first, to "iostream.h", and the last, to "DEALER.H", are there for obvious reasons. The other four—to the standard C++ libraries "stdlib", "time.h", "ctype.h", and our own library of utility functions ("UTILITY.H")—are there because we make use of functions that come from each of these libraries. We mentioned earlier that there are several more or less standard libraries that come with most C++ implementations. These include many standard mathematical functions, I/O routines, and a wealth of functions for time and date calculations, string processing, and so on. It is well worth your time to explore the documentation that came with your version of C++, so you can become familiar with the functions and data structures that the libraries provide for you.

```
//---------------------------DEALER.CPP-------------------

// This is the definition file for class Dealer

#include <iostream.h>       // for cin, cout
#include <stdlib.h>         // for rand, srand
#include <time.h>           // for clock
#include <ctype.h>          // for toupper

#include "UTILITY.H"        // for WaitForUser
#include "DEALER.H"         // for obvious reasons

void Randomize()
// COMPILER-SPECIFIC: sets the random number generator's seed.
{
    unsigned int seed = unsigned(clock());
    srand(seed);
}

Dealer::Dealer()
// the way our classes are organized, all that a dealer need
```

```
    // explicitly do to prepare for a game is shuffle the deck
    // and clear out its own hand
    {
        Shuffle();
        numCards = 0;
    }


    void Dealer::PlayGame()
    // continues dealing and evaluating hands until there are no
    // cards remaining to deal
    {
        cout << "\n\nGame on!!!\n\n";
        do
        {
            DealHand();              // deal and display each hand.
            FindBestHand();          // determine and display the winner.
        }
        while (!EndOfDeck());
    }


    void Dealer::DetermineResults()
    // after all hands are done, display the player's final "pot"
    {
        cout << "\n\nPLAYER #1 started with a pot of 10\n";
        cout << "*** FINAL POT: " << p.pot << '\n';
    }


    void Dealer::ShowHand(int startCard)
    // display the dealer's hand starting with card startCard;
    // at the start of a game, the first card can be hidden from
    // the player
    {
        cout << "\nDealer's hand: \n";
        for (int i = startCard; i < numCards; i++)
            hand[i].Display();
        // display the value showing by determining the hand's value,
        // ignoring the value of the first (hidden) card
        cout << "*** Value showing: " << HandValue(startCard) << '\n';
    }


    int Dealer::HandValue(int startCard)
    // determine the numeric value of the dealer's hand
    // beginning with card startCard
    {
        int v;
        int total = 0;
```

```
        for (int i = startCard; i < numCards; i++)
        {
            v = hand[i].GetVal();
            if (v <= 10)
                total += v;
            else if (v <= 13)    // it's a face card
                total += 10;
            else                 // it's an ace
                total += 11;
        }
        return (total);
}


void Dealer::Shuffle()
// shuffles the deck by switching each card
// with a randomly selected card
{
        Randomize();                    // Initialize the random number generator.

        for (int i = 0; i < 3; i++)     //Shuffle 3 times.
        }
            for (int j = 0; j < 52; j++)  // Rearrange each card (0-51).
            {
                int r = rand() % 52;    // Pick a location to swap j-th card with
                Card c = d.cards[j];
                d.cards[j] = d.cards<r>;
                d.cards<r> = c;
            }
        }
        d.topCard = 0;                  // no cards dealt yet
}


void Dealer::DealHand()
// deals a complete game to the player and the dealer
{
        StartHand();            // start the game by dealing 2 cards to each
        DealPlayerCards();      // deal the rest of player's cards
        DealDealerCards();      // deal the rest of dealer's cards
}


void Dealer::StartHand()
// start the game by dealing 2 cards each to the player and the dealer
// and displaying the resulting hands
{
        p.numCards = 0;
        numCards = 0;
        DealACardToPlayer();
```

```
        DealACardToDealer();
        DealACardToPlayer();
        DealACardToDealer();
        p.ShowHand();              // show player's hand
        ShowHand(1);               // show dealer's hand (except for first card)
    }

void Dealer::DealACardToPlayer()
// take the top card of the deck and place it in player's hand, and
// increment the number of cards in the hand, and the top card of the deck
{
        p.hand[p.numCards++] = d.cards[d.topCard++];
}

void Dealer::DealACardToDealer()
// take the top card of the deck and place it in dealer's hand, and
// increment the number of cards in the hand, and the top card of the deck
{
        hand[numCards++] = d.cards[d.topCard++];
}

void Dealer::DealPlayerCards()
// deal additional cards to the player so long as they are asked for,
// there is room in the hand, and the total is less than 21
{
        char ans;
        do
        {
            cout << "\nDo you want another card ";
            cout << "(Y for yes, N for no)? ";
            cin >> ans;
            ans = toupper(ans);
            if (ans == 'Y')
            {
                DealACardToPlayer();
                p.ShowHand();
            }
        } while ((ans == 'Y') && (p.HandValue() < 21) && (p.numCards <= 5));
    }

void Dealer::DealDealerCards()
// deal cards to the dealer so long as the total is less than 17
// and there is room in the hand
{
        ShowHand(0);
        // make sure to count all cards, even the hidden one
```

```
        while ((HandValue (0) < 17) && (numCards <= 5))
        {
            DealACardToDealer();
            ShowHand(0);
        }
}


void Dealer::FindBestHand()
// compare the hand of the two contestants to find out who,
// if either, won.
{
    // get and display the two final hand scores
    int pVal = p.HandValue();
    int dVal = HandValue(0);

    // it's a draw if both are "over" or if they're equal in value
    if (((pVal > 21) && (dVal > 21)) ||
        (pVal == dVal))
        cout << "hand was a draw\n";
    // player wins with a better legal hand, or if computer is "over"
    else if (((pVal <= 21) && (pVal > dVal)) ||
        (dVal > 21))
    {
        cout << "Player #1 wins hand\n";        // player wins,
        p.pot++;                                // so update pot
    }


    // computer wins with a better legal hand, or if player is over
    else if (((dVal <= 21) && (dVal > pVal)) ||
        (pVal > 21)
    {
        cout << "Computer wins hand\n";         // computer wins,
        p.pot--;                                // so update pot
    };

    WaitForUser();
}


int Dealer::EndOfDeck()
// check to see that we have enough
// cards left to deal a new hand; we need (at most)
// 10 cards. Returns 1 = yes, 0 = no.
{
    return (d.topCard >= 42);
}
```

Most of the function definitions in "DEALER.CPP" are simple enough that they require little explanation. This is, at least in part, a reflection of our design. The fact that we have separately declared and defined classes for each of the high-level objects in our program yields many small, easy-to-implement, logically cohesive functions. The most complicated function definition is that of *Dealer::Shuffle*. The heart of the routine is the collection of statements

```
for (int i = 0; i < 3; i++)
    {
        for (j = 0; j < 52; j++)
        {
            r = rand() % 52;

            c = d.cards[j];
            d.cards[j] = d.cards[r];
            d.cards[r] = c;
        }
    }
```

Notice that we have two loops here, one inside the other. The statement body of a while, do, or for loop can be any statement at all: an expression statement, a compound statement, an if or switch statement, or even another loop statement. In case the statement body of a loop is itself a loop, the entire inner loop will be performed, as many times as necessary, for each iteration of the outer loop. If, for instance, we had a pair of *nested loops* like this:

```
for (int i = 0; i < 3; i++)
        for (j = 0; j < 2; j++)
            cout << "i = " << i << "\tj = " << j << '\n';
```

the output would be

```
i = 0    j = 0
i = 0    j = 1
i = 1    j = 0
i = 1    j = 1
i = 2    j = 0
i = 2    j = 1
```

> If a loop is nested within another, the inner loop iterates most rapidly.

We can see that the inner, *j*, loop makes two iterations for each *i* value in the outer loop. In *Shuffle,* then, the outer loop says, in effect, "Do everything in the inner loop three times." The inner loop is where the real work of shuffling goes on:

```
for (j = 0; j < 52; j++)
{
    r = rand() % 52;

    c = d.cards[j];
    d.cards[j] = d.cards[r];
    d.cards[r] = c;
}
```

This inner loop performs its statement body 52 times (once for each card in a deck), for values of *j* ranging from 0 to 51. The first statement in the loop body, *r = rand( ) % 52*, uses the library routine *rand*, which returns a randomly chosen integer. By finding the remainder of that number and 52, we are setting *r* to a random number in the range 0 to 51. The next three assignment statements swap the contents of the array elements *d.cards[r]* and *d.cards[j]*, as illustrated in Figure 5.11.

There's another part of the definition file for *Dealer* that we need to look at: the constructor *Dealer::Dealer*. It appears that this function does nothing more than shuffle the deck and assign the dealer zero cards. Hold on, though— how can we shuffle a deck before we've initialized it? In fact, if you look through the program, you'll find that there is no place where the player object *p* and the deck object *d* of a dealer are ever explicitly declared or initialized. The reason, remember, is that C++ does it implicitly.

In our case, then, as soon as we call *Dealer* to construct a new *Dealer* object, the constructors for its member data *p* and *d* are automatically invoked, with no intervention required on our part. That is to say, when we create an instance of class *Dealer*, we automatically get an initialized instance of a *Player*, and an initialized, ready-to-use *Deck*.

The Finished Program: The File "PIP5.CPP"

Now that we have all the classes we need to play our card game, we are ready to finish the job by filling in the details of the main function. We've mentioned before that an advantage of the object-oriented approach to program design is that the last part is almost always the easiest. In our program we see that all we need to do to play a game is (1) create a new dealer, (2) instruct the dealer object to play a game, and then (3) tell the dealer object to determine the winner of the game. Our main function, then, would look like this:

```
void main()
{
    Dealer theDealer;
    theDealer.PlayGame();
    theDealer.DetermineWinner();
}
```

FIGURE 5.11
Swapping two elements in an array

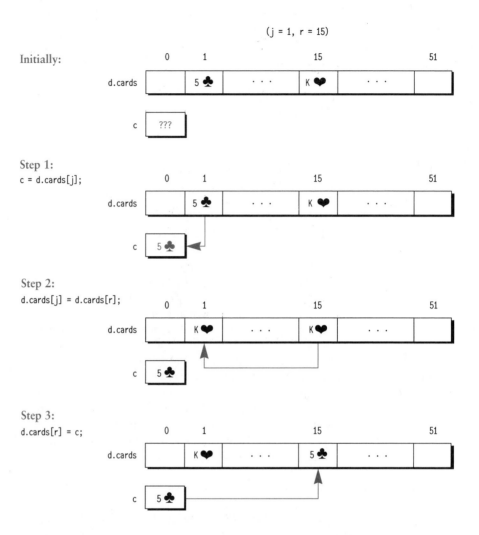

If you look through the main file, you'll see that all we've done is embed the preceding three lines into a loop that allows the user to play more than one game without restarting the program, using the UTILITY library function *ReadyToQuit*.

```
//----------------------PIP5.CPP--------------------

// This program uses classes Deck, Player, and Dealer
// to play a simple game of blackjack. The player may
// draw up to five cards, and the dealer acts like the
// "house" in that it must draw if under 17. All aces are
// counted as 11.
```

```
#include "UTILITY.H"          // for ReadyToQuit, Terminate
#include "DEALER.H"           // for classes Dealer, Player, and Deck

void main()
{
    do
    {
        // create a dealer, which implicitly creates
        // a player and a new deck of cards
        Dealer theDealer;

        // start a game
        theDealer.PlayGame();
        theDealer.DetermineResults();
    }
    while (!ReadyToQuit());

    Terminate();
}
```

5.4 SUMMING UP

▶ An array is an indexed collection of objects of the same type.

▶ Array indices begin with zero.

▶ An array is declared by describing the type and number of elements. The declaration double data[5], for example, declares an array of five doubles, indexed from 0 to 4.

▶ Elements of an array are accessed using the [ ] selector after the array name, so data[0], data[1], data[2], data[3], and data[4] are the elements of the array declared by double data[5];.

▶ The array selector brackets may contain any numeric expression. Don't count on C++ to make sure that the value of the expression is a legal index. Check array ranges in your program.

▶ The typedef specification permits you to give a name to any type. A typedef specification looks like a declaration, except that it begins with the word typedef and has the type synonym where the object name would be in a declaration.

▶ Arrays may be initialized using an initialization list like those that are used to initialize classes.

▶ Arrays of characters may be initialized with strings. A string has a '\0' terminator that will be placed in the array, along with the other characters in the string.

▶ If the elements of an array are objects with constructors, the constructors may be used in an initialization list. If the elements have default constructors, these constructors will be invoked implicitly when the array is declared, unless the program invokes other constructors.

▶ Arrays may be passed as arguments to functions. Arrays may not be assigned to each other and they may not be used as return values of a function.

▶ When loops are nested within each other, the inner loop iterates most rapidly.

▶ An enumeration is a user-defined collection of identifiers. An enumeration is a numeric type, so most numeric operators can be used with enumerations. Some operators that can't be used on enumerations are ++, − −, <<, and >>.

▶ If a class contains member data that are objects of another class, and if those classes have default (no-argument) constructors, then those constructors will be called at the start of the constructor for the class that contains them.

▶ A class cannot include objects of its own type as members.

5.5 EXERCISES

1. Given the following declarations, tell which of the statements are incorrect and why they are.

```
typedef char CharArray[64];
class Page
{   int numLines;
    CharArray theLine[50];};

CharArray thisLine;
Page thisPage;
```

a. ```
for (int i = 0; i < 64; i++)
      cin >> thisPage[i][3];
```
b. ```
for (int line = 0; line < thisPage.numLines; line++)
    for (int ch = 0; ch < 64; ch++)
        cout << thisPage.theLine[line][ch];
```
c. `thisPage.theLine[3] = thisLine;`
d. `thisPage.CharArray[3][1] = thisLine[2];`
e. `return thisPage;`

2. Given the following declarations, tell which of the statements are incorrect and why they are.

```
const int CLASS_SIZE = 35;
const int NUM_TESTS = 3;

enum Grades {F, D, C, B, A};
typedef int Distribution[5];
typedef int Gradebook[CLASS_SIZE][NUM_TESTS]
Distribution csDept;
Gradebook cs241;
```

a. ```
for (Grades g = F; g <= A; g++)
      cout << csDept[g];
```
b. ```
double sum = 0.0;
      for (int ex = 0, sum = 0; ex < NUM_TESTS; ex++)
          sum += Gradebook[2][ex];
      double average = sum / 3;
```
c. ```
for (int student = 0; student < CLASS_SIZE; student++)
   {   for (int test = 0; test < NUM_TESTS; test++)
          cout << '\t' << cs241[student][test];
          cout << '\n';   }
```
d. ```
cout << cs241[4];
```

3. Given the declarations of Exercise 1, how many elements are contained in the following objects?

a. *thisLine*
b. *thisPage*

4. Given the declarations of Exercise 2, how many elements are contained in the following objects?

a. *csDept*
b. *cs241*

5. Write declarations that would be appropriate to store the following information:

a. The current state of a game of checkers.
b. An inventory item in a bookstore, consisting of a name, a price, and the number on hand.
c. An inventory for an entire bookstore.

6. Write declarations that would be appropriate to store the following information:

a. A rectangle, for display on a computer screen.
b. A collection of no more than 100 rectangles.
c. The number of students in a class whose average falls in one of the ranges 0–20, 21–40, 41–60, 61–80, 81–100.

7. Consider the following two data types, named *Data1* and *NumArray*:

```
class Pair
{    double x, y; }
typedef Pair Data1[7];

typedef double NumArray[7];
class Data2
{    NumArray x, y;}
```

   a. Draw diagrams of *Data1* and *Data2*, as we have done in the text for other class declarations.
   b. How many numbers do each of these types contain?
   c. What types must *d* and *e* be for the identifiers below to make sense?

   ```
   d[3].x       and      e.x[3]
   ```

   d. Which of the two types would be a better conceptual choice to represent the coordinates of seven points in the plane? Which would be better to represent a week's worth of high temperatures in Xenia, Ohio, and Ypsilanti, Michigan?
   e. Write a declaration that would replace both of these types, not using classes.

8. Write a program that reads 25 integers and prints the value of any number that appeared more than once among the inputs. How would you solve this problem if you weren't allowed to use arrays?

9. Let's consider what would be necessary to write a grade-keeping program. Suppose that a course has twenty students and that each student will have integer scores for ten quizzes. Each student will have a name consisting of no more than thirty characters, and each quiz will have a positive weight, which is some real number.

   a. Write a declaration for a class for this problem. You might want to look at part b before you do this part.
   b. For the following tasks and your declaration, describe how you would get the needed information.
      i.   The name of the *n*th student.
      ii. The (weighted) average of the quiz scores for the *n*th student.
      iii. The (unweighted) average of the scores of all students on quiz *n*.
      iv. The class average; namely, the average of the weighted averages of all students.
      v.   The names of the students with averages less than the class average.

10. Do Exercise 9 assuming that a course may have from zero to twenty students and that each student may have scores for zero to twenty quizzes.

For Exercises 11–16, assume that we have the following declarations:

```
const int SIZE = 200;
typedef int NumArray[SIZE];
```

11. Write the definition of the function

    ```
    void Copy(int n, int sourceStart, int destStart, NumArray a)
    ```

    that copies *n* elements of array *a*, starting at index *sourceStart*, to the locations starting at index *destStart*. In this exercise, you may assume that the array segments indicated all lie within the array and do not overlap.

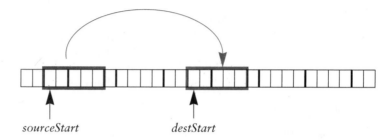

12. a. Do Exercise 11, allowing for the possibility that the segments overlap.
    b. Modify part a so that the function checks whether the segments do not fit in the array (as would happen, for instance, if *destStart* + *n* was larger than *SIZE*).

13. Write a function void Reverse(NumArray a) that will reverse the contents of *a*, swapping *a*[0] and *a*[*SIZE* – 1], *a*[1] and *a*[*SIZE* – 2], and so on.

14. a. Write a function int AreEqual(NumArray a, NumArray b) that returns 1 if the two arrays are element-by-element equal and returns 0 if not.
    b. Do part a by overloading the == operator rather than writing a function.

15. What does this function do? Trace its action on the array {5, 2, 8, 3} and then guess.

    ```
    void Mystery(NumArray a)
    {   for (int i = 0; i < SIZE - 1; i++)
        {   int m = a[i];
            int p = i;
            for (int j = i + 1; j < SIZE; j++)
                if (a[j] < m)
                {   m = a[j];
                    p = j;
                }
            int t = a[i];
            a[i] = a[p];
            a[p] = t;
        }
    }
    ```

16. A common programming task is to find the index of an element in an array, as we did in Section 5.1, when we found the position of the first instance

of 0 in an array. In the text example, we found the element by a *linear search,* inspecting each element of the array in turn until we either found a zero or ran out of elements to inspect. If the array is sorted in order from smallest to largest, though, we can search more efficiently (think about a phone book—it's much easier to find a name than a number, because the phone book is sorted by name). A *binary search* in a sorted array works like this:

> Set *lowerBound* to –1.
> Set *upperBound* to *SIZE* – 1.
> As long as *lowerBound* is less than *upperBound*:
>   Set *middle* to (*upperBound* + *lowerBound* + 1) / 2.
>   If *numberToFind* < a[*middle*]:
>   Set *upperBound* to *middle* – 1,   // Look in lower half
>   else
>   Set *lowerBound* to *middle* .   // Look in upper half
> Return *lowerBound*.

a. Trace the action of this algorithm to find the index of 73 in the array {3, 13, 27, 54, 55, 60, 65, 68, 70, 73, 82, 83, 90, 101, 119}.

b. Trace the action of this algorithm to find the index of 74 in the array above. The answer should be the same as for part a, since the algorithm finds the position at or after which the sought-for element would reside.

c. Write a function *int Position(int n, NumArray a)* that returns the position at or after which the element *n* is or would be in the array *a*.

17. These three segments are intended to compute the sum $a[0] + a[1] + a[2] + a[3] + a[4]$. Do they all do that?

```
// Sample 1
for (int sum = 0, i = 0; i < 5; i++)
    sum += a[i];
```

```
// Sample 2
int sum = 0, i = 0;
while (i < 5)
{   sum += a[i]; i++;}
```

```
// Sample 3
int sum = 0, i = 0;
do
{   sum += a[i]; i++}
while (i < 5);
```

18. Write the for loop in Sample 1 of Exercise 17 so that the loop body is empty. In other words, rewrite the loop so that all work is done in the header.

19. In Samples 2 and 3 of Exercise 17, show that order matters by interchanging the order of the statements in the loop body to { *i*++; *sum* += *a*[*i*] }. What do the loops do now?

20. Write the following bounded linear search with a do loop, and comment on the readability of your solution.

```
int i = 0;
while ((i < 5) && (a[i] != 0))
        i++;

if (i == 5)
    cout << "There are no zero values in the array";
else
    cout << "The first zero element has index " << i;
```

21. We have mentioned several times that C++ will allow you to be excessively cute at the expense of being understandable. What does this segment do? Do we gain anything by eliminating the iteration part of the header?

```
for (int i = -1; ++i < 4; )
    a[i] = b[i];
```

22. Write the definition of the test function *Deck::ShowDeck( )* we mentioned in the text.

23. C++ cannot read or write enumerated types unless you tell it how to do so. In this exercise, suppose we have the declaration

```
enum Days {SUN, MON, TUE, WED, THU, FRI, SAT};
```

   a. Fix part of this shortcoming by writing the definition of the function *void WriteDay(Days d)* that displays the identifier corresponding to the argument *d*.
   b. (Harder) Fix the other part of the shortcoming by writing the function *Days ReadDay()* that reads characters from standard input and returns the value corresponding to the characters read.

24. There are many ways to shuffle a deck of cards, other than the one we used in the PIP. The *riffle shuffle,* for instance, divides the deck into two piles and then recombines the deck by alternately inserting the top card of each pile. As a simple example, if the deck originally contained the "cards" 1, 2, 3, 4, 5, 6, 7, 8, we would cut the deck into the piles 1, 2, 3, 4 and 5, 6, 7, 8, and combine the cards alternately, yielding 1, 5, 2, 6, 3, 7, 4, 8.

   a. Rewrite *Shuffle* to perform a riffle shuffle.
   b. With lots of practice, one can learn to perform a perfect riffle shuffle. This is a useful skill, since if we start with a fresh deck and perform a perfect riffle shuffle, we can then predict exactly the arrangement of the

deck. Modify *Shuffle* so that it performs the riffle shuffle a random number of times, say in the range 1 to 10.

c.   What happens when we perform eight riffle shuffles on a deck of 52 cards? How might one take advantage of this?

25. Many times, we don't need all of the space in an array. If, for example, we have an array that stores quiz scores for a student, we might have no scores at the start of the term and ten scores at the end of the term. We could represent a *dynamic array* by the following declaration:

```
class DynamicArray
{
public:
    // Member functions go here.
private:
    int num;            // the current number of scores (=< 10),
                        // stored in quiz[0] ... quiz[num - 1]
    int quiz[10];       // the quiz scores
};
```

Write member functions for the class *DynamicArray* that

a.   add a new quiz score (make sure there's room, first);

b.   update the *k*th score (make sure *k* is valid, first);

c.   display the contents;

d.   return the average of the scores (what if *num* is zero?).

26. This is an interesting routine:

```
for (int i = 1; i <= 100; i++)
    a[i] = 1;

for (int i = 2; i <= 100; i++)
    for (int j = 1; j <= 100 / i; j++)
        a[i * j] = !a[i * j];

for (int i = 1; i <= 100; i++)
    if (a[i])
        cout << i;
```

a.   What is its output?

b.   (Hard) Why?

c.   (Harder) Generalize it.

27. Suppose that we had declared the type *CharArray* by

```
typedef char CharArray[64];
```

Write a function *void Delete(CharArray a, int n)* that will delete the element in position *n* from the array *a*, moving all elements with index higher than n down one position to fill the "hole" left by the deleted element. You should fill in the missing character in position 63 with a '\0' null character.

28. Write a function *void Insert(CharArray a, char c, int n)* that will insert a new character c in position n, after first moving the elements in positions n and above up one position to make room for the new character. You'll lose the character in position 63—that's okay.

6

POINTERS AND
REFERENCES

It's impolite not
to point.

Up to now, all the objects we've talked about—whether they were types built into C++, like integers, or instances of classes that were defined by the programmer—have all had the same nature. That is, there was a simple correspondence between the name of an object and the data that the object represented. This correspondence was so fundamental that you probably gave it no thought: The information in an int variable *sum,* for example, is accessed by referring to the name *sum.* The information in the first card of an instance, *d,* of class *Deck* (from the Chapter 5 PIP) is accessed by the slightly more verbose, but still direct, *d.cards*[0].*val.* In this chapter, we'll explore two new data types, *pointers* and *references,* that deviate from this direct name:data correspondence. Pointers and references are *derived types,* like classes and arrays, and like those compound types they allow you to construct new types from others. We'll also see how these new types are used to represent dynamic arrays (arrays that can change their number of elements) and function arguments that can be modified.

OBJECTIVES

In this chapter, we will

▶ Describe the pointer and reference types and show how they can be used to make our programming easier and more flexible.

▶ Discuss the relation between pointers, arrays, and character strings.

▶ Show how pointers can be used to implement dynamic arrays.

▶ Describe reference types and show how they can be used to implement modifiable function arguments.

6.1 POINTERS

Marginal notes like this often contain pointers, too. See the first marginal note in Chapter 1.

A *pointer* is an indirect reference to an object of a specified type. From the computer's perspective, a pointer is nothing more than the address of a location where an object of a given type may be stored. In other words, a pointer object does not contain the information we want, but rather contains a reference to the information. This may sound intimidatingly opaque, but in other contexts you use indirect references all the time. Take this text, for example: If you look in the index, you'll see that it's nothing but a collection of pointers to locations in *The Object Concept*. If you want to find out what a compiler is, you look under "Compiler"; you won't find the information you want there, but you will find where to find the information.

Pointers are also a common feature of natural languages such as English. We call them pronouns. In the sentence "As John and Mary entered the theater, he said he wanted some popcorn," we understand that "he" is an indirect reference to "John," so we may consider "he" to be a pointer.

We declare a pointer by using the unary * operator* on the left of the name of the pointer. In the declarations below, we have declared two variables: n is an integer, and p is a pointer to an integer.

```
int n;          // an integer
int *p;         // a pointer to an integer
```

As with other data types, at the time of declaration, you cannot assume that pointers point to any useful data. All you know after having made the declarations above is that n will refer to an integer and p will refer to an address of a memory location (which we call the *target* of the pointer) where an integer may be stored. We'll show you how to initialize both a pointer and its target shortly, but for the time being, assume that n has the value −16 and that the target of p, which we refer to as *p, has the value 101, as pictured in Figure 6.1. The pointer object p is located in memory at address 7884 and contains the value 9004. Therefore p points to memory location 9004. The details of which addresses are used to store which data items are handled invisibly for us by C++, so we can ignore them and just think that p points to some integer-sized location.

The syntax of pointer declarations is slightly tricky. The * operator has the same precedence as the other unary operators, like ++ and !, and groups from

---

* This *, although it looks like the multiplication operator, serves an entirely different purpose and has a different syntax. It modifies what's on its right (like the ! operator), rather than operating on what's on its right and left (like %).

FIGURE 6.1
Two ways of thinking
about pointers

Memory picture (what really goes on)

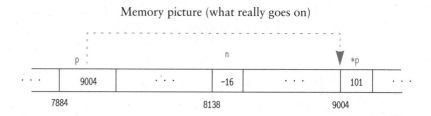

The way we can think of things

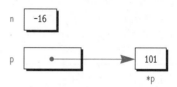

the right, so the * operator attaches itself to the variable to its right, not the type name to its left. This means that in the declaration

```
int *p, n;        // a pointer-to-int and an int
```

the correct interpretation is

```
int (*p), n;
```

To declare both *p* and *q* as pointers to integers, we would have to write

```
int *p, *q;
```

Since blanks in declarations are ignored, some people prefer to place the * operator adjacent to the type name, as in int* p. Your authors tend to place the * next to the type, rather than the variable, except in instances like the ones above, where placing the * next to the variable emphasizes the nature of the variable.

We mentioned that the target of a pointer is written exactly as the pointer was declared (in a way similar to the way array elements are written just as the array was declared—with square brackets). Thus, if *p* is a pointer to an integer, that integer is named *p* and behaves just like a normal integer object, which in fact it is. For example, all of these are legal statements:

```
int *p, *q, n;            // two pointer-to-ints and an int
n = -16;                  // set n to -16
*p = 101;                 // set *p to 101
*q = n + *p;              // set *q to 85
```

A pointer is declared by writing *typeName* *variableName*;. Once a pointer, *p*, has been declared, the object to which it points is written *p* and may be treated like any other variable of type *typeName*.

Although all pointers are addresses, C++ treats pointers to different types as having different types themselves. If, for instance, we had the declarations

```
int* ip;
double* dp;
```

the pointers *ip* and *dp* would be considered to be of incompatible types, so it would be an error to write

```
dp = ip;                    // ERROR: can't assign pointers to different types
```

although it would be legal (but confusing) to have an assignment with an implicit type cast between their targets, like this:

```
*dp = *ip;
```

There's a special pointer value that can be used as a signal in C++ programs. The *NULL pointer* has value zero, distinguishing it from all valid addresses. Knowing this allows us to test whether a pointer p is the NULL pointer by evaluating the expression (p == 0). NULL pointers are used only as signals that something has happened, as we'll see shortly, and never have targets. In other words, if p is a NULL pointer, it is never correct to refer to its target $*p$ (since there isn't one).

Pointers and Arrays

At this point, you have every right to ask why anyone would bother to invent pointers in the first place. We will discuss pointers and some of their more interesting uses in detail in subsequent chapters. For now, we'll concentrate mainly on one valuable feature of pointers, one that ties them closely to arrays.

Arrays in C++ are different from other types in that the name of an array object also can be used as a pointer to the first element in the array. For example, if we have the declaration

```
double a[10];
```

the name *a* can not only be used to refer to an array of ten floating point numbers, but is also used as a pointer to the first element in the array, $a[0]$. In other words, if we continue our example by writing

```
double* p = a;
```

then p and a both refer to the same array, as we illustrate in Figure 6.2. To refer to the array element with index 6, for example, we could use any of the following expressions:

```
a[6]
p[6]
*(p + 6)
```

The last expression, $*(p + 6)$, illustrates a useful features of pointers: Since pointers are really addresses, which are really numbers, we can do arithmetic

FIGURE 6.2
An array name also can be used as a pointer to the first element in the array.

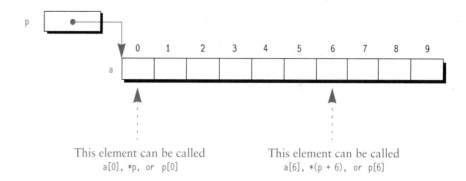

This element can be called
a[0], *p, or p[0]

This element can be called
a[6], *(p + 6), or p[6]

on them. Since the compiler has been told that p is a pointer-to-double, it can use the size of an object of double type to calculate the address of the memory location that is six elements beyond $*p$.

> The name of an array also can be used as if it were a pointer to the first element in the array.

This equivalence between arrays and pointers to the first elements of arrays explains something we did in the last chapter that would have seemed illogical if we had explained it in full detail at that point. Recall that functions in C++ are intended to return a single value (unless the return type is void, in which case they don't return anything). When we described the action of functions, we mentioned specifically that functions cannot modify the values of their arguments. As we said, what happens when a function is called is that the actual arguments are evaluated and their values are used to initialize the formal arguments. This process is illustrated in Figure 6.3.

FIGURE 6.3
A function makes local copies of its arguments. Any modifications to the arguments modify only the local copies.

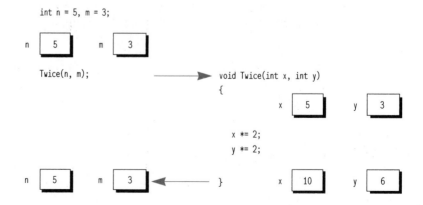

For example, when we shuffled the deck of cards in PIP5, the heart of the process was swapping two cards in the deck. We might have tried to encapsulate that action into a function like this:

```
void Swap1(Card c1, Card c2)
{
    Card temp = c1;        // Save the value of c1,
    c1 = c2;               // replace c1's old value with the value of c2,
    c2 = temp;             // and replace c2's value with c1's original.
}
```

There's nothing syntactically wrong with this function. It would compile correctly, but if we had called it in the *Shuffle* function by writing

```
Swap1(d.cards[j], d.cards[r]);
```

nothing noticeable would have happened in the function *Shuffle*. The array *d.cards* would have remained unchanged, because the function *Swap1* would have correctly interchanged its *local copies*—*c1* and *c2*—of the actual arguments *d.cards[j]* and *d.cards[r]*, rather than the values of the arguments themselves.

Suppose, though, we had written *Swap* this way:

```
void Swap2(Card *c, int firstIndex, int secondIndex)
{
    Card temp = c[firstIndex];
    c[firstIndex] = c[secondIndex];
    c[secondIndex] = temp;
}
```

If we then made the call

```
Swap2(d.cards, j, r);
```

the *j*th and *r*th cards in the array *d.cards* would have been swapped exactly as we intended. Why? Because we're not modifying any of the arguments, *d.cards.*, *j*, or *r*. Remember that *d.cards* is an array, and hence its name is actually a pointer to the start of the array—an address, in other words. The *Swap2* function doesn't modify the address of the start of the array: The array is still in the same memory location it was before. To be sure, *Swap2* modifies the contents of the array, but that modification does not modify the (pointer) argument *d.cards*, so—for arrays, at least—we can get around the fact that functions can't change their arguments.

We illustrated swapping arrays in Figure 5.11.

> Although functions cannot modify their arguments, if an array is used as an argument to a function, the function can modify the contents of the array.

It's not obvious at first glance why C++ equates arrays and pointers to their first elements. The reason becomes clearer when you think about what goes on when a function is called. We know that when a function is called, the actual arguments are copied to initialize their corresponding formal arguments. Copying, obviously, involves moving data and, especially for potentially large data collections like arrays, this process can take a considerable amount of time. Copying a pointer, however, is very fast since the size of a pointer is the same, regardless of the size of its target. This being the case, it makes good design sense for C++ to pass a reference to an array rather than to send an entire array to a function. You can use this to your advantage: When you need to send a function a large object, consider instead sending a pointer to the object, just as we did in *Swap2*.

When you pass a pointer to a large object, but don't ever intend the function to modify the object (as, for instance, if we wanted simply to display the contents of an array), it's a good idea to make this explicit to the reader by declaring the argument to be a pointer to a constant object, like this:

```
void Display(const VeryBigObject *v);
```

There's a possibility for confusion when defining constant pointers. Should we think of them as potentially changeable pointers to objects that can't be modified or as unmodifiable pointers to objects that can be altered? The word const modifies whatever comes next. This means that C++ will interpret

```
const VeryBigObject *v
```

as "*v* is a pointer to a constant object of type *VeryBigObject*." In other words, if *w* was a pointer to a *VeryBigObject*, we could assign *v = w*, modifying *v*, but we couldn't make any changes to its target **v*.

The declaration

```
const TypeName *v
```

establishes *v* as a pointer to an object that cannot be modified. Use this form of declaration if you are passing a pointer to a large object and don't intend the function to modify the object.

The new and delete Operators

How do we give a pointer a target? As far as we know now, the only way to give a pointer something to point to is if we already have declared an array, since arrays are referred to by pointers to their first elements. If that was all we could do with pointers, there would hardly be any sense in having them in C++, except perhaps to confuse programmers. The main virtue of pointers is that they permit us complete control over the lifetimes of their targets. That is, C++ provides us with operators that allow us explicitly to create and destroy the targets of pointers (and, hence, any type of object) dynamically—as our program is running.

Consider the types of objects and declarations we've discussed so far. In the definition

```
{ int p = 0; . . . }
```

the object *p* is created when execution reaches the point of its definition and is destroyed as soon as execution leaves the block in which *p* is defined. If we gave *p* file scope by declaring it outside of any block, its lifetime would begin at its definition and persist until the program completed its execution. For the kinds of objects we've seen so far, those are the only possible lifetimes: perpetual or created and destroyed implicitly along with their blocks.

Most of the time, these two forms of lifetimes are perfectly sufficient for our programming purposes. The difficulty comes from the fact that all computers have a limited amount of memory available for storing objects. A computerized phone directory, for instance, might start its life with very few entries, but we would want to allow it to grow much larger as the user adds names and numbers. If we wrote such a program with ordinary objects, we would have to declare a data structure (probably an array) that would be large enough to hold all the entries we anticipate the user would ever need, whether or not it ever would be fully used. Clearly, our program would make much better use of memory if we could define a *dynamic* data structure to represent the phone book, one which could grow and shrink as entries were added and removed. This is precisely why C++ provides us with pointers and the supporting operators new and delete.

The unary operator new is used to construct a new target for a pointer. It has the same precedence as ++ and !. It takes a type name on its right and returns a pointer to the new target, or returns the NULL pointer, 0, if there is no available room in memory for the requested target. For example, if we wrote

```
int* p;
p = new int;
```

the first statement would construct an uninitialized pointer-to-int *p* and the second would instruct the computer to find an integer-sized location in memory, return a pointer to that location, and assign that pointer to *p*, as we illustrate in Figure 6.4.

> The operation new *TypeName* returns a pointer to a newly created object of type *Typename*.*

Of course, since new returns a pointer, we could use that pointer to initialize *p* in a single definition, so we could combine the two statements above into one, as

```
int* p = new int;
```

---

* Caution: Some implementations of C++ allow new to apply only to user-defined types, so new int would be an error. That's not much of a problem, as we rarely use pointers to integers, anyway.

FIGURE 6.4

Using new to build a target for a pointer

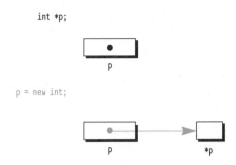

Notice in Figure 6.4 that the target of *p*, *p*, doesn't contain any useful information. Making a new target does not generally give it a value. We would have to do that ourselves by writing something like

```
*p = -54;
```

We can use new to make a target for a pointer to any type, including user-defined types. If, for instance, we wanted to make a pointer to a *Fraction* object like those described in Chapter 2, we could write

```
Fraction* fp = new Fraction;
```

In this case, the target would indeed contain useful information. Since the *Fraction* class has a default constructor, that constructor is invoked to initialize the target.

Recall from Chapter 2 that the no-argument, default constructor for *Fraction* sets the object to the fraction 0/1.

> If new is used to make a target of a user-defined type that has a default constructor, that constructor is invoked implicitly to initialize the target.

We can use other constructors as well, if we have them available. We could, for instance, initialize the target of *fp* to contain the fraction 3/7 by invoking *Fraction*'s two-argument constructor:

```
Fraction* fp = new Fraction(3, 7);
```

If we have pointers to classes, we can access member data and functions of their targets by using the usual dot operator. Consider this simple example:

```
class Pair
// A class representing ordered pairs of integers (x, y)
{
public:
    Pair();                    // Construct the pair (0, 0)
    void Show();               // Display the elements
    int x, y;                  // the two elements of the pair
};
```

We know we can make a pointer, *p*, to a *Pair* object by writing

```
Pair* p = new Pair;              // remember, this calls the constructor
```

Having done this, *p* points to a *Pair* object with value (0, 0). That object is known as **p*, and we can access its member data and functions by using the dot operator:

```
cout << "The first component is " << (*p).x;
cout << "Here's the entire pair: ";
(*p).Show();
```

We need the parentheses, since the dot operator has a higher precedence than *. Without parentheses, the expression **p.x* would be incorrectly interpreted as the nonsensical **(p.x)*. Because we use pointers to objects so frequently, C++ provides the *arrow operator,* -> (a minus sign followed by a greater-than sign), to simplify access. The arrow operator has precedence between ++ and /, and it allows us to write the previous lines like this:

```
cout << "The first component is " << p->x;
cout << "Here's the entire pair: ";
p->Show();
```

The operator `delete` is the inverse of the `new` operator, in that `delete p` destroys the target of the pointer *p*, leaving *p* pointing to no useful target.* If *p* is the NULL pointer, nothing happens (since the NULL pointer never has a target, anyway). We'll discuss `delete` in more detail when we discuss the PIP for this chapter. All we need to know now is that `delete` provides us with a means of destroying what we created so we can use memory more efficiently. There are two cautions we must observe when using `delete`: First, the target to be deleted must have been created by `new`; and second, after having deleted the target of a pointer *p*, it is no longer legal to dereference *p* by referring to **p*, unless we first give *p* something to point to.

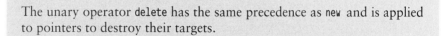

The unary operator `delete` has the same precedence as `new` and is applied to pointers to destroy their targets.

Dynamic Arrays

Using the operators `new` and `delete` with arrays (which, as we've seen, are referred to by names that are also pointers) allows us to solve an interesting programming problem that we mentioned in passing earlier. The situation can be described

---

* What actually happens is a bit complex. C++ sets aside an area of memory, called the *free store* or *heap,* for the targets of pointers. The operator `new` instructs the computer to find an unused (i.e., free) area in the free store large enough for the indicated type and returns the address of the newly created object. When we call `delete`, C++ instructs the computer to return the indicated storage to the list of available storage locations that can be used as targets.

generally as follows. In many programs we use arrays to store collections of objects, such as the entries in a phone directory. When we write a program to manipulate the directory, we don't know how large the directory will be. Indeed, its size will change, potentially radically, over time as the program is used.

Without pointers, we are constrained to a solution—declaring the array to be large enough to hold as many entries as we think will ever be put into the directory—that has two unpleasant side effects. First, for almost all of the directory's life it will be wasting some of the computer's limited memory by allocating it for entries that are not yet defined. Indeed, when this hypothetical program is first run nearly all of the space reserved to hold the array of entries is not being used. Equally unsettling is the prospect that no matter how large we declare the array, our directory may eventually outgrow it. After perhaps months of uneventful use, we will attempt to create a new entry, and the program will crash (either literally or figuratively) because there is no space left in our array.

A better solution would be to have an array that could somehow shrink and grow to meet the changing storage needs of the program. The good news (you knew this was coming) is that C++ allows us to describe such a beast as follows. Imagine that we have declared a class *Entry* to hold individual phone directory entries and a class *Directory* to hold the entire collection of entries (you'll see full descriptions of these classes in this chapter's PIP).

The first step is to declare class *Directory* to contain a pointer to an *Entry*, rather than an array of *Entry*s. That is, our declaration for *Directory* would include a number

```
Entry* entryList;
```

Notice that all this does is allocate space for a pointer (admittedly a pointer to an *Entry* object) in our *Directory* class. We leave it to the constructor function for class *Directory* to use the new operator to allocate space for an array of entries as follows:

```
entryList = new Entry[5];
```

This not only allocates enough storage to hold an array of five entries, but also assigns the starting address of that storage to our pointer in class *Directory, entryList*. Since *entryList* is now a pointer that happens to have as its target the first element of an array, we can refer to our entries just as we would with any array of entries, as *entryList[i]*.

The beauty of this arrangement is its flexibility. Should our demand for entries exceed five (in this case), we can reallocate a larger array, as say

```
EntryList* newList = new entry[20];
```

We then can copy successive entries from the old list to the new one using

```
newList[i] = entryList[i];
```

and do two final bits of housekeeping:

```
delete entryList;
entryList = newList;
```

These final statements help us satisfy our original concerns about storage efficiency. We first free all of the storage we had previously associated with pointer *entryList*. Don't worry, this doesn't destroy the pointer *entryList* itself. It simply returns the previous target of the pointer to the computer's list of available storage locations, and renders *entryList* targetless.

The next statement reestablishes a target for *entryList* by assigning it the value of pointer *newList*. Now, both pointers have the same value (an address) and, thus, the same target—the newly declared, larger array of entries.

Using this technique gives our program the effect of having dynamic arrays. How such arrays are managed and controlled (under what program conditions are they expanded? How big is each growth spurt? Are arrays to be shrunk when they are being underutilized?) depends completely on the programs that use them. We will see a complete example of such a program in this chapter's PIP.

Pointers and Strings

We know a great deal more about C++ than we did when we first introduced the topic of strings in Chapter 5. Let's look back quickly at what we presented there through our more experienced eyes, in the hope of gaining a better understanding of this somewhat slippery subject.

Strings are slippery in C++ because there is no predefined string type built into the language. C++ strings are implemented as arrays of characters. This explains, in large part, why we have seen three distinct notations for referring to strings. We have seen strings referred to as arrays of characters, as string literals, and as pointers to characters, all of which are illustrated in the following statements.

```
char string1[15] = "Object Concept";
char* string2 = string1;
```

Knowing what we now know about arrays and pointers, these notations are perfectly consistent with one another. All arrays in C++ are implemented in terms of pointers. The name of any array denotes a constant pointer, the address of its first element, so the name of a string denotes a pointer to its first character. Given the previous declarations, the expressions *string1[0]*, *string1*, and *string2* all refer to the character 'O'.

These pointers receive their values in one of three ways. They can be used in an explicit string declaration (char s[20]), in which case the allocated address of *s[0]* is associated with variable *s*. They can be assigned a string literal (char* s = "Hello"), in which case the address of character 'H' is assigned to *s*. Or they can be assigned another string address (as in our example above, string2 = string1), in which case *string2* and *string1* both point to the same character in memory.

Despite the ease with which the array names and pointers are interchanged, beware a common misconception. Declaring a char* (pointer to char) neither creates nor allocates storage for a string. While a char* can receive a value at any time, a string cannot receive a value, at least in the sense of a list of characters, until it has been explicitly allocated via an array declaration. In short, remember that while we interchange pointers and array names freely in C++, a pointer is a single value and an array (including any string) refers to a collection of values.

Because strings are meant to refer to collections of characters, they have additional notational overhead associated with them. That is, in order for C++ to recognize that we intend to treat a collection of characters in memory as a single string, we must somehow designate it as such. We do so by appending the string terminator character, '\0', to the end of each string.* In programming terms, we describe C++ strings as being "zero-terminated." Thus, our string *string1*, as previously declared, would be represented internally as pictured in Figure 6.5. Notice that we have allocated one extra space to hold the terminating zero required for a string.

Strings can be initialized by using string literals or by using standard array initialization notation, such as:

```
charstring1[]={'O','b','j','e','c','t',' ',
               'C','o','n','c','e','p','t','\0'};
```

In both cases, the result will be like that pictured in Figure 6.5. In the first case, the terminating zero is there by virtue of the fact that "Object Concept" is a string literal, and in recognition of this C++ equipped the storage allocated to hold it with its own terminating zero. In the second case, wherein we initialize the array in character-by-character fashion, we must provide the string terminator ourselves.

The advantage of imposing the notational overhead of zero-terminators on C++ strings is that it allows C++ to recognize collections of characters as strings and to overload various of its primitive built-in operators to accommodate them. For example, we just saw that one can initialize a string variable with a

FIGURE 6.5

How C++ represents and refers to strings

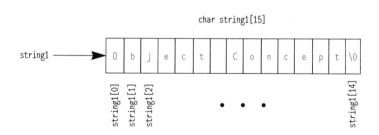

* Remember the escape mark ('\') is used to specify nonprinting characters; e.g., '\t' for tab, and '\n' for newline. The character '\0' is the character with code zero.

string literal. We can also send strings (either literals or variable) directly to stream cout using the insertion operator, as in:

```
cout << string1;
cout << "Object Concept";
```

We even can use the extraction operator to read sequences of (printing) characters and to create a well-formed string, as in:

```
char anotherString[20];
cin >> anotherString;
```

When we extract a string using >>, characters are extracted until a white space (a space, tab, or return character) is seen. The white space is pushed back on the incoming character stream. The function

```
get(char* string, int length, char delimiter = '\n')
```

extracts up to *length* characters, storing them in *string*. If a character equal to *delimiter* is seen, it is pushed back in the input stream and extraction stops. For example, if we wanted to get a name of no more than twenty characters to place in the string *s* we could write

```
char s[20]
cin.get (s, 20);          // We're using the default delimiter here
```

The function

```
getline(char* string, int length, char delimiter = '\n')
```

acts like get, except that it extracts the terminating delimiter instead of inserting it back on the stream. You'll see that this is a very useful function, as it allows us to get a string and not leave the return character on the stream to be misinterpreted by the next input operation.

The library header file, named "string.h," contains declarations for a number of standard string processing functions. These functions accomplish a number of useful operations on strings such as string-to-string assignment, string comparisons, and determining a string's length. Knowing how strings are implemented, we can easily imagine how such functions are implemented.

For example, determining the length of a C++ string, *s*, given a pointer to its first character is simply a matter of counting the number of characters until the terminating zero is encountered. This algorithm could be implemented in a number of ways, perhaps the most straightforward of which is

```
int strlen (const char* s)
{    int i = 0;
     while (s[i] != '\0')
          i++;
     return i;
}
```

We can accomplish the identical processing equally concisely by taking advantage of the fact that when referring to the string terminator, the value of *s[i]* is NULL. Therefore, an empty for loop could also be used, as follows:

```
int strlen (const char* s)
{   for(int i = 0; s[i]; i++);
    return i;
}
```

Just for the sake of illustration, we could also accomplish our length calculation using pointer arithmetic. The version of *strlen* below is like the first version above, with a pointer value substituted for the subscripted array in the original.

```
int strlen (const char* s)
{   int i = 0;
    while (*s++ != '\0')
        i++;
    return i;
}
```

No matter how it is implemented, the *strlen* function is representative of C++'s string handling functions. It exploits the standard implementation of strings (as zero-terminated arrays of characters) and is declared in the standard library file "string.h." A number of other functions are similarly declared in "string.h." The most useful of them are described in the following examples.

Example 1

```
int strcmp (const char* s1, const char* s2)
```

This statement compares strings *s1* and *s2* for lexicographic order (essentially, alphabetical ordering based on character codes). It returns 0 if the two strings are equal, a negative number if *s1* precedes *s2* lexicographically, and a positive number if *s2* precedes *s1*.

Again, in the interest of developing our facility with strings, we can provide two candidate implementations for function *strcmp*. The first is array based, and the second is pointer based.

```
int strcmp (const char* s1, const char* s2)
{   int i = 0;
    while ((s1[i] != '0') && (s1[i] == s2[i]))
        i++;
    //return the comparison of first differing characters
    return (s1[i] - s2[i]);
}

int strcmp (const char* s1, const char* s2)
{
    while ((*s1) && (*s1 == *s2))
    {
```

```
        s1++;
        s2++;
    }
    //return the comparison of first differing characters
    return (*s1 - *s2);
}
```

◁

Example 2   char* strcpy (char* s1, const char* s2)

This statement copies the string pointed to by *s2* into the array pointed to by *s1*, returning a pointer to the newly assigned copy (*s1*). Note that storage must be allocated for array *s1* prior to calling *strcpy* and that array *s1* must be large enough to hold the full length of *s2*. Remember, too, that no matter how this routine is implemented, it is defined with full knowledge of how C++ represents strings. That is, *strcpy* assumes that *s2* points to a well-defined C++ string and copies all of *s2's* character data through and including its zero terminator. Following are two different definitions of *strcpy*.

```
char* strcpy (char* s1, const char* s2)
{
    for (int i = 0; s2[i] != '\0'; i++)
        s1[i] = s2[i];
    s1[i]=s2[i]; //copy the terminator
    return s1;
}
```

```
char* strcpy (char* s1, const char* s2)
{
    char* temp = s1;
    while (*s2)
        *s1++ = *s2++;
    *s1 = *s2;
    return temp;
}
```

◁

Pointers as Links: A Preview

Although this is not the place to go into all of the uses of pointers, we should mention that one of the most important uses is to provide links from one object to another. For example, rather than representing a list of integers by using an array, we could instead represent it as a linked collection of *nodes*, each containing an integer and a pointer to the next node in the list, like this:

```
struct Node
{
    int value;          // the integer stored in the node
    Node* link;         // a pointer to the next node in the list
};
```

FIGURE 6.6
Using pointers to
link objects

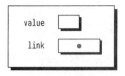

A single node

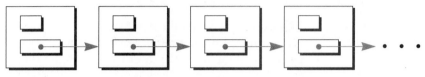

A linked collection of nodes

Having done this, we could use the pointer member data* to provide access to other nodes in the list, as we illustrate in Figure 6.6. The advantage here is that our list never takes up any more space in memory than it has to: When we need a new entry in the list we use new to make one, and when we're finished with an entry we use delete to remove it. In both cases, we have to manipulate the pointer links to maintain the integrity of the list, but you'll see in Chapter 11 that this isn't so hard to do.

6.2 REFERENCES

Let's return to the problem of swapping the values of two objects. *Swap1* is such a simple and useful function; surely there must be some way to write a function that actually does swap its arguments. After all, we may want to interchange the values of two objects, even if they're not in the same array or are not array elements at all. We know that a function can modify the targets of pointers, even if it can't change the pointers themselves. What we need, then, is to be able to say something like this:

```
void ModifiedSwap(Card* p1, Card* p2)
// Here, p1 and p2 are pointers to cards, rather than cards.
{
    Card temp = *p1;          // copy the target of p1
    *p1 = *p2;                // move target of p2 into target of p1
    *p2 = temp;               // move temp into target of p2
}
```

---

* Although a class cannot contain member data of its own type, there is no prohibition about classes containing member data that *points* to other objects of their type.

In fact, this would do exactly what we want. The pointers *p1* and *p2* aren't modified, but there's no prohibition against modifying what they point to, so *ModifiedSwap* would interchange the values of (the *targets* of) its arguments, **p1* and **p2*, more or less as we wanted.

There's a big problem here, though. How do we call *ModifiedSwap?* The two formal arguments are pointers to cards, rather than cards. To swap two cards, we need pointers to the cards and not the cards themselves. What we need is the opposite of the * operator—something that, when given an object, returns a reference to that object. Guess what? C++ has just what we want.

Reference Types

An object may be defined to be a *reference type* by using the unary & operator to the left of the reference object. For example, if we had written

```
int n = 10;
int& r = n;                    // r is a reference to n
```

we would be defining *r* to be a reference to the object *n*. In other words, after the previous definitions, *n* and *r* would be two different names for the same integer object.* If we then make the assignment

```
r = 20;
```

we not only would be setting the value of *r* to 20 but, because *r* and *n* have been defined to be names for the same object, we also would be setting the thing we call *n* to 20.

There are two sources of potential error when declaring references. First, a reference must obviously be a reference to *something,* so every reference declaration must also be a definition telling us what the reference object refers to. Second, once a reference has been defined, it may not then be redefined to be a reference to another object. Both possible errors are illustrated below:

```
double sum, average;
double& total = sum;
double& value;                 // error: nothing to refer to
double& total = average;       // error: can't redefine a reference
```

> A reference must be defined to refer to a variable when it is declared, unless the reference declaration is part of a formal argument to a function. Once a reference has been defined, it cannot be changed to refer to another object.

---

* Also known as *aliases.*

Reference Arguments

Using reference types as function arguments gives us a simple and more concise way to modify the arguments of a function. Suppose we wrote our swapping routine like this:

```
void SimpleSwap(Card& r1, Card& r2)
// Here, r1 and r2 are references to cards.
{
    Card temp = r1;             // copy the target of r1
    r1 = r2;                    // move target of r2 into target of r1
    r2 = temp;                  // move temp into target of r2
}
```

If *c1* and *c2* were cards, we could then call *SimpleSwap(c1, c2)* and the swap would be made as we intended, through a little C++ sleight of hand. The call would have the effect of defining the references in the argument like this:

```
Card& r1 = c1;
Card& r2 = c2;
```

Now the function would modify the local objects *r1* and *r2* as usual, but because *r1* and *r2* were reference objects referring to *c1* and *c2*, the result would be to modify their aliases, *c1* and *c2*, as well, thereby swapping as we wished (whew!).

> If you need to modify an argument to a function, make that argument a reference type in the function declaration.

In general, we prefer to avoid overuse of reference arguments. Certainly there are times when reference arguments are useful—as in *SimpleSwap,* for instance—and we wouldn't advise that you never use reference arguments. Using reference arguments as a matter of course, however, tends to deviate from the notion that a function should return at most a single object. More important than style is readability. Notice that there's no way to tell from a function call whether the function being called modifies its arguments. To discover whether it does, we have to hunt down the function declaration, and that may be several pages removed from its call, or even in another file. When we call a function that modifies its arguments, we generally alert the reader with a comment to that effect, unless the action of a function is obvious from its context or its name (like *Swap,* for instance).

6.3 MORE INPUT AND OUTPUT

We gave a brief introduction to the classes *ostream* and *istream* back in Chapter 2. Since the definitions of the operators << and >> involve both pointers and reference types, this is a good place to look at these two classes in a bit more detail.

If you look at the C++ header files in the standard libraries that came with your compiler, you'll find the declaration of the class *ostream*. This is the class that C++ uses for output, and we've provided a skeletal listing here. We have intentionally omitted many details here, not only because we want to avoid confusion, but also because library designers frequently include what might be called "nonstandard" member functions and operators that they consider useful to a programmer. You'll almost certainly find many declarations in your *ostream* class that we haven't included here. You can use these other functions, but remember that they might not be recognized if you try to compile your program on another implementation of C++.

```
class ostream
// . . .
{
public:
//-------------- Overloads of << Operator --------------
    ostream& operator<<(const char* string);
    ostream& operator<<(char c);
    ostream& operator<<(int n);
    ostream& operator<<(double v);
    // (operators for many other predefined types, like
    // unsigned int, long, pointers, and so on, omitted here)
};
```

Let's take a closer look at the declaration of the overloads* of the operator <<. Suppose we wish to display the value of the int object named *i*, followed by a return to the next line. We've done things like this many times; we'd write the statement

```
cout << i << '\n';
```

Here's what really goes on. First, since << groups from the left, the expression is evaluated in this order:

```
((cout << i) << '\n')
```

The characters go to **cout** in this case; we could define and use a different *ostream* object than **cout** if we wished to send the output to a different place, such as a file. We'll see this process in Chapter 9.

The leftmost << operator converts the internal representation of *i* to characters and sends them to the *ostream* cout. But all this is a side effect, as we saw with the assignment operator =. In terms of evaluating the expression, what's important is that << returns a reference to the *ostream* object, cout, on its left. Substituting the returned reference back into the original expression yields

```
(cout << '\n')
```

---

* The operator << is overloaded because the predefined definition of << is a *bit shift* operator, which shifts the bits of an object to the left, changing 00001101 to 00011010, for instance. We won't discuss the bit shift operators in detail.

This expression is evaluated as the first was. The newline character is sent to cout and the expression again returns a reference to cout, which—since the expression is now fully evaluated—is then ignored as execution passes to the next statement.

Observe that the two << operators in the example are different. The leftmost one, as indicated by its argument, is the one declared as

```
ostream& operator<<(int n);
```

The rightmost one, which takes a char as its argument, is the one declared for characters:

```
ostream& operator<<(char c);
```

We now can see how to define overloads for types of our own. If we wanted to display fractions, for example, we could declare our own overload of << to be a friend of the *Fraction* class by writing

```
friend ostream& operator<<(ostream &s, Fraction f);
```

and then define it by

```
ostream& operator<<(ostream& s, Fraction f)
// Inserts the numerator, a '/' character, and the denominator
// into the ostream s, and then returns a reference to s.
{
    s << f.numerator << '/' << f.denominator;
    return s;
}
```

Having done that, we could then use our overloaded << as we do all the others. That is, to display a fraction *f*, all we'd have to do is write

```
cout << f;
```

You may have noticed that our overload of << has a different declaration than the ones in *ostream*. To display an integer, the declaration in class *ostream* is

```
ostream& operator<<(int n);
```

while our program-defined overload had this declaration:

```
friend ostream& operator<<(ostream &s, Fraction f);
```

Our fraction operator is declared to be a friend and has an *ostream* argument as well as an argument for the object to be displayed. The reasons for the two differences make sense now that we understand how C++ handles classes. First, our version of << must be declared a friend in order for it to have access to the private data members *numerator* and *denominator*. The *ostream* << operators are member functions, so they are already part of the class and so do not have to be granted access to other members of *ostream*. Second, since the *ostream* operators are members of class *ostream*, we do not need to mention explicitly the object they belong to, so we don't need the first argument ostream &S that we do need for the *Fraction* overload.

Input: The Class *istream*

The *istream* class is used for input. Its declaration looks like the following, where we have again omitted many declarations that are probably in your version of C++:

```
class istream
// . . .
{
public:
//------------- Overloads of >> Operator -------------
    istream& operator>>(char* string);
    istream& operator>>(char& c);
    istream& operator>>(int& n);
    istream& operator>>(double& v);
    // (operators for many other predefined types, like
    // unsigned int, long, pointers, and so on, omitted here)

//------------- Utility Routines -------------
    istream& get(char* string, int length, char delimiter = '\n');
    istream& get(char& c);          // Extract a single character.
    int get();                      // Get one character, and return it in an int.
    istream& getline(char* string, int length, char delimiter = '\n');

//------------- Constructor, destructor -------------
// . . .


private:
// . . .
};
```

As with *ostreams*, we know there is a standard, predefined *istream* object, called cin, that refers to the standard input device (the keyboard, for our purpose). This class is somewhat more complex than *ostream*, due mainly to the fact that we have more control over what our program sends to the screen than we do over what a user might type on the keyboard.

Notice for now how each of the overloads of the extraction operator >> (except the one defined for strings) uses reference parameters. Extraction is, after all, intended to modify its argument by reading a new value for it. The string extractor accomplishes the same effect by using a pointer to the arrays of characters.

We can overload extraction for any user-defined type in much the same way we did with the insertion operator. Such overloads would take the same general form as this *Fraction* extractor:

```
friend istream& operator >> (istream& a, Fraction& f);
```

Remember that the second argument of the operator, a *Fraction* in this case, must be a reference parameter.

6.4 DESIGNING THE PIP: A PHONE DIRECTORY

The PIP for this chapter is a simple electronic phone directory. Conceptually, the directory is much simpler than the soda machine we developed in Chapter 3, and is organized very much like the deck of cards we defined in Chapter 5. In terms of organization, a phone directory is clearly a list of entries, each one consisting of a name, a phone number, and an address. A natural choice, then, is to define a class for entries and then make a directory class containing an array of entries. We'll begin at the bottom level of this organization by defining the *Entry* class.

As usual, we need to specify the member data that each entry object will contain, along with the member functions we'll use to manipulate the data. We've already implied that the data should be three arrays of characters, one each for the person's name, phone number, and address. We could, of course, have chosen to make the phone number an integer large enough for seven digits; we chose an array of characters to permit phone numbers like "859–4785 ext 328." As we do so often, we will make the member data private and restrict access by using public member functions. Of course, we'll need a constructor to initialize each of the three data items (setting each to blank strings), and since a common operation in a phone book is to look up an entry by name, we'll declare a function *char* GetName()* that will return a pointer to the first element in the name array. Using a pointer allows us to circumvent the C++ prohibition against functions returning arrays.

> We first saw the prohibition against returning arrays at the end of Section 5.1.

There is one part of the *Entry* class that illustrates something we haven't done before. Now that we know how to do so, we'll overload the insertion and extraction operators << and >> so that we can use them to display and get the name, number, and address of an entry. We will have to declare these operators as friends of the *Entry* class so that they may have access to the private member data items. We've illustrated the *Entry* class in Figure 6.7.

Once we've defined an entry, we need to describe a *Directory* class that maintains a list of entries. An array of entries is a natural choice, and that's what we'll use. What operations would be appropriate for a phone directory? As is often the case in computerized applications of familiar real-world tasks,

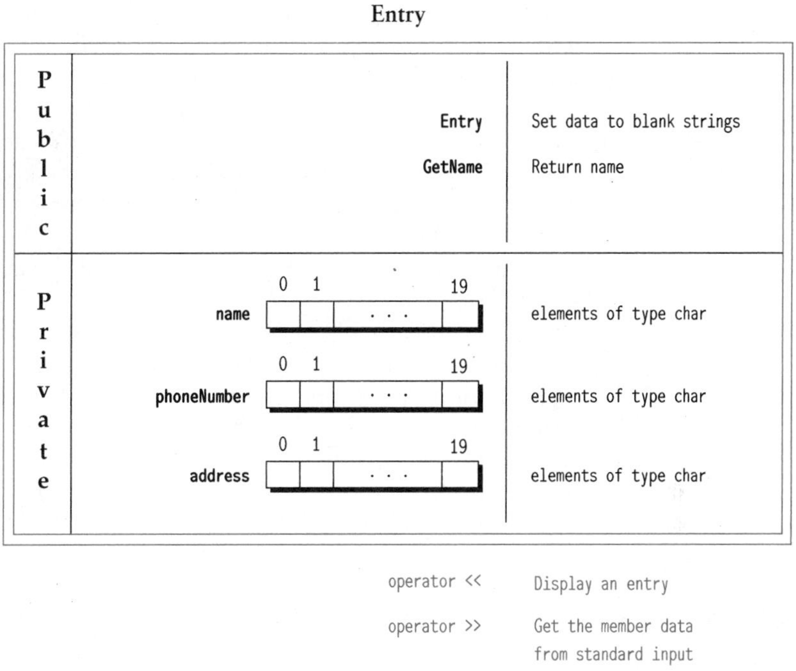

FIGURE 6.7

The class *Entry*

this question is most easily answered in natural, real-world terms. We'd like to be able to

1. Create a new, empty *Directory.*
2. *Insert* a new entry into the directory.
3. *Lookup* the data in an entry, given a person's name.
4. *Remove* the entry corresponding to a given name.
5. *Update* the entry corresponding to a given name.

We might be lucky enough at this early design stage to recognize that the last three activities all have a common function. In each case, we are given a name and have to find the index of the entry, if any, that contains that name. Rather than write the same code three times, we'll factor out the common activity into a separate, private, function *int FindName(char* aName),* which will search through the array of entries and return the index of the element containing *aName.*

Now, how large should we make the array of entries? You've read enough of this text by now to suspect that we have a hidden agenda here, and indeed we do. Just as the rest of the PIPs you've seen, this one was tailored to illustrate the material of the chapter. In particular, we will make the array dynamic so that it can grow and shrink during the program's execution. Rather than storing the array "in" the directory, the *Directory* class will instead just keep a pointer to the array and use new to build the array in the free store. We will begin with a pointer to a very small array, and we'll keep two integers as additional member data: One, *currentSize,* will keep track of the current number of entries in the array and the other, *maxSize,* will keep track of the maximum possible number of entries we can fit in the current directory. Then, when the user attempts to insert a new entry into a full array, the program will create a new array twice the size of the old one, copy the entries into the new array, adjust *maxSize,* and use delete to destroy the old array. We will use a private member function, *Grow( ),* to do this, and have it called when needed by the public *Insert* function.

If you look at Figure 6.8, where we've illustrated the *Directory* class, you'll see all of the member data and functions we've mentioned, along with one function we haven't mentioned yet. The function *~Directory* is a *destructor,* which we will describe in more detail shortly. Its purpose here is to "clean up" when a *Directory* object is no longer needed by deleting the entry list.

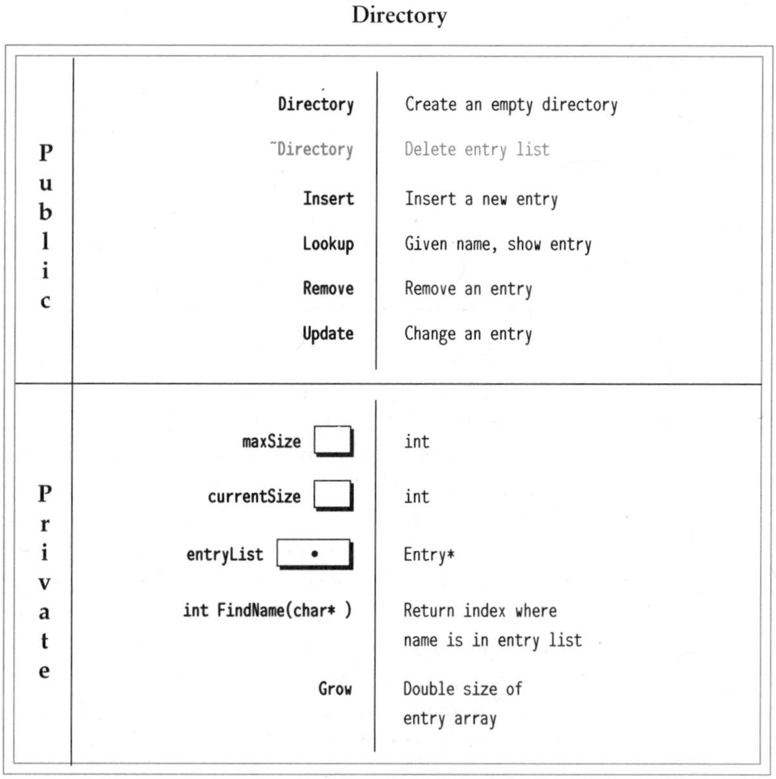

FIGURE 6.8

The class *Directory*

Directory

6.5 EXPLORING THE PIP

The PIP for this chapter consists of five files, as dictated by our declare-define-use approach. "ENTRY.H" and "ENTRY.CPP" contain the declarations and definitions of the class *Entry*, along with the operator overloads of << and >> for *Entry* objects. The files "FONEBOOK.H" and "FONEBOOK.CPP" (not "PHONEBOOK", since some systems limit filenames to eight characters) contain declarations and definitions of the class *Directory*, and the file "PIP6.CPP" contains the main function along with some utility functions.

Entries: The Files "ENTRY.H" and "ENTRY.CPP"

An entry in our directory is quite simple, containing as it does just three arrays of characters—*name, phoneNumber,* and *address*—along with a constructor that sets each of these three strings to a single blank and an access function that returns the value of the *name* data member. As we mentioned, we also declare friend overloads of the << and >> operators, to get from the keyboard and display on the screen the three member data items.

```
//---------------- ENTRY.H----------------

// Declarations for class Entry for a phone directory

#include <iostream.h>           // so we can overload the iostream operators

class Entry
{
    friend istream& operator >> (istream& a, Entry& e);
    friend ostream& operator << (ostream& a, Entry e);
public:
    Entry();                // initializes all values to blanks
    char* GetName();        // returns the name in an entry
private:
    char name[20];          // A name is 20 characters.
    char phoneNumber[20];   // so is a phone number
    char address[20];       // and so is an address.
};
```

In "ENTRY.H", notice that we have included *<iostream.h>*. We need this, of course, since otherwise the compiler would have no way of recognizing the names *istream* and *ostream* that we use in the operator overloads. Notice, too, that the *Entry e* in the argument lists of the overloads is a reference parameter in >> and not in <<. This is because in doing input we want to modify the argument *e* by setting its member data. The output operator doesn't modify the argument and so doesn't need to be a reference.

```
//---------------- ENTRY.CPP -----------------

// Definition of class Entry for a phone directory.
// Note that although we need iostream.h, we don't mention it here,
// since <iostream.h> is already included in "ENTRY.H".

#include <string.h>                              // for strlen, strcopy
#include "ENTRY.H"                               // for class Entry

//---------- Overloaded (friend) I/O operators ----------

istream& operator >> (istream& s, Entry& e)
// This overloads the extraction operator for entries. To read an
// entry from the keyboard, we can just use >> with cin.
{
    cout << "\nType name, followed by RETURN or ENTER: ";
    s.getline(e.name, 20);                       // Gets a name; discards newline.

    cout << "\nType phone number, followed by RETURN or ENTER: ";
    s.getline(e.phoneNumber, 20);                // Gets a phone; discards newline.

    cout << "\nType room number, followed by RETURN or ENTER: ";
    s.getline(e.address, 20);                    // Gets an address; discards newline.

    return s;                                    // Required by operator type
}

ostream& operator << (ostream& s, Entry e)
// This overloads the insertion operator for entries. To display
// an entry on the screen, we can just use << with cout.
{
    int i;

    s << '\t' << e.name;                         // Display name (after tabbing).
    // Display remaining blanks, so that data lines up on screen.
    for (i = strlen(e.name) + 1; i < 20; i++) s.put(' ');

    s << '\t' << e.phoneNumber;                  // Display phone number.
    for (i = strlen(e.phoneNumber) + 1; i < 20; i++) s.put(' ');

    s << '\t' << e.address;                      // Display address.
    s << '\n';

    return s;                                    // required by operator type
}
```

```
//---------- Member functions ----------

Entry::Entry()
// This constructor for class Entry initializes the name, phone
// number, and address to be blank strings.
{
    strcpy(name, " ");
    strcpy(phoneNumber, " ");
    strcpy(address, " ");
}


char* Entry::GetName()
// Return the name part of an entry.
{
    return name;
}
```

The definition of the overload of the operator >> is simple enough. The operator will take a reference to an *istream* (cin, in this program) as its first argument and a reference to an entry as its second, and like all such overloads, it returns to the program a reference to the *istream* it saw as its left argument. The action consists of three similar steps: Display a prompt to the user and use the *istream* function *getline* to get the name, number, and address, discarding the newline character each time so it doesn't get read by the next input operation.

The definition of << is handled similarly. The only tricky part here is that after displaying the name and phone number we pad the display with blanks so that all the strings line up in tabular form. The line

```
for (i = strlen(e.name) + 1; i < 20; i++)
    s.put(' ');
```

uses the string function *strlen* to find the length of *e*'s *name* datum and then uses the *istream* function *put* to display (19 – *length*)more spaces, guaranteeing that each field in the display will take up exactly 19 characters.

The constructor *Entry* uses the string function *strcpy* to initialize each data string to a single blank. This function returns a pointer to the destination string, which we don't need (since we're only interested in its side effect of setting the target of its argument), so we simply call the function and ignore its returned value.

The Directory: The Files "FONEBOOK.H" and "FONEBOOK.CPP"

The header file containing the declarations of the *Directory* class needs no explanation, except perhaps to remind you that we use a pointer to the array *EntryList* in the class declaration rather than using the array itself.

```
//---------------- FONEBOOK.H ----------------


// Declarations for class Directory, where a directory
// is a collection of Entries, declared in "ENTRY.H".

#include "ENTRY.H"

class Directory
{
public:
    Directory();                        // Set up empty directory of entries
    ~Directory();                       // Deallocate the entry list.
    void Insert();                      // Insert an entry into the directory.
    void Lookup();                      // Look up a name in the directory.
    void Remove();                      // Remove an entry.
    void Update();                      // Update an existing entry.
    void DisplayDirectory();            // Display the current directory.

private:
    int maxSize,                        // the maximum number of entries
        currentSize;                    // the current number of entries
    Entry* entryList;                   // pointer to the list of entries
    void Grow();                        // Double the maximum size, when required.
    int FindName(char* aName);          // Return index of an entry, given a name.
};
```

Most of the real work in this program is done in the definition file
"FONEBOOK.CPP"

```
//---------------- FONEBOOK.CPP ----------------


// Definitions for class Directory

#include <string.h>                 // for strcmp
#include "FONEBOOK.H"

Directory::Directory()
// Set up empty directory of entries.
{
    maxSize = 5;
    currentSize = 0;
    entryList = new Entry[maxSize];
}


Directory::~Directory()
// This destructor function for class Directory
```

```
// deallocates the directory's pointer to its entry list.
{
    delete entryList;
}


void Directory::Insert()
// Insert a new entry into the directory.
{
    if (currentSize == maxSize)
    // If the directory is full, grow it.
        Grow();
    cin >> entryList[currentSize++];
    // Use overloaded >> to read new entry.
}


void Directory::Lookup()
// Display the directory entry for a name.
{
    // Prompt the user for a name to be looked up
    char aName[20];
    cout << "\tType the name to be looked up, followed by ENTER: ";
    cin.getline(aName, 20);

    int thisEntry = FindName(aName);
    // Locate the name in the directory.

    if (thisEntry == -1)
        cout << aName << " not found in current directory\n";
    else
    {
        cout << "\nEntry found: ";
        cout << entryList[thisEntry];
        // Use overloaded << to display entry.
    }
}


void Directory::Remove()
// Remove an entry from the directory.
{
    // Prompt the user for the name to be removed.
    char aName[20];
    cout << "\nType name to be removed, followed by ENTER: ";
    cin.getline(aName, 20);

    int thisEntry = FindName(aName);
```

```
    // Locate the name in the directory.

    if (thisEntry == -1)
        cout << aName << " not found in directory";
    else
    {
        // Shift each succeeding element "down" one position in the
        // Entry array, thereby deleting the desired entry.
        for (int j = thisEntry + 1; j < currentSize; j++)
            entryList[j - 1] = entryList[j];

        currentSize--;          // Decrement number of entries.
        cout << "Entry removed.\n";
    }
}


void Directory::Update()
// Update an existing directory entry by reentering
// each of its values (name, phone, and room number).
{
    cout << "\nPlease enter the name of the entry to be modified: ";
    char aName[20];
    cin.getline(aName, 20);

    int thisEntry = FindName(aName);

    if (thisEntry == -1)
        cout << aName << " not found in current directory\n";
    else
    {
        cout << "\nCurrent entry is: \n";
        cout << entryList[thisEntry];
        // Display the current entry.

        cout << "\nReplace with new entries as follows: \n";
        cin >> entryList[thisEntry];
        // Get new values for entry.
    }
}


void Directory::DisplayDirectory()
// Display the current directory entries
// on the standard output (the screen).
```

```
{
    if (currentSize == 0)
    {
        cout << "\nCurrent directory is empty.\n"
        return;
    }

    // Display a header.
    cout << "\n\t***NAME***\t\t***PHONE***\t\t***ADDRESS***\n\n";

    for (int i = 0; i < currentSize; i++)   // For each entry, send it
        cout << entryList[i];.               // to output using overload >>.
}


void Directory::Grow()
// Double the size of the directory's entry list by creating
// a new, larger array of entries and changing the directory's
// pointer to refer to the new array.
{
    int newSize = 2 * currentSize;           // Determine the newsize.
    Entry* newList = new Entry[newSize];      // Allocate a new array.

    for (int i = 0; i < currentSize; i++)     // Copy each entry into
        newList[i] = entryList[i];            // the new array.

    delete entryList;                         // Remove the old pointer,
    entryList = newList;                      // establish the new pointer,
    maxSize = newSize;                        // and reset the table size.
}


int Directory :: FindName(char* aName)
// Locate a name in the directory. Returns the
// position of the entry list as an integer if found,
// and returns -1 if the entry is not found in the directory.
{
    for (int i = 0; i < currentSize; i++)              // Look at each entry.
        if (strcmp(entryList[i].GetName(), aName) == 0)
            return i;                        // If found, return position and exit.

    return -1;                               // Return -1 if never found.
}
```

Let's first look at the dynamic array that the directory uses to store the list of entries. The constructor, *Directory*, looks like this:

```
Directory::Directory()
// Set up empty directory of entries.
{
    maxSize = 5;
    current = 0;
    entryList = new Entry [maxSize];
}
```

We begin with a five-element array, setting *maxSize* to 5. We indicate that there are no valid entries in the array by setting *currentSize* to zero, and we use new to set the pointer *entryList* to point to the first element of an array of five entries. Since *Entry* has a default constructor, it will be invoked implicitly to initialize each of the entries in the array.

Any class may have a *destructor* function. Unlike constructors, a class may have only one destructor. A destructor's name is the class name preceded by a tilde ("squiggle," in programmer-ese). A destructor must have an empty argument list. The purpose of a destructor is to handle any tasks that must be done before a class object is destroyed (like displaying some data before saying goodbye, for instance). A program may explicitly call a destructor for an object; the destructor is also implicitly invoked when a class object goes out of its scope. We haven't introduced destructors yet because we've had no need for them, but there is a good reason to use one here.

If we didn't have a destructor for the *Directory* class, every time a directory object was destroyed its *entryList* pointer would also be destroyed, leaving the target array to which it pointed stranded in the free store. That is to say, the array would still be occupying storage, but there would be no pointer pointing to it. If we had a program that created and destroyed a number of large directories, sooner or later the free store would become completely cluttered with unreferenced arrays, leaving no available room for subsequent calls to new.* In *Directory*'s destructor, we explicitly destroy the array of entries by calling

```
delete entryList;
```

The situation is a little more complicated if the array to be destroyed has elements that are themselves class objects. If the array's objects were members of a class that had a destructor, that destructor should be called for each element before the array itself was destroyed. C++ will do that for us, but we need to specify for the compiler that the pointer target is an array so that it will invoke the constructor as many times as needed. We do this by using

---

* Once a target loses all pointers to itself, it is impossible to ever get to the target again, so it stays as garbage in the free store until the program quits (and may even remain after that). Some languages, like LISP and Smalltalk, include automatic *garbage collection,* destroying any targets that lose all their references. C++ does not.

square brackets between the word delete and the pointer to the array to be destroyed.

As if that weren't confusing enough, some older versions of C++ require you to specify the size of the array, as **delete [20] p**. Ask your instructor which form you must use.

Suppose (1) *p* is a pointer to an array, (2) the elements of the array are class objects, and (3) the class has a destructor. To invoke the destructors for each element and destroy the array, you must write

```
delete [] p;
```

If any of the three conditions above does not hold, you invoke delete in the usual way:

```
delete p;
```

Now we can see how the private *Grow* function works. When *Insert* discovers that there's no room in the array for a new entry, it calls *Grow*. This function first sets a local variable *newSize* to twice the *currentSize*. It then constructs a new array of *newSize* entries:

```
Entry* newList = new Entry[newSize];
```

Now that the new array is available, the contents of the old array are transferred to the new one using a for loop, as follows:

```
for (int i = 0; i < currentSize; i++)
    newList[i] = entryList[i];
```

Finally, the old array is deleted (which is safe, since it was originally created as a result of invoking new), the pointer to the entry list is set to point to the new array, and *maxSize* is set to its new value:

```
delete entryList;
entryList = newList;
maxSize = newSize;
```

Before we leave the *Directory* class, we'll explore the *Remove* function. Recall that this function asks the user for the name of the entry to be removed. It then calls *FindName* to locate the index of the entry to be removed. *FindName* uses a *linear search* to find the required entry, looking at the *name* datum of each entry in turn, until it finds a match (at which point it exits both the loop and the function, returning the index) or runs out of elements to inspect.

```
int Directory :: FindName(char* aName)
{
    for (int i = 0; i < currentSize; i++)
        if (strcmp(entryList[i].GetName(), aName) == 0)
            return i;                    // If found, return position and exit.

    return -1;                           // Return -1 if never found.
}
```

The test for matching names uses the string function *strcmp* to compare the test name, *aName,* with the name in the *i*-th entry, which is accessed by the entry's *GetName* member function. In case *FindName* finds a match and returns an index, *thisEntry,* the function *Remove* removes the entry by shifting each higher-indexed entry down one position, as we show in Figure 6.9. The last thing *Remove* has to do (a necessary task that's often forgotten) is to decrement *currentSize,* reflecting the fact that there is now one fewer entry in the directory than there was before.

The Main Program: The File "PIP6.CPP"

The file "PIP6.CPP" contains the main function, along with some menu-handling functions that are very similar to those in the *User* class that we used in Chapter 4's soda machine program. The action of the main function should be quite familiar by now: It creates a new *Directory* object, displays a menu of available operations, and keeps getting command characters from the user and executing the functions corresponding to those commands until the user signals his or her intention to quit the program by typing the character 'Q'.

```
//---------------- PIP6.CPP -----------------

// Test program and general support functions
// for phone directory

#include <ctype.h>              // for toupper
#include <iostream.h>           // for cin, cout
#include "FONEBOOK.H"           // for class Directory

void ShowMenu()
// Display the main program menu.
{
    cout << "\n\t\t*** PIP 6 PHONE DIRECTORY ***";
    cout << "\n\tI \tInsert a new entry into the directory";
    cout << "\n\tL \tLook up an entry";
```

FIGURE 6.9
Deleting an element
in an array

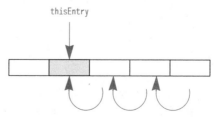

Note: We must do the shifts from here   . . .   to here.

```
        cout << "\n\tR \tRemove an entry";
        cout << "\n\tU \tUpdate an entry";
        cout << "\n\tD \tDisplay the entire directory";
        cout << "\n\t? \tDisplay this menu";
        cout << "\n\tQ \tQuit";
    }


    char GetAChar(char* promptString)
    // Prompt the user and get a single character,
    // discarding the Return character.
    // Used in GetCommand.
    {
        char response;                  // the char to be returned
        cout << promptString;           // Prompt the user
        cin >> response;                // get a char
        response = toupper(response);   // and convert it to uppercase
        cin.get();                      // Discard newline char from input
        return response;
    }


    char Legal(char c)
    // Determine if a particular character, c, corresponds
    // to a legal menu command. Returns 1 if legal, 0 if not.
    // Used in GetCommand.
    {
        return((c == 'I') || (c == 'L') || (c == 'R') ||
               (c == 'U') || (c == 'D') || (c == '?') || (c == 'Q')));
    }


    char GetCommand()
    // Prompts the user for a menu command until a legal
    // command character is entered. Return the command character.
    // Calls GetAChar, Legal, ShowMenu.
    {
        char cmd = GetAChar("\n\n>");               // Get a command character.

        while (!Legal(cmd))                 // As long as it's not a legal command,
        {                                       // display menu and try again.
            cout << "\nIllegal command, please try again . . .";
            ShowMenu();
            cmd = GetAChar("\n\n>");
        }
        return cmd;
    }
```

```
void main()
{
    Directory d;                    // Create and initialize a new directory.

    ShowMenu();                     // Display the menu.

    char command;                   // menu command entered by user
    do
    {
        command = GetCommand();                 // Retrieve a command.
        switch (command)
        {
            case 'I': d.Insert();           break;
            case 'L': d.Lookup();           break;
            case 'R': d.Remove();           break;
            case 'U': d.Update();           break;
            case 'D': d.DisplayDirectory(); break;
            case '?': ShowMenu();           break;
            case 'Q':                       break;
        }
    } while (command != 'Q');
}
```

6.6   SUMMING UP

▶ A pointer is an indirect reference to an object. To declare a pointer to an object of type *TypeName,* we write *TypeName * pointerName.* The object to which a pointer p points is *p.

▶ There is only one pointer literal. The NULL pointer has value 0.

▶ The dereference operator, *, has the same precedence as the other unary operators like ++, and like them it groups from the right.

▶ if p is a pointer to a class object, member functions and data may be accessed by using the arrow operator –>.

▶ An array is accessed by a constant pointer to the zero-th entry in the array. For arrays, either pointer or array notation may be used interchangeably.

▶ If an array is used as a function argument, the function can modify the contents of the array.

▶ The declaration const TypeName *p; makes p a pointer to a constant object of type *TypeName.*

▶ The new operator creates an object in the free store and returns a pointer to that object, so in the definition int* p = new int; the pointer p is set to point to a new integer object. If there is no room in the free store to create the new object, new will return the NULL pointer.

▶ If new is used to create a pointer to a class object, that object's default constructor will be called implicitly after the object is created. When creating a new class object, one can also call its constructor explicitly.

▶ A class may have a destructor, which is invoked when a class object is destroyed. There may be at most one destructor for a class, and it must have no arguments. The name of a destructor is always ~*ClassName*.

▶ The delete operator removes an object from the free store. The expression delete p may only be used if *p* points to an object that has been created by new.

▶ If delete is called on a pointer to a class object, that object's destructor will be called implicitly before the object is destroyed.

▶ If *p* is a pointer to an array, the deletion command must include array brackets, as delete [] p when the array elements are class objects with destructors. The destructors for the array elements will be called before the array is destroyed.

▶ A reference type is defined by *TypeName* & *name1* = *name2*, where *name2* is an object of type *TypeName*. A reference is an alias for the object it is defined to be.

▶ The primary use of reference types is in formal arguments of functions. An argument of reference type may have its value modified by the function.

▶ A string in C++ is a zero-terminated array of characters, and so may be referenced by a pointer to char. The library <string.h> contains a number of string-processing functions.

▶ The stream operators << and >> return references to an *ostream* or an *istream*, respectively. We can define overloads of these operators for output and input of user-defined classes.

6.7 EXERCISES

1. Suppose we have the following declarations

```
SomeClass *p, *q;
```

Draw pictures as we did in Figure 6.4 to show the state of the program after each of the following sequence of statements.

```
p = new SomeClass;
q = new SomeClass;
q = p;
delete p;
```

2. What's wrong with this program segment?

```
double* p, q;
*p = 1;
q = p;
cout << "q points to " << *q;
```

3. Given these declarations,

```
int *pi, *pj, i, j;
double *px, *py, x, y;
```

identify the incorrect statements below.

```
i = 100;
pi = 1024;
pj = 0;
*pi = i;
px = pi;
pi = 2 * pi;
cout << "pj contains the address " << pj;
if (pi < pj)
    cout << "pi's target is before pj's in memory";
```

4. You can declare pointers to almost any type, including pointers. Given the following

```
int** p, n;
n = 2;
**p = n;
```

what can you say about the types and values of *p*, **p*, and ***p*? Draw a picture.

5. If *p* and *q* are strings (i.e., are zero-terminated), what does this loop do? Recall that * and ++ have the same precedence and group from the right, and that we're using the postincrement form of ++.

```
while (*q)
    *p++ = *q++;
```

6. How would you check whether two pointers *p* and *q* were aliases; that is, whether they pointed to the same object?

7. What sort of object is *x* in each of these declarations? Remember, [ ] has higher precedence than *.

```
int *x[10];
int (*x)[10];
```

8. In C++, functions can return pointers and references, just as they return other types. This can lead to interesting (if mysterious) results. Suppose, for example, we had defined the following function:

```
int& Max(int i, int j)
{
    if (i >= j)
        return &i;
    else
        return &j;
}
```

What would happen if we later made this peculiar-looking statement, with a function call on the left?

```
Max(x, y) = 0;
```

9. The operator &, when used in an expression, returns the address of its operand and so can be used to initialize a pointer. After executing the definitions

```
int a[] = {10, 19, 6};
int* ptr = &a[1];
```

what is the value of *ptr?

10. Write *Swap* so that it swaps the values of two pointers to integers. In other words, if *p* and *q* are two pointers, after calling *Swap*(*p*, *q*), *p* will point to what used to be *q*, and *q* will point to what used to be *p*.

11. This function is supposed to return the index of the first instance of the char *c* in the string *str*, and to return −1 if *c* doesn't appear in *str*.

```
int strchr(char* str, int c);
{   int i = 0;
    while ((*str != c) && (*str != '\0'))
    {   str++; i++; }
    if (*str == c)
        return i;
    else
        return -1;
}
```

It appears as if we have a problem since the function moves the pointer *str* away from the start of the string. Explain why we don't have a problem.

12. Use the string functions to write char* DeleteTail(char* src, int n), which returns all but the last *n* characters of the string *src* and returns the empty string if *src* has *n* or fewer characters.

13. After executing these statements

```
char t[5], u[10];
char *p;
t = "food";
u = "dog";
p = u;
```

what would be the result of this statement?

```
p = strcat(u, strncpy(t, "bonehead", 4));
```

14. Here's a first-class example of why people say that C++ is hard to understand. What does this function do?

```
void Mystery(char* p, const char* q)
{   while (*p++ = *q++); }
```

15. Write your own version of *strlen*.

16. Write a function char* Difference(char* s1, char* s2) that will compare *s1* and *s2* and will return the tail of *s1*, starting at the first character where *s1* and *s2* don't match. For example, if we had *s1* = "unintelligent" and *s2* = "under" or "un", then the function would return "intelligent". If all of *s1* matches the start of *s2*, the function should return the empty string '\0'.

17. We want to write a function char* Remove(char* src, int index, int n) that will return the string that results when we delete *n* characters from *src*, starting at position *index*. In other words, *Remove* will remove the characters at positions *index, . . . , index + n – 1.*

    a. What preconditions on *index, n,* and the length of *src* does this function require to be true when it is called?
    b. Write the function assuming that the preconditions are satisfied.
    c. Write the function in such a way that it checks whether the preconditions are satisfied and does the best it can if they are not.

18. a. Write the definition of an overload for >> that gets an integer, a character (the '/', one hopes), and another integer and uses them to construct a fraction.
    b. Write an overload for << that displays a fraction in the form "*numerator / denominator.*"

19. What would happen in *Directory::Remove* if we had shifted the array elements down starting at the top of the array, using this loop?

```
for (int j = currentSize; j > thisEntry; j--)
    entryList[j - 1] = entryList[j];
```

20. Suppose we rewrote *Directory::Insert* in the following way:

```
void Directory::Insert()
{
    if (currentSize == maxSize)
        Grow();

    Entry newEntry;
    cin >> newEntry;
    if (currentSize == 0)
        entryList[0] = newEntry;
    else
```

```
        {
            int i = 0;
            while ((strcmp(entryList[i].GetName(),
                        newEntry.GetName()) < 0)
                    && (i < currentSize))
                i++;
            for (int j = currentSize -1; j >= i; j --)
            entryList[j + 1] = entryList[j];
            entryList[i] = newEntry;
        }
        currentSize++;
}
```

What does this new version of *Insert* do now? What, if any, advantage do
we gain with this new version?

7

PROCESS I: ORGANIZING AND CONTROLLING CLASSES

It is easier to see the picture when you are outside the frame.

See Chapter 9 for more about the process of programming.

This chapter is quite different from those that have preceded it in this second section of the text. Whereas the previous chapters are dedicated primarily to introducing and illustrating the C++ language, in this chapter we will see almost nothing new about C++. We will concentrate instead on using effectively those features of C++ that we have already seen. We have repeatedly described the combination of C++, object-oriented programming, and the Declare-Define-Use approach as a powerful problem-solving tool. We believe this so strongly that we think our three-pronged tool and the process it embodies merit a separate chapter of their own, in which we can provide you with more specific advice on how to use C++ to represent and solve problems. In short, this is a chapter about the process of programming.

Our intent is that this chapter will allow you to catch your breath and to gain some additional experience with C++ before we begin to describe, in the next chapter, some of the language's more advanced features. We will walk you through the development of a complete sample program, pointing out along the way how many of the programming techniques and language features we have discussed earlier come into play in solving a nontrivial problem. Doing so allows us to shift temporarily our focus from the C++ language per se to what computer scientists refer to as the "software life cycle." That is, we will illustrate by example the processes whereby a program is specified, designed, implemented, tested, and revised, and identify for you those attributes of a program that facilitate these processes.

OBJECTIVES

In this chapter, we will

▶ Provide a brief history of software engineering and introduce the notion of a software life cycle.

▶ Explain how our use of C++ and the Declare-Define-Use approach support all life-cycle activities.

▶ Show how programs can be organized using files to support the process of program linking.

▶ Describe an interesting problem, the simulation of an elevator, and show how it can be modeled and implemented in C++.

▶ Review many of the C++ language features that were introduced in earlier chapters.

▶ Discuss how our solution to the elevator problem—and how well-written programs in general—lend themselves readily to maintenance and extension.

7.1 SOFTWARE ENGINEERING

Since this chapter is devoted to describing more formally the process we have advocated throughout the text for developing C++ programs, it makes sense to begin by recounting the relatively brief history of such studies. In the early days of modern computing, the primary expense for any computing installation was the computer itself. The first commercial machines were large and unreliable and cost millions of dollars in today's money. The expenses associated with these machines had mostly to do with purchasing them, building climate-controlled rooms to house them, and repairing them. The costs associated with actually using the machines, including writing programs for them, were insignificant by comparison.

By the mid-1960s, however, the amount of money spent in the United States on software surpassed for the first time the amount spent on hardware. As hardware costs continuously decreased and software costs, particularly those associated with repairing and maintaining existing programs, escalated dramatically, people from both inside and outside the computing professions began to recognize a growing crisis in the business of producing software. Indeed, by the end of the decade numerous books and articles appeared that recounted horror stories of failed software projects, missed deadlines, and incorrect, unfixable, and unmaintainable programs—all of which translated into lost investments. The software business was under fire, and Edsger Dijkstra was convinced that he knew where to lay the blame.

In what was to become an influential series of papers, Dijkstra argued persuasively that programming should be recognized as a "human activity." His premise was that in writing programs we should take into account rather than ignore our conceptual and memory limitations and that we should organize our programs in ways that help us manage and understand them better. This approach to programming was motivated by his practical experience, which indicated that certain programming practices of the day hindered our ability to write and understand programs because they served to obscure the logical organization of a program.

In hindsight, Dijkstra was among the first to recognize what we said at the outset of this text: Programs are written for people as well as for computers. He effectively shifted our collective focus from merely getting programs to run to writing programs that could be understood and managed by people (and as a result made to run). In so doing, he encouraged the software community to reconsider how the processes, methods, and languages being used to produce programs affected the quality of the programs being produced.

We can see in Dijkstra's early work the first seeds of what is now a thriving subfield of computer science: software engineering. As the name implies, the subfield is devoted to the task of making software development more like an engineering discipline and less like the practice of voodoo. Software engineers have devoted a great deal of energy to developing, experimenting with, and refining programming techniques and tools that are intended to make both the process of producing software and the resulting programs more formal, controllable, and predictable. For example, software engineers have developed methods for specifying program requirements and notations for expressing them. They have described program design techniques, notations, and criteria by which designs can be evaluated.

Modern programming languages and environments (like your implementation of C++) represent the state of the art in software engineering research. Automated tools for recording and tracking system requirements and for performing systems analysis are commonplace in industry and the business world. Formal measures of program quality—"software metrics"—have been proposed and evaluated. A variety of management and cost estimation techniques have been either borrowed from other disciplines (including psychology, engineering, and economics) or developed originally to help in the process of coordinating the activities of increasingly large teams of programmers. Even the processes of program testing and review have been subject to formal analysis and description. All in all, software engineering attempts to provide us with an understanding of programs and the programming process and with tools that reflect this understanding.

7.2   THE TRADITIONAL SOFTWARE LIFE CYCLE

Among the best-known byproducts of software engineering research, and certainly the most relevant to our focus in this chapter, are the "life cycle" models that have been defined to describe the activities involved in writing a program. A software life cycle attempts to identify and specify carefully each phase of the programming process and to make explicit the relationships between the phases. A number of such models exist, and most recognize the five phases depicted in Figure 7.1 as central to the programming process.

These phases may sound somewhat intimidating, but they are little different from those described at the end of a typical English handbook for writers. In the course of your schooling, you've often been advised that to write a paper you must define your topic carefully, prepare an outline, write a first draft, read your draft, and revise what you write. You may even have been told that "writing is rewriting" and that you should be prepared to repeat the entire process as often as necessary. The phases of the software life cycle codify this common-sense approach and apply it to the task of writing programs. Let's look briefly at each phase individually in the context of programming.

Specification

Specifying a program means that you articulate fully what your program is expected to do. You ask yourself questions like these: What information will the program require as input? What will be the format of the input? What output should the program produce, and in what format? What should the program look like to the user? Unless you have complete answers to these kinds of questions, it is pointless to continue, as you'll be working without a clear goal in mind.

FIGURE 7.1
The standard software life cycle

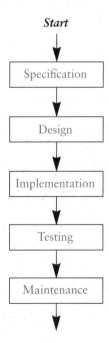

At this stage in your programming career, this phase is usually performed for you by your instructor. A well-conceived programming assignment will specify a program thoroughly, and if it doesn't, you have the responsibility to ask for either a clarification or additional information. In the real world, you might be asked not only to write a program to perform an ill-defined task, but to do so for users who have no computing experience and thus have some difficulty expressing their requirements for the program. In such cases this phase can be laborious, frustrating, and protracted. Indeed, as potential users of the program see it evolve, their expectations of it—and, quite possibly, of you— may change. Ideally, the result of this stage should be a document detailing all decisions made about the program's requirements, which can serve as a reference point for all subsequent phases.

Design

With a detailed specification in hand, you can proceed to designing your program. You can think of this as the "outlining" phase, in which you identify the major components of your program and describe the relationships between them. Historically (or, at least, prior to the advent of the object-oriented paradigm), components of a program took the form of steps in an algorithm. That is, a program was described in terms of its functional components. High-level design might identify a main program and the subprograms it must call to perform the basic processing tasks required of a program. It also might specify the order in which subprograms are to be called and the input and output requirements of each subprogram. At a more detailed level, a design also could provide a step-by-step description of the processing to be accomplished by each major subprogram.

As you have seen, when expressing a design in object-oriented terms, the components of a program tend to correspond to the agents (or objects) in the program domain. We describe a problem in terms of the things (as opposed to the activities) from the program specification, and we associate processing activities with the agents that perform them.

In either case, the design phase is intended to decompose the problem that your program addresses into smaller, less complex subproblems and to impose an organization on those subproblems. In so doing, the focus remains on what your program is intended to accomplish, not on how it is to accomplish anything. You will find yourself addressing questions like these: What are the principal components of the program? Which components communicate with each other? What information must be available to each component? How can these components best be organized to accomplish the goals of the program?

Implementation

Having identified and described the components of your solution, you can at last proceed to what most people think of when they hear the term "programming." If your specification and design are consistent with one another, and if you have described the components of your problem clearly and in enough detail, this coding phase amounts to a more or less straightforward translation of your low-level design into a particular programming language. These are some big "ifs," however. In practice, attempting to express your solution in a programming language often reveals complications that were unanticipated in either the specification or the design phases and may dictate the need for some backtracking.

Your task in this phase is not merely to translate your design into code, but to do so with style. You will want to make effective and efficient use of the chosen programming language. You will want the resulting code to be readable and logically clear and to reflect as directly as possible your understanding of the problem. Finally, you should document your code, primarily at this stage with internal comments, so that the connections between your program specification, your design decisions, and your program are made explicit.

Testing

Another advantage of writing clear and well-documented code is that doing so will facilitate the activities involved in testing (or "debugging") your program. Testing encompasses a great deal more than simply running your program on a variety of inputs and verifying that the outputs are what you expect. You should, of course, subject your program to extensive self-testing, and you should do your best to choose input conditions that will exercise all aspects of your program. Detecting errors, however, can be tough (often errors don't turn up until a program has been used for some time), and this is part of your job in this phase. In this age of "user-friendly" programs, you probably will want to let others who are not familiar with the program (or even programming) run the program. The odds are good that a potential user of the program will run the program—and thus test it—differently than will its author.

Once errors are detected, they must be fixed, and this may have repercussions to any and all previous life-cycle phases. Sometimes, an error can be the result of a misuse or misunderstanding of the programming language. In other cases, errors may result from unclear specifications or less than optimal choices made during design. In all cases, the more readable and better documented your program is, the easier it will be for you or someone else to isolate the source of an error and eliminate it.

Maintenance

As with the specification phase, maintenance entails a collection of activities that often are ignored in classroom assignments. For example, it is not often that an instructor changes an assigned program's specification after you have begun work on it and asks you to revise your program accordingly. Nor is it likely that your instructor would ask you to take one of your working programs and implement it again for a different programming language or on a different computer. In the real world, many programmers spend most of their time responding to precisely these types of requests. Again, the better documented your program is, and the more clearly linked it is with the original specification and design, the easier it will be to adapt your program to such changes.

As we have hinted, these phases of the software life cycle are often more of an ideal than they are a reflection of the real programming process. In fact, the phases are related in a variety of ways to the extent that work done in one phase will regularly influence, or even dictate, work done in another phase. A request made to maintain or extend a program after it has been written can necessitate a complete redesign. Errors detected during testing can point to ambiguities in a program's specification. Difficulties encountered in the implementation phase may reflect incorrect assumptions made during low-level design. Clearly, the term "programming" encompasses a wide range of related problem-solving activities, and any particular interpretation of the software life cycle must address them all.

7.3   THE DECLARE-DEFINE-USE APPROACH, REVISITED

The Declare-Define-Use approach and C++ constitute a software development methodology.

The coupling of our Declare-Define-Use approach to program development with the programming language C++ is but one interpretation of the software life cycle. We regard it as a particularly useful interpretation for many reasons. First, it addresses most of the programming activities just described in a consistent, holistic manner. Further, it does so with a minimum of notational overhead. That is, we use C++ as both a programming language and as a design medium, thus eliminating the need for additional confounding specification or design "languages."

Finally, because we perform many design, implementation, testing, and maintenance activities all in the context of C++, the connections between the life-cycle phases are clearer than they are in many other methodologies. We can, for example, see our design decisions as they manifest themselves in our implementation. We can test parts of our implementation individually and isolate errors with relative ease. We can even extend programs without having to start over from scratch.

By now you are probably familiar with the basic notions of the Declare-Define-Use approach (which, from this point on, we'll abbreviate as "DDU"). We'll provide you with another concrete and full-blown example of DDU in action later in this chapter. For now, let's review it in light of our description of the software life cycle. In the process, we'll describe how and where each programming activity fits into our approach. We'll also do our best to offer more specific advice on how to use DDU with C++ to their—and your—best advantage.

Before doing so, we should make clear our assumptions and expectations of DDU. First, it is not intended to address directly the activities that are normally associated with program specification. As we mentioned earlier, a carefully articulated program specification is essential to the success of any realworld project. It helps clients identify and record their presumptions and demands for a program and allows the record to serve as a baseline for all subsequent program development activities. Still, the processes whereby a problem is identified and the requirements for a program are made explicit are somewhat independent from and prerequisite to more directed program development. Indeed, an extensive collection of separate languages and automated tools have been developed for the expressed purpose of supporting system analysis and specification activities. In our academic setting, however, we have the luxury (albeit temporary) of assuming that these activities have been performed with rigor before we begin designing and implementing our program.

The second significant assumption that underlies DDU as a programming methodology is that it is linked inexorably with C++. Many other schemes for developing programs claim to be language independent; that is, they are described as working well with any programming language. Our experience indicates that such claims, while well intentioned, are misleading. The fact is that most program development techniques presume, at the very least, that a certain type of programming language (for example, procedural, functional, or object oriented) will be used and that certain features will be available to a programmer. We not only want to make our language assumptions explicit, but we also want to take full advantage of the features of C++ that support effective program development (the ability to distinguish header files from implementation files, the availability of program libraries, and the language features that support classes).

Figure 7.2 depicts the DDU methodology as we have implicitly described it in earlier chapters. It is considerably different from the standard life-cycle model. Perhaps the biggest difference is that the DDU is more of an iterative model than a linear one (note the arrows returning to the top of the diagram). The standard model presumes a linear ordering to its phases (allowing, in theory, for some modest backtracking). According to the standard model, a program is designed before it is implemented and implemented before it is tested. While this is all still true for the DDU approach, it is true on a small, rather than large, organizational level. The DDU approach could more accurately be characterized as "design, implement, test, maintain; design, implement, test, maintain; . . ." in which each repetition of the cycle applies to a distinct class in the problem domain.

Another significant difference between the DDU approach and a linear life cycle is that the DDU provides numerous and explicit opportunities for revising previously written code, as indicated by the upward-pointing arrows. The activity of integrating new code with that which is already completed is a fundamental part of the DDU life cycle. As classes are individually declared, defined, and tested, they are integrated and retested in the context of other classes. These more global tests may indicate a need to revise the new class being tested, or they may dictate that an earlier design or implementation choice

FIGURE 7.2
The DDU life-cycle
model

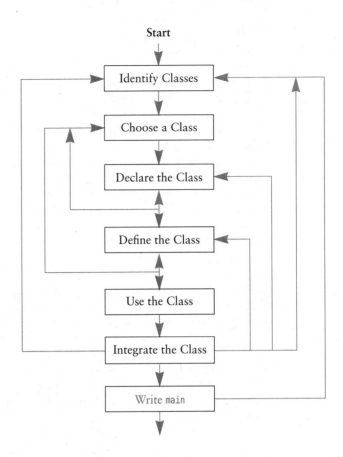

for another class be reconsidered. We'll see examples of this type of change in the chapter's PIP.

A third, and more subtle, distinctive feature of the DDU model is its lack of attention to an overall main program. Unlike many other methodologies, we do not begin the development process by considering what the entire program is to do or how it is to operate. On the contrary, the ultimate main function—the one that will instigate and control the processing of all classes—is the last function to be written. Indeed, the expectation is that by the time you write the final main function (there will be other main functions written along the way serving as "drivers" to test class definitions) you will have successfully tested and debugged all parts of the program, and the main function will merely be exercising pretested code.

Finally, look at Figure 7.3, in which we overlay the standard life-cycle activities on our DDU model. Most interesting to us are the relative sizes of the boxes devoted to design (high- and low-level) and to testing. Indeed, if you apply the DDU approach rigorously, you will find, as we have, that most of your time is spent working on your program's design and on testing the code written

FIGURE 7.3
Comparing the standard and DDU life cycles

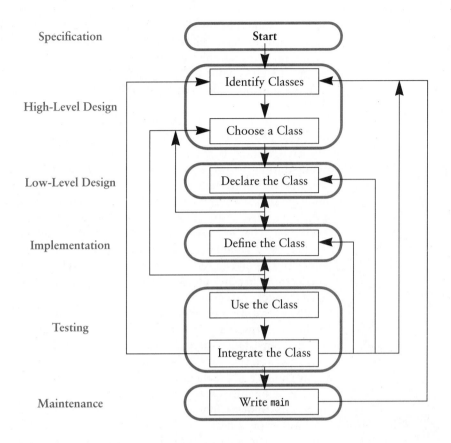

to support the design. The writing of the code itself (the implementation phase) can be one of the easiest and least time consuming steps in the development process. This feature, to be sure, is as much a testimony to object-oriented programming and to C++ as it is to our DDU approach.

Having noted our assumptions and the general features of the DDU life-cycle model, we can now reexamine the steps in the model individually, starting with the first. The process of identifying the classes to be used in describing a problem from a problem specification is the key step in any object-oriented design technique. Clearly, all subsequent life-cycle activities depend on which classes are chosen at this high-level design stage.

We have described informally our technique for identifying classes in our explanations of all of the previous PIPs. We can't offer too much more explicit guidance other than to remind you of two of our basic rules of thumb for identifying classes: (1) Most nouns (in particular, those that serve as the subjects of sentences) from the program specification can be implemented as classes, and (2) when in doubt, and when applicable, refer to reality. That is, think of what your program is intended to model or control (for example, a digital watch, a soda machine, a card game, or an elevator), and choose classes that reflect your understanding of that reality at a level that is appropriate for your program. For example, it's probably overkill to describe a soda machine in terms of a class named *SubAtomicParticles*. For the sake of our program, dispensers, buttons, and coin returns describe the reality at a much more useful level.

One additional note about the identification of classes is in order before we describe how to implement them. As we mentioned, the iterative nature of the DDU model is meant to encourage continual reevaluation of decisions made during the process of developing a program. Note the arrows in Figure 7.2 that return to the step in which we identify our classes. They are there to indicate that if you proceed with the development process and recognize that you have missed an obvious class, or you have just realized how useful it would be to define a new class, you can do so at any point. Conversely, if what looked like a valuable class turns out to be so trivial as to be subsumed by another class, you can redesign your classes to reflect this. The point here is that no decision, in particular your choice of classes, is irrevocable according to the DDU model.

The reason we decided to isolate the process of choosing a class to implement as a separate step is that it makes explicit an important feature of the DDU model. DDU dictates that you work on declaring, defining, and using one class at a time, and so you must choose one class to focus your efforts on. Your choice may be dictated by the impression that one class will be particularly easy or difficult to write. Perhaps you will recognize one class as being necessary to describing another. For example, one class may be a component of another (as a deck is composed of cards), or one class may need to refer to another (as a soda machine refers to its selection buttons). No matter what criteria you base your class choice on, it is subject to revision according to the DDU model. That is, if you get to the point of declaring or defining a class and realize that you would be better off implementing another class first, the model (as indicated by the upward arrows that return to the "Choose a class" step) allows you to reconsider your choice of class and to proceed without losing any of your work.

The next three steps, in which you declare, define, and use a class, are the heart of the DDU model. Whereas the identification of classes constitutes what is generically referred to as high-level design (the identification of a program's components), the "Declare the class" step accomplishes the low-level design of a particular component (see Figure 7.3). Even at this low level , we are still free to think primarily in terms of what data and processing a class is to embody and do not have to worry about how the processing is to be achieved.

One of the beauties of C++, as we have repeatedly pointed out, is that it supports this level of design description by allowing us to write separate header files. In writing a header file to describe a class, we specify in full detail the member data and member functions of the class, but need not commit ourselves to how the functions will be implemented. In most implementations of C++ we can even compile the header file separately to verify that our class declaration is in the proper format and is consistent with the declarations of other related classes.

> To declare a class, you write its header file.

The class definition phase ("Define the class") comprises much of what is traditionally described as implementation (see Figure 7.3 again), which is why we refer to ".CPP" files as "implementation files." Defining a class serves both to provide the algorithmic meat that implements the design specified in the corresponding header file and to verify the design. Notice that the arrow connecting the Declare and Define steps in the DDU life cycle is double headed. This is meant to indicate that there can be considerable interaction between these steps. It often happens, for example, that as you attempt to implement a particular header file you run into some problems. It may be that a certain function proves very difficult to define, or you may realize that a function needs to access some private data from another class. Many of us tend to interpret such difficulties as shortcomings in our programming abilities or as indications of our lack of understanding of the problem at hand. The fact is that they are almost always indications that something is wrong with your design. These types of problems often can be eliminated by rearranging your header files rather than by hacking at your implementation code.

> To define a class, you write its implementation file.

> Difficulties in defining a member function often indicate problems with the declaration of the related classes.

Remember, too, that in most versions of C++ implementation files are like header files in that they can be separately compiled. This ensures that your code is grammatically sound from a C++ standpoint and is consistent linguistically with any other included files.

Another reason we are not shy about linking the DDU approach explicitly with C++ is that C++ allows one to test classes individually. This "local testing" is what we expect to be accomplished in the "Use the class" phase. At this point in the life cycle, you have declared and defined a class. You may be confident that your class description is compilable, but as yet you have no real indication that it "works"—that is, that it behaves as you intend it to. Before running off and concentrating on describing another class, it is always worth the effort to test each class in isolation so that you will trust it when you use it in the larger context of your program. To do this, we resort to writing a main function that exercises as fully as possible your class definition. We have referred to such main functions as "driver programs" because they test-drive (or exercise) a particular class in your program.

> To use a class, you write a driver program that tests the class as completely as is possible. The time you spend testing classes individually will more than pay for itself when it comes to testing your complete program.

Although driver programs are, almost by definition, extraneous to your ultimate main program, they can be written to test explicitly all parts of a class definition. A well-written driver program will invoke as many of the class's member functions as possible and will indicate clearly the result of each function call. In fact, it is often worth writing a few additional functions to be used solely by the driver program to display in a readable and unambiguous form the values of member data as they are manipulated by member functions. These additional functions are usually simple to write, and will help the testing process considerably. Remember, the goal of this phase is to gain confidence in code that you have already written. Any effort you invest in writing a good driver program will result in increased confidence. We'll show you an example of a driver program in our discussion of this chapter's PIP.

The practice of writing driver programs is so useful to program development, and so often overlooked, that the DDU model gives you multiple explicit opportunities to practice. The DDU step labeled "Integrate the class" is meant to describe what might be called "global testing," and this, too, is accomplished by means of a driver program. That is, to integrate a newly defined class one writes a driver program that tests it in the context of all those classes that were previously developed and tested. Clearly, this step is most crucial in cases where classes are related in interesting ways (like those in our PIP describing an elevator and its riders). In such cases, a driver program can make use of both classes as they will most likely be used in the ultimate main function and can help you specifically test that interaction. Even in cases where there is little interdependence between classes and this step seems straightforward, it is usually worth performing just to make sure that there are no unforeseen conflicts between classes.

> To integrate a class you write a driver program that exercises the class in the context of other classes that refer to it.

The programming activities normally associated with program maintenance are embodied, to the extent that they can be in the DDU model, in the final step. As we said before, the more rigorously one adheres to the DDU life cycle, the easier it is to write a main function—the global driver program—that activates an integrated, tested, and useful collection of classes. Still, no `main` function is ever "final." As users gain experience with a program, they can decide that a desired feature has been left out, or that they would like the program to perform some additional operations. These changes will be noticed first in the context of a `main` function and will, most often, have repercussions to all previous life-cycle activities. That is why Figure 7.3 contains an arrow from its "Write `main`" step back to the start of the program development process.

Finally, notice that even within this seemingly prescriptive methodology there is considerable room for variation. In fact, because of the constant testing of new code and the regular integrating of new code with previously written code, each program ultimately will evolve according to a different path through the DDU life cycle. The DDU not only allows for this variability, it encourages it in the name of good software engineering practice.

7.4 FILES, LINKAGE, AND THE DDU

The DDU life-cycle model owes much of its ability to support good software engineering practice to the C++ language. For example, it is difficult to imagine developing a program according to this incremental (one class at a time) and iterative (repetitive and subject to continual revision) approach without the facilities that C++ provides for making use of predefined program libraries, for describing our own classes in separate files, and for distinguishing header files from implementation files. Indeed, the DDU model presumes these facilities and exploits them. We have done the same in the course of developing our PIPs. That's why we consider the DDU model and C++ to be so intimately related. As our programs become increasingly complex and are composed of larger numbers of files, it behooves us to take a quick look at how C++ makes everything fit together and work.

We touched earlier on the notion of program "linkage." Informally speaking, linking is the process whereby distinct object files are combined into a single working program. Fortunately for us, it is handled automatically by most implementations of C++. The toughest part of linking a program is not so much the physical gathering of distinct files into a single piece of code. Rather, it is in ensuring that the contents of the files that compose a program are consistent with one another. Consistency, in this sense, means that every identifier (name) used in the program has an unambiguous interpretation.

More formally, C++ maintains consistency between program files by associating with each identifier a linkage property that describes its accessibility to other files. That is, each identifier is recognized as having either internal linkage, external linkage, or no linkage. As the names imply, identifiers with *internal linkage* are accessible only from within the file in which they are declared. Such identifiers are considered completely independent from those used in any other program file. Identifiers with *external linkage*, on the other hand, are accessible to all files that make up a given program. Put another way, every instance of an identifier with external linkage is assumed to refer to the same object or function. Distinct instances of an identifier with internal linkage are assumed to represent the same object or function only with a single file. An identifier's linkage is different from its scope, which we also discussed earlier. The scope of an identifier describes its accessibility within a single file and is determined by the location of the identifier's declaration within the file. Linkage refers to accessibility across files and is specified as follows.

We can specify an identifier's linkage explicitly by declaring it as either static (internal) or extern (external). We will see examples of explicit linkage declarations later. More often, we rely on the default rules that C++ uses to determine an identifier's linkage. For example, in C++ it is assumed, unless specifically noted otherwise, that local variables, constant identifiers (those declared with const), type names other than those naming classes (like enumerated types, for example), and inline functions all have internal linkage. Similarly, C++ assumes that global variables, predefined functions, and class names have external linkage.* Formal typedefs and function parameters are considered to have no linkage.

These default linkages make it clear why our PIPs have worked as they have. We have used separate header files to declare our classes, which by default have external linkage and thus can be accessed from other files. Member function names clearly have external linkage, as evidenced by the fact that we regularly define them in separate implementation files and often invoke them from a main function, which is in yet another file. We have at different times declared global variables in header and in implementation files. In both cases, they have external linkage by default. Local variables and constants, on the other hand, have always been declared, defined, and used in a single file, since their linkage as determined by C++ is internal.

C++ enforces these linkage rules by imposing a restriction on identifiers with external linkage. It is possible to have multiple declarations for an identifier, but such declarations must conform to the standard of "type-safe linkage." That is, every declaration for a given external identifier must describe the same kind of entity and must ascribe to it the same type information. For example, if one declaration of an external identifier describes it as an integer variable, so must all declarations. Similarly, if an identifier with external linkage is declared as a void function, all other declarations of that identifier must declare it to be of the same basic form. When this restriction is violated, the linker cannot disambiguate the multiple declarations for the same identifier, and it reports an error.

Speaking of multiple declarations, there is one important and useful feature of C++ that relates directly to how the DDU approach deals with declarations that are spread across many files. The ability to build a program from preexisting code files is predicated on the include directive that is implemented by the

---

* There is one rather unlikely situation, which we are choosing to ignore for now, in which a class name would have internal linkage by default.

C++ preprocessor. Remember, the C++ preprocessor performs the automatic textual editing of your source code so that it can be presented to the compiler in a complete and cohesive form. As we begin to build our own collections of reusable classes, and as our programs grow in complexity, unrestricted use of the include directive can lead to a few practical problems.

For example, imagine (and this shouldn't be that hard to do—just look at this chapter's PIP) that you have defined two classes, both of which make use of one of the C++ libraries, say "iostream.h". The declarations of these classes would both, then, presumably begin with the preprocessor command *#include* *<iostream.h>*. At one level this is somewhat inefficient if you are to build a program using both of these classes. After all, how many copies of the *iostream* header file do you need to include in order for the compiler to make sense of your program? While multiple declarations of the items in "iostream.h" won't keep your program from compiling (all declarations will be type-safe because they are exact duplicates), they will certainly add unnecessarily to its size.

What would happen, however, if the header file that was included more than once in our program contained definitions of, say, global constants, as such files often do? In this case, our program would not merely be inefficient. It would not even link, thanks to C++'s intolerance for multiple definitions for the same identifier. Given that the *iostream* header file does indeed contain some definitions, it is surprising that any of our PIPs have linked.

They have, of course, and have done so as a result of another C++ preprocessor feature that allows us to check for and guard against multiple file inclusions. You can see this feature by examining the header file for any of the C++ libraries. Looking, for example, at the file "iostream.h", you will see that it begins with (some variation of) the following preprocessor directives

```
#ifndef _IOSTREAM_H
#define _IOSTREAM_H
```

and ends with the directive

```
#endif
```

These commands, which surround the body of the header file, accomplish what is referred to as "conditional compilation." That is, they guarantee that the declarations and definitions that they enclose will be included only once in a given program no matter how many times the header file is included in the files that comprise the program.

If you translate "ifndef" as "if not defined," you can imagine how the preprocessor reacts to these commands. In effect, it regards them much like C++ regards a simple if statement. When told to include file "iostream.h" into the program currently being compiled, the preprocessor is instructed by the #ifndef statement to look into the current program to see if an identifier has been defined with the name _IOSTREAM_H. If it hasn't ("if not defined"), it goes ahead and defines one (#define) and includes all of the declarations and definitions that follow it, up until the #endif command. If such an identifier already has been defined in the current program, which would likely be the result of file "iostream.h" already having been included in the program, the preprocessor ignores all of the statements up to the #endif command, thereby not including them again in the linked program.

In fact, every library C++ header file begins and ends with a similar combination of preprocessor commands that refer to a distinct identifier. One common practice is to construct an identifier from the name of the header file. Thus, the file "stdlib.h" might begin in your implementation, as it does in ours, with the statements:

```
#ifndef _STDLIB_H
#define _STDLIB_H
```

Fortunately for us, the use of these preprocessor directives is not restricted to the C++ code libraries. We can use them ourselves in the class header files that we create. In general, a header file named "MYCLASS.H" should begin with the directives:

```
#ifndef _MYCLASS_H
#define _MYCLASS_H
```

and should end with an #endif command. While sometimes unnecessary, it is a good idea to describe all header files as "conditionally compilable." Doing so renders your classes safe in the sense that they can then be included in any number of other classes and programs without fear of multiple inclusion. Even more important, doing so affords your classes with a level of security and ease of use consistent with those of the other C++ libraries. This is what we strive for when we define classes of our own. It's the object-oriented way.

7.5 PROGRAM IN PROGRESS: RIDING AN ELEVATOR

As we said earlier, this chapter's PIP is not intended to illustrate any new features of C++. While it certainly will serve as an excellent review of many of those parts of the language that we have discussed in previous PIPs, its primary purpose is to provide a vehicle for examining the program development process as we have described it in this chapter. We will walk you through the DDU life cycle as it applies to our PIP, which simulates an elevator and its riders. Along the way, we will point out the design issues we confronted, the design decisions we made, and the implications of these decisions to the resulting code and to the way it is organized. As promised, you will see the DDU approach in action. Equally important, you will see that there is no one "correct" design for this (or probably any) program. Many alternative designs—all justifiable from a software engineering perspective and all derivable from the DDU approach—can lead to effective, working, and workable programs.

Preliminaries: Program Specification

The problem we want our PIP to address is that of simulating an automatic elevator (that is, one in which there is no human operator). Just as with real elevators, riders may call for the elevator from and exit to any floor in the building that contains it. The elevator should remain idle until a request is made for service, and should then continue to operate until all requests have been satisfied. For the sake of simplicity, we will assume that all passengers behave in an expected manner. That is, when passengers request service from a particular floor, they are expected to board the elevator as soon as it stops at that floor (so in this model there is no changing your mind and taking the stairs). Also, on entering the elevator each passenger will request to be taken to a single floor and will leave the elevator as soon as it reaches that floor. Finally, there is no maximum capacity for our elevator. Any number of passengers may ride at one time.

Our program interface requirements are quite modest. To test the program some number of riders will be created and placed at random floors in the building. Floor numbers will be entered from the keyboard to simulate the pushing of the elevator's floor buttons. Regarding output, we would like to be kept aware of the elevator's and its passengers' actions (including indicating which floor the elevator is on, in which direction it is heading, when riders enter the elevator, and when riders depart). Within these constraints, we want our simulated elevator to act as much like a real one as possible.

STEP 1: IDENTIFY CLASSES In describing the DDU methodology we mentioned that there are in general two places to begin your search for classes when presented with a problem like this one. The first is the problem specification and the second is reality (or your understanding of it as it pertains to what your program is to model). Both serve us well in this example. The two nouns that occur most frequently in the program specification, and as the subjects and objects of its sentences, are "elevator" and "rider." The idea of creating classes to describe each of these entities is confirmed by our real-life experience with elevators. The elevator itself is clearly an object with its own properties and actions. Similarly, the agents who interact with the elevator most directly are those humans who intend to ride it.

We could describe some classes that are more detailed than "elevator"— say, buttons, cables, lights, floor, or door. We could equally well describe classes that are more general than "rider," such as human. Neither approach does us much good given the scope of our program. If we were in the elevator building business, we might be concerned with simulating in detail the inner workings of one or more of the elevator's mechanisms. We, on the other hand, are most interested in the general behavior of the elevator as it pertains to its riders. Riders of elevators do not normally worry about how the elevator's cables work or how its doors open (beyond, of course, expecting that they work as they should). Similarly, although there is a much wider range of behaviors that we could model in elevator riders (how they walk, eat, or read the lettering on the elevator's buttons, for example), these behaviors are far beyond the scope of what our program is intended to model. We are concerned with our riders only to the extent that they interact with our simulated elevator.

STEP 2: CHOOSE A CLASS Since our design requires only two classes, *Elevator* and *Rider,* our choice of which class to implement first is reasonably narrow. It is also, in this case, quite straightforward. As we just said, the reason we have informally named a class "Rider," as opposed to, say, "Human," is that we are interested in a person's behavior only as it relates to elevators. Think about what elevator riders do. They get on elevators. They get off elevators. They push an elevator's buttons. All of a rider's behavior that we want to model is described in terms of an elevator. In short, whereas an elevator can exist, can be described, and can even be tested without riders, it is tough to describe a rider without reference to an elevator. This indicates to us that it might help to define the *Elevator* class first. We'll see later that the DDU approach and C++ would allow program development to proceed directly no matter in which order we choose to implement our classes.

STEP 3: DECLARE THE CLASS *ELEVATOR* Having described our problem to the extent that we have identified and described in general terms two classes, it is now time to turn our attention to the low-level, more detailed description of each class. Our ultimate goal for this step is a header file describing an elevator as a C++ class. Thus, we should be thinking of describing an elevator in terms of its data and functions. We usually start by describing a class's data, since the member functions often refer to it.

As was the case with the high-level decisions we made in recognizing *Elevator* and *Rider* as classes, our guiding lights in low-level design are our evolving program specification and reality. Both sources confirm what we have illustrated in Figure 7.4. An elevator's member data include (1) a collection of on/off buttons, one for each floor of the building, (2) an indicator of the floor the elevator is currently on, and (3) an indicator of the direction the elevator is heading.

Some of the member functions of the Elevator class are equally obvious when we think of an elevator's actions. An elevator clearly must be able to move from floor to floor, hence the function *MoveToNextFloor.* As part of this process the elevator must somehow "decide" which move to make among the alternatives at any given time. This decision process will be implemented by the function *ChooseMove.* In choosing a move, an elevator takes into account whether any of its floor buttons are on, as these indicate riders' service requests. So, we have included in the class description a function, *ButtonsPushed,* that will check the elevator's buttons and return a value that indicates whether any are on.

Our interface requirements (and good programming practice) indicate a need for two additional functions. We said in our program specification that our program should keep its user informed about the activities and location of the elevator. Thus, we have included in our class description a function, *Dis-*

FIGURE 7.4

The class *Elevator*

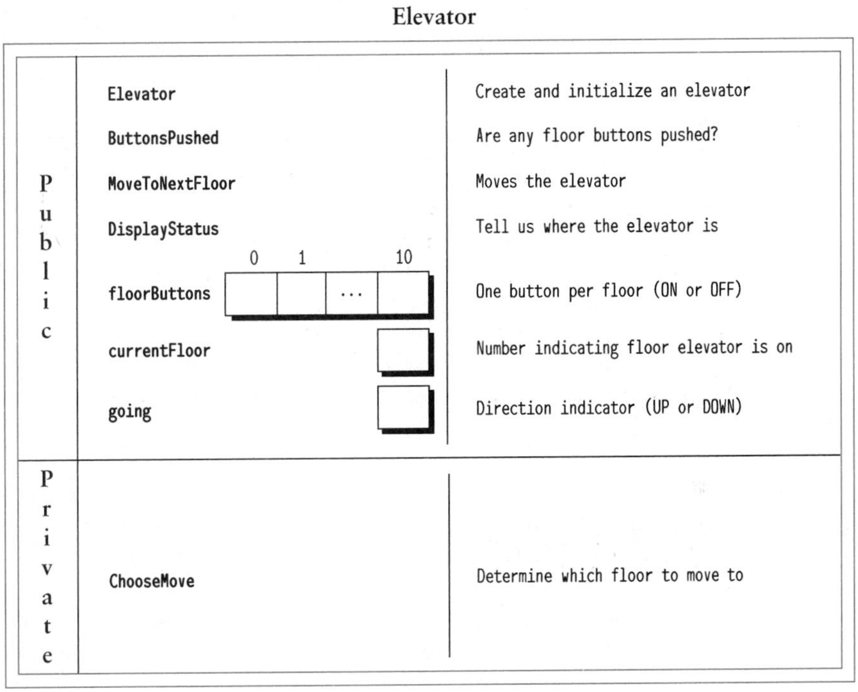

Elevator

playStatus, for that purpose. Even had our specification not called for it, it is a good idea from a software engineering perspective to include such a function in most classes, as it can be used effectively to monitor, test, and debug your code as you develop it. Similarly, we include a class constructor for *Elevator* even though we may not be sure at this juncture of its specific role.

One issue we have glossed over to this point is how we decided which of *Elevator*'s members should be public and which should be private. These are critical decisions (which, of course, can be reconsidered later) in that they will certainly affect how we implement the *Elevator* class and others that refer to it. They are also pretty straightforward ones if, again, we think about our class in realistic terms.

When you board an elevator, what information is available to you? Can you, for example, determine what floor the elevator is on? Can you tell which direction the elevator is heading? Can you see which of its floor buttons are on? The answer is yes in all cases, indicating that all of *Elevator*'s member data can be described as public. So too can function *ButtonsPushed* because as a rider of the elevator you can easily make such a determination.

The other public functions are described as such for more pragmatic reasons. In general, a class constructor, like function *Elevator,* must be declared as public so that *Elevator* objects can be declared and initialized from within other class implementations and other programs. Given that we will probably want to invoke function *DisplayStatus* from within the implementation of class *Rider* (say, when a rider gets on or gets off of the elevator) and will certainly invoke it at various other points in the program to interact with the user, we make it public as well. Function *MoveToNextFloor* could go either way, but our program specification gives us a clue that leads us to describe it as public, too. We described the elevator as continuing to move from floor to floor until all service requests have been satisfied. This sounds to us like our main program will contain a loop that will repeatedly invoke *MoveToNextFloor*—and indeed it will.

ChooseMove, on the other hand, is a good example of a member function that should be private to its class. Both reality and programming sense bear this out. While we, as riders of an elevator, expect the elevator to move from floor to floor, we have neither control nor direct knowledge of the algorithm it uses for choosing between floors. From a software engineering standpoint, no other class or program should have access to this function that embodies the elevator's control mechanism. Notice, too, that by making the function private to the class, we can easily change the floor-choosing algorithm without affecting any other class or program that uses class *Elevator*.

The C++ header file for class *Elevator* that appears here reflects almost directly our design-level description of the class. We have declared two enumerated types, *Direction* and *Button,* to improve the readability of both our class declaration and its eventual definitions. For example, we now can declare member data *going* as being of type *Direction* (DOWN or UP), and can describe the elevator's floor buttons as an array of type *Button* (OFF or ON). We also have included an integer constant to refer to the number of floors in the building.

```
// ----------ELEVATE1.H----------
// Declaration file for class Elevator

#ifndef ELEVATE1_H_
#define ELEVATE1_H_

const int FLOORSINBLDG = 10;    // predetermine the number of floors

enum Direction {DOWN,UP};       // possible directions for the elevator

enum Button {OFF,ON};           // each floor button can be on or off


class Elevator
{
public:
    Elevator();                 // builds a new elevator on ground floor
    int ButtonsPushed();        // are there any floor buttons ON?
    void MoveToNextFloor();                 // moves elevator
    Button floorButtons[FLOORSINBLDG+1];    // the floor buttons
    int currentFloor;                       // where elevator is now
```

```
        Direction going;            // which direction is it heading
        void DisplayStatus();       // tells us where elevator is

private:
        int ChooseMove();           // private function to determine which
                                    //   floor to move to next
};
#endif // ELEVATE1_H_
```

STEP 4: DEFINE THE CLASS *ELEVATOR*   The definition of class Elevator is more interesting from a design perspective than it is for its use of C++. The fact that the member function definitions that it includes are by and large quite simple is testimony to the reasonableness of our class design. As we mentioned earlier, extremely complex function definitions are most often a reflection of a less than optimal class declaration.

```
// ----------ELEVATE.CPP----------
// Definition file for class Elevator

#include <iostream.h>               // for cin, cout
#include "ELEVATE1.H"               // for Elevator declarations
#include "UTILITY.H"                // for WaitForUser

Elevator::Elevator()
// This function creates a new elevator, places it at the ground
// floor, directs it up, and turns all of its buttons off.
{
    currentFloor=1;
    going=UP;
    for (int i=0; i<FLOORSINBLDG+1; i++)   // for each button
            floorButtons[i]=OFF;           //   turn it off
}


int Elevator::ButtonsPushed()
// This function returns 1 if any of the elevator's floor
// buttons are still on.  Otherwise, it returns 0.
{
    for(int i=1; i<FLOORSINBLDG+1; i++)    // check all buttons
        if (floorButtons[i]==ON) return 1; // if any one is on, return true
    return 0;                              // else, return false
}


int Elevator::ChooseMove()
// This function determines which floor to move to, as follows. It
// tries to move to the closest floor that needs service, in the same
// direction as the elevator is currently headed.  If no floors need
```

```
// service in the same direction, it "turns around", and tries again.
{
    for(int t=1; t<=2; t++)              // loop twice to change direction
    {
        if (going==UP)                  // try moving up
        {   // check to see if any higher floors need service
                for (int i=currentFloor;i<FLOORSINBLDG+1; i++)
                if (floorButtons[i]==ON)  return i;
                going=DOWN;                // if nothing up, head down
                continue;                  // and try again
        }
        else                            // try moving down
        {   // check to see if any lower floors need service
                for (int i=currentFloor; i>0 ; i--)
                if (floorButtons[i]==ON)  return i;
                going=UP;                  // if nothing down, head up
                continue;                  // and try again
        }
    }
    return -1;                          // if no moves possible, return -1
}


void Elevator::MoveToNextFloor()
// This function moves the elevator to the closest floor requiring service
{
    int newFloor=ChooseMove();          // determine which floor to move to
    if (newFloor==-1)                   // if no moves needed
        cout << "Elevator stopped at floor " << currentFloor;
    else
    {                                   // if a move is possible
        currentFloor=newFloor;          // change to new floor
        floorButtons[currentFloor]=OFF;// turn that floor's light off
        DisplayStatus();
    }
}


void Elevator::DisplayStatus()
// This function displays the current status of the elevator on the screen
{
    cout << "\nElevator is currently stopped at floor " <<
                currentFloor << " heading ";
    if (going==UP)
        cout << "up\n";
    else
        cout << "down\n";
    WaitForUser();
}
```

The comments in each definition do a pretty good job of describing each function. Two features of this file warrant additional explanation. The first is our description and use of the *floorButtons* array. We have declared it to be an array of buttons of size *FLOORSINBLDG* + 1, thus creating eleven buttons (referenced as *floorButtons*[0], *floorButtons*[1], . . ., *floorButtons*[10]) for a building of ten floors. We did so to make our definitions reflect our understanding of the program a bit more directly. Basically, we felt more comfortable, and found it easier to write the function definitions, thinking about the first floor as *floorButton*[1] as opposed to *floorButton*[0]. The effect of this decision is that (particularly when the user of the program enters an integer from the keyboard to signify which floor button he or she wants to push) we don't have to subtract 1 from that value to have it match our array declaration. In short, declaring the elevator to have an extra floor button is a workaround of C++'s zero-subscripted arrays.

The most complex function definition by far is that of *ChooseMove*. In a nutshell, the algorithm finds the next floor requiring service (either a pickup or a drop-off) in the same direction the elevator is currently moving. It does so by checking the elevator's floor buttons. The outermost for loop is executed twice in case the elevator needs to change direction. The function uses return statements to return the floor number found and to kick out of both inner loops. If no buttons are ON in either direction, the function returns a value of –1 (not zero, because there is a *floorButton*[0]) to indicate this.

STEP 5: USE THE CLASS *ELEVATOR* At this point, according to our DDU life cycle, we should write a driver program to exercise and test our definition of class *Elevator*. Given that our overall mission is to see how the elevator works with riders, this driver program will most likely be thrown away when it comes time to write our final main program. Still, it will help us tremendously in writing the final program if we have confidence beforehand that class *Elevator* works as expected. Then, if problems arise, we can look elsewhere to track them down.

The question we now face is: How can we test class *Elevator* without any riders? The answer, again, lies equally in our understanding of the reality our program is attempting to model and in the code we have developed to describe it. In realistic terms we can think of ourselves as the elevator installers. Our job, then, is to "build" an elevator and to test it before any riders are allowed on it. Testing it in this case probably amounts to pushing some buttons and seeing if the elevator responds as it should. In programming terms, we can accomplish these activities by writing a driver program that invokes each of *Elevator*'s member functions in a variety of circumstances, as illustrated by the main program here.

```
// ---------- DRIVER1.CPP ----------
// A driver program to test class Elevator

#include <iostream.h>
#include "ELEVATE1.H"
```

```
void main()
{
    // "Build" a new elevator, and check it out
    Elevator e;
    e.DisplayStatus();

    // Turn some of its floor buttons on "manually"
    e.floorButtons[4] = ON;
    e.floorButtons[7] = ON;

    // See which floor it would choose, move there
    // and turn off that floor button
    e.MoveToNextFloor();

    // Turn another button ON to present elevator with a choice
    e.floorButtons[2] = ON;

    // Move to the next floor and turn off that floor button
    // Make sure it chose the "right" floor
    e.MoveToNextFloor();

    // Move to final floor and turn off that button
    e.MoveToNextFloor();

    cout << "\nWe made it!!!\n";
}
```

If you run this program (which relies, of course, on files "ELEVATE1.H" and "ELEVATE.CPP") in your C++ environment you would not only get a good feeling for how a program can make use of our *Elevator* class, but you also would gain some confidence that the class is implemented properly. In this simple, ten-line program we have invoked, either explicitly or implicitly, each of *Elevator*'s member functions (note that function *MoveToNextFloor* calls both *ChooseMove* and *DisplayStatus*) and have accessed and manipulated each of its member data. Note, too, that when confronted with the choice of moving to floor number 7 or to floor 2 (after stopping at floor 4), the elevator correctly moved to floor 7 (because it was already heading up), and later returned to the second floor. Finally, see how useful function *DisplayStatus* is at this stage of our program development. Because we declared it as a public member of class *Elevator* we can use it directly whenever we want to check on the state of an elevator (for example, after it was created).

STEP 6: DECLARE THE CLASS *RIDER*   Since at this point we have defined only one class (and there is nothing to integrate it with) and have identified only two classes (and therefore have no other choice), we can proceed directly to designing class *Rider*. We put off doing so originally because we thought *Rid-*

er would be dependent on class *Elevator,* and indeed it is. The good news, of course, is that we have already designed, implemented, and tested class *Elevator,* so we can refer to it in describing a rider as we see fit and with some confidence.

In describing a rider, as we do in Figure 7.5, two data items immediately come to mind: a floor from which the rider requests service (*startFloor*) and a floor to which the rider wants to be delivered (*destinationFloor*). One piece of rider information is less obvious, but equally important: the rider's status.

In our description of this PIP we consider a person a rider as soon as that person hails the elevator. At that point, as in the real world, the rider is not actually on-board the elevator, but is waiting for it. Such riders-in-waiting are as important to the elevator's behavior as are its on-board customers, since they represent as yet unfulfilled service requests. Indeed, riders remain important to the elevator until they have been served.

Notice, too, that from a rider's perspective the status of a rider affects directly how the riders will respond to the elevator. For example, if the riders are waiting for the elevator, they will (according to our program specification) get on the elevator when it arrives at their floor. Similarly, if they are currently on board the elevator, they will get off the elevator when it reaches their destination. Obviously, riders cannot get off an elevator if they are not on board, and cannot get on an elevator if they already are! We have included as a data member of class *Rider* an element meant to indicate a rider's status. We also added an identification number so that our program can refer to riders as they come and go from the elevator.

With regard to member functions for class *Rider,* we have implicitly described most of them already. Our simulated riders must be able to perform the

FIGURE 7.5
The class *Rider*

Rider	
P **Rider**	Create a new rider for an elevator
u **GetOn**	Getting on an elevator
b **GetOff**	Getting off an elevator
l **PushButton**	Push any of the elevator's buttons
i **SelectFloor**	Choose a floor once on elevator
c **Respond**	Decide whether to get on or off
P **s**	WAITING, ABOARD, or SERVED
r **startFloor**	Floor from which service requested
i **destinationFloor**	Rider's destination
v **number**	A rider id

basic operations that we normally associate with real elevator riders. That is, they must be able to push a button from a particular floor outside the elevator to hail it (which we describe in function *PushButton*), to get on the elevator when it stops to pick them up (function *GetOn*), to push one of the elevator's floor buttons from inside the elevator to select a destination floor (*SelectFloor*), and to leave the elevator when it stops at the destination (*GetOff*).

Two additional member functions will come in handy, as well. The first, as you might guess, is a class constructor for *Rider*, which will define, locate, and initialize a new rider. The need for the second, which we named *Respond*, is probably less obvious. Our problem specification, again, gives us a clue that such a function might be necessary. In it, we mentioned that we are writing the program on the assumption that riders get on and get off the elevator as expected; that is, as soon as the elevator arrives at the floor they have signaled it from or directed it to. Still, it is the rider, not the elevator, who recognizes that he or she should get on or get off the elevator at a given floor and responds accordingly. Nothing in our previous description of class *Elevator* alludes to this recognition and response, and rightfully so. It is every rider's responsibility to recognize, for example, that the elevator has reached his or her destination floor and to get off the elevator. Function *Respond* is meant to describe a rider's decision about what to do when the elevator arrives at each floor.

The decisions about whether class *Rider*'s members should be described as public or private are not quite as clear as they were for class *Elevator*. For example, is a rider's status public information in the sense that other classes in our program should have direct access to it? What about a rider's destination? Should another part of our program be able to cause a rider to get on or get off an elevator? Answers to such questions are subjective at best, so we'll take a safe (and quite standard) approach to describing *Rider*'s members.

Generally speaking, a good first crack is to make all member data items private and all member functions public. This approach has two immediate advantages. First, it tends to hide and therefore protect a class's data, leaving it accessible to the class's member functions (which are those that are most likely to use it anyway). Second, it makes using and testing the class easy since its public member functions can be invoked directly from a driver program. One final advantage of this approach is that it can be reconsidered later, as we shall see.

> When in doubt, declare member data as private and member functions as public. You can always revise your declarations later.

The step from high-level design description to C++ header file is also a bit more complicated in the case of class *Rider* than it was for class *Elevator*. The listing of file "RIDER.H" that follows shows simple descriptions of *Rider*'s data items (the relevant floor and ID numbers are all expressed as integers, and we created an enumerated type to represent a rider's status). The function headers, though, are not quite as straightforward. Each includes a non-empty parameter list, and each refers indirectly to an elevator (which explains why the file includes file "ELEVATE1.H").

These repeated references to elevators from within class *Rider* should not be surprising given our high-level descriptions of these classes. First, we said from the start that class *Rider* was likely to be dependent on class *Elevator* (remember, you can't be an elevator rider without an elevator). In addition, our descriptions of all of class *Rider*'s member functions refer to elevators. A rider gets on and gets off an elevator. A rider pushes an elevator's buttons to hail it, selects a floor by pushing another of its buttons, and responds to an elevator's opening its doors. Thus, each function is described as having a parameter of type pointer-to-*Elevator* to indicate which elevator the rider should act on. We use a pointer object for reasons of efficiency, as described in Chapter 6.

Function *PushButton* is described as having a second parameter of type int to indicate which floor the rider is on when hailing the elevator. The lone constructor function for class *Rider* also takes parameters in addition to an *Elevator* pointer. The first parameter (*num*) is used to set the ID number for a particular rider, and the third (*start*) is an integer indicating which floor the rider starts from.

```
//----------RIDER.H----------
// Declaration for an elevator rider.

#ifndef _RIDER_H
#define _RIDER_H

#include "ELEVATE1.H"                          // for class Elevator

enum Status {WAITING,ABOARD,SERVED};
// a rider is in one of these states

class Rider
{
public:
    Rider(int num, Elevator* e, int start = 1);
    // builds a new rider
    void GetOn(Elevator* e);                    // getting on
    void GetOff(Elevator* e);                   // getting off
    void PushButton(Elevator* e, int thisFloor);
    // to hail elevator
    void SelectFloor(Elevator* e);
    // to choose floor once on elevator
    void Respond(Elevator* e);                  // the user responds to where
                                                // the elevator is
```

```
private:
    Status s;                   // the rider's state
    int startFloor;             // the floor from which service was requested
    int destinationFloor;       // the rider's destination
    int number;                 // a rider number, for id purposes only
};
#endif // RIDER_H_
```

STEP 7: DEFINE THE CLASS _RIDER_   Perhaps the most interesting feature of the definition file for class _Rider,_ listed as "RIDER.CPP", is how the member functions interact and depend on one another. To create and initialize a rider (using constructor function _Rider_), we set the rider's status and starting floor number and allow the rider to respond (by calling function _Respond_) to the elevator. Responding to the elevator involves checking its current location and, based on the rider's status, either getting on (_GetOn_) or getting off (_GetOff_). After getting on an elevator the rider selects a floor (_SelectFloor_), which in turn involves pushing a button (_PushButton_). Notice, too, how the _PushButton_ function serves the dual purpose of hailing the elevator (when called from within _Rider_'s constructor) and selecting a destination floor once aboard the elevator (from within function _SelectFloor_).

When reading through "RIDER.CPP" one almost gets the impression that nothing is ever getting done by _Rider_'s member functions. They seem merely to be calling one another. In fact, these definitions describe the processing activities of a rider at a perfectly suitable level, given our original specification. After all, a rider doesn't really do much to an elevator beyond get on it, get off it, and push some buttons—but there's the rub. By pushing and turning on the elevator's buttons in the statement

```
e-> floorButtons[thisFloor] = ON
```

the rider implicitly directs the elevator to perform a particular function. The only real "thinking" a rider has to do (and this is reflected clearly in the code) is to decide how to respond when the elevator stops at a particular floor in function _Respond_.

```
//----------RIDER.CPP----------
// Definition file for an elevator rider.

#include <iostream.h>
#include "RIDER.H"

Rider::Rider(int num, Elevator* e, int start)
// Create a new rider for a particular elevator.
// The rider is placed at a floor, pushes the button on that floor
// to request service, is assigned an identifying number, and is
// given a chance to respond to where the elevator is.
{
    s = WAITING;
    startFloor = start;
```

```cpp
    number = num;
    PushButton(e, startFloor);
    cout << "\n\nPassenger " << number << " is waiting at floor "
            << startFloor << '\n';
    Respond(e);
}


void Rider::Respond(Elevator* e)
// This function embodies the rider's response to where the
// elevator is. It allows the rider to get on or get off the
// elevator, if the location of the elevator is relevant to the
// rider.
{
    if ((s == WAITING) && (e->currentFloor == startFloor))
    {   // if the rider is waiting, and the elevator arrives
        GetOn(e);
        return;
    }
    // if the rider is on the elevator, and arrives at destination
    if ((s == ABOARD) && (e->currentFloor == destinationFloor))
    {
        GetOff(e);
        return;
    }
}


void Rider::GetOn(Elevator* e)
// This function simulates the rider entering the elevator.
// The rider's status changes, and the rider "pushes" a floor
// button
{
    s = ABOARD;
    cout << "\nPassenger " << number
            << " enters elevator at floor "
            << e->currentFloor << '\n';
    SelectFloor(e);
}
void Rider::GetOff(Elevator* e)
// This function simulates the rider getting off the elevator.
{
    s = SERVED;
    cout     << "\nPassenger " << number
            << " leaves elevator at floor "
            << e->currentFloor << '\n';
}
```

```
void Rider::PushButton(Elevator* e, int thisFloor)
// Simulate a rider request for service, either by
// pushing a button on a floor or by pushing a button in the
// elevator.
{
    e->floorButtons[thisFloor] = ON;
}


void Rider::SelectFloor(Elevator* e)
// Simulate the rider pushing a floor button
// from inside of the elevator.
{
    cout << "\nTraveling to which floor (1-"
         << FLOORSINBLDG << ") ? ";
    cin >> destinationFloor;
    PushButton(e, destinationFloor);
}
```

STEP 8: USE AND INTEGRATE THE CLASS *RIDER*   We could write a
new driver program to test explicitly our definition of class *Rider*. We might,
for example, declare an elevator and then check to see if a rider can get on
and get off of it effectively. From a simulated rider's perspective, the net effect
of getting on an elevator is merely that one of the elevator's floor buttons gets
pushed and a message gets printed. As we described before, the only interesting behavior implemented by class *Rider* is in function *Respond,* wherein a
rider decides what if any action to take when the elevator stops at a floor. We
also saw that by invoking function *Respond* we start a chain of calls that can
include every one of *Rider*'s member functions. In short, it seems that the two
classes that comprise this program are so intimately related that one cannot
fully test the *Rider* class without setting an elevator in motion. As a result, we
have chosen to write a single main function that will at once use class *Rider*
and integrate it with class *Elevator.*

The following file containing our driver program is listed as "PIP7.CPP".
With not too much effort its main function can become our "final" main program. Thinking back to our program specification, we wanted to create some
number of riders and place them at various floors in a building. We accomplish
this by first declaring and initializing an elevator, which we need in order to declare any riders. We then make use of three standard C++ functions to produce
random integers. Functions *clock* and *srand* are used to initialize the random
number generator, and function *rand* is used here to produce random floor
numbers. We convert the integer returned by function *rand* into one that is in
the acceptable range of floor numbers by using the C++ modulo operator (%).

Once we have our riders (four in this case) created, placed within our
building, and having requested service, we set our elevator in motion. Accord-

ing to our original specification, the elevator is to continue operating until all service requests have been satisfied. The while loop wherein the bulk of the processing occurs reflects the fact that for our implementation of an elevator, all service requests manifest themselves as pushed buttons on the elevator console. The loop, described clearly in the code, simply moves the elevator to the next floor requiring service (as determined by the elevator) and gives each of our four riders an opportunity to respond to the elevator "opening its doors" at that floor. To verify that all service requests have been satisfied, we display each rider's status. If our program worked correctly, all riders will have been SERVED.

```cpp
// ---------- PIP7.CPP ----------
// Test program to exercise classes
// Elevator and Rider.

#include <iostream.h>          // for cin, cout
#include <stdlib.h>            // for rand, srand
#include <time.h>             // for clock
#include "RIDER.H"            // for class Rider
#include "UTILITY.H"          // for Terminate

void main()
{
    Elevator e1;                 // create a new elevator

    // initialize random number generator, so we can use it below
    int s = int(clock());
    srand(s);

    int aFloor;

    // create 4 randomly placed riders
    aFloor=((rand() % FLOORSINBLDG) + 1);
    Rider r1(1, &e1, aFloor);

    aFloor=((rand() % FLOORSINBLDG) + 1);
    Rider r2(2, &e1, aFloor);

    aFloor=((rand() % FLOORSINBLDG) + 1);
    Rider r3(3, &e1, aFloor);

    aFloor=((rand() % FLOORSINBLDG) + 1);
    Rider r4(4, &e1, aFloor);
```

```
    // process all requests for service from riders
    while (e1.ButtonsPushed())      // continue as long as buttons still on
    {
        e1.MoveToNextFloor();       // move to a floor requiring service
        r1.Respond(&e1);            // give each rider a chance to get
        r2.Respond(&e1);            //    on or off the elevator
        r3.Respond(&e1);
        r4.Respond(&e1);
    }

    // Make sure all requests have been satisfied
    cout << "\nRider 1 status: " << (int) r1.s;
    cout << "\nRider 2 status: " << (int) r2.s;
    cout << "\nRider 3 status: " << (int) r3.s;
    cout << "\nRider 4 status: " << (int) r4.s;

    cout << "\n\nElevator returned to ground floor having";
    cout << "\nprocessed all requests for service.";

    Terminate();
}
```

STEP 9: RECONSIDERING SOME DECISIONS If, as often reported, hindsight is really 20/20, why not use it to evaluate our working program and to see if the program can be improved in any way.? Remember, a programmer's goal isn't merely to produce a *working* program. It is as important to produce a *workable* program—one that lends itself readily to error detection, error elimination, modification, and extension. There are countless alternative designs and implementations of an elevator, some better than others. Even just considering our version, there are many improvements one could suggest that would result in a slightly more workable program. We'll describe briefly three such suggestions here, and leave you to accomplish a few others yourself in the lab exercises for this chapter.

One suggestion has to do with what might be considered the excessively public nature of class *Elevator*. Look back at *Elevator*'s header file and notice how nearly all of its members are public. Our original motivation for describing them as such was that our real-life experience with elevators dictated it. For example, the elevator's current floor, its direction, and its floor buttons represented publicly available information to a user of the elevator. Our implementation of class *Rider* bore this out. A rider needs access to this information in order to respond to the elevator's moves.

There are two good reasons for reconsidering this decision. The first has to do with the fact that although much of an elevator object's member data and functions must be accessible to its riders, it need not be accessible to any other classes that might be part of a program involving an elevator (say, a "building" class). In other words, only a rider of an elevator is privy to the elevator's information. Our program declares much of an elevator's information as publicly available to any object of any type.

This declaration not only fails to reflect clearly our understanding of the problem our program is intended to model, but is also dangerous from a programming perspective. In general, the more tightly we control which parts of a program have access to which information, the more workable the overall program is. Currently, any part of a large program of which class *Elevator* was a part can change an elevator's direction or floor number. If our elevator malfunctioned in some way while running in another program, we would have no idea where to begin our search for the programming problem. Indeed, the entire program (conceivably comprising many classes) would have to be examined. On the other hand, if we make explicit the relationship between classes *Elevator* and *Rider,* and take care to make private (or to "hide") as much of an elevator's member information as possible, such a problem would be much easier to track.

Fortunately for us, the C++ *friend* descriptor that we saw in earlier PIPs allows us to accomplish this by merely rearranging our header file as follows. By declaring class *Rider* as a friend to class *Elevator,* riders gain access to all of *Elevator*'s members, including the private ones. We can now describe most of *Elevator*'s members as private. We have left three functions as public ones because each is accessed from our main program, as per our program specification. If the *Elevator* and *Rider* classes were to be included in a more extensive main program, we could further encapsulate them (in, perhaps, a "Rider/ Elevator" class) and probably hide even those functions. Note, too, that we don't have to change a single line of class *Elevator*'s definition (in file "ELEVATE.CPP") to accommodate these changes in its header file and thus achieve this increased protection for our program.

```
// ----------ELEVATE.H----------
// Declaration file for class Elevator

#ifndef _ELEVATE_H
#define _ELEVATE_H

const int FLOORSINBLDG = 10;   // predetermine the number of floors

enum Direction {DOWN,UP};      // possible directions for the elevator
enum Button {OFF,ON};          // each floor button can be on or off

class Elevator
{   // Since nearly all of Rider's member functions
    // need access to the private data of Elevator
    // we make the entire Rider class a friend of Elevator

    friend class Rider;
```

```
public:
    Elevator();                    // builds a new elevator on ground floor
    int ButtonsPushed();           // are there any floor buttons ON?
    void MoveToNextFloor();        // moves elevator

private:
    int ChooseMove();              // Determine which floor to move to next
    Button floorButtons[FLOORSINBLDG + 1];
    // the collection of floor buttons
    int currentFloor;              // where elevator is now
    Direction going;               // which direction it is heading
    void DisplayStatus();          // tells us where elevator is
};
#endif
```

We can make a similar type of change to class *Rider* in the interest of program protection. Looking back at our original declaration of *Rider,* we left all
of its member functions as public on the grounds that doing so would produce
a class whose data were protected and whose functions were easy to test. Having completed our testing of the class, though, we now see that the only member information accessed from outside of *Rider*'s class definitions are its
constructor function (as usual), its *Respond* function, and its status. Rewriting
our declaration of class *Rider* as follows, wherein most of it member information is now described as private, yields, again, a better-protected implementation of the class at virtually no cost to us. Just as with class *Elevator,* we don't
have to change a single line of *Rider*'s definition file to accommodate this
change.

```
//----------RIDER.H----------
// Declaration for an elevator rider.

#ifndef _RIDER_H
#define _RIDER_H

#include "ELEVATE.H"                   // for class Elevator

enum Status {WAITING,ABOARD,SERVED};   // a rider is in one of these states

class Rider {

public:
    Rider(int num, Elevator* e, int start=1);   // builds a new rider
    void Respond(Elevator* e);                  // the user responds to where
                                                // the elevator is
    Status s;                                   // the rider's state
```

```
private:
    int startFloor;          // the floor from which service was requested
    int destinationFloor;    // the rider's destination
    int number;              // a rider number, for id purposes only
    void GetOn(Elevator* e);  // getting on the elevator
    void GetOff(Elevator* e); // getting off the elevator
    void PushButton(Elevator* e, int thisFloor);   // to hail elevator
    void SelectFloor(Elevator* e); // to choose floor once on elevator
};
#endif
```

The third and final suggestion we would make to produce a slightly better C++ program is the simple one of taking advantage of code that we have already written. At various points in our PIP we ask the user of the program to hit a key to continue processing. We have, you may recall, written a few simple functions to accomplish this type of processing and incorporated them into a file called "UTILITY." It wouldn't take much to have our PIP include file "UTILITY.H" and make use of its functions *WaitForUser* and *Terminate*. The result would be a PIP that not only is easier to read but also relies on previously tested and debugged C++ code that we have great confidence in. That, after all, is what software engineering is all about.

7.6 SUMMING UP

▶ Software engineers study all aspects of the process of program development.

▶ The activities involved in developing a program are collectively referred to as the "software life cycle."

▶ Our Declare-Define-Use (DDU) approach to program development is a software life cycle that is explicitly linked to the C++ programming language.

▶ The DDU model is an iterative one in which we design, implement, and test classes one at a time.

▶ The DDU model provides for regular and explicit opportunities to reconsider design decisions and to revise code.

▶ To declare a class in the DDU model, we write its header file.

▶ To define a class in the DDU model, we write its implementation file.

▶ To test and integrate a class in the DDU model, we write driver programs that thoroughly exercise the class.

▶ The DDU model relies directly on C++'s facilities for linking many files together to produce a working program.

▶ Type-safe linkage allows for an external name to be declared more than once, as long as all declarations describe the same type of object.

▶ We can avoid multiple definitions of a name in a program by using the C++ preprocessor. Surrounding a header file (for example, "MYCLASS.H") by

```
#ifndef _MYCLASS_H
#define _MYCLASS_H
{body of header file}
#endif
```

calls for conditional compilation, and protects against multiple definitions.

▶ Workable programs are programs that work and, further, lend themselves readily to testing, maintenance, modification, and extension.

▶ A final program is never done.

7.7 EXERCISES

1. Describe the historical trends that led to the development of software engineering.

2. Using our graphic description of the DDU approach (Figure 7.3), describe the steps that we followed in developing each of the PIPs for Chapters 1–6.

3. Why did we explicitly couple the DDU approach with the programming language C++? Was this necessary? Would other programming languages have worked as well?

4. What are the differences between a "working" and a "workable" program? How does the DDU approach support the development of the latter?

5. Read the following brief program specification. Produce a list of issues that you would want clarified before attempting to write such a program.

   Write a program that reads characters and displays the number of words entered.

6. Identify what you think would be useful classes from the following program specification.

   Write a program that simulates a car wash. Your program should describe some number of vehicles entering the car wash. Each vehicle should be sprayed, washed, rinsed, and dried. The driver of each vehicle is responsible for paying the cashier.

7. For each of the following collections of classes, specify in what order you would choose to implement them and describe the reasons for each ordering.

   a. *Automobile, Engine*
   b. *Customer, Salesperson*
   c. *Point, Triangle, Line*
   d. *Passenger, Airplane, Flight*

8. Draw a class diagram (like that in Figure 7.4, for class *Elevator*) to describe each of the following classes:

   a. an automated teller machine (an "ATM")
   b. a rational number
   c. a digital watch

9. For one of the classes you described in Exercise 8, write its C++ header file. Include comments that indicate why members are declared as private or public.

10. Although we chose not to do so in developing our PIP, we could have written a driver program to test explicitly our *Rider* class. Write a driver program for class *Rider* now.

8

INHERITANCE

A rose is a rose is
a flowering plant
is a plant.

One of the most important features of C++, as we have said repeatedly throughout this text, is that it allows us as programmers to use the predefined data types of the language to define our own useful, high-level classes. Once defined, a class takes on many of the properties of a predefined type. Most notably, it can be used to help define other classes. We saw this feature in action when we described a digital timer as containing two digital displays and when we designed our soda machine to contain several dispenser objects. These "part-of" relationships between classes allow us to build a new class by composing existing types and classes.

There is another powerful relationship that can be directly expressed by C++ to extend the notion of type even further. Just as we think, for example, of dogs as types of animals, classes can be derived from one another to form "is-a" relationships. Doing so allows the "derived class" (dog) to inherit the properties—the data and functions—of the more general "base class" (animal). Further, the derived class can tailor the inherited data and functions to its specific needs and extend them to include additional information and functionality. Organizing classes in "is-a" hierarchies has two practical advantages. First, doing so allows classes to share information. We need not describe the functions and data of a derived class that come from its base class, since they are already described in the base class. Second, classes arranged as hierarchies can be used to model a wide range of interesting real-world phenomena that are naturally described in such terms.

OBJECTIVES

In this chapter, we will

▶ Introduce in general terms the notions of hierarchical relationships and inheritance.

▶ Describe the C++ facilities for defining hierarchies and inheritance—base and derived classes.

▶ Review how classes control access to member data and functions and introduce a new level of member control, *protected* access.

▶ Show how to declare, define, and use derived classes.

▶ Explain how C++ combines its general facilities for polymorphism with derived classes to model heterogeneous lists.

▶ Develop our PIP, a payroll processor, which illustrates many of the characteristics of derived classes.

8.1 HIERARCHY AND INHERITANCE

Zoology is the study of animals. Zoologists study, among other things, how animals interact with one another and with their environments. They also study how different species of animals are related to one another. A great deal of research and effort has been expended in developing a taxonomy, or a naming and classification scheme, for the animal kingdom. Doing so entails an understanding of each animal's physical and behavioral traits so that commonalties and differences between species can be recognized. Animals are named and categorized based on the common and distinguishing traits.

A typical (highly abbreviated) animal taxonomy is presented in Figure 8.1. It is presented in chart form to make clear the relationships between each of the different subkingdoms and the groups within each subkingdom. This chart shows, for example, that both Anthropoda and Chordata are subgroups of the Metazoa subkingdom. This tells us that both subgroups share the defining characteristics of the Metazoa class (that is, that they are many-celled animals with digestive cavities). It also tells us that animals classified as either Anthropoda and Chordata are distinct from Protozoa (one-celled animals) and from Parazoa (many-celled animals without digestive cavities).

While Anthropoda and Chordata share the defining characteristics of the Metazoa subkingdom, they are separate subgroups of that subkingdom because each has features that distinguish it from other Metazoans. All Anthropoda, for example, have identifiable heads, thoraxes, abdomens, and three or

FIGURE 8.1
A taxonomy of the
animal kingdom

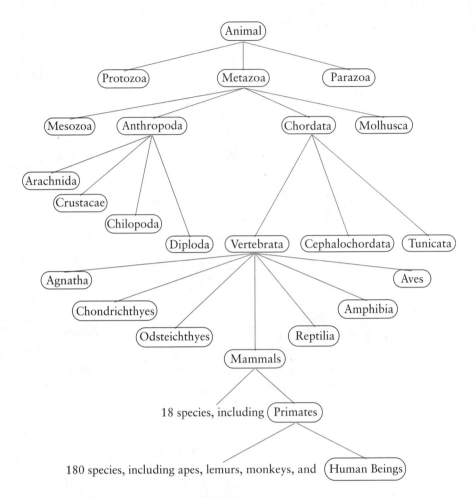

more pairs of legs. Chordata, on the other hand, have rod-like structures, called notochords, that support their bodies.

We humans could, according to this chart, be described as Animals, Metazoans, Chordata, Vertebrata, Mammals, and/or Primates. We share the defining traits of each of these categories, but are different (or so we believe) from every other subcategory in some fundamental way. It may be that we have distinctive properties, such as our skin, hair, skeleton, internal organs, or circulatory, digestive, nervous, or respiratory systems. Or we may differ from another animal subcategory by virtue of our behavior—our eating habits or how we move, reproduce, migrate, or defend ourselves.

Whereas a background in zoology is necessary to appreciate the differences between the multitude of classifications needed to describe the animal kingdom, some things are directly obvious to us from the chart. Such charts represent hierarchies of information. That is to say, the information is presented to reflect an ordering of rank or class. Species listed toward the top of the chart are more general than are those listed near the bottom. A line connecting species indicates a subclass relationship. So, for example, Primates are a subclass of Mammal, which is a subclass of Vertebrata. A subclass relationship indicates that the subclass "is-an" example of the more general class, with additional specificity. Thus, a Mammal is a Vertebrata, with all of the defining characteristics of that more general class and with additional specific characteristics of its own (Mammals, unlike other Vertebrata, feed their young on mother's milk). This sharing of traits between a general class and its subclasses is called *inheritance*. We describe the subclass as inheriting the properties and behaviors of the superclass.

Subclasses can do more than inherit and extend the properties and behaviors of their superclasses. They also can customize them to suit their own purposes. For example, all Primates eat, sleep, move, and reproduce, so these behaviors can be said to be among the defining common characteristics of the entire class. Still, as we walk through the Primate section of the zoo, we see each individual species perform these same basic behaviors slightly differently. Each Primate subclass has imposed its own interpretation on these general actions and performs them accordingly.

The organization of our taxonomy chart tells us more than simply which classes are subclasses of others. It also tells us implicitly that classes are not related to one another, or at least not closely related. For example, although Reptiles and Mammals share the properties and behaviors common to all Vertebrates, the chart indicates to us that there are distinguishing features of a Reptile that Primates (a subclass of Mammal) do not share. Similarly, there are features common to all Mammals that a snake does not have. In short, the strictly hierarchical nature of the chart not only helps us organize information, but it also serves to localize information; that is, make it apply to a well-defined area of the chart.

Finally, representing information hierarchically is as economical as it is expressive because it eliminates redundancy to a great degree. Once, for example, we have expressed the fact that all Primates have five fingers and five toes, we need not duplicate that information when describing the 180 Primate subclasses. Having said these properties apply to all Primates, and having indicated which species inherit properties from class Primate, we imply that any Primate subclass, such as Human Beings, has these properties.

8.2   BASE AND DERIVED CLASSES

Since one of the goals in the design of the language was that it provide facilities for modeling high-level concepts, it should not be surprising that hierarchical relationships like those we described are more or less directly expressible in C++. Just as in our animal world example, the key to expressing such relationships is the ability to describe super- and subclasses. In C++ parlance, we refer to them as *base* and *derived* classes, respectively.

Informally, we can think of each entry on our animal taxonomy chart as corresponding to a C++ class. Class Animal, the highest-level, most general class in our hierarchy, serves as the base class for three derived classes: Protozoa, Parazoa, and Metazoa. Each of these classes, in turn, serves as a base class for other derived classes. Looking further down the chart, we can describe class Mammal as a base class from which class Primate is derived. The Human Being class is derived from class Primate. By virtue of these derivations, class Human Being would inherit all of the data and functions described in class Primate as well as those from all classes from which Primate was either directly or subsequently derived.

Let's change examples now so that we can talk about base and derived classes and about inheritance more directly in terms of C++. Any problem domain that lends itself to hierarchical descriptions will do, but we'll pick one that not only yields a more interesting program than would the animal kingdom, but also has something to do with computer science. We will describe a drawing program, like the one we used to generate the figures in this text, as a hierarchy of C++ classes.

A drawing program helps its user to define and manipulate a drawing by combining geometric objects such as circles, lines, and rectangles. These objects may be moved around the screen, re-sized, and colored, as specified by the user. Suppose we were responsible for that part of a drawing program that kept track of the objects in a drawing. How would we go about designing it?

The mere fact that we keep talking about geometric *objects* indicates that it might be a good idea to provide a collection of classes like *Rectangle, Circle,* and *Line* to represent the objects that make up a drawing. Notice, too, that all of these classes have common members. For example, each geometric object has an extent—the maximum and minimum horizontal and vertical coordinates of the object. Each object also will be capable of drawing itself, erasing itself, and moving itself to a new location. If we think a bit more about this problem, we might notice that two-dimensional objects like circles and rectangles differ from one-dimensional objects like lines and arcs in that two-dimensional objects may be filled with a pattern. One-dimensional objects, by contrast, do not enclose any region we could fill. It appears that we have described a natural hierarchy here, which we illustrate in Figure 8.2.

Design Guideline 7. If two or more classes are logically related and share member functions and data, consider "factoring out" the common elements into a base class.

The first step toward translating our hierarchy chart into C++, the results of which follow, is to recognize that each entry in the chart will become a class and then to start declaring classes with the topmost class in the hierarchy. Class *GeometricObject* looks like many other classes we have declared. It contains

FIGURE 8.2

A hierarchy of geometric objects

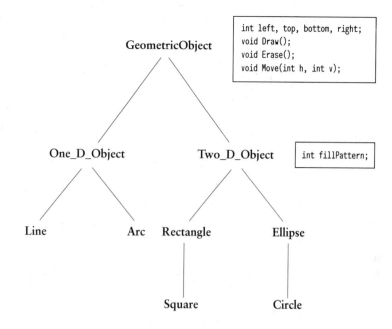

four data members (integers describing an object's extent) and three functions for drawing, erasing, and moving the object. Its only feature of note is that all of its members are quite intentionally declared to be public. You may be able to guess why this is the case. For the moment, let's just say it has something to do with the fact that we want *GeometricObject* to serve as a base class for the other classes in our hierarchy.

```
class GeometricObject
{
public:
    int left, top, bottom, right;
    void Draw();
    void Erase();
    void Move(int h, int v);
};
```

Defining the other classes requires that we make use of C++'s facility for declaring derived classes. To signify that class *Two_D_Object* is to be derived from base class *GeometricObject*, we declare it as follows:

```
class Two_D_Object : public GeometricObject
// This class is a derived class of GeometricObject
{
public:
    int fillPattern;
};
```

Notice that the header for the class declaration has been expanded to include a "base list"—a list of classes from which *Two_D_Object* is to be derived.* In our example, we indicate that class *Two_D_Object* is derived from class *GeometricObject*. This allows class *Two_D_Object* to inherit the four public member data items and the three public member functions of class *GeometricObject* and to refer to them just as if they were its own. Class *Two_D_Object* adds its own data member (an integer describing the fill pattern) to the information provided to it by its base class, *GeometricObject*. This inheritance is illustrated in Figure 8.3.

Similarly, we would declare the *Rectangle* class to be derived from *Two_D_Object* by writing:

```
class Rectangle : public Two_D_Object
{
    // Any members and functions specific to rectangles
};
```

This class would inherit the member functions and data from its base class, *Two_D_Object*, including those that *Two_D_Object* inherited from its base class, *GeometricObject*. For example, if we had declared *thisRect* to be an object of the *Rectangle* class, all of the following would be legal statements:

```
cout << thisRect.top;          // Display the top of the extent of thisRect.
thisRect.Move(32, -8);         // Move thisRect right and up.
thisRect.fillPattern = 1;      // Use fill pattern number 1.
```

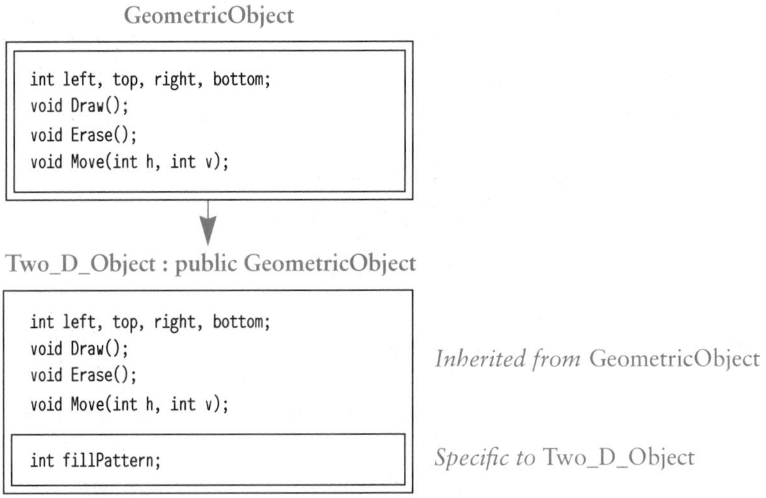

FIGURE 8.3
A derived class inherits members from its base class.

GeometricObject

```
int left, top, right, bottom;
void Draw();
void Erase();
void Move(int h, int v);
```

Two_D_Object : public GeometricObject

```
int left, top, right, bottom;
void Draw();
void Erase();
void Move(int h, int v);
```
Inherited from GeometricObject

```
int fillPattern;
```
Specific to Two_D_Object

* This is called a "base list" because there can be more than one base class for a derived class. That is to say, a class can be derived from many base classes, inheriting properties from all of them. In such cases, we no longer have strictly hierarchical relationships, but rather "multiple inheritance."

To declare a class to be derived from a base class, follow its name by the name of the base class, as

```
class DerivedClassName : public BaseClassName
```

The derived class will have access to all public member data and functions of the base class, just as if they were public members of the derived class.*

Notice that a derived class is usually more specific than its base class, as for example a rectangle is a special case of the more general class of two-dimensional geometric objects. This usually implies that the derived class will have more member data and functions than the base class: those that are inherited from the base class along with any others that are specific to the derived class.

8.3   INHERITANCE AND ACCESS CONTROL

Introducing inheritance into our C++ repertoire allows us to model directly and efficiently any hierarchical problem domain. It also creates a number of interesting questions that must be attended to by programmers. For instance, why were we careful in our preceding example to declare all of the member data and functions of class *GeometricObject* as public? Presumably, we did so to afford classes that are derived from *GeometricObject* access to these members. But doesn't inheritance provide derived classes of *GeometricObject* with their own copies of all member data and functions—including those described as private? Here's an explanation.

Although derived classes in C++ inherit everything—all member data and functions—from their base classes, they are still regarded as separate classes from their base classes. As separate classes they are subject to the access constraints imposed on members by the base class. Therefore, if a data item is declared to be private to a base class, it is inaccessible to *any* external classes—including those that are derived from the base class. The private data in a base class is inherited by its derived classes, but we can think of such data as maintaining a private residence in the base class. Thus, it is directly accessible only to the member functions of the base class or to friends of the base class. Such data is indirectly accessible to derived classes through any publicly defined inherited functions.

---

* We could also declare the base class to be private rather than public. Doing so still gives the derived class access to all the public members of the base class, but they would be treated as private, rather than public, to the derived class.

In terms of our drawing program, we could expand class *Two_D_Object* to include a function, *FindCenter,* that determines the coordinates of the center of the figure, as below.

```
class Two_D_Object : public GeometricObject
// This class is a derived class of GeometricObject
{
public:
    int fillPattern;
    void findCenter(int&, int&);
    // We use reference parameters so that the
    // function can return two values
};
```

As declared, function *FindCenter* would have direct access to integer values *left, top, bottom,* and *right,* inherited from base class *GeometricObject.* If, on the other hand, those data members had been declared as private to class *GeometricObject,* function *FindCenter* would not be able to use them directly in its calculations. We could, as we have done in other examples, provide member functions in class *GeometricObject* to access the private data members, and as long as these functions were declared as public, *FindCenter* (and any other functions in derived classes) could use them.

Situations like this raise another question about access control. Is there a way to make members of a base class accessible to classes that are derived from it but not to any other classes, in much the same way that the secret of the de la Poer Curse is passed on from the senior de la Poers to their children but is never mentioned outside the family? C++ provides a third level of access control, the *protected* level, for just this purpose. We have intentionally avoided discussing the protected level until now because its utility lies in the access it affords to derived classes.

> Class member functions and data that are declared protected may be accessed by objects of that class, by friends of the class, *and* by objects in a derived class, but they may not be accessed by any other object.

In our example, we probably would not want users of any of our classes to have direct access to the extent members *left, top, bottom,* and *right,* so we would declare them to be protected. Doing so makes them accessible only to the members of classes directly derived from class *GeometricObjects.* On the other hand, we might very well want the member functions *Draw, Erase,* and *Move* to be accessible to users of the *Rectangle* class, so we would declare them to be public members of the base class:

```
class GeometricObject
{
public:
    // These are accessible by any object, including those of
```

```
        // derived classes (where they also have public access).
        void Draw();
        void Erase();
        void Move(int h, int v);
protected:
        // These members can be used only by GeometricObject
        // and its derived classes (where they also have protected
        // access).
        int left, top, bottom, right;
private:
        // Anything declared here is inaccessible outside of this
        // class. Even derived classes cannot use these members.
};
```

8.4   CREATING AND DESTROYING DERIVED CLASSES

Here's another interesting dilemma that is a by-product of our ability to derive classes from one another. Think about what happens when, in our drawing program, we declare a *Rectangle* object. We are in effect declaring three objects from three different but related classes: one *Rectangle,* one *Two_D_Object,* and one *GeometricObject.* Generally speaking, this is not much of a problem for C++. What happens is that the default constructors for each class in the derivation chain are activated, beginning with the most general, highest-level class. In our example in which we have not declared any constructors, this means that the system-generated constructors for classes *GeometricObject, Two_D_Object,* and *Rectangle* are invoked in that order to create a *Rectangle* object.

If we had declared constructors of our own for any of these classes, things would be slightly more interesting. In particular, imagine that our class declarations were extended as follows:

```
class GeometricObject
{
public:
        // These are accessible by any object, including those of
        // derived classes (where they also have public access).
        void Draw();
        void Erase();
        void Move(int h, int v);

        // Here are the new constructors
        GeometricObject();
        GeometricObject(int t, int l, int b, int r)
                    {top = t; left = l; bottom = b; right = r;};
        protected:
            // These members can be used only by GeometricObject
```

```
        // and its derived classes (where they also have
        // protected access).
        int left, top, bottom, right;
    private:
        // Anything declared here is inaccessible outside of this
        // class. Even derived classes cannot use these members.
    };


class Two_D_Object : public GeometricObject
// This class is a derived class of GeometricObject
{
public:
    int fillPattern;
    void findCenter(int&, int&);
    // We use reference parameters so that the
    // function can return two values


    // Here are the new constructors
    Two_D_Object();
    Two_D_Object(int t, int l, int b, int r, int fill):
                GeometricObject(t,l,b,r)
                {fillPattern = fill;};
};


class Rectangle : public Two_D_Object
// This class is a derived class of Two_D_Object
{
public:
    // Here are its constructors
    Rectangle ();
    Rectangle (int t, int l, int b, int r, int fill):
                Two_D_Object(t,l,b,r, fill)
                {};
};
```

Notice that each class declared above now has a pair of user-defined, public constructor functions, one for default declarations and another for parameterized declarations. If we simply declare an object to be of type *Rectangle,* like

```
Rectangle r;
```

our three default constructors will be invoked in the order prescribed by our hierarchy:

```
GeometricObject(); Two_D_Object(); Rectangle();
```

If, on the other hand, we declare a *Rectangle* object using our parameterized constructor, like

```
Rectangle r(10, 20, 100, 200, 3);
```

we have the option of specifying directly how the constructors in our chain of derived classes will be invoked. We do so by attaching an *initialization list* to the definitions of our constructor functions.

Notice how the parameterized constructors for classes *Rectangle* and *Two_D_Objects* have been defined. As part of the declaration header for each, we include calls to constructors for the base classes that will be invoked before the body of the constructor for the derived class. Look closely at the definition of the parameterized constructor for class *Two_D_Object*. In its definition we have provided an initialization list that tells the processor which *GeometricObject* constructor to use and which parameters to provide it with. Initialization lists are particularly useful when defining constructor functions of derived classes because constructors for base classes cannot simply be called from within a derived class constructor. Since class *Two_D_Object* is derived from base class *GeometricObject*, a *GeometricObject* constructor still will be invoked before the constructor for class *Two_D_Object* and thus before the function body that follows the initialization list. The list, though, allows us to control explicitly which version of our constructors gets called and how they are parameterized. The initialization list provided in the definition of *Rectangle*'s parameterized constructor explicitly invokes the constructor for class *Two_D_Object*, which in turn invokes the *GeometricObject* constructor. The order of constructor invocation is not affected by the use of an initialization list. The body of the *Rectangle* constructor need not be empty, but is in this case because all of the necessary initializations have been accomplished by our chain of base and derived constructors.

It should be noted that destructors for base and derived classes operate in much the same way as do constructors. The only significant difference is that the order of invocation is reversed for destructors. That is, when an object of a derived class is destroyed, the destructor for the derived class is invoked first, and then the destructor for its base class is invoked.

Initialization lists become increasingly useful in cases in which we have multiple inheritance, that is, a class derived from two or more base classes. In such cases, there is no clear order for invoking constructors and destructors, and initialization lists can be used to resolve these ambiguities.

8.5 DEFINING DERIVED CLASSES

Recall our earlier discussion of the animal kingdom. We have seen how C++ lets us describe the salient features of such a hierarchy using base and derived classes and inheritance. We also mentioned that certain animal behaviors, like eating or sleeping, are common to multiple species, but are interpreted differently in each case. In C++ terminology, this phenomenon is described as *polymorphism*. Informally, polymorphism means that we can use the same name to take on a number of different meanings and leave it up to the compiler or processor to determine which interpretation of the name to use in different contexts.

We already have seen many examples of how C++ supports varying degrees of polymorphic behavior. The overloading of function names and operators are good examples. We have seen that function names within a single class description can be overloaded as long as their parameter lists differ. We also have seen that function names in distinct classes can be overloaded in any manner without regard for parameter lists. Function overloading gets even more interesting when we talk of base and derived classes.

In our drawing program, each geometric object is capable of drawing itself, but the definition of the *Draw* function would be different for each class. The classes *GeometricObject*, *One_D_Object*, and *Two_D_Object* will never have any objects of their own that would appear on the screen. The program would deal with ellipses, rectangles, lines, and arcs, but the three highest-level classes are "abstract" in the sense that their only purpose is to provide member functions and data to their derived classes. This means that their member functions would also be of a very general nature and so would need to be redefined in their derived classes.

For example, the *Draw* function of *GeometricObject* might do nothing more than ready the area defined by *left, top, bottom,* and *right* for drawing. Having done that, the *Draw* function of *Two_D_Object* might set the system's fill pattern to the correct number. Finally, the *Draw* function of *Rectangle* would draw the borders of the rectangle and fill it with the selected pattern. When a derived class redefines a function inherited from its base class, we say that the derived class *overrides* the base class definition.

In our example, we might have the following definitions (among others, of course):

```
void GeometricObject::Draw()
// Initialize the rectangle in which we'll do the drawing.
{  . . . }


void Two_D_Object::Draw()
// This has the same name as an inherited function, so we're
// overriding it here
{
    GeometricObject::Draw();
    // It's okay to call the inherited function.
    // We might also want to do other things in the definition,
    // as well.
}
```

```
void Rectangle::Draw()
// This is another override. This time, we're overriding the
// Draw function from the base class Two_D_Object.
{
    // We might do some processing here,
    Two_D_Object::Draw();
    // and call the base class Draw function
    // and, finally, do the actual drawing of the rectangle.
}
```

Given these admittedly sketchy definitions, a main program like the following would work fine.

```
main()
{   // create three distinct objects
    GeometricObject g;
    Two_D_Object t;
    Rectangle r;

    // invoke each object's version of function Draw
    g.Draw();
    t.Draw();
    r.Draw();
}
```

The reason this program would work is that there is no ambiguity in terms of which version of function *Draw* should be invoked. The C++ compiler can tell (as can we), just from looking at the preceding listing, which *Draw* function to invoke based on the declared types of the objects involved. Since variable *r* is explicitly declared as an object of class Rectangle, there is no question that *r. Draw()* refers to the *Draw* function declared as part of that class.

Confusion sets in when we think more realistically about our drawing program trying to maintain a collection of *GeometricObject* objects in an interactive fashion. The first difficulty arises from the fact that an interactive program would allow its user to create and manipulate any combination of available objects. That is, there may in a single drawing be some rectangles, some circles, some lines, and so on. Second, it would greatly simplify our program if we were able to treat this collection of objects in a uniform way. Each object is, after all, a derived version of our abstract class *GeometricObject*. We should be able to say something like: "For each of these geometric objects, draw it."

We have described a drawing as what computer scientists refer to as a "heterogeneous list." That is, a drawing is a list of related but different kinds of objects. In our program, we will have a list of *Rectangle, Circle,* and *Line* objects, each of which "is-a" *GeometricObject* yet has its own method for drawing itself. It would be lovely if in C++ we could simply create an array of

GeometricObject objects and draw all of the objects in a drawing by looping through the array as follows:

```
GeometricObject GO[10];
    .

    .

    .
for (int i = 0; i < numberOfObjects; i++)
    GO[i].Draw();
```

But we can't for two reasons. The first is clear if you put yourself in the role of the C++ compiler and look again at the code just presented. Based on the declarations and the code you see, it seems perfectly obvious which version of function *Draw* to invoke for each iteration through the loop: the one declared and defined as part of class *GeometricObject*. That is, after all, the declared type of array *GO*.

Second, think about the problem of creating objects and assigning them to the array. Since the user of the program would be creating objects that are instances of derived classes, like *Rectangle, Circle,* and *Line,* and these objects contain more information (member data and functions) than does any plain old *GeometricObject* object, C++ won't let us assign, say, a rectangle to occupy a space in array *GO*. What to do?

It almost goes without saying that C++ provides a way out of this dilemma (why else would we have belabored the point?). In fact, the kind of polymorphism introduced by heterogeneous lists is what is most commonly referred to as "polymorphism" when speaking of object-oriented programming. C++ handles polymorphism in derived classes by declaring potentially ambiguous function names to be *virtual functions*. We'll explain virtual functions in detail shortly. For now, look at how they can be used, along with pointers and references, to accomplish the goals of our drawing program.

Step 1: Instead of creating an array of *GeometricObject* objects, create an array of *pointers* to *GeometricObject*.

```
GeometricObject* GO[numberOfObjects];
```

Step 2: Create individual, derived objects.

```
Rectangle r;
Circle c;
Line l;
```

Step 3: Put the addresses of these derived objects into our array.

```
GO[0] = &r;
GO[1] = &c;
GO[2] = &l;
```

Step 4: Draw a collection of *GeometricObject*s by iterating through the array.

```
for (int i = 0; i < numberOfObjects; i++)
    GO[i]->Draw();
```

Step 5: Change the declaration of the function to be overridden (*Draw,* in this case) in the most abstract class (*GeometricObject,* in this case), as shown here.

```
virtual void Draw() = 0;
```

The two critical steps are the first and the last. By declaring an array to hold pointers to *GeometricObject* objects, C++ allows us to assign to our array a pointer to any derived type of *GeometricObject* (in part, since a pointer occupies the same amount of space regardless of the type of object it points to). More formally, C++ will coerce a pointer to a derived type into a pointer to its base type.

The final step, declaring *GeometricObject::Draw* to be a virtual function, allows the C++ processor to disambiguate the reference to function *Draw* within the for loop. By describing function *Draw* as "virtual" and indicating that we will not be defining the function for this abstract class (that's essentially what the "= 0" notation means), we identify it as one that (1) will be overridden by classes derived from *GeometricObject* and (2) will be disambiguated (or, in computer science parlance, "bound" to a particular interpretation)— based not on how array *GO* was declared but on the types of the objects pointed to by *GO*. So, if *GO[0]* points to a *Rectangle* object, *GO[0]->Draw()* will invoke function *Draw* as defined and declared in class *Rectangle*. We'll see additional examples of derived classes, inheritance, protected members, and virtual functions in this chapter's PIP.

8.6 PROGRAM IN PROGRESS: A PAYROLL PROGRAM

Our PIP for this chapter illustrates all of the aforementioned features of derived classes in the context of a program for printing the payroll checks for a small company. The company's employees are categorized hierarchically, as they are in many companies, to reflect the method by which their pay is calculated and the benefits or deductions to which they are subject. The hierarchy chart in Figure 8.4 describes the relationship between the employee categories.

We describe the categories as follows: Everyone who receives a paycheck from our company is considered an employee. Each employee has identifying information (a name, address, and social security number) and a net pay that

FIGURE 8.4
The *Employee* payroll
hierarchy

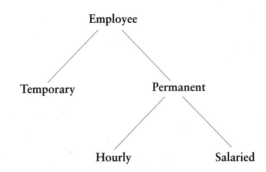

he or she will receive for a given pay period. There are two basic distinctions between temporary employees and permanent ones. First, temporary employees (like contractors, consultants, and other part-time help) are paid at an hourly rate for the number of hours worked and are subject to no payroll deductions. All permanent employees are, for the sake of this highly simplified example, subject to a fixed deduction (the same amount for all permanent employees) to cover their company benefits.

There are, as shown by the hierarchy chart, two types of permanent employees. Permanent hourly employees have their pay calculated like those of temporary employees. That is, hourly employees are paid based on an hourly rate and the number of hours worked. Unlike temporary employees, they are subject to the aforementioned payroll deduction. Salaried employees, as you would expect, are paid a fixed salary for each pay period. This descriptive information is presented in the context of the employee hierarchy in Figure 8.5.

We want our program, first off, to declare and define classes to reflect our employee hierarchy. As our ultimate processing goal, we want the program to be capable of soliciting or accepting input data describing employees and their pay-related information and to print checks for the employees that reflect both the pay data entered and the employee's class. As we have seen repeatedly, if we are complete and careful about how we organize and describe our classes, most of the program's processing requirements will be met quite naturally.

Declaration: The File "EMPLOYEE.H"

As opposed to creating distinct header files to describe each individual class, we will instead write a single header file to declare our entire employee hierarchy. We justify this on three grounds. First, the base class *Employee* and its derived classes are all so intimately related that declaring them in separate files would obscure the relationships. Second, it is unlikely that any program would want to make use of any of these classes in isolation of the others. Third, this program is small enough that we have less of a need to decompose the program to

FIGURE 8.5
Inheritance in the
Employee payroll

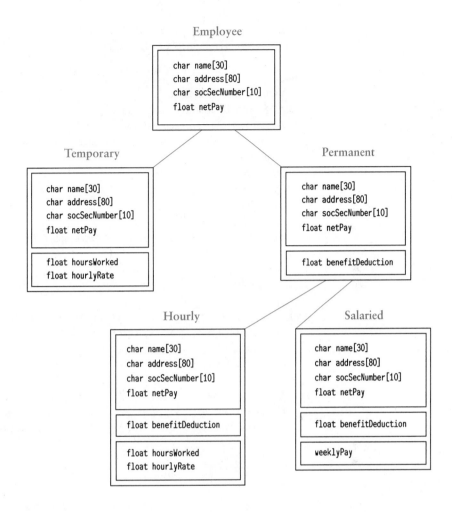

make it more manageable. The listing for our declaration file, "EMPLOY-EE.H," follows.

```
// ----------EMPLOYEE.H----------
// Declarations for class Employee and its
// derived classes. Class Employee has two directly
// derived subclasses, Temporary (employees who work on
// an hourly basis and get no company benefits) and Permanent.
// Permanent employees (all of whom have a benefit deduction)
// are further subdivided into Hourly and Salaried classes.

#ifndef _EMPLOYEE_H
#define _EMPLOYEE_H
```

```
class Employee
// the information common to all employees
{
public:
    virtual void PrintCheck() = 0;
    // a virtual function that will be
    // implemented for each derived class
protected:        // accessible to derived classes only
    float netPay;
    Employee();
    Employee(char* n, char* a, char* ssn);
    char name[30];
    char address[80];
    char socSecNumber[10]; // leave an extra space for terminator
};

class Temporary: public Employee
{
public:  // Public so that they can be invoked from main()
    Temporary(char* n, char* a, char* ssn, float hw, float hr);
    Temporary();
    void PrintCheck();

private:                        // Temporary is an Employee with
    float hoursWorked;          // a number of hours worked, and
    float hourlyRate;               // an hourly rate of pay.
};

class Permanent: public Employee
{
// This is public so that it can be initialized externally
public:
    // Permanent is an Employee with
    // a fixed deduction for benefits.
    static float benefitDeduction;

// All is protected so that it is only accessible to derived
// classes
protected:
    Permanent(char* n, char* a, char* ssn);
    Permanent();
    void PrintCheck() = 0;
    // redeclared as virtual, to be implemented
    // in further derived classes
};
```

```
class Hourly: public Permanent
{
public:
    Hourly(char* n, char* a, char* ssn, float hw, float hr);
    Hourly();
    void PrintCheck();
private:
// Hourly is a Permanent with a number of hours worked,
// and an hourly rate.
    float hoursWorked;
    float hourlyRate;
};


class Salaried: public Permanent
{
public:
    Salaried(char* n, char* a, char* ssn, float wp);
    Salaried();
    void PrintCheck();

private:
// Salaried is a Permanent with a weekly salary.
    float weeklyPay;
};


#endif // _EMPLOYEE_H
```

The first thing to notice about the declarations in file "EMPLOYEE.H" is how closely they conform to our formal hierarchical description. This, of course, is less a testimony to our programming prowess than to the quality of the support C++ provides us for expressing hierarchical relationships. We can see, for example, that *Temporary* and *Permanent* are declared as derived classes from base class *Employee*. Class *Permanent* then serves as a base class for its own derived classes, *Hourly* and *Salaried*. Also, each class declares data members that match the information we described as being part of the class. Since name, address, social security number, and net pay are common to all employees, those data items are declared as members of class *Employee* and are inherited by all of its derived classes. Similarly, the benefit deduction applicable to all permanent employees is a member of class *Permanent, hoursWorked* and *hourlyRate* are members of both class *Temporary* and class *Hourly*, and data item *weeklyPay* is a member of class *Salaried*.

Let's review briefly how we can control access to our classes and their members. We'll look at one class at a time, ignoring for now function *PrintCheck* and its various overrides, which we'll return to later.

Employee: All data members are protected and so are both inherited by and accessible to all classes derived directly from *Employee*—in this case, classes *Temporary* and *Permanent*. The member data of class *Employee* is not publicly accessible to any function (like main, for example) that is outside of its derivation chain. This works out fine, since we will not be invoking, say, *Employee*'s constructors directly from our main function. Rather, we will be creating specific kinds of employees (like temporary, hourly, and salaried), but will never declare a variable to be solely of type *Employee*. Note, too, that for each class we provide two constructors. The constructors with non-null parameter lists are used to create employees with pre-specified data values. The default constructors will solicit data values for employees interactively from the user of the program.

Temporary: In this case, we have no protected members (only public and private members) for good reason. Class *Temporary* does not serve as a base class for any derived classes, so it would be useless to declare any members as protected (or would be equivalent to declaring them as private). We declare data values *hoursWorked* and *hourlyRate* as private since only *Temporary*'s member functions (its constructors and its *PrintCheck* function) need access to them. The constructor functions are public because, unlike for class *Employee*, we will want to declare *Temporary* objects directly from our main function.

Permanent: Again, this class is serving as a base class for two derived classes and so describing its member functions as protected makes sense. Access to these functions is thus constrained to classes (publicly) derived from *Permanent*. Data member *benefitDeduction* is declared as public because its value will be set from outside of *Permanent*'s member functions. It is declared as *static* because, according to our program description, it is uniform for all permanent employees. Remember that in the context of a class declaration, a member value declared as *static* means there is, in effect, a single copy of the member for all objects of the class.

Hourly and Salaried: Both of these classes share the access attributes of class *Temporary*, in the following senses. First, they are derived classes that don't serve as base classes, so there is no reason to protect members. Second, we will want access to their member functions from our main function, since we will want, for example, to create hourly and salaried employees directly. Finally, their data members (*hoursWorked, hourlyRate,* and *weeklyPay)* should all be controlled from within their member functions and so are declared as private.

In reviewing the listing of "EMPLOYEE.H" one can't help but notice the member functions associated with each class that were not described explicitly in our employee hierarchy charts. We already mentioned briefly the pairs of constructor functions provided for each class. We will see more clearly how these work and how they are related to one another when we look at their definitions. Let's consider now function *PrintCheck*. It is a perfect candidate for what we described earlier as a virtual function.

Our first clue as to the nature of function *PrintCheck* comes from our program description, wherein we mention the processing goal of printing checks for all employees. While this goal could be implemented in a number of ways using conventional function overrides, we opted to have our program build a list of employees and then loop through the list to print checks. Clearly our list of employees will be heterogeneous (some employees will be temporary, some will be hourly, and some will be salaried), and we will rely on C++'s propensity for polymorphism to print checks. We'll describe the check-printing procedure in full detail shortly, but now must take care to declare our classes to allow for polymorphism.

We declare *PrintCheck* as a pure virtual function (that is, one with no definition at this level of our hierarchy that must be implemented by derived classes) in class *Employee*. We do not have to respecify the keyword "virtual" since C++ assumes that all overrides of function *PrintCheck* within our derivation chain are also virtual. *PrintCheck* is redeclared as part of each derived class. It is also clearly described as virtual (with no required definition) in class *Permanent*, since *Permanent*'s version of *PrintCheck* must also be overridden by its derived classes. In those classes that will actually define their own versions of *PrintCheck* (*Temporary, Hourly,* and *Salaried*), the function is declared like a normal member function. Notice that in all declarations of *PrintCheck*, the function is described as having the identical return type (void) and an identical (empty) parameter list.

Definition: The File "EMPLOYEE.CPP"

There are precious few functions to implement for our *Employee* classes, and those that must be defined are quite straightforward in their processing requirements. By and large, the most interesting aspects of our definitions file have to do with how our classes are organized hierarchically, which in turn influences directly how our definitions interact with one another. File "EMPLOYEE.CPP" is listed below.

```
// ----------EMPLOYEE.CPP----------
// Definition file for class Employee and
// its derived classes.

#include <iostream.h>      //for cin, cout
#include <string.h>        //for strcmp
#include "EMPLOYEE.H"      //for Employee declarations

float Permanent::benefitDeduction = 100.00;
// Define static variable for class Permanent

Employee::Employee()
// The default constructor for class Employee solicits from the
```

```
// standard input (keyboard) values for the data common to all
// employees.
{
    cout << "\nType employee name, followed by <Enter>: ";
    cin.getline(name,30);

    cout << "\nType employee address, followed by <Enter>: ";
    cin.getline(address,80);

    cout << "\nType social security number, followed by <Enter>: ";
    cin.getline(SocSecNumber,10);
}


Employee::Employee(char* n, char* a, char* ssn)
// This constructor is used when any kind of employee object is
// created with supplied parameters.
{
    strcpy(name,n);
    strcpy(address,a);
    strcpy(socSecNumber,ssn);
}


Temporary::Temporary()
// This is the default constructor for a Temporary employee. It
// solicits values from the user for the hours worked and hourly
// rate.
{
  cout << "\nType number of hours worked, followed by <Enter>: ";
  cin >> hoursWorked;

  cout << "\nType hourly rate, followed by <Enter>: ";
  cin >> hourlyRate;
}


Temporary::Temporary(char* n, char* a, char* ssn,
                            float hw, float hr): Employee(n, a, ssn)
// This is the constructor for Temporaries declared with
// parameters. It invokes the Employee constructor to retrieve
// the basic employee data.
{
  hoursWorked = hw;
  hourlyRate = hr;
}


void Temporary::PrintCheck()
// Calculates the pay for a Temporary,
```

```
// and fills in the
// rest of the check.
{
  netPay = hoursWorked * hourlyRate;
  cout << "\n\n_____";
  cout << "\n\nPAY TO THE ORDER OF: " << '\t' << name;
  cout << "\n\t\t\t" << address;
  cout << "\n\t\t\t" << socSecNumber << '\n';
  cout << "\nEMPLOYEE CLASS: Temporary";
  cout << "\n\nHOURS: " << hoursWorked;
  cout << "\nRATE: " << hourlyRate;
  cout << "\n\nTHE AMOUNT OF ***************$" << netPay << '\n';
  cout << "\n\n_____\n\n";
}


Permanent::Permanent()
{
// the value of static member benefitDeduction is supplied above
}


Permanent::Permanent(char* n, char* a, char* ssn):
                        Employee(n, a, ssn)
// The parameterized constructor for Permanent employees merely
// invokes the Employee constructor to fill in the rest of the
// employee data.
{
// the value of static member benefitDeduction is supplied above
}


Hourly::Hourly()
// The default constructor for Hourly employees. This solicits
// values for the number of hours worked and the hourly rate.
{
  cout << "\nType number of hours worked, followed by <Enter>: ";
  cin >> hoursWorked;

  cout << "\nType hourly rate, followed by <Enter>: ";
  cin >> hourlyRate;
}


Hourly::Hourly(char* n, char* a, char* ssn, float hw, float hr):
                        Permanent(n, a, ssn)
// The parameterized constructor for Hourly employees. This
// function first invokes the Permanent employee constructor
// (which, in turn, invokes the Employee constructor) to fill in
```

```
// the Permanent employee data, and then fills in the hourly
// information from its parameters.
{
  hoursWorked = hw;
  hourlyRate = hr;
}


void Hourly::PrintCheck()
// Prints an Hourly employee's check by: calculating the net pay,
// then printing the rest of the check.
{
    netPay = (hoursWorked * hourlyRate) - benefitDeduction;
    cout << "\n\n_____";
    cout << "\n\nPAY TO THE ORDER OF: " << '\t' << name;
    cout << "\n\t\t\t" << address;
    cout << "\n\t\t\t" << socSecNumber << '\n';
    cout << "\nEMPLOYEE CLASS: Hourly";
    cout << "\n\nBENEFITS DEDUCTION: " << benefitDeduction;
    cout << "\nHOURS: " << hoursWorked;
    cout << "\nRATE: " << hourlyRate;
    cout << "\n\nTHE AMOUNT OF ***************$" << netPay << '\n';
    cout << "\n\n_____\n\n";
}


Salaried::Salaried()
// The default constructor for Salaried employees. This function
// solicits and records a value for the weekly salary. The other
// member data for salaried employees is solicited by the
// constructors for Permanent and Employee classes, which are
// invoked implicitly.
{
    cout << "\nType weekly salary, followed by <Enter>: ";
    cin >> weeklyPay;
}


Salaried::Salaried(char* n, char* a, char* ssn, float wp):
                        Permanent(n, a, ssn)
// To construct a Salaried employee using parameters, we
// explicitly invoke the Permanent constructor, and then fill in
// the value for weekly pay.
{
  weeklyPay = wp;
}


void Salaried::PrintCheck()
```

```
// This function calculates the net pay
// and fills in the data for the
// Salaried employee.
{
    netPay=weeklyPay-benefitDeduction;
    cout << "\n\n_____";
    cout << "\n\nPAY TO THE ORDER OF: " << '\t' << name;
    cout << "\n\t\t\t" << address;
    cout << "\n\t\t\t" << socSecNumber << '\n';
    cout << "\nEMPLOYEE CLASS: Salaried";
    cout << "\n\nBENEFITS DEDUCTION: " << benefitDeduction;
    cout << "\nSALARY: " << weeklyPay;
    cout << "\n\nTHE AMOUNT OF **************$" << netPay << '\n';
    cout << "\n\n_____\n\n";
}
```

We should start analyzing our file at the beginning, with what is indeed an organizational matter. Remember that we declared a static variable, named *benefitDeduction,* as part of class *Permanent.* This data member was declared to be static because it was to be fixed and uniform for all permanent employees. Declaring the value as static has the effect of creating a single instance of the variable to be shared by all *Permanent* objects. Where, though, does this static variable get its value? It can't be initialized at its point of declaration within the class declaration, and it doesn't make sense to reinitialize it repeatedly from within a constructor that is executed with the creation of each instance of class *Permanent.* From our listing we can surmise the solution. We define a static class member outside of its class declaration at a point prior to its use. We have thus defined *benefitDeduction* to have value 100.00 at the beginning of our definition file for the rest of the class.

The only versions of virtual function *PrintCheck* that require definitions are those from classes where *PrintCheck* was overridden by a standard (not purely virtual) function—that is, in classes *Temporary, Hourly,* and *Salaried.* In each case the *PrintCheck* function calculates the *netPay* appropriate for the class and displays the employee and pay rate information in check form on the screen. We will see shortly how these definitions allow C++ to determine the correct version of *PrintCheck* to be invoked from within the main function.

Each pair of class constructors (one pair for each class) operates in roughly the same manner, as we described earlier. The default constructor for each class solicits employee and payroll data from the user (via the screen and keyboard) to create an employee record. The parameterized constructors create employee records by filling in the data members with the supplied values. Again, what is interesting about the constructors is a result of the fact that we are dealing with base and derived classes arranged in a hierarchy.

Since, for example, every time we create a salaried employee, we are implicitly creating a permanent employee as well as an employee, the constructors for all three of these classes will be invoked. If we rely on our default constructors (that is, simply declare a Salaried employee by `Salaried s;`), C++ takes care of everything for us. Before invoking the default constructor for class *Salaried,* the default constructors for classes *Employee* and *Permanent* will be invoked, in that order. Similarly, declaring an hourly employee as `Hourly h;` would invoke the default constructors for classes *Employee, Permanent,* and *Hourly* to be called in order. Creating a temporary employee as `Temporary t;` would invoke class *Employee*'s default constructor and then that for class *Temporary.*

The punch line in terms of defining the default constructors for our employee classes is that each default constructor need only solicit those values that it supplies to its class. The values for its inherited data members will be solicited for and provided by the default constructors of its base class(es). You can see this is the case in our definition file. The default constructor for *Salaried* need only retrieve a value for its data member *weeklyPay.* The values needed to initialize the inherited data members of a *Salaried* employee are provided by the default constructors for classes *Permanent* and *Employee.*

The organizing principle behind the parameterized constructors is essentially the same. Creating a *Salaried* employee using a parameter list, like

```
Salaried s("Sparky Anderson","Detroit, MI","345678901",1000.00)
```

still involves the invocation of constructors for classes *Employee, Permanent,* and *Salaried* in order. This is dictated by how we defined our hierarchy and by C++. As programmers, though, we need to exercise some control over how these constructors get invoked. Specifically, we can control which versions of the constructors get called and how parameters are sent to these constructors. As we have seen, one way to exercise such control is by using initialization lists.

Notice how the parameterized constructor for class *Salaried* is defined. It still supplies a value (by means of assignment from one of its parameters) only for its data member that is not inherited from its base classes *(weeklyPay).* Before doing so, though, it explicitly invokes from its initialization list the parameterized constructor for base class *Permanent,* sending it the parameters it needs to create a *Permanent* object. The parameterized constructor for class *Permanent* passes that information to *Employee*'s parameterized constructor using the same technique. When you run this program in lab you will see concrete evidence that the correct versions of the constructors for our employee hierarchy get invoked and that they get invoked in the right order.

Use: The File "PIP8.CPP"

Speaking of running the program, we need a `main` function to do so. File "PIP8.CPP" exercises our employee hierarchy quite thoroughly and fulfills the original processing requirements of our program.

```
// -----------PIP8.CPP----------
// Main program to test class Employee
// and its derived classes.
```

```cpp
#include <iostream.h>          // for cin, cout
#include "EMPLOYEE.H"          // for Employee classes
#include "UTILITY.H"           // for SetNumeric, WaitForUser, Terminate

#include <conio.h>  // clrscr      ***IMPLEMENTATION DEPENDENT***
inline void ClearScreen() {clrscr();}; ***IMPLEMENTATION DEPENDENT***

void main()
{
    ClearScreen();

    // Create an array to hold (pointers to) our Employees
    Employee* pip8Emps[6];

    // Create checks via initialized declarations
    // and place them in our array
    cout << "\n\nCreating a temporary employee pay record . . .";
    Temporary t("Clipper Decker","Clinton, NY","123456789",40.0,5.25);
    pip8Emps[0] = &t;
    WaitForUser();

    cout << "\n\nCreating an hourly employee pay record . . .";
    Hourly h("Sparky Hirshfield","Deansboro, NY","234567890",30.5,8.50);
    pip8Emps[1] = &h;
    WaitForUser();

    cout << "\n\nCreating a salaried employee pay record . . .";
    Salaried s("Fenton Sugarman","Boston, MA","345678901",500.00);
    pip8Emps[2] = &s;
    WaitForUser();

    // Creating checks using our interactive constructors,
    // and place them in our array
    cout << "\n\nEnter data for a temporary employee pay record: . . .";
    Temporary* tEmp = new Temporary;
    pip8Emps[3] = tEmp;

    cout << "\n\nEnter data for an hourly employee pay record: . . .";
    Hourly* hEmp = new Hourly;
    pip8Emps[4] = hEmp;

    cout << "\n\nEnter data for a salaried employee pay record: . . .";
    Salaried* sEmp = new Salaried;
    pip8Emps[5] = sEmp;
```

```
        // Set format flags for numeric output
        SetNumeric();

        // Now, print all checks, letting C++ determine the
        // appropriate version of PrintCheck depending upon
        // the type of the Employee
        for (int i = 0; i < 6; i++)
        {
            ClearScreen();
            pip8Emps[i]->PrintCheck();
            cout << "\n\n\n";
            WaitForUser();
        };

        Terminate();
};
```

There is slightly more to this main function than was the case in previous PIPs. "PIP8.CPP" does more than simply create a few objects and exercise their member functions. It also exploits C++'s facility for polymorphism. Not coincidentally, it accomplishes this by following precisely the technique we described earlier for creating and manipulating heterogeneous lists.

The program begins by creating an array of *Employee* pointers. It then proceeds to fill the array with six employee objects, three created via parameterized constructors and three via default constructors. In each case, what gets stored in the array is not the *Employee* object itself, but rather the address of the object. Remember, this is essential because the C++ compiler will not coerce between base and derived types, but will coerce pointers of derived types to pointers of base types.

Having created the array of employee data (which is heterogeneous by virtue of the fact that we are dealing with different derived *Employee* types), the program easily prints the check (easily, given the time we invested in defining our classes, and thanks to C++'s facility with virtual functions).

The loop that accomplishes the printing of the checks simply cycles through the *Employee* array and invokes the *PrintCheck* function. You and I—and, fortunately, C++—know that this *PrintCheck* is overridden for each of our derived *Employee* classes, and C++ is smart enough to determine which interpretation of *PrintCheck* to use given the type of each *Employee* record pointed to by the employee array.

8.7 SUMMING UP

▶ Many real-world problems lend themselves to hierarchical description, in which common and distinguishing traits are the basis for a system of classification based on "is-a" relationships.

▶ C++ expresses "is-a" relationships in terms of *base* and *derived classes*.

▶ To declare a class as derived from a base class, its header takes the form:

class *DerivedClass*: public *BaseClassName*

▶ Publicly derived classes inherit all member data and functions from their base classes. They have direct access only to the public and protected members of the base class.

▶ Base class members declared to be *protected* are accessible only to members of the base class and to those of classes derived from the base class.

▶ When declaring an object from a derived class, constructors are invoked for each class in the derivation chain, beginning with the most abstract class. Destructors for derived classes are invoked in the reverse order.

▶ *Initialization lists* can be used for controlling which version of base class constructors get invoked and how parameters are passed to them.

▶ When a member data item is designated as *static*, a single instance of that item is created for all instances of the class.

▶ Generally speaking, *polymorphism* refers to C++'s ability to associate many meanings with a single name. In the context of derived classes, it refers to the ability to distinguish between instances of classes derived from a common base class.

▶ A member function declared as *virtual* can be overridden in derived classes and is used to implement heterogeneous lists.

8.8 EXERCISES

1. Draw charts to represent the following as class hierarchies. In each case, make the term provided the topmost class in the hierarchy.
   a. restaurants
   b. household pets
   c. bank accounts

2. Declare the bank accounts hierarchy that you defined above as a collection of C++ classes. Justify the access control you provide to each class member.

Answer questions 3–6 in terms of the declarations for class GeometricObject and its derived classes found in Section 8.2.

3. What would the implications be if data members *top, left, bottom,* and *right* of class *GeometricObject* were declared as private?

4. How would a program using these declarations behave differently if we removed the initialization list from *Rectangle*'s parameterized constructor?

5. Write a main function that uses our declarations to animate a scene. That is, the main function should create three objects, draw them, erase them, move them, and draw them again at a new location.

6. Extend and fill in the class declarations to make function *Draw* a pure virtual function that is overridden in both class *Two_D_Object* and class *Rectangle*.

7. Why can't we assign a derived class to a base class instance in C++?

8. Why can't a static member variable be defined within the body of a constructor for the class in which it is declared?

9. a. Write a series of class declarations to describe an evaluator for arithmetic expressions. Think of an expression as being in one of five forms:

an integer	// evaluates to the integer
plus (exp_1, exp_2, ... exp_n)	// evaluates to ($exp_1 + exp_2 + \cdots + exp_n$)
minus (exp_1, exp_2)	// evaluates to ($exp_1 - exp_2$)
times (exp_1, exp_2, ... exp_n)	// evaluates to ($exp_1 \times exp_2 \times \cdots \times exp_n$)
divide (exp_1, exp_2)	// evaluates to (exp_1 / exp_2)

    Declare class *Expression* as a base class, and describe its member functions *Evaluate* and *Display* as virtual functions.

    b. Write definitions for class *Expression* and for all of its derived classes. Then, write a main function to read an expression from the keyboard, evaluate it, and display its value.

10. Given the informal declarations below, list every member that each of the following objects has direct access to.

    a. object *parent1*
    b. object *child1*
    c. object *friend1*

```
class AParent
{   friend class AFriend;
private:
     p1, p2;
protected:
     p3, p4;
public:
     p5, p6;
};

AParent parent1;
```

```
class AChild
{
private:
    c1, c2;
protected:
    c3, c4;
public:
    c5, c6;
};

AChild child1;

class AFriend
{
private:
    f1;
protected:
    f2;
public:
    f3;
};

AFriend friend1;
```

11. Show the output that would be produced by function main, below.

```
#include <iostream.h>

class FirstBase
{ private:
    virtual void f1() {cout << "\nFirst base f1 \n";};
    void f2() {cout << "\nFirst base f2 \n";};
    void f3() {f1(); f2();};
    void f4() {cout << "\nFirst base f4 \n";};
public:
    FirstBase() {};
    void f5() {f3();};
    void f6() {cout << "\nFirst base f6 \n";};
    void f7() {f6();};
};
```

```
class LouGehrig
{ private:
    void f1() {cout << "\nLou f1 \n";};
    void f4() {cout << "\nLou f4 \n";};
public:
    LouGehrig () {};
    void f5() {f1();};
    void f6() {cout << "\nLou f6 \n";};
    void f7() {f4();};
};

main()
{
    FirstBase first;
    LouGehrig lou;

    first.f5();
    lou.f5();

    first.f6();
    lou.f6();

    first.f7();
    lou.f7();
}
```

9

PROCESS II: WORKING WITH CLASSES

I warn you that what you're starting to read is full of loose ends and unanswered questions.

In this chapter, our second devoted expressly to the process of programming, we will concentrate on making the most of the C++ we already know to produce working and workable programs. Our first "process" chapter, Chapter 7, described the DDU approach to program development, focussing primarily on the early stages of the life cycle. Software engineering studies indicate, though, that most of a professional programmer's time is spent performing the later life-cycle activities such as documenting, debugging, and revising existing code. These are the activities we'll work on here.

Most of this chapter revolves around our PIP, in which we take on the task of writing a rather formidable sounding application—a word processor. Instead of merely describing the program, we'll walk you through a rather typical scenario in which you are handed a program that someone else has written and told to "finish it up." Doing so involves, first, understanding the problem specification and the original code—not always an easy task, as you will see. You then must detect, isolate, and repair errors in the use of the C++ language (syntax errors), errors in how the program is organized and how classes are controlled (linker errors), and errors that produce incorrect or undesired program behavior (run-time errors). We have intentionally loaded our PIP with examples of each type of error, and will provide you with some guidelines and hints for effectively addressing them.

At the end of the chapter you'll be able to look back and compare the version of the program that you were originally handed with the one that has benefited from your analyses and revisions. The comparison may surprise you. Our hope is that it will help you appreciate further the virtues of workable programs.

OBJECTIVES

In this chapter, we will

▶ Provide you with a problem specification for a line-oriented word processor and a PIP that attempts to implement it.

▶ Describe how programs can be built from existing code libraries and review the libraries that support streams and strings.

▶ Discuss program documentation techniques, and show you how they can be used to improve the readability of our PIP.

▶ Discuss and provide examples of compiler errors, in general and in the context of our PIP, and show you how to eliminate them.

▶ Discuss and provide examples of linker errors, in general and in the context of our PIP, and show you how to eliminate them.

▶ Discuss and provide examples of run-time errors, in general and in the context of our PIP, and show you how to eliminate them.

▶ Review the properties of workable C++ programs.

9.1 PROGRAM IN PROGRESS: A WORD PROCESSOR

Our PIP for this chapter is a word processing program that by today's standards is rather simplistic and somewhat limited in its functionality. To those of us who are old enough to remember the first commercial word processors, the PIP approximates the state of the art from around 1975. The program provides for basic editing of a document on a line-by-line basis. That is, it allows its user to insert lines (one at a time, in a specified position within the document), to delete a line, to change a line (by retyping the entire line), and to display a range of lines in the current document. It also allows the user to save a document to a disk file and to retrieve one from a disk file. Only one document may be open for editing at a time.

All of these characteristics are illusrated graphically in our description of class *Document* (Figure 9.1). From this description you get the feeling that we are using many of our established programming techniques to represent a document. It appears clear, for example, that we described the document's text as a dynamic array (using a pointer to the text, keeping track of the number of lines, providing a *Grow* function and a class destructor). Some features, on the other hand, appear new (saving and retrieving from files and *OCString*). The key to understanding these new features is in understanding how our program makes use of existing program libraries.

FIGURE 9.1
The class *Document*

Document

Public		
	Document	Construct empty document
	Document(int)	Construct a document of specified size
	~Document	Free up text storage
	InsertLine(int)	Add a line at specified position
	DeleteLine(int)	Remove line at specified position
	ChangeLine(int)	Change line at specified position
	Display(int, int)	Display lines in specified range
	Save	Store document to disk file
	Retrieve	Read document from disk file

Private		
	maxLines ☐	int
	numberLines ☐	int
	ShiftLines(int, int)	Move lines of text from specified position up or down
	Grow	Double size of text array
	text ▣	OCString*

9.2 BUILDING PROGRAMS FROM LIBRARIES

Even given its modest description, the fact that we can talk in an introductory programming text about writing a reasonably complete word processor is impressive by any standards, and it is most directly a testimony to C++'s facility with program libraries. This PIP, more than any of the others we have presented, is a great example of how existing libraries can be composed with relative ease to build an interesting program. The resulting main function is deceptively simple because most of the dirty work is performed in the libraries. Some of these libraries are provided by C++ (like those that support stream I/O), and others (like *OCString*) we wrote ourselves. Once written and tested, they become part of our C++ construction kit for building working and workable programs.

Let's take a few pages to review a couple of the more important libraries that we have used regularly in developing our PIPs. It turns out that these libraries, which support most directly streams and strings, are vitally important to any program that manipulates textual data—and no program does that any more than a word processor, even a simple one like our PIP.

Streams, Revisited

We have discussed streams in dribbles (how appropriate) throughout the text. We introduced them briefly as a means for accomplishing basic I/O back in Chapter 2. We discussed them again in Chapter 6 in the context of references and showed how we could overload the extraction and insertion operators to work for programmer-defined classes. We return to the topic of streams for a final time here to fill in the remaining holes in our presentation.

Almost all of the programs we have developed throughout this text have made use of C++'s facilities for input and output. For example, in many programs we have used statements like:

```
char ans;
cout << "Do you wish to run the program again?";
cout << " (Y for yes, N for no):";
cin >> ans;
cout << '\n';
```

We have avoided discussing too many of the details of how such statements and operators work, beyond warning you that any program that attempts to perform such operations must include header file "iostream.h." Class *iostream* is but one of a large and intricately related group of standard C++ classes that are provided to implement a wide range of I/O operations and data. The kinds of streams we are most concerned with in this chapter are those that accomplish program input (that is, where the source of data is either the keyboard or a data file, and the destination for the data is our program), and program output (where our program is the data source, and the screen or a data file is its consumer). That portion of the class hierarchy for C++ streams that supports these types of I/O is pictured in Figure 9.2.

Clearly, this arrangement of classes is not a simple hierarchy. Class *iostream*, for example, is derived from both classes *istream* and *ostream*. Still, the notions we discussed in Chapter 8 of derived class and inheritance apply here. The classes near the top of the diagram provide more general stream data, operators, and functions, and those nearer the bottom describe more specific versions of these. Things become a bit more clear, too, once you realize that, in general, the prefix "i" designates a class devoted to program input, prefix "o" designates an output class, and prefix "f" designates a class that supports external files.

Our programs have accomplished the input and output that they have to date by making use of two (of the four) predefined and open streams that are provided to all C++ programs. Stream cin is an object derived from class *istream*. Class *istream* is the one that provides us with an extraction operator, >>, which is overloaded to accommodate most of the standard C++ data types, as declared next. These operators are public members of class *istream*, which, not coincidentally, is declared in file "iostream.h." Class *istream* also provides two versions of function get, for extracting individual characters and strings from a stream. Function get differs from the extraction operator in that get can be used to read white space (or blanks), but the extraction operator ignores blanks.

FIGURE 9.2
Part of the C++ class
hierarchy for
streams

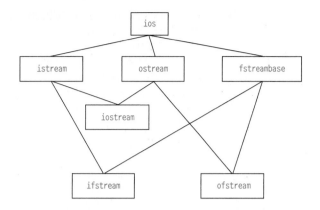

```
istream& operator>> (int& i);
istream& operator>> (double& d);
istream& operator>> (char& c);
istream& operator>> (char* s);
istream& get(char& c);
istream& get(char* s, int n, int ch='n');
```

So with regard to our program's input and output capabilities, the picture begins to make sense. Stream cin is a predefined, open stream that is automatically associated with the standard input device (which for most implementations is the keyboard). Being an *istream* object, cin has extraction operators as public members, so that when we ask a user to input a value, like

```
int i;
cin >> i;
```

the appropriate version of the extraction operator is applied to cin. Remember, too, how each of cin's listed members returns an *istream* reference. This is what allows us to chain input requests together, as in

```
int i;
double d;
cin >> i >> d;
```

Our experience with program output is similarly explained. Stream cout is a predefined object of class *ostream*. It, too, has public operators and function members, but these define insertion operators for most C++ types (char, int, double, char*), as well as put functions for inserting individual characters and strings into streams. These operators and functions return references to *ostream* objects, so that they can, as we have seen, be chained together. Header file "iostream.h" contains the declarations for both classes *istream* and *ostream*.

Restricting ourselves to using the streams that are predefined for us in "iostream.h" limits our programming ability considerably. Many programs, including our PIP for this chapter, require external data files to be useful. At first glance, all of the effort expended in describing and defining a complex network of classes, each with its own collection of data, operators, and functions, just to accomplish basic keyboard input and screen output seems like considerable overkill.* The major advantage to doing so is that we can regard external data files as streams of characters, and interact with them very much like we interact with the standard input and output streams.

Looking back at the inheritance chart for stream classes, we included three classes that support directly external data files as streams. Class *fstreambase*, as its name implies, serves as the base class for two derived classes, *ifstream* and *ofstream*. The general mechanisms for establishing connections between program and data files are provided by the base class. The derived classes are devoted to prescribing how files can be used as input streams to programs (*ifstream*) and as output streams from programs (*ofstream*). The similarity between how we interact with files and how we interact with the standard C++ streams is no coincidence. Classes *ifstream* and *ofstream* are also derived from the general classes *istream* and *ostream*, respectively.

Unlike the more general input and output streams, there are no predefined standard *ifstream* or *ofstream* objects. So, if our program is to make use of file streams, it is up to us to declare, initialize, and use them ourselves. Informally, initializing a file stream involves three steps. First, a stream must be associated with a particular file by means of the latter's file name. Second, that file must be connected temporarily to our program, so that the stream is effectively "attached at both ends." Finally, we must indicate in which direction information is to flow. An input file stream sends data from a file to a program. An output stream sends data in the opposite direction.

Consistent with many of the C++ classes we have made use of, we can declare and initialize *fstreams* in one step, using constructors of the appropriate type. To create an *ifstream*, for example, we can use the following procedure:

```
char fileName[30];
cout << "\nOpen which file?";
cin >> fileName;
ifstream fInput(fileName);
```

Variable *fileName* is a string used in this case to hold a name entered from the keyboard by the user of the program. That string (a string literal can be used as well) is supplied to a constructor for class *ifstream*, which accomplishes the initialization steps described above. That is, in one declaration we have (1) declared variable *fInput* to be an *ifstream* object, (2) associated *ifstream fInput* with a particular file, (3) connected that file to our program, and (4) established the direction of the stream so that it flows from the external file to our program.

The declaration

```
ofstream fOutput (fileName)
```

---

* To be sure, this approach is justified at least in part by the need to keep C++ compatible with earlier implementations of C.

would accomplish the analogous declaration and initialization of an *ofstream* object. In this case, of course, the stream's flow would be from our program to the specified external data file.

Although there is some overhead associated with declaring file streams, using them is quite consistent with using the standard streams. File stream *fInput*, as declared above, is after all both an *ifstream* and an *istream*. We saw before that class *istream* provides its instances with a variety of member extraction operators. So, to extract data from a file stream, we simply use that file stream's versions of the extraction operator. That is, we can retrieve data from file *fileName* simply by:

```
int i;
char c:
fInput >> i >> c;
```

Similarly, we can send data to the file associated with stream *fOutput* by using the insertion operators that it has inherited from base class *ostream*, like this:

```
fOutput << i << c;
```

The base class for all streams, class *ios*, provides to its derived classes many data members and functions that can be used to control the flow of data in a stream. For example, a group of related data members and functions describes and sets the formatting properties for the stream. Many of these "format-state flags" are described in Appendix B. Another group of member functions detects error conditions as they arise from attempts to use the stream.

Function *eof()*, for example, returns true if an end-of-file condition was detected when trying to use the stream for input. Function *fail()* returns true if any attempt at input or output did not succeed (possibly as the result of some temporary condition). If function *bad()* returns true, that indicates a severe failure, most likely the result of something being wrong with the stream itself. Function *good()* returns true if the three preceding functions all return false—in other words, if all went well with the most recent attempt to access the stream. The following code illustrates some of these stream member functions.

```
istream ist;
ist >> aValue;

while (!ist.fail())
{ //process aValue
    . . .
}

if (ist.eof())
{ //detected end of input, terminate processing
    . . .
}
```

```
else if (ist.bad())
{ //report serious error with stream ist
    . . .

}
```

One final feature of *ios* should be noted about the use of these stream monitoring functions. Class *ios* provides us with operators that allow us to use stream objects as boolean control expressions. In essence, these operators convert a stream reference, like *ist,* to true (non-zero) if *ist.fail()* is false and to false if *ist.fail()* is true. This allows us to abbreviate control expressions like

```
while (!ist.fail()) . . .
```

as

```
while (ist >> aValue) . . .
```

So far we have barely scratched the surface in describing C++'s facility with and support for streams. Because, in part, of the external nature of these facilities to C++, there is considerable variation across language versions in the details of how streams are implemented. We have intentionally discussed only the most uniform parts of the stream libraries. We leave it to you to investigate, both in the lab and on your own, the details of your specific environment. Knowing what you do about streams and, more generally, about C++, you are quite well prepared to carry on.

Strings Revisited

C++ strings are implemented as zero-terminated arrays of characters. The abilities to initialize a string and to extract individual characters from a string via subscripts are examples of C++'s more general facility with arrays. Similarly, the ability to handle strings on input and output derives from overloading the insertion and extraction operators, which themselves are defined in program libraries for streams. Indeed, C++'s ability to deal with strings is not really part of the language but is embodied instead in one of its program libraries.

The library header file named "string.h" contains declarations for a number of standard string processing functions. In Table 9.1, we list ten common ones. If you inspect the file "string.h" in your implementation of C++, you may find functions that we don't list here, but you will almost certainly find the ten we do describe. In the table we use the following notations.

dest is of type char*, a string that will be modified.
src is of type const char*, a string that will not be modified.
n is usually unsigned int. Its type may be different in different implementations, but it will always be some integral type. In the table, we call it *size_t*.
c is a char.

TABLE 9.1

Sample string manipulation functions from library/string.h/

Copy functions

`char* strcpy(dest, src)`	Copies *src* to *dest*, returns a pointer to *dest*.
`char* strncpy(dest, src, n)`	Copies at most *n* characters of *src* to *dest*, returns a pointer to *dest*.

Concatenation functions

`char* strcat(dest, src)`	Concatenates *src* on the end of *dest*, returns a pointer to *dest*.
`char* strncat(dest, src, n)`	Concatenates at most *n* characters of *src* on the end of *dest*, returns a pointer to *dest*.

Comparison functions

`int strcmp(src1, src2)`	Compares *src1* to *src2*, returns negative, zero, or positive value, depending on result.
`int strncmp(src1, src2, n)`	Compares the first *n* characters of *src1* and *src2*, returns negative, zero, or positive value, depending on result.

Search functions

`char* strchr(src, c)`	Returns a pointer to the first instance of *c* in *src*, or NULL pointer, if not found.
`char* strrchr(src, c)`	Returns a pointer to the last instance of *c* in *src*, or NULL pointer, if not found.
`char* strstr(src1, src2)`	Returns a pointer to the first instance of *src2* in *src1*, or NULL pointer, if not found.

Length function

`size_t strlen(src)`	Returns the length of *src*, not counting '\0'.

Here are some examples to illustrate how the string functions operate:

```
char s[10], t[5], u[10];
char *p, *q;
int i;
strcpy(s, "dog");        // s has 6 unused spaces
strcpy(t, "food");       // used up all the space in t

p-strcpy(u,s);           // p points to u, which contains "dog"
q = strcat(s,t);         // q points to s, which contains "dogfood"
q = strchr(s, 'g');      // q now points to the 'g' in s[2],
                         // so q refers to the string "gfood"
i = strlen(q);           // i is 5, the length of "gfood"
i = strcmp(p, s);        // i has a negative value, since
                         // "dog" < "dogfood" in lexicographic order
i = strncmp(p, s, 3);    // i is zero, since the first three
                         // characters of "dog" and "dogfood" match
```

Since the copy and concatenation functions return pointers to strings, we can use them as arguments to other functions, like this:

```
p = strcat(u, strncpy(t, "bonehead", 4));
```

We need to mention only a few things here. First, in the copy and concatenation functions, it is your program's responsibility to ensure that there is enough room in *dest* to perform the operation. Second, the comparison functions rely on what is known as the *lexicographic* order on strings of characters, and that order is based on the order of the numeric codes for the set of characters. A string *s* is lexicographically less than a string *t* if either of the following conditions are met:

1. The first n (≥ 0) characters of *s* and *t* are equal, but $s[n + 1] < t[n + 1]$.
2. The first n (≥ 0) characters of *s* and *t* match, but *s* has exactly n characters, and *t* has more than n characters.

Under this order, "brains" < "brawn" and "hot" < "hottenhot", and the empty string, "", with no characters (except, of course for the invisible terminator '\0'), is less than any other string.

As we gain more experience designing and developing classes we have come to expect a great deal from them. We expect a class to provide us with a variety of constructors that will allow us to declare and initialize objects conveniently and safely. We expect any standard operators that are relevant to the class being defined to be overloaded in order to be consistent with the other interpretations of the operators. And we expect full (or as nearly so as we can get) functionality. That is, the class should be implemented so that it can be used wherever and whenever needed. The bad news is that, according to our not unrealistic demands, the C++ string library doesn't go far enough to elevate strings to a near-C++ type.

The good news, as we saw back in Chapter 6, is that knowing how C++ represents strings allows us to declare and define our own collection of string processing functions. We have done precisely that, and we have expressed it as a class named *OCString*. The class is so named for two reasons. First, we wanted to make sure it would not be confused with any classes named *String* that might be available to you in your C++ environment. Second, class *OCString* is a class in the Object Concept sense of that term—a useful, high-level collection of information that fits neatly into the C++ landscape. We'll start by reviewing the header file for class *OCString*.

```
// ---------- OCSTRING.H ----------
// This file contains the declaration of the
// Object Concept version of class OCString.
#ifndef _OCSTRING_H
#define _OCSTRING_H

#include <iostream.h>              // for istream, ostream
```

```
class OCString
{
public:
// We define three different String constructors and one
// destructor.
    OCString();                  // creates empty string
    OCString(char* array);
    // constructor using a standard C++ string
    OCString(OCString& Other_String);
    // constructor using an OCString
    ~OCString();
    // destructor for our Strings

    int GetLength();             // returns current length

    // We overload operators for assignment, subscripting,
    // equality, extraction, and insertion
    OCString& operator=(const OCString& str);
    char& operator[](int i);

    friend int operator== (const OCString& str1,
                                  const OCString& str2);
    friend istream& operator>>(istream& is, OCString& str);
    friend ostream& operator<< (ostream& os, OCString& str);

private:
    char* s;                 // pointer to the first character of the string
    int length;              // current length of the string
};


#endif
```

These declarations illustrate, in a somewhat curious combination, many of the C++ features we have made use of in earlier examples and PIPs. *OCStrings* are a lower level of object than, say, a soda machine, a deck of cards, or a company payroll, in that they are not programming ends unto themselves. Rather, they are programming means. We develop a class like *OCString* as a support class, if you will, that will serve us in developing other, higher-level, classes. The fact that C++ provides some library support for strings indicates that strings are closer to a programming data type than to a class of real-world objects.

Consistent with this interpretation, the *OCString* class is composed primarily of constructors, destructors, and overloaded operators. It declares a constructor for defining an empty *OCString* object and two copy constructors for initializing *OCString* objects from either a C++ string or another *OCString*. Notice how the member data does not declare any static storage for the *OCString*'s characters, but instead includes a char pointer, *s*. We have chosen to implement *OCStrings* dynamically (using `new` and `delete`), and so the requests for storage allocation will be made by the constructors on demand. The class destructor will free the storage pointed to by *s* when an object is destroyed.

The class declaration also describes five overloaded operators that apply directly to *OCStrings*. For example, we want to be able to assign one *OCString* to another, so we overload the assignment operator to accomplish this. We pass the assignment operator an *OCString* reference in the interest of efficiency, but protect its value by declaring it as a *const* parameter. Like all good assignment operators, this one returns a reference to the type of object being assigned to. This enables assignment expressions to be strung together in standard C++ style.

The selection, or subscript, operator is also overloaded, taking as usual a single integer parameter to serve as a subscript. We know when dealing with *OCStrings* that the value returned will be a character reference.

The overloaded equality operator is designated as a friend to class *OCString* because it clearly applies to two distinct *OCString* objects (both passed as constant references). It returns 1 to indicate that the two *OCStrings* are identical both in length and in character data, and returns 0 otherwise.

The programming-type nature of this class dictates that we use conventional access control. That is, all member functions are declared as public so that they are accessible to any user of the class, and all member data (in this case, a pointer to our character array, and an integer indicating the string's current length) are declared as private.

We will not at this point delve into the definition file for class *OCString* for three reasons. First, we gave you a hint of how we would implement some of the member functions back in Chapter 6 when we were discussing pointers and strings. Second, we have provided a copy of the file (named "OCSTRING.CPP") on your lab disk. You are free to look at it in lab. Most important, you don't need to be concerned with, or even see, the definition file in order to make use of *OCStrings*. Just as you have used streams without knowing the details of how they are implemented, you can use *OCStrings* knowing just what you know from reading the class declaration. That's why C++ supports the notion of distinguishing header from implementation files, and that's why program libraries are so powerful and useful for building complex programs.

9.3 DOCUMENTING PROGRAMS

Much of the advice we offer in this chapter will sound like plain old common sense applied to the task of working with programs. For example, it seems obvious that when we begin to work with an existing program (particularly one written by someone else) it would help tremendously if we understood the program. That is to say, we should have a clear understanding of the problem specification, of how the program addresses the problem, and of the code itself. Perhaps less obvious is the fact that the degree to which we understand the program is likely to reflect not only its clarity of expression and its design but also its style.

Part of a program's style is how well it communicates to its (human) readers. There are many forms of documentation that may accompany a program in the interest of helping it to communicate with its readers. Program documentation can include, for instance, detailed requirements specifications, functional specifications, user interface specifications, design documents that show how the program is decomposed and how its pieces are organized and coordinated, class hierarchy charts, flow charts that express algorithms in graphical form, formal test plans and testing procedures, and a variety of review documents that record the results of formal evaluations at various stages in the program's development. These types of documents are typically written in English or some structured subset thereof.

Throughout this text we have relied primarily on the C++ language for expressing our understanding of a program. We have done so in part because the problems we have dealt with are relatively simple and quite well defined. Still, all programs are expected to communicate directly from their source code listings, and this is the type of documentation we want to focus on here. In particular, we want to demonstrate the degree to which the effective use of comments and sensible choices for variable names can influence a program's understandability.

We have done our best to provide you with well-commented code that uses communicative variable names. To appreciate the value of readable code, read through the following listing. Do you recognize it?

```
// File F1
Class Ft
{
    friend Ft operator+ (Ft f1, Ft f2)
public:
    Ft(int t, int b = 1);
    Ft();
    void Gt();
    void Sw();
    double Evl();
private:
    int nt;
    int dt;
}
```

Does the listing make sense to you at all? Can you tell what it represents, aside from the fact that it appears to declare a class? Does it help if we tell you that "Ft" stands for "Fraction"? This listing, believe it or not, is a defiled version of the header file for class *Fraction* from our Chapter 2 PIP. Here is the original file:

```
// ---------- FRACTION.H ----------
// This file declares the Fraction class

class Fraction
{
    // operator overload, so we can do fractional arithmetic
    // using a familiar operator
    friend Fraction operator+ (Fraction f1, Fraction f2);

public:
    // All member functions are public so that they can be used
    // by programs that need fractions.
    Fraction(int n, int d = 1);        // Set numerator = n,
                                       // denominator = d.
                                       // if no second argument, default
                                       // to 1
    Fraction();                        // Set numerator = 0,
                                       // denominator = 1.

    void Get();                        // Get a fraction from keyboard.
    void Show();                       // Display a fraction on screen

    double Evaluate();                 // Return the decimal value of a
                                       // fraction

private:
    // The member data is private so that users of the class cannot
    // alter it, except implicitly through the constructors.
    int numerator;                     // top part
    int denominator;                   // bottom part
};
```

While the stylistic differences between these two listings go wholly unappreciated by the C++ compiler, the differences are profound in their effect on how these listings communicate to us humans. The second version communicates clearly what the first obscures—that we have defined a C++ class to represent a high-level concept with which we are already familiar. Interestingly enough, the primary differences between the listings are that the second includes descriptive comments and uses carefully chosen names for all its identifiers. Also interesting is that while the C++ compiler does not appreciate these differences, it supports them. That is, we are (almost) free to name identifiers and to use comments however we please.

What makes for a good identifier name? We present a few basic guidelines here—all of which are subject to interpretation. Again, these may sound like common sense, but notice how they coincide with how we tend to specify problems. Following these guidelines tends to minimize the need for translating between a problem specification and a program. The same words that we used to describe the problem can be used to write the program.

1. An identifier should almost always be an English word. The only exception is when a variable is used temporarily to represent a place holder, such as a control variable in a loop.* Otherwise, it makes good sense to provide every identifier with a readable name that conveys what it is intended to represent.

2. In general, nouns should be used for class objects, types, and quantities.

3. In general, verbs should be used to describe functions (except, obviously, class constructors).

4. Names should be precise. For example, *beanCounter* is a better name than *counter,* and *totalAmountPaid* is better than *total.*

5. Names should be unambiguous, so that *GetChar* is better than just *Get* (which could apply to any type of value).

6. Names should conform to some stylistic conventions of their own. In this text, for example, we have adopted the conventions of capitalizing the names of all functions and classes and leaving variable and object names uncapitalized. Similarly, we decided to capitalize the second and subsequent parts of variable names (like *totalAmountPaid)* when a name is composed of two or more words.

We also can offer some general guidelines for including comments in a program listing. Like identifier names, when used effectively comments can serve to connect a program listing to a problem specification or a design document. It doesn't help to be overly prescriptive about how to comment a listing, but it is very difficult to provide too many comments. Some comments, though, are more valuable than others, and that's what we're trying to steer you toward.

1. Include comments at the head of every file, at every declaration, at the head of every function, at any compound control structure (loops, conditionals), at any tricky or unusual code, and anywhere else that requires explanation.

2. Comments should be in English. Don't simply reiterate what the C++ statement says. For example,

```
c = length;     // assign length to c -- BAD!!!
                // save current length so that we can restore it
                // later -- BETTER!
```

3. Comments should relate parts of the program to one another. Critical relationships between classes (like derived and base classes) and functions

---

* Even in these situations, a variable name can communicate in varying degrees. It is customary (although probably only because of an historical accident) to use variable names beginning with 'i' for integer values. Other common practices include using 'r' to designate real values, 'f' to designate floats, 's' to designate strings, and 'p' to designate pointers.

(where one depends on a value returned by another) should be noted explicitly in the code.

4. Comments, like identifiers, should conform to some style standards of their own. You may, for example, prefer comments to occur on individual lines. Or you may prefer to see them attached to lines of code. Wherever you place them, they should be easily detected. Lining comments up vertically with one another helps in this regard.

Let's turn now to the first piece of code of our PIP for this chapter and see how it holds up in light of our informal documentation guidelines. The problem, as you recall, is to describe a text document that can be created, edited, saved, and retrieved in a line-by-line fashion. The listing for file "DOCUMENT.H", follows. If it is clear to you how we have used C++ to describe our problem domain, the documentation has done its job.

```
// ---------- DOCUMENT.H ----------
// This file declares class Document, which serves
// as the basis for our PIP for Chapter 8, a line-
// oriented word processor.

#ifndef _DOCUMENT_H
#define _DOCUMENT_H

#include "OCSTRING.H"          // for class OCString

class Document
{
public:
    Document();                // create default document of 10 lines
    Document(int i);           // create document of specified size
    ~Document();               // destructor frees document storage
    void InsertLine(int);      // insert new line at specified position
    void DeleteLine(int);      // delete line from specified position
    void ChangeLine(int);      // change the line at specified position
    void Display(int, int);    // display range of lines on screen
    void Save();               // save text to a file
    void Retrieve();           // retrieve text from a file

private:
    int maxLines;              // current maximum for number of lines
    int numberLines;           // current number of lines of text
    void ShiftLines(int, int); // shift lines up or down by one position
    void Grow();               // expand text array to fit more lines
    OCString* text;            // points to the start of the text,
                               //  so we can make it grow dynamically
};


#endif
```

This file does a pretty good job of conforming to our guidelines for comments and for identifiers. It begins with clear English comments describing its contents. The class declaration also begins with a comment that relates it to the others declared in the file. Individual comments are supplied to describe class members, particularly where their roles may not be obvious (*ShiftLines*). Comments appear both as individual lines (prior to the code they describe) and attached to specific lines. In all cases, they line up neatly and are clearly visible.

The names chosen for identifiers similarly add to the readability of the file. Indeed, most of the names come, as they should, from our informal program specification. In it, we speak of documents and lines of text. These names become class names in our file as dictated by our DDU approach to program design. The verbs we used to describe the operations we want to perform on our objects (insert, change, delete, save, and retrieve) have been used to name member functions applicable to objects. Other member names were chosen carefully to describe a document as a dynamic array (*Grow, maxLines, numberLines*).

Other simple stylistic features contribute to the readability—and hence, the understandability—of a source listing. Notice, for example, how in our *Document* header file the include statement is listed explicitly near the top. It doesn't have to be, but it is safer that way (because it guarantees that the included declarations will be there before they are referenced), and we have gotten into the habit of doing so. The effect is that the reader of our code comes to expect any include statements to appear prior to any other declarations and need not look around for them. Note, too, that the include has an attached comment describing why (for which of its declarations) it has been included in this file.

Of all of the documentation techniques we have described for improving a program's readability, the deliberate use of spacing is representative in the most ways. First, it is completely ignored by the machine as it reads your program. Spacing is provided to help the human reader of the program. Second, it is remarkably easy to do, requiring almost no thought beyond deciding on what style suits your reading fancy. In fact, it is easier to write comments when you are first typing your program than it is to go back and attempt to add your comments or spaces to an already working program. The problem with adding documentation in any form to a working program is that you may wind up with a program that no longer works. It is far too easy to disturb a working program by, for example, a misplaced brace or comment symbol.

In short, we recommend that you take our documentation guidelines to heart, and that you make them part of your program development technique from the beginning. By investing a minimum amount of time in the relatively simple task of documenting your code carefully as you create it, you stand to save yourself considerable time performing the inevitable and difficult debugging tasks that come later in the the life cycle. Documentation is intended, after all, to help human readers, and you as the author of your program certainly qualify.

9.4 COMPILING PROGRAMS

A clearly documented program is a significant first step toward working with a program. But, as we were careful to point out, no matter how helpful documentation is to a human reader, it is completely ignored by the computer in its attempts to understand a program. In order to make the computer understand our programs, we must write the program in a programming language. Programming languages, like C++, differ from natural languages, like English, in many ways. Perhaps the most critical distinction is that programming languages are constrained to the extent that they can be translated unambiguously by a program (the C++ compiler) into the primitive machine codes that the computer on which it is running understands. The same cannot be said for any natural language.

In order to accomplish such a translation, it is necessary to specify a programming language fully in terms of both its syntax and its semantics. That is, we must describe what constitutes a well-formed statement in the language and what the meaning of each well-formed statement is in terms of its effect on the machine. In describing C++ to you we have done this, but in a decidedly casual manner. When, for example, we described C++'s simple assignment operator, we told you how to write an expression that uses it, and what effect such an expression would have on your program when it was evaluated. When you as a programmer misunderstand or misuse an assignment operator in the semantic sense, your program may produce incorrect results or behave in some otherwise unexpected way. We'll talk about semantic errors later in this chapter. If you make a syntactic error when writing an assignment expression, your program won't even get to the point of running. The C++ compiler will not "understand" your program to the extent that it can perform the necessary translation, and it will give up trying.

If we are to describe the notion of syntax to a computer, we must be considerably more precise than we are in describing the language's grammar rules to one another. Indeed, most programming language manuals contain detailed specifications of the grammar rules for the language being described. These rules describe in a complete and formal way the syntactic knowledge a programmer must have to write a C++ program. We're not expected to memorize them in this form, but knowing how to read these rules can come in handy when confronted with a particularly sticky syntax error. A small portion of the grammar rules for one implementation of C++ appears in Figure 9.3.

These rules, for example, describe a name as having four different possible forms (it can be an identifier, an operator_function_name, a conversion_function_name, or a qualified_name). A qualified_name, in turn, can take any of five forms, each of which begins with a class-name followed by two colons (::). As assignment expression has two forms, as prescribed by the grammar. One is a conditional expression, which itself has two general forms. The other is composed of a unary expression, followed by any one of

FIGURE 9.3
Part of a C++
grammar

```
name
    identifier
    operator_function_name
    conversion_function_name
    qualified_name
qualified_name
    class_name :: identifier
    class_name :: operator_function_name
    class_name :: conversion_function_name
    class_name :: class_name
    class_name :: ~class_name
conditional_expression
    logical_OR_expression
    logical_OR_expression ? expression : conditional_expression
assignment_expression
    conditional_expression
    unary_expression assignment_operator assignment_expression
assignment_operator
    =
    *=
    /=
    %=
    +=
    -=
    <<=
    >>=
    &=
    ^=
    |=
```

the permissible assignment operators, followed by an assignment expression. Ultimately, these rules are spelled out fully to describe the structure of every well-formed statement in the language, down to the level of the individual characters involved.

Not coincidentally, these rules are used to guide the development and behavior of the C++ compiler. The compiler (which itself is just a program) accepts as input a program, which it regards as a string of characters. It then attempts to interpret the program according to the rules specified by the C++ grammar. If the input program conforms to one of the many recognized forms for a complete program, we say the program compiled successfully. Practically speaking, this means that our program was well formed from a grammatical standpoint, that the compiler recognized it as a C++ program, and that the compiler was able to translate it.

When our program somehow violates the grammar rules as interpreted by the compiler, the compiler alerts us to this fact by providing us with a list of syntax errors. Most modern compilers, which would include all C++ compilers, are quite adept at isolating and identifying syntax errors in our programs. Along with a detailed description of its version of the C++ grammar, most programming manuals include lengthy lists of errors that are detected by the C++ compiler and the error messages the compiler will produce when it detects these errors. While both the details of the C++ grammar and the error messages the compiler produces vary across environments, the types of error messages listed in Figure 9.4 are quite common.

In its attempts to help us make effective use of the language, the C++ compiler not only reports syntax errors as they are detected, but also does its best to locate them for us. Many of the errors listed in Figure 9.4 are straightforward to fix, especially if we are told the line in which the error was detected. A missing ";" at the end of a declaration or a missing "," within a parameter list are obvious oversights and quick fixes, to say the least.

Other errors point out discrepancies that must be resolved in order to compile the program. If we are told that there is an "extra parameter in call" to a particular function, that means either we declared the function with the wrong number of parameters (if it is a function that we have defined, and not one belonging to a standard C++ library), or we have invoked the function with an extra parameter. The error is signaled when it is detected (at the point of the function call), but the error could be in one of a few places. In this case, and others like it (including, for example, complaints about type mismatches, too many or too few parameters, multiple declarations, and missing declaration), the source of the error may not be quite so obvious. Fortunately, the point at which the error was detected usually provides a good indication of where to look.

FIGURE 9.4
Some typical compiler error messages

```
identifier is not a member of struct
, expected
: expected after private/public/protected
cannot find class::class() to initialize base class
cannot modify a const object
compound statement missing }
declaration missing ;
duplicate case
extra parameter in call
function function should have a prototype
misplaced else
multiple declaration for identifier
subscript missing ]
too few parameters in call
type mismatch in parameter number in call to function function
undefined symbol identifier
```

Some error messages can be classified as "best guesses" by the compiler. That is, they represent the compiler's attempt to understand the program, and they show up when the compiler can no longer make any syntactic sense out of a portion of the program. It may report an error like "compound statement missing }" or "misplaced else" long after the real source of the error (a missing '}', misplaced comment symbol, extra '{', or missing if). In these cases, the error messages tell us the point at which the compiler gave up trying to understand the program. These types of syntactic errors are the toughest to track down because they could have resulted from simple errors at any previous point in the listing.

We can offer a few guidelines for isolating and repairing syntax errors. Before describing them, we should remind you of two things. First, error messages attempt to describe in English what the compiler perceives to be a misuse of the C++ language. Read these messages carefully, trying to imagine the processing that was going on from the compiler's perspective. It is, after all, only a program reading a series of characters that we happen to believe conforms to the C++ grammar. If you don't understand an error message, look for a more verbose description in the C++ language manual for your particular implementation. As we said, these manuals usually contain fuller explanations of the grammar and the syntax error produced by the compiler.

Second—and this is very important—remember that syntax errors are detected as your program is being compiled. That means that your program has not been run and, in fact, cannot be run until the errors are repaired. The point is that in attempting to track down syntax errors you need not consider whether the algorithms expressed by your function are correct. Nor should you worry about your program's flow of control (which functions call which functions, and in what order). Such considerations are superfluous because your program never got to the point of running. When trying to fix syntax errors the only ordering that you need to take into account is the physical ordering of code in the file being compiled (paying attention, of course, to any include directives and inline function definitions).

Here, then, are a few basic techniques for repairing syntax errors.

1. Look first at the line of code where the error is indicated. If the error is purely grammatical (like a missing punctuator), the source of the error is probably close at hand.

2. If the error message indicates some discrepancy in your program (too many . . ., too few . . ., or a mismatch of some kind), look first at the line where the error is indicated. If the source of the error is not evident, look earlier in the file (or in any programmer-defined included file) for references to each of the identifiers that occur in the indicated line. For example, if a function is called in the indicated line, look back to find its declaration and make sure it matches with how it is being used at the point of error.

3. If the error message describes something more substantial than a missing punctuation mark (like an undeclared identifier, misplaced else, or

missing declaration), start from the indicated line and work backward toward the beginning of the file. Make sure, for example, that identifier names are spelled correctly and used consistently.

A version of the definition file for our *Document* class follows. The bad news is that we have included a few syntax errors. The good news is that we don't expect you to detect them with the naked eye. Rather, we'll show you error messages as they might be produced as a result of trying to compile the file and then show you how the sources of the errors can be detected and repaired.

```cpp
// ---------- DOCUMENT.CPP ----------
// WITH SYNTAX ERRORS
// The definition of class Document, for
// use in our word processor of PIP9.

#include <iostream.h>        // for cin, cout
#include <fstream.h>         // for ifstream, ofstream
#include "DOCUMENT.H"        // for class Document
#include "OCSTRING.H"        // for class OCString
#include "UTILITY.H"         // for Swap

Document::Document()
// constructor creates a default document of 10 lines,
// and allocates storage for document
{
    maxLines = 10;
    numberLines = 1;
    text = new OCString[maxLines+1];
};

Document::Document(int i)
// constructor sets maximum and current number of lines,
// and allocates storage for document
{
    maxLines = i;
    numberLines = 1;
    text = new OCString[maxLines+1];
};

Document::~Document()
// This destructor function for class Document
// deallocates, first the OCStrings that comprise
// the text of the document, and then the
// document's pointer to its text.
{
    delete [maxLines+1] text;
};
```

```
void Document::InsertLine(int lineNum)
// This function inserts a new line of text at
// the position specified by parameter lineNum.
{
    // Use class OCString and its overloaded I/O operators
    // to read in a new line.
    OCString newLine;
    cout << "Type new line, followed by <Enter>:\n";
    cin >> newLine;

    if(numberLines == maxLines)             // if we have to expand text array
        Grow();                             //    do it

    if (lineNum < 1)                        // if line number is too small
        lineNum = 1;                        //    assume we'll insert at start

    if (lineNum > numberLines)              // if line number is too big
        text[numberLines+1] = newLine;      //    insert at the end

    else
    {                                       // normal insertion involves . . .
        ShiftLines(1,lineNum);              //    moving lines to make space, and
        text[lineNum] = newLine;            //    copying the line into our array
    }
    numberLines++;                          // in any case, we have one more line
}


void Document::DeleteALine(int lineNum)
// This function removes a line of text from
// a document by shifting lines up.
{
    if((lineNum < 1) || (lineNum > numberLines))// if illegal line specified
        cout << "\n*** No such line.\n";    // don't assume anything!
  else
    {
        cout << "\nDeleting line " << lineNum << ". . .\n";
        ShiftLines(-1,lineNum);             // shift lines in array up
        numberLines--;                      // one fewer line now
    }
}


void Document::ChangeLine(int lineNum)
// This function uses OCString assignment
```

```
// to replace an existing line with a new
// one provided by the user.
{
    if((lineNum<1) || (lineNum > numberLines))      // Can't replace a line
        cout << "\n*** No such line.\n";            // that doesn't exist
    else
      {
          cout << "Current line " << lineNum << ":" ;   // Show the old line
          cout << "\n\t" << text[lineNum] << '\n';
          cout << "Enter new line: \n\t";
          cin >> text[lineNum];                      // Read the new one
      }
}


void Document::Display(int start, int finish)
// Display a range of lines from the document
// on the screen. The hardest part is making
// sure the line numbers make sense.
{
    if (start > finish)
        Swap (start, finish);
    if (start < 1)
        start = 1;
    if (( finish > numberLines) || (finish < 1))
        finish = numberLines;

    // use loop and OCString's overloaded insertion operator
    // to display each line of text in the range
    for (int lineNum = start; lineNum <= finish; lineNum++)
    {
        cout << "\n" << lineNum << ":\t";
        cout << text[lineNum];
    };
    cout << "\n\n";
}


void Document::Save()
// This function writes a document to a disk file.
// The user provides a file name, and the function
// opens that file and connects it to this program.
{
    char fileName[30];
    cout << "\n\nSave document in what file? Type full file name";
```

```
        cout << "\nfollowed by <Enter>: ";
        cin >> fileName;

        ofstream f(fileName);

        // Now send the document one line at a time to the open file
        // Notice that we start with line #1, to be consistent with
        // the user's counting
        cout << "\nWriting file: " << fileName << '\n';
        for(int thisLine=1; thisLine <= numberLines; thisLine++)
            f << text[thisLine] << '\n';

        // Close the file for safety's sake
        f.close();
}


void Document::Retrieve()
// This function reads a document from a disk file.
// The user provides a file name, and the function
// opens that file and connects it to this program.
{
        char fileName[30];
        cout << "\n\nOpen which document? Type full file name";
        cout << "\nfollowed by <Enter>: ";
        cin >> fileName;

        ifstream f(fileName);

        // Since a file to be input must exist before reading it,
        // we check to make sure it does, and re-prompt if we
        // can't open the file name specified
        while (!f)
        {
            cout << "\nSpecified file cannot be opened. Try again...";
            cout << "\n\nOpen which document? Type full file name";
            cout << "\nfollowed by <Enter>: ";
            cin >> fileName;
            ifstream f(fileName);
        }
        // Read the file in, one OCString at a time, starting
        // with line #1 of the document (leaving text[0]
        // uninitialized -- that's OK because we don't access it!)
        cout << "\nReading file: " << fileName << '\n';
        numberLines=1;
```

```
    while(f >> text[numberLines])
    {
        if (numberLines == maxLines)
            Grow();
        numberLines++;
    }
    // the last read failed, so decrement the number of lines
    numberLines--;
    f.close();
}


void Document::ShiftLines(int direction, int start)
// This function moves lines of text one position up
// or down in our document, depending on the value
// of parameter direction (+1 means move lines down,
// making a space; -1 means move lines up, deleting
// a line). Parameter start indicates the line number
// from which the moving is to begin.
{
    int i;
    if (direction>0)
    // We want to make space, so copy lines "down"
    // starting from the last line
        for(i=numberLines+1; i>= start+1; i--)
            text[i]=text[i-1];
    else if (direction < 0)
    // We want to remove a line, so move lines "up"
    // starting from the specified line
        for(i=start; i<=numberLines-1; i++)
            text[i]=text[i+1];
}


void Document::Grow()
// Doubles the size of the dynamic array that holds
// the document's text. Called whenever we run out
// of space when trying to insert a new line.
{
    int newSize=2*maxLines;              // double the size of current text
    OCString* newText = new OCString[newSize+1];
    // create a new array of that size
    for (int i=1; i<=maxLines; i++)      // copy all lines into new array
        newText[i]=text[i];
    delete[] text;
    text=newText;                        // make our document point to new text
    maxLines=newSize;                    // set new maximum size
}
```

We compiled this file using a few different compilers. While there were differences both in which errors were detected and in the language used to describe the errors, the following messages describe in general terms the errors that were most commonly detected and their locations in the source file. We will discuss them briefly, and in order.

Error #	Location	Message
1	cout expression (InsertLine)	*unterminated string*
2	cin expression (InsertLine)	*statement missing ;*
3	first if expression (InsertLine)	*possibly incorrect assignment*
4	third if statement (InsertLine)	*undefined symbol numLines*
5	function header (DeleteALine)	*Document::DeleteALine is not a member of class Document*
6	function header (Save)	*declaration syntax error*
7	last (empty) line of file	*compound statement missing }*

Error #1 is an example of a straightforward syntax error detected exactly at the source of the problem. It reports an unterminated string (that is, a missing closing quote for what appears to be a string literal) right where we neglected to include a double quote symbol. Interestingly enough, this misuse of C++ also was the source of error message #2, which reported a missing ';' in the subsequent line. It appears that by leaving the quote out, we confused the compiler sufficiently so that it never detected the semicolon that is quite obviously there. At any rate, by placing a double quote between the /n and the colon in the cout expression in *InsertLine* both errors are resolved.

Error #3 isn't really a syntax error at all, but was flagged as a "warning" by our compilers as a "possibly incorrect assignment." What happened is that the compiler interpreted the expression *numberLines=maxLines* as an assignment statement. Since such statements return values (in this case, the value of *maxLines*), these values can serve as boolean indicators that would make sense (at least syntactically) following the keyword if. Although it is legal syntactically, using an assignment statement in this context is unusual, not to mention confusing. The writers of the compiler must have recognized this, and prepared the compiler to detect and flag such situations. The punch line here is that, just as the compiler suggested, we really intended to compare *numberLines* and *maxLines* for equality (==) and not assign one to the other.

Errors # 4 is an example of the discrepancy type of error we described earlier. In this case, we have used the name *numLines,* when the data member of class *Document* that we really intend to refer to is named *numberLines* in the *Document* class declaration. The error message reports what the compiler regards as an "undefined symbol." What has happened from our perspective is that a symbol has been used in a class member definition that is not itself a defined member of the class. Changing the identifier to match the name used in the class declaration fixes the problem.

Another discrepancy type of error is reported in message # 5. Function *DeleteALine* is not recognized as a member function of class *Document*, because it isn't. Function *DeleteLine* is, of course, and once again, we have apparently used two different names to refer to the same function. We could change the name in the class declaration to match that used in the definition, but then if we invoke the function from elsewhere in our code using the name as first declared (which seems likely), we'll introduce new errors. Changing the name in the function definition header is the most direct fix here.

The compiler does a good job of detecting and isolating error # 6, found in the header for function *Document::Save*. What it doesn't do particularly well is explain its findings. One of our compilers produced the vague message "declaration syntax error" and another reported that "the size of Document was unknown", neither of which seemed to have much to do with where the error was signaled. We looked up the second error message in the appropriate C++ language manual and found that such a message gets produced in a variety of circumstances, including when a single colon (instead of the required "::") is used between a function header and its opening left brace. How the compiler comes up with this interpretation may be known only to those who wrote the compiler. Indeed, we might never have known this had it not been for the explanation in the manual. At any rate, inserting the second required colon takes care of the problem.

The most baffling error of all is the last one, # 7, which signals a missing '}' at the very last line of the file. Given that this line is empty, the only thing clear about this error is that it is one in which we will have to resort to backtracking through the file. The only—but significant—hint we have is that the computer seems to be missing a closing brace somewhere. The best way to proceed, then, is to work backward, matching opening and closing braces to make sure they come in pairs. Remember, too, that spacing is ignored by the compiler. Even though an open and close brace are lined up somewhere in the file, that doesn't mean the compiler regards them are "matching" in the sense that they begin and end a compound statement. Cutting to the chase, we can direct you to the definition of function *Document::Retrieve*. Notice the compound statement that comprises the body of the `while` loop. There is no closing brace there, and that is the source of the rather distant error message.

One final note is in order about a message that doesn't appear in our list. In the definition for function *ShiftLine* we intentionally referred to an identifier, *test,* in the body of the function's first for loop. As in error # 4, we should have referred to variable *text* the correct name of the data member of class *Document*. Clearly this is an error, but it went undetected by two of our compilers. This is a good indication of how syntax errors can be interrelated. Probably because of the confusion suffered by the compiler as a result of either error # 6 or error # 7, this error did not get reported. The punch line, again, is: Take the compiler's error messages, particularly those that do not make clear or immediate sense, with equally healthy doses of salt and common programming sense.

9.5 LINKING PROGRAMS

Before we move on to examine a main function that uses the classes we have compiled for our PIP, let's consider briefly some common errors that can occur when we call on C++ to link our programs. Since C++ environments differ in the details of which program preparation tasks are explicitly performed by compilers and which are performed by linkers, we'll take a less formal point of view here. When we say we are interested in "linking errors," we mean any errors that occur as a result of attempts to integrate program libraries into a cohesive running program. In some C++ environments the errors we describe in this section are reported as compiler errors. In others they are explicitly referred to as linker errors. In all cases, they tend to point out problems with getting distinct files of code to refer to one another correctly.

By far the most common cause of these linker-type errors is the misuse of the include directive. If, for example, you forget to include a library file the contents of which are referenced by the program you are writing, you will probably get a list of error messages when you try to run your program. These messages will point to every identifier described in the missing library file and claim they are "undeclared." They are declared, of course, but not in your file. When the compiler cannot locate a declaration for an identifier, it doesn't know the type of object the identifier refers to, and it gets confused. The compiler sometimes reports other seemingly unrelated errors (like "missing ;" or "expected") that reflect its confusion.

The same kind of confusion results if you use an include directive to refer to a file that doesn't exist. If in our "DOCUMENT.CPP" file, we had mistakenly included file "DOCS.H" (like #include "DOCS.H") instead of file "DOCUMENT.H," we probably would get a message to the effect that no such file exists, and so it could not be included. Then we would be subjected to the same barrage of "undeclared" or "unrecognized" symbols as we were before.

A third variation on the misuse of the include directive is as follows. Most C++ environments provide programmers with a facility for combining separate files into a single program (sometime referred to as a "make" facility). When you include in your program one of the standard C++ library header files, the corresponding definition file (if it is separate) is effectively tacked onto your program as well. When your program includes a header file that is programmer defined (like DOCUMENT.H), C++ does not know which file contains the definitions that match the declarations contained in the file. In these cases, we must indicate which definition files are to be linked to our program.

This allows for the following possibility. You use the `include` directive properly and include in your program the correct header file that your program needs to reference. In building your program, however, you might forget to specify the definition file corresponding to the header file that you have included. In these cases, your program will probably compile correctly (assuming, of course, that there are no other errors). After all, the compiler has access to all of the declarations it needs. When, C++ tries to link your program, actually composing the definition files so that they can reference one another, it realizes something is missing. At that point, it signals any identifiers that are defined in the missing ".CPP" file as being "undefined."

Combining files into a single program also opens the possibility of multiple declarations for individual identifiers. We first discussed this possibility in Chapter 7 and offered a suggestion for protecting against such occurrences (using `#ifndef` . . . `#endif` around our header files). The problem still can occur if we define, say, constants or inline functions in definition files. What happens, then, if we define them as well in the file containing a main program? What happens is that when we go to run our program we get an error message indicating that these identifiers have "already been defined."

Another linker-type error that we have already discussed results from applying incorrect access control to class members. Again, in our PIP, if the constructor functions for class *Document*, say, were declared in the class declaration as private (instead of public, as they are now), we would not have access to them from a `main` function. Even if we properly included the file "DOCUMENT.H" in our `main` program file, we would not be able to declare an object of type *Document* (thereby invoking one of its constructors). An attempt to do so would result in an error message indicating that *Document::Document* is not accessible. This is yet another example of what we call a discrepancy error, in which the problem may not be where the error is signaled. The source of the error in this case is back in the header file that declares class *Document*.

In fact, most of the linker-type errors we have discussed result from similar discrepancies. The good news is that, like the *Document::Document* example, most of the messages provide reasonably clear indications as to where the sources of the errors are. The following hints for avoiding these errors primarily take the form of reminders or of additional commenting guidelines.

1. Comment all `include` directives to indicate why the specified file is being included (that is, which of its declarations are being used in the current file). This not only makes clear why the file was included, but also will help you recognize if the file is no longer needed.
2. Check file names in `include` directives carefully to make sure they match their intended files exactly.

3. Remember to use the `#ifndef` . . .`#define` . . . `#endif` directives around all programmer-defined header files to avoid multiple declarations.

4. Define inline functions, globally useful constants, and any machine-dependent code in header files. This makes it easy to change them by localizing the change to the file that other programs will include. It also reduces the chance for multiple declarations.

5. Comment all class declarations to describe why access control is used as it is. For each class member, it should be clear why the member is controlled as it is.

9.6 RUNNING PROGRAMS

We are at last ready to run a program involving our *Document* class, and this is where things get really exciting. Having reached the point where a program successfully compiles and links, it is natural to assume that it will run, and run correctly. While it may happen that way, it is equally (far more?) likely that you will encounter a runtime error or two.

Run-time errors are those that occur after your program has been completely translated and while it is in the process of running (hence, the name). They come in two basic flavors: *fatal* and *logical*. Both types are the result of a programming error and, in both cases, analysis of the error (determining what caused the error, where the source of the error is, and how to fix the error) is often much tougher than for any of the errors we have discussed so far. We cannot rely merely on listings of the program's files to analyze a runtime error. Rather, we must take into account both the flow of control through the program (which functions call which others) and the value of every data object involved in the computation that caused the error.

Most C++ environments include support for runtime error analysis (or "debugging"). Most allow you to step through a program in a controlled manner (one C++ instruction at a time) so that you can see explicitly the flow of control. They also let you observe the values of selected data objects as the objects are used in calculations. Together these facilities, when used effectively, can provide you with a clear picture of how the computer is evaluating your code. Such an understanding is, needless to say, essential to understanding why the computer is producing a runtime error.

A listing of the file containing the `main` function for this chapter's PIP follows. Briefly, our program is intended to exercise the *Document* class in three steps. First, it asks the user of the program if an existing document should be opened to begin the processing. If the user responds affirmatively, a body of text is read in from a disk file (by calling function *Document::Retrieve*) and stored as the *text* in a newly created *Document* object. Otherwise, the *text* member for the new *Document* object is defined as empty (as prescribed by the *Document* default constructor).

Once a *Document* object has been created and initialized, it is up to the user of the program to manipulate it. This is implemented by the while loop, wherein the program repeatedly displays the menu of commands, accepts a command from the user, and invokes (using free function *ProcessDocument-Menu*) the appropriate manipulator function. This process continues until the user types 'Q' at the menu prompt, indicating a desire to quit the program.

Before quitting, the program gives the user the opportunity to invoke the document's *Save* function, which sends the text portion of the current document to a disk file.

```
// ---------- PIP9.CPP ----------
// A program (and a support function) that combines
// our User, String, and Document classes to make
// a simple, line-oriented word processor.

#include <iostream.h> // for cin, cout
#include <ctype.h>    // for toupper
#include "DOCUMENT.H" // for class Document (includes class OCString)
#include "USER2.H"    // for class User (revised for this program)

void ProcessDocumentMenu(char c, int p1, int p2, Document d)
// This function serves the purpose of associating commands and
// parameters received from our menu with operations performed
// on Document objects.
{                                  // Choose an operation to perform
    switch(c)                      // based on the value of char c. . .
    {   case 'I': d.InsertLine(p1);   // insert a line a position p1
                  break;
        case 'C': d.ChangeLine(p1);   // change the line at position p1
                  break;
        case 'D': d.DeleteLine(p1);   // delete the line at position p1
                  break;
        case 'P': d.Display(p1, p2); // display the range of lines p1-p2
                  break;
        case 'Q': return;            // simply return to quit
    };
}

void main()
{
    Document d;   // creates a new, empty document
    char ans;

    // Either leave the document blank, or read one in from disk
    cout << "\n\nType N to start a new document, or O to open an existing";
    cout << "\ndocument. Then hit <Enter>: ";
```

```
cin >> ans;
ans=toupper(ans);
if (ans=='0')
    d.Retrieve();

// Create our menu, and the necessary variables to read commands
User u;
char command;
int param1, param2;

// The menu loop continues to get and process commands until
// a quit command is entered
do
{   u.ShowMenu();
    u.GetMenu(command, param1, param2);
    ProcessDocumentMenu(command, param1, param2, d);
} while(command != 'Q');

// Give the user a chance to save the current document
// before terminating
cout << "\n\nType S to save current document, or X to exit without";
cout << "\nsaving. Then hit <Enter>: ";
cin >> ans;
ans = toupper(ans);
if (ans == 'S')
    d.Save();
}
```

This program will compile and link with our *Document* declaration and definitions files, but it will produce a few errors when we ask C++ to run it (which you will in lab). Despite the unfortunate choice of terms, "fatal" errors tend to be somewhat easier to detect and recover from than are logical run-time errors because we often receive some information from the computer about the error it detected before it quit running the program. The good news is that this information typically includes an error message and a location indicating which instruction caused the error. The bad news (you knew this was coming . . .) is that this information tends to describe the symptoms of the error and not necessarily its real cause.

The place to start with all fatal errors is where the error was signaled. We then want to work backward, if necessary, getting as much information as we can about any and all of the functions and data objects involved in the evaluation that led to the error.

Logical run-time errors are the toughest of all errors to track down for one simple reason: As far as the computer is concerned, there is no problem. That is, when a program contains a logical error it runs completely through to what the computer regards as a normal termination. The problem from our perspective is that the program produces results that we neither expected nor desired. Since the computer did not detect a problem, it provides us with no clues as to what went wrong, aside from the output it produces. It becomes our task in such cases to work backward from the program's output, trying our best to ascertain why the program behaved as it did. The following list provides a few more general guidelines that will help you in this often frustrating but frequently satisfying task.

1. Become familiar and comfortable with the debugging tools provided by your C++ environment. When used effectively, nothing gives you a better-informed picture of how the computer is evaluating your program.

2. When analyzing runtime errors, do your best to "play computer." That is, put yourself in the role of computer looking dispassionately at your program as a series of instructions to follow. Do your best to forget what you, as its author, *want* the program to do, and try to concentrate on what it *did* do.

3. In tracing backward through a program, start at the point of error (if there is an error reported), and proceed logically through the program. If no error was reported, begin tracing from the code that directly produced the first signs of incorrect behavior in the program's output.

4. In tracing backward through your code, examine every function and data item related however remotely to the error. Pay careful attention to the values of array subscripts, formal and actual parameters, and pointers.

5. Be systematic and thorough, because the computer is. Don't rule out any possible source of error until you are sure of the cause.

6. Avoid at all cost the "fix and pray" approach to debugging. Do your best to understand the real source of an error before attempting to fix it. Otherwise you may find yourself adding new code or changing existing code based on incomplete information, and you are likely to introduce more errors than you eliminate.

9.7 SUMMING UP

▶ An identifier should almost always be an English word. The only exception is when a variable is used temporarily to represent a place holder, such as a control variable in a loop. Otherwise, it makes good sense to provide every identifier with a readable name that conveys what it is intended to represent.

▶ In general, nouns should be used for class objects, types, and quantities.

▶ In general, verbs should be used to describe functions (except, obviously, class constructors).

▶ Names should be precise. For example, *beanCounter* is a better name than *counter,* and *totalAmountPaid* is better than *total.*

▶ Names should be unambiguous, so that *GetChar* is better than just *Get* (which could apply to any type of value).

▶ Names should conform to some stylistic conventions of their own.

▶ Look first at the line of code where a syntax error is indicated. If the error is purely grammatical (like a missing punctuator), the source of the error is probably close at hand.

▶ If a compiler error message indicates some discrepancy in your program (too many . . ., too few . . ., or a mismatch of some kind), look first at the line where the error is indicated. If the source of the error is not evident, look earlier in the file (or in any programmer-defined included file) for references to each of the identifiers that occur in the indicated line.

▶ If a compiler error message describes something more substantial than a missing punctuation mark (like an undeclared identifier, misplaced else, or missing declaration), start from the indicated line and work backward toward the beginning of the file.

▶ Comment all include directives to indicate why the specified file is being included (that is, which of its declarations are being used in the current file).

▶ Check file names in include directives carefully to make sure they match their intended files exactly.

▶ Remember to use the #ifndef...#define...#endif directives around all programmer-defined header files to avoid multiple declarations.

▶ Define inline functions, globally useful constants, and any machine-dependent code in header files.

▶ Comment all class declarations to describe why access control is used as it is. For each class member, it should be clear why the member is controlled as it is.

▶ Become familiar and comfortable with the debugging tools provided by your C++ environment.

▶ When analyzing runtime errors, do your best to "play computer."

▶ In tracing backward through a program, start at the point of the routine error (if there is an error reported), and proceed logically through the program. If no error was reported, begin tracing from the code that directly produced the first signs of incorrect behavior in the program's output.

▶ In tracing backward through your code, examine every function and data item related however remotely to the error.

▶ Be systematic and thorough, because the computer is. Don't rule out any possible source of error until you are sure of the cause.

▶ Avoid at all cost the "fix and pray" approach to debugging. Do your best to understand the real source of an error before attempting to fix it.

9.8 EXERCISES

1. Evaluate each of the following variable names as either good or bad. If it is good, describe in English what it refers to. If it is bad, say why it is bad and offer an alternative.

   a. xr7
   b. thisLine
   c. charPointer
   d. fileName
   e. this

2. Evaluate each of the following function names as either good or bad. If it is good, describe in English what it refers to. If it is bad, say why it is bad and offer an alternative.

   a. GetIt
   b. ALINE
   c. CountWords
   d. process
   e. SendToDiskFile

3. Look at the listing of file "FRACTION.H" in the text. Write out (by hand) what you think the file looks like to the C++ compiler as it prepares to check the syntax of the file. Compare this version with the listing of file "F1" that precedes it in the text.

4. Find the list of compiler error messages in your C++ language manual. Find three errors that you think would be characterized as discrepancy errors, as we described in the chapter.

5. Find the syntax errors in the following program segments. Use the computer and your compiler to verify your analysis. Assume appropriate declarations have been made in each case.

   a.
```
void DisplayFindings(int s, float d, int t)
{
    cout << "The car travelled at a speed of "
            << d << "mph\n"
    cout << "The car travelled a distance of "
            << s << "miles\n;
    cout << 'The car travelled at a speed for "
            << t << "minutes\n";
}
```

b.
```
int LinearSearch(IntArray arr, int size, int val)
    {
    \\ This function searches for value val in array arr,
    \\ and returns its position, or -1 if not found
        for (int i = 0, i <= size, i++)
        {   if (arr[i] = x) return i;
        return -1;
    }
```

6. Find a full description of the grammar for your version of C++. Compare it to the grammar rules found in Figure 9.3. Is the notation used to describe each the same? Can you see similarities in the content of the two sets of rules?

7. Why are logical runtime errors often the toughest of all error types to detect and repair?

8. If your program includes a file (like #include <iostream.h>) that is not required to compile or link your program, no error message is produced. Why not? What would be involved in detecting this type of "error"?

9. We recommend in the guidelines for addressing both compiler and runtime errors that you work "backward" from the reported spot of the error. What precisely does "backward" mean in these two contexts?

10. What do you think we mean when we tell you that in analyzing runtime errors you should do you best to "play computer"? How can automated debugging tools help you play computer?

11. Write a program that performs "lexical analysis" on a C++ program file. That is, your program should accept as input a C++ file (start with a header file) and produce on the screen a list of the individual words and punctuation marks that constitute that part of the input program that is subjected to C++'s syntax rules (which is just about everything other than comments).

10

CLASS ACTIONS III: ALGORITHMS

God is in the details.

The vast majority of most real-world programs, no matter what language they're written in, are quite simple in a computational sense. A commercial-grade word processor or a spreadsheet program, for instance, may very well be tens of thousands of lines long, but the vast majority of the work done by such programs is conceptually simple, involving little more than storing and retrieving information, responding to actions by the user, and managing the details of displaying menus and windows. If you think back over the PIPs we have used so far in this text, you'll see that once we have designed a program as a collection of cooperating objects, the actions each object can perform generally involve very simple manipulation of the object's member data, such as reporting values and elementary modification.

There are times, however, when an object has to be manipulated in a way that is not as simple as displaying the values of its member data. Once we turn our attention to computational tasks that are not entirely trivial, we find that it is often not enough just to get the job done. Instead, an important consideration now comes to the fore: how to get the job done *efficiently*. Obviously, a program that takes two hours to manipulate one of its objects is less desirable than one that performs the same task in two seconds, all other things being equal.

Algorithm: The sequence of actions needed to perform a computational task.

We have seen that there are generally many ways to perform the same task, depending on which *algorithm* we use. The study of algorithms, which we introduce in this chapter, is devoted to finding appropriate measures of the "efficiency" of algorithms, to studying and classifying the various types of algorithms, and to comparing the efficiency of various algorithms that perform the same task. In one sense, the study of algorithms has an ecological nature based on the need to conserve the two scarce resources of any computer: the time it takes to complete a task and the amount of storage space the algorithm requires.

OBJECTIVES

In this chapter, we will

▶ Investigate several ways of searching for an element in a list.

▶ Learn how to design functions that call themselves.

▶ Design and implement an array-like class to represent lists of integers.

▶ Discuss measures we can use to express the time it will take for an algorithm to run.

▶ Compare the efficiency of two algorithms that sort a list of elements.

10.1   SEARCHING FOR AN ELEMENT IN A LIST

The problem of searching a list for an element meeting some condition can be expressed in a number of different forms. In this section and the next, we will consider three variants on this problem. The first two will involve the same basic idea—inspecting each element in turn—and the last will use an entirely different technique.

Finding the Smallest Element

For our first example of searching, let's consider the problem of finding the location of the smallest element in an array of integers at or after a given location. We can describe this problem in precise terms as follows:

In: An array, *a*, of integers, occupying indices 0 to *end*.
      An index, *start*, assumed to be in the range 0 . . . *end*.
Out: The index of the smallest element in the collection a[*start*], . . . , a[*end*].
      If there are duplicate copies of the minimal element, return the
      smallest index among the duplicates.

For example, if the array *a* was {13, 18, 9, 2, 28, 2, 16, 7, 5}, with *end* = 8 and a start index of *start* = 0, the algorithm would return 3, the index of the first 2. Similarly, if we began our search at position *start* = 6, the algorithm would return 8, the index of the smallest element in the subarray {16, 7, 5}.

We begin designing this algorithm by asking the same question we have used in past algorithm design problems: "How would I do this if I had to do it manually?" It seems that a simple way to proceed would be something like, "Look at elements a[*start*] to a[*end*] in turn, and for each element that is less

Remember, C++ array indices always start at 0, so the highest index in this nine-element array is **8**.

than the minimum we've seen so far, keep track of where the new minimum is and what its value is. After we've looked at each element, return the location of the minimum we found." That's almost simple enough to translate directly into C++: We'll use a for loop, since we know the starting and ending indices, and in the loop we'll use an if statement to compare the value of the current element with the minimum we've seen so far. But how will we do the first comparison before we've seen any minimum? Hmm. . . . Why not start by letting *a*[*start*] be the minimum, and then look at the elements from *a*[*start* + 1] to *a*[*end*]? If we do that, we can write our function with little difficulty. We assume in our definition that we have defined a type *IntArray* that represents arrays of integers (which, in fact, is what we'll do in this chapter's PIP).

```
int FindMin(IntArray a, int start, int end)
// Finds the index of the first minimal element in the
// subarray a[start] ... a[end].
// NOTE: this requires that start <= end and that both indices
// are legal positions in the array a.
{
    int     min = a[start],      // smallest value seen so far
            where = start;       // location of the smallest value

    // Look at each element, from start + 1 to end.
    for (int i = start + 1; i <= end; i++)
        if (a[i] < min)          // Is a[i] a new minimum?
        {
            min = a[i];          // If so, record it,
            where = i;           // and record its location.
        }
    return where;                // Return the index of the minimal element.
}
```

Finding a Particular Element (I)

Our second search problem sounds very much like the first: Given an integer *x*, find the index in the array of the first instance of the value *x*. This differs from our first problem in two important ways, though. First, there will always be a minimal element, but there may not be any instance at all of a match for *x*. Second, we will always have to search to the end of the array to find the minimal element, but once we find a match for *x*, we can stop our search right there.

We can deal with the possibility of no matches easily enough: We simply will decide to return the dummy index −1 if our algorithm fails to find a match. With this extra condition, we can describe the problem as follows:

In: An array, *a*, of integers, occupying indices 0 to *end*.
     An integer, *x*.

Out: The index, *r*, of the first element in the collection *a*[0], . . . , *a*[*end*], for which *a*[*r*] == *x*. If there is no value matching *x* in the array, return −1.

Notice here that we have simplified the problem slightly by assuming that the start index is always zero. In our example, where a = {13, 18, 9, 2, 28, 2, 16, 7, 5}, if the sought value x is 2 our function will return the index, 3, of the first instance of 2. If $x = 10$, the function should return the dummy index –1, since 10 is not in the array.

Linear search: The process of searching a list by examining each element in turn.

As we've said many times in the past, a good design principle is not to write new code if what we need to do can be accomplished by a simple modification of an existing routine. We could design this algorithm almost exactly as we designed *FindMin*, using what is known as a *linear search*, but it would be a waste of time to continue searching after we found a match. What we should do is leave the loop as soon as we find a match, and C++ provides us with exactly what we need. We'll simply use a return statement to break out of the function (and hence out of the loop) when we find a match.* Our function now takes the following form:

```
int Find(IntArray a, int x, int end)
// Finds the index of the first element with value x in the
// array a[0] ... a[end].
// NOTE: this requires that end is a legal position in the array.
{
    for (int i = 0; i <= end; i++)
        if (a[i] == x)              // Did we find a match?
            return i;               // if so, jump out with the index.

    return -1;                      // We can only get here if we didn't find
                                    // a match.
}
```

10.2 DIVIDE AND CONQUER: FINDING A PARTICULAR ELEMENT (II)

Here are two similar-sounding problems; which one could you perform faster using a conventional phone directory?

1. Find someone's phone number, given his or her name.
2. Find the name of a subscriber, given his or her phone number.

Clearly, you could perform the first task far more quickly than the second. In fact, the second task would be almost completely impractical except for extremely small telephone books. The reason is obvious—the entries in phone books are sorted by name, not by number. That means that to find a name, given

---

* Some authorities would object to this, arguing that programs are easier to understand if the only exit from a loop is at the beginning or end. In the Exercises, we will explore a way of writing the loop so that the exit case will test for a match.

a number, one couldn't do much better than to perform a linear search. That is, you'd have to start with the first number, go on to the second, the third, and so on, until either the number was located or the end of the book was reached. In the first problem, though, we gain a considerable advantage from the fact that the entries are in the form of a *sorted list,* with the first name in alphabetic order first, followed by the second, and so on. In a sorted list, we could look at the middle element of the list and compare that element with our target element, and then use that information to decide where to search next, as below.

```
int RFind(SortedArray a, int x, int start, int end)
// Return the array index where x is, or where it belongs,
// if it's not in the array.
{
    if (start == end)                  // No need to search one-element lists
        return start;
    else
    {
        int middle = (start + end) / 2;      // Find middle index.

        if (x < a[middle])                   // x can only be in the left
                                             // half.
            return RFind(a, x, start, middle);
        else if (x > a[middle])              // x can only be in the right
                                             // half.
            return RFind(a, x, middle + 1, end);
        else
            return middle;                   // We found x.
    }
}
```

Recursion

This algorithm is an example of a *binary search,* and, appearances aside, the idea behind it is very simple. To find an element, x, in a sorted list that is stored in array locations *start* to *end,* we look at the element in the middle of the list (or as close to the middle as possible). If the list has only one element or if x is the middle element, we're done, and we return the position of x or the position where x would belong. On the other hand, if x is less than the middle element we know that we must search for it in the first half of the list. Similarly, if x is greater than the middle element, we know that we must search for it in the second half of the list.

In the latter two cases, we perform our search by passing the smaller problem to another copy of *RFind.* There's nothing that forbids a function from calling itself; such functions are called *recursive.* The basic idea behind a recursive algorithm is to design a function in such a way that it solves a problem (finding an element in a list) by solving a smaller instance of the problem (determining which half of the list the element is in and finding the element in the half-size list). We know the recursive algorithm *RFind* will terminate eventually, since (1) at each stage we reduce the size of the problem to be solved, and (2) we have a way of solving the smallest problem we could ever see, since *RFind* quits immediately if it is ever given a list of size 1.

> To solve a problem recursively, we must design a function that handles two possibilities:
>
> 1. The *exit* case, in which the problem can be solved immediately.
> 2. The *recursive* case, in which we solve the problem based on solutions to one or more smaller problems.
>
> Failing to handle both cases invariably will lead to a function that, at best, exhibits unpredictable behavior and at worst leads to serious run-time errors.

A recursive solution to a problem is like successfully jumping out of an airplane. We can get to the ground safely from a given height if and only if two conditions are satisfied: first, that our parachute will open at a certain height (the exit case) and, second, that from any altitude we can get closer to the height at which our parachute will open (the recursive case). Once we are confident that both conditions are satisfied, we can close our eyes and jump, secure in the knowledge that the details will be handled correctly. Recursion often takes a bit of getting used to, largely because people (at least non-computer-science people) tend not to think in recursive terms. In thinking about recursion, it's important to realize that we are not calling the same function, but rather are invoking a duplicate copy of the function to work on a smaller version of the problem.

> Lurking inside many problems is a smaller version of the same problem. Often we can solve the original problem by using a solution to the smaller one. The key to recursive design is to ask, "How could I solve this problem if I already had a solution to the smaller one?"

Figure 10.1 illustrates the action of this binary search when we look for the element 17 in the array containing 3, 8, 12, 17, 24, 30, 39, 44, 54. We see that three calls to *Find* are required, first to look for 17 in the positions 0 to 8, then to look for 17 among positions 0 to 4, and finally to look for (and successfully find) 17 in positions 3 and 4.

Binary search is *much* faster than a linear search. To find an element in a list of 1000 numbers, for example, at the very worst we'd need to look in sublists

FIGURE 10.1
Searching for 17 in a
sorted list

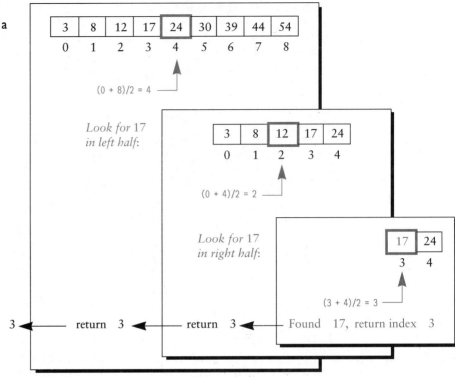

of size 1000, 500, 250, 125, 63, 32, 16, 8, 4, 2, and 1, for a total of 11 function calls. Even in a list of a million elements, we'd require at most 21 calls to find any element, an enormous improvement over the million probes it might take with a linear search.*

10.3 SAFER ARRAYS: THE *IntArray* CLASS

The PIP for this chapter will allow you to experiment firsthand with the sorting and searching algorithms we present in this chapter. As we've seen, it's very natural to use arrays to store the lists of numbers we represent, so that's what we'll do. Unfortunately, C++ arrays have a major deficiency: We cannot rely on C++ to check that the references we make to an array are legal. If, for example, we have declared an array, `int a[10]`, of ten integers and later refer to the array el-

---

* For the mathematically inclined, it's not hard to see that it takes at most $1 + \log_2 n$ probes to find an element in an array of n elements. This, by the way, is why the game Twenty Questions works so well. If the questions are chosen well, 20 questions will serve to identify any element out of a collection of a million items.

ement *a*[*i*], C++ will cheerfully accept this as legal, even if *i* happens to have the value 2000. If this happens, say, as part of an assignment expression, we may wind up modifying the value of some other program variable or even—heaven forbid!—the code of the program, of the C++ compiler, or of the operating system of the computer itself.*

Declaring Safe Arrays

With this in mind, we have designed a class that acts just like arrays of integers, but with safeguards built in to catch array indices that are outside the bounds of the array. In doing this, we are embarking on a course similar to that which we followed in Chapter 9: We are writing our own improved version of a class that is built into C++. To do this, we want to make things as natural as possible for the user, which means we should try to declare our class so that it at least has all the functionality of "standard" arrays of integers in C++, along with any other modifications we wish to include.

```
//================ INTARRAY.H ===============

// This class implements arrays of integers, with bounds-checking.

#include <iostream.h>

class IntArray
{
    friend ostream& operator<< (ostream& os, const IntArray& a);
public:
    IntArray();                 // Construct a 10-element IntArray of zeros.
    IntArray(int n);            // Construct a zero IntArray of size n.
    IntArray(const IntArray& a);            // copy constructor
    ~IntArray() { delete data;};            // destructor

    Length() { return (upper + 1);};
    int& operator[] (int i) const;
    IntArray& operator= (const IntArray& a);


private:
    int upper;                  // the upper bound on array indices
    int* data;                  // pointer to the array elements (indices
                                // 0 .. upper)
};
```

---

* Although many operating systems detect and forbid references into "sensitive" areas of memory, one cannot assume that this will always happen. A good rule of thumb here is Murphy's law of memory references: "An erroneous reference into memory will always be to the location that will cause the most bizarre and catastrophic consequences."

If we think about what we can do with arrays of integers, we see that, in fact, there isn't really much we can do. We can construct an array of zeros, with or without specifying the size of the array; we can use the subscript operator [ ] to refer to an element in an array; and we can pass arrays as arguments to functions. The first three of these actions are declared in the header file "INTARRAY.H" as follows:

```
IntArray();
IntArray(int n);
int& operator[] (int i) const;
```

The subscript operator deserves scrutiny because its return type is a reference to an int, rather than just an int value. We need to do this because we frequently use a subscripted array element on the left side of an assignment and hence need to be able to modify that element. We can do so only if we have a reference to its location. Notice as well that this member operator is declared to be constant, meaning that we are not allowed to modify the object. This seems to contradict what we just said, but the apparent contradiction is explained when we look at the *IntArray* member data.

We represent an *IntArray* object by a pointer to the array of *data* values, along with an integer, *upper,* that keeps track of the largest possible index in the *data* array. Figure 10.2 illustrates the (private) member data of an *IntArray* object. Representing integer arrays this way means that the subscript operator cannot modify the two member data items. Even if the subscript operator does result in modifying the contents of the array, it doesn't change the pointer to the *data* items or the value of *upper.*

The remaining four member functions and one friend operator are included primarily to address what we consider to be deficiencies in C++ arrays.

```
friend ostream& operator<< (ostream& os, const IntArray& a);
IntArray(const IntArray& a);
~IntArray() { delete data;};
Length() { return (upper + 1);};
IntArray& operator= (const IntArray& a);
```

The insertion operator << and the assignment operator = are included because C++ arrays do not support output and assignment, both of which, as you'll see, are quite easy to implement for our class. Similarly, it would be useful to be able to ask an array, as it were, how large it is. We can almost do that now, using the sizeof operator, except that sizeof returns the size in memory,

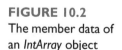

FIGURE 10.2
The member data of an *IntArray* object

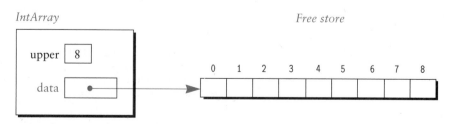

rather than the number of elements, and so might differ from one implementation of C++ to another, depending on how much space the implementation uses to store integers. We might consider overloading sizeof, except that C++ won't let us, so we must declare our own member function, *Length*. Notice that *Length* is so simple that we chose to place its definition in the header file.

Although C++ provides a default destructor if one is not specified in the class declaration, we need to define our own here, since *data* points to an array in free store. If we relied on the default constructor, an object's *data* pointer would be destroyed when, for example, the object passed out of its scope, but the array to which it pointed would not be. Notice that here, as with *Length*, the destructor's definition is short enough to warrant its inclusion in the header file.

The last operator to consider is what is called a *copy constructor*.

```
IntArray(const IntArray& a);
```

We have seen many times so far that C++ will do some things for us even if we don't tell it explicitly to do so, and this is another example. A copy constructor is, roughly speaking, a constructor-by-assignment.

> The copy constructor for an object is invoked whenever (1) an object is defined to have the value of another object of the same type, (2) an object is passed to a function by value, and (3) an object is returned by a function.

The following example uses all three kinds of calls to the *IntArray* copy constructor:

```
IntArray ZeroTail(IntArray a, int n)          // (2) here
// Zeros out all entries from index n on.
{   IntArray r = a;                            // (1) here
    for (int i = n; i < Length(a); i++)
        r[i] = 0;
    return r;                                  // (3) here
}
```

Notice that the copy constructor is invoked whenever we pass an object by value. This implies that we must declare the argument for the copy constructor by reference; passing it by value would mean that the copy constructor would be invoked, circularly and illegally, in its own definition.

> The copy constructor for a type *Typename* is declared with a reference argument:
>
> ```
> Typename (const Typename&);
> ```
>
> Declaring the reference argument constant is not absolutely necessary, but is good practice, since it indicates that the argument value will not be modified.

Recall that the five operators we are not allowed to overload are :: (scope resolution), . and .* (member access), sizeof, and ?: (compound conditional).

Although C++ will provide a copy constructor for us if we don't write one (as it will provide a destructor and assignment operator), we must supply our own here because we want to make a copy of the array *data* points to, rather than simply make a copy of the pointer itself. Just copying the pointer (called a *shallow clone,* in the jargon) would result in two objects pointing to the same array in free store. This would mean that any modification of one object's array would result in an invisible modification of the other's array. Such aliasing can lead to errors that are exceedingly difficult to detect and fix.

> If you design a class with pointers in its member data, it is always a good idea to provide the class with its own copy constructor, assignment operator, and destructor, rather than relying on the implicit ones C++ will generate.

Defining Safe Arrays

In defining the member functions of *IntArray,* we built in two different kinds of safeguards. First, as we've already mentioned, we made sure that whenever we refer to an array index, it is a legal index in the array (namely, between 0 and *upper,* inclusive). We need to do this checking in the operator [ ], obviously, but we also need a check in the constructor that builds an array of a specified size, since there's no reasonable way to build an array with –1 elements, for instance.

The second safeguard takes care of a situation that is less likely to happen in practice but has a similar potential for disaster. When we construct an array or assign one array to another, we use new to set aside space in free store for the *data* array. In a program that uses a large number of arrays, we might find at some point that there simply isn't room in the free store for any new arrays. When new is unable to allocate any more space in the free store, it returns a zero pointer (also called a *null pointer*) to indicate failure. We would want to be notified if this happened, because our program would no longer work as expected, so after each call to new we check the value of the *data* pointer and take appropriate action if the pointer has value zero.

```
//---------- INTARRAY.CPP ----------

#include <iostream.h>          // for cerr
#include <stdlib.h>            // for exit
#include "INTARRAY.H"


ostream& operator<< (ostream& os, const IntArray& a)
{
    for (int i = 0; i <= a.upper; i++)
        os << a.data[i] << '\t';
    return os;
}
```

```
IntArray::IntArray()
// Construct a 10-element IntArray of zeros.
{
    upper = 9;
    data = new int[upper + 1];
    if (data == 0)
    {
        cerr << "Out of memory in IntArray()" << endl;
        exit(1);
    }
    else
        for (int i = 0; i < 10; i++)
            data[i] = 0;
}


IntArray::IntArray(int n)
// Construct a zero IntArray of size n.
{
    if (n <= 0)
    {
        cerr << "Illegal size argument (" << n << ") in IntArray(int n)" << endl;
        exit(1);
    }
    else
    {
        upper = n - 1;
        data = new int[n];
        if (data == 0)
        {
            cerr << "Out of memory in IntArray()" << endl;
            exit(1);
        }
        else
            for (int i = 0; i < n; i++)
                data[i] = 0;
    }
}


IntArray::IntArray(const IntArray& a)
// Copy constructor
{
    upper = a.upper;
    data = new int[upper + 1];
    if (data == 0)
    {
```

```
            cerr << "Out of memory in IntArray()" << endl;
            exit(1);
        }
        else
            for (int i = 0; i <= upper; i++)
                data[i] = a.data[i];
    }


int& IntArray::operator[] (int i) const
// ovarload of subscript operator
{
    if ((i < 0) || (i > upper))
    {
        cerr << "Illegal array index [" << i << ']' << endl;
        exit(1);
    }
    return (data[i]);
}


IntArray& IntArray::operator= (const IntArray& a)
// Assign one array to another
{
    int u = ((a.upper < upper) ? a.upper : upper);

    if (a.upper != upper)
        cerr << "Size mismatch: (" << upper << ") != (" << a.upper << ')' << endl;

    for (int i = 0; i <= u; i++)
        data[i] = a.data[i];

    return *this;
}
```

Let's look first at the constructor *IntArray::IntArray(int n)*, which builds an array of *n* zeros. This function has both safeguards we mentioned in the introduction to this section. The first thing the function does is check that *n* could be the size of an array:

```
if (n <= 0)
{   cerr << "Illegal size argument (" << n;
    cerr << ") in IntArray(int n)" << endl;
    exit(1); }
```

This segment uses the *ostream* cerr, which is defined as part of C++, to report error messages. It also uses the function *exit()*, declared in "stdlib.h," whose job is to force an immediate and tidy exit from the program.* For example, if the constructor was called with $n = -1$, this segment would send the message

```
Illegal size argument (-1) in IntArray(int n)
```

to the ostream cerr (which normally results in the message being displayed on the screen) and then would terminate the program, completing any pending business like function returns and output operations. If the value of n is legitimate, the constructor then tries to allocate space for the *data* array. As before, if the attempted allocation fails, an error message is displayed and exit is called to terminate the program.

```
upper = n - 1;
data = new int[n];
if (data == 0)
{   cerr << "Out of memory in IntArray(int n)" << endl;
    exit(1); }
```

Finally, if all went as it should, the function fills the *data* array with zeros and returns.

If you look at the default constructor *IntArray::IntArray()*, you will see that we did the same checking to make sure new succeeded. The copy constructor, *IntArray::IntArray(const IntArray& a)*, acts exactly like the two other constructors, except that it sets the size of the object being constructed to the same as the size of its argument, and it copies the values of the argument's *data* array, rather than setting the object's *data* elements to zero.

The overload of the assignment operator has a different check built into it. Since the *IntArray* class is designed to represent arrays of different sizes, it could happen that a user of this class might try to assign an array of size 10 to one of size 8, or vice versa. This should not be a fatal error, but it should certainly be brought to the user's attention. If a is an array of size 10 and b is an array of size 8, the assignment b = a would result in the loss of two elements, and the assignment a = b would leave the last two elements of a in an unpredictable state.

Our operator handles this by checking whether the sizes are the same. If they are not, it displays a warning but does not call exit.

```
if (a.upper != upper)
{
    cerr << "Size mismatch: (" << upper;
    cerr << ") = (" << a.upper << ')' << endl;
}
```

---

* The argument for exit is ignored in some implementations. In others, the argument is displayed so that the programmer can use different arguments to get an idea of where the exit was invoked.

It uses the compound conditional to find the smaller of the two upper indices.

```
int smallerUpper = ((a.upper < upper) ? a.upper : upper);
```

After that, it copies the smaller number of elements from the argument to the object and returns a reference to the object itself, using the implicit pointer, *this,* to the object.

```
for (int i = 0; i <= smallerUpper; i++)
    data[i] = a.data[i];
return *this;
```

10.4 SORTING

We've seen that finding an element in an array is much faster if the array is sorted from smallest to largest. But how does one go about sorting an array of numbers? Here's a good place to ask whether we can find a solution by looking at what other people have done. There are *many* different ways to sort a list—the standard reference, *Sorting and Searching* (*The Art of Computer Programming,* vol. 3), by Donald Knuth, is 723 pages long! We'll begin with a simple (but not particularly efficient) sorting algorithm, called *SelectionSort.* This technique is the one that people often use to sort a hand of cards in a card game.

To use *SelectionSort,* one finds the smallest element in the list, marks where in the list it was found, and then swaps the smallest element with the first element in the list, thus putting the smallest element at the front of the list. The algorithm then finds the largest remaining element and swaps that into the second position in the list, and continues this process with the third-largest, the fourth-largest, and so on, until the entire list has been sorted from smallest to largest. The outline of *SelectionSort* is presented below. Notice that we modify the array argument *a,* so we need to make it a reference argument.

```
void SelectionSort(IntArray& a, int start, int end);{
    int k;
    for (int i = start; i < end; i++)
    {
        // Find the location, k, of the smallest element from
        // i. .. end;
        // Swap the elements a[i] and a[k];
    }
}
```

Figure 10.3 traces the action of *SelectionSort* on a list of five integers. At each stage, the figure indicates where we begin looking for the smallest element, the location of the smallest element, and that portion of the array that is already sorted.

FIGURE 10.3
An example of
SelectionSort

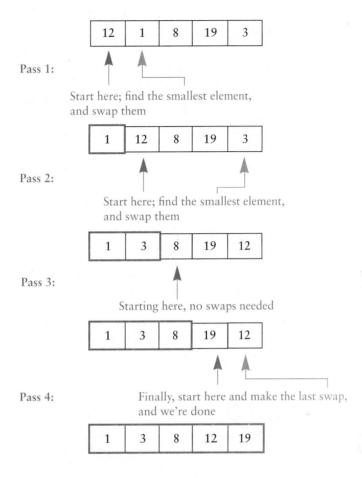

Pass 1:

Start here; find the smallest element,
and swap them

Pass 2:

Start here; find the smallest element,
and swap them

Pass 3:

Starting here, no swaps needed

Pass 4:

Finally, start here and make the last swap,
and we're done

The next step is to fill in the details of the routines that find the minimum element and swap two elements, and here's where code reuse comes in handy. We've already written and verified a swapping routine and saved it in our *Utility* library, so all we have to do is reference it from our program. Similarly, we just finished defining *FindMin*, so we make use of it as well. In finished form, *SelectionSort* looks like this:

```
void SelectionSort(IntArray& a, int start, int end)
{
int k;
    for (int i = start; i < end; i++)
    {
        k = FindMin(a, i, end)
        Swap(a[i], a[k]);
    }
}
```

10.5 ANALYSIS OF ALGORITHMS

We have seen *SelectionSort* in action; it's simple enough to understand, but it turns out that it isn't frightfully efficient. The drawback to *SelectionSort* is that it repeatedly uses a linear search on the unsorted part of the array to find the next element to be inserted. It's not that the repeated calls to *FindMin* are redundant; the inefficiency stems from the basic idea behind *SelectionSort*, which forces us to inspect the same elements over and over again.

Saying that *SelectionSort* is inefficient is somewhat imprecise. What exactly do we mean by the efficiency or inefficiency of an algorithm? One way to measure this is to count the statements that are executed when the algorithm runs and to express this as a function of the size of the data being sorted. The advantage of this method is that it ignores the running speed of different computers. An algorithm that takes n^2 steps to run on an input of size n may run in $0.087n^2$ seconds on a desktop computer and $0.000026n^2$ seconds on a fast supercomputer, but the essential behavior is the same on both machines: Double n and the algorithm will take four times longer; triple n and the algorithm will take nine times longer.

For example, the number of statements *SelectionSort* takes to sort an array of n elements depends on how long it takes to find the minimum element in the range i to n. We clearly have to inspect each of the $n - i + 1$ elements to find the minimum. So the time it takes to perform *SelectionSort* will be n, to find the first element, plus $(n - 1)$, to find the second, and so on, for a total sum of $n + (n - 1) + (n - 2) + \cdots + 2 + 1$. What is that sum? Well, if we group the first and last terms we get $(n + 1)$. If we group the second and the next-to-last we get $(n - 1 + 2)$, which is also $(n + 1)$. In fact there are $n/2$ such pairs, each equal to $n + 1$, so the running time of *SelectionSort* on an array of size n is just

$$n + (n - 1) + (n - 2) + \cdots + 2 + 1 = (n + 1)(n / 2)$$

or approximately $(n^2) / 2$. This kind of analysis can get pretty tricky, but the essential idea is simple enough: To estimate the time an algorithm takes to run, we can count the number of steps it takes on inputs of size n, expressing our answer as a *timing function* for the algorithm.

Big-O

When we estimate the timing function of an algorithm on inputs of size n we can for the most part ignore any constant multiples and concentrate on the terms that involve n. For purposes of estimation, two algorithms that run in time $2n^2$ and $10n^2$ may be lumped together in the class of n^2 algorithms and considered as substantively different from those in the class of, say, 2^n algorithms. Let's see why we can get away with this simplification. Suppose we have two algorithms, A and B, that do the same thing, but in different ways, and that by counting statements performed on inputs of size n we find that A

runs in time $10n^2$ and B runs in time 2^n. Which one is faster? Look at the first few values of n in Table 10.1.

For n up to 9, the 2^n algorithm has smaller timing function values, so B runs faster. Once n is 10 or more, the $10n^2$ algorithm takes over and thereafter is much faster than the 2^n one. The multiplicative constant in front of n^2 makes the n^2 algorithm slower for a while, but eventually the 2^n algorithm dominates and takes more time for all other values. If we had increased the multiplicative constant to 200 and compared $200n^2$ against 2^n, we would have observed the same behavior, except that the crossover point would be later—16, rather than 10.

> In the long run, a constant multiple will have no effect on the relative behavior of the timing function of an algorithm. An n^2 algorithm will eventually beat an n^3 algorithm, no matter what multiplicative constants are in front of the terms. Any *polynomial*-time algorithm with timing function n^k, for some fixed k, will eventually beat an *exponential* algorithm like 2^n or 3^n. Similarly, a *logarithmic* algorithm, with timing function no larger than $\log n$, will eventually beat any polynomial algorithm.

Logarithmic algorithms are very efficient; polynomial algorithms are at least worth the effort of programming; but exponential algorithms are so inefficient that they aren't practical for all but the smallest data sets, no matter how fast the computer is that executes them. Consider Table 10.2, in which we compare some timing functions. The logarithmic algorithm is clearly the winner. Notice that doubling the size of the input increases the timing by a single time unit. Also look at the columns for $n\log_2 n$ and n^2. Notice how much more slowly the $n\log_2 n$ column increases. Finally, look at the column for the exponential function 2^n. An algorithm with this timing function might be practical for inputs of size 16 or (on a fast computer) 32, but even on a computer that can execute a trillion operations per second (far faster than anything you can buy

		$10n^2$	2^n	*Faster*
TABLE 10.1	n	*(A)*	*(B)*	*Algorithm*
Comparison of the	5	250	32	B
running times of two	6	360	64	B
algorithms	7	490	128	B
	8	640	256	B
	9	810	512	B
	10	1000	1024	A
	11	1210	2048	A
	12	1440	4096	A

TABLE 10.2
Relative growths of
some functions

n	$\log_2 n$	$n\log_2 n$	n^2	2^n
8	3	24	64	256
16	4	64	256	65,536
32	5	160	1,024	4.3×10^9
64	6	384	4,096	1.8×10^{19}
128	7	896	16,384	3.4×10^{38}
256	8	2,048	65,536	1.2×10^{77}

today) it would take 213 days to execute on an input of size 64. For inputs of
size 128, it wouldn't finish for ten billion billion years!

> Exponential-time algorithms are infeasible, except for the smallest prob-
> lems, no matter how much computational power is available.

There is a convenient shorthand that computer scientists use to express timing functions. We say that a timing function, $T(n)$, is "big-O" of another func-
tion, $f(n)$, if there are two constants, $k > 0$ and $N \geq 0$ such that $T(n) \leq |kf(n)|$, for
all $n \geq N$. In other words, T is big-O of f (which we write as $T(n) = O(f(n))$) if
T is eventually always beaten by some multiple of f, as illustrated in Figure 10.4.

FIGURE 10.4
Graphical represen-
tation of big-O

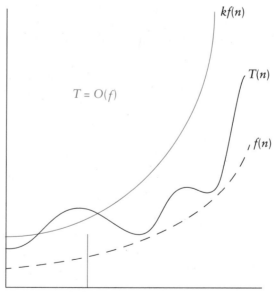

After this point, $T(n)$ is always
less than a multiple of $f(n)$.

By this definition, the quadratic functions $4n^2$ and $89n^2 + 233n + 101$ are both $O(n^2)$. A function that is constant, or never rises above a fixed value, is said to be $O(1)$. An algorithm with a $O(1)$ timing function is about as good as we can hope for, since it takes no more than a constant amount of time to execute, no matter what the size of the input is.

In simple (and, we admit, somewhat sloppy) terms, the definition of big-O can be taken to mean "Identify the fastest-growing part of T; any function that grows at least as fast as that part can be used in $O(\ )$." Don't worry if big-O and timing seem confusing now: There will be plenty of time to cover these topics in subsequent courses. For now, keep in mind that the way an algorithm is expressed may have significant implications to its feasibility. Computer scientists know that there is a practical side to program style.

10.6 FASTER SORTING

SelectionSort is what we called a $O(n^2)$ algorithm, since its running time is no worse than a multiple of n^2. That's not terrible, but we can do better if we scrap the whole idea and start fresh, using the idea of binary search as a basis for sorting. The power of binary search comes in part from the fact that it solves the problem of finding an element by dividing the problem in half. This *divide-and-conquer* scheme appears in many programming applications, and it often leads to a better (faster) solution than would be obtained by an attack on the entire problem at once. In this section, we'll talk about a divide-and-conquer algorithm for sorting.

Suppose we have a list of numbers that we wish to sort, and suppose we were willing to settle for a "partial" sorting with the following property: After the partial sorting, the list will be divided into a left and a right sublist, in such a way that every element in the left sublist was less than or equal to every element in the right sublist. For example, starting with the list 4, 5, 2, 1, 3, we might be content to wind up with the arrangement 3, 1, 2; 5, 4. In this arrangement, every element in the left sublist 3, 1, 2 is less than or equal to every element in the right sublist 5, 4. Does this lead to anything useful? It sure does.

Notice that the left sublist is in its correct position. The *elements* of the sublist aren't where they should be, but the sublist itself is. The same, of course, holds for the right sublist. Here's the clever part: What happens if we apply the same partial sort, *recursively*, to the left and right sublists? Nothing we do to either sublist alters the fact that the lists are where they should be, and every time we apply the partial sort to a sublist, we'll wind up with two smaller sublists, each of which is now in its correct position. For example, the sublist 3, 1, 2 might wind up as 2, 1; 3 and the right sublist must necessarily become the two smaller lists 4; 5. Now our entire list looks like 2, 1; 3; 4; 5. That's almost perfectly sorted and indeed becomes perfectly sorted as soon as we do a partial sort on the sublist 2, 1. We illustrate this algorithm, called *QuickSort*, in Figure 10.5.

FIGURE 10.5
QuickSort in action

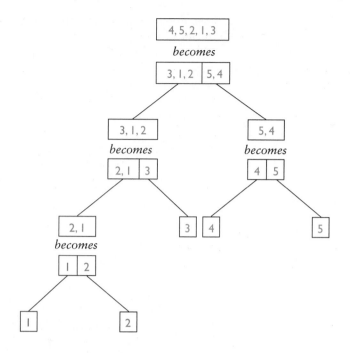

FIGURE 10.5
QuickSort in action

QuickSort is almost too good to be true. Since the elements in every sublist are no further from their correct—sorted—positions than the size of the sublist, as long as we can guarantee that at every stage a sublist will be split into nonempty sub-sublists, we will eventually wind up with a collection of lists of size one, each of which consists of a single element in its correct position. *QuickSort* is basically a function that makes three function calls: one to split the list and two recursive calls to sort the sublists. It looks like this:

```
void QuickSort (IntArray& a, int start, int end)
// Sorts a[start] ... a[end] in place.
{
    if (start < end)        // We don't need to sort a 1-element list
    {
        // Rearrange a into two subarrays, from start .. split
        // and from split+1 .. end, in such a way that every
        // element in the left part is less than or equal to
        // every element in the right part.
        int split = Partition(a, start, end);

        Quicksort(a, start, split);
        // Now sort the left sublist,
        Quicksort(a, split + 1, end);
        // and the right sublist.
    }
}
```

This seems too simple to be right, but based upon our understanding of recursion it seems like it has to work. *QuickSort* clearly works correctly on lists with a single element (that's our exit case), and if it sorts lists of size smaller than *n*, it will certainly work on lists of size *n* (that's the recursive part, after we invoke *Partition* to produce the two sublists).

Of course, all the real work of *QuickSort* is done by the helper procedure *Partition*. The idea behind *Partition* is also rather clever: We work our way inward from *start* and *end*, and every time we find a pair of elements that are in the wrong sublists, we swap them.

1. Pick an array value, *pivot*. We'll rearrange the list by putting on the left all values ≤ *pivot* and on the right all values ≥ *pivot*.
2. Use two indices, *left* and *right*. We'll walk these indices toward each other, using them to swap array elements as we go.
   a. Begin with *left* = *start* − 1 and *right* = *end* + 1.
   b. As long as *left* is less than *right* do the following three steps:
      i. Keep increasing *left* until we come to an element a[*left*] ≥ *pivot*.
      ii. Keep decreasing *right* until we come to an element a[*right*] ≤ *pivot*.
      iii. Swap a[*left*] and a[*right*].
   c. Do one last swap of a[*left*] and a[*right*].
3. Return *split* equal to *right*.

Figure 10.6 shows how *Partition* works on the list 4, 5, 2, 1, 3. After two swaps it is done, having produced the sublists 3, 1, 2 and 5, 4.

The code for *Partition* follows. To get a better picture of how *QuickSort* works, refer to Figure 10.7, where we show the contents of the sublists that are used in each of the nine function calls that the algorithm makes when given the initial list 4, 5, 2, 1, 3.

```
int Partition (IntArray& a, int start, int end)
// This routine rearranges the portion of the array a so that each
// element in a[start] .. a[split] is less than or equal to each
// element in a[split + 1] .. a[finish].
{
    int top = end + 1, bottom = start - 1;
    int pivot = a[start];
    while (top > bottom)
    {
        do {    bottom++; } while (a[bottom] < pivot);
        do {    top--; } while (a[top] > pivot);
        Swap(a[top], a[bottom]);
    }
    Swap(a[top], a[bottom]);
    return top;
}
```

FIGURE 10.6

Tracing the action of
Partition

Begin with *pivot* = 4, the starting element.

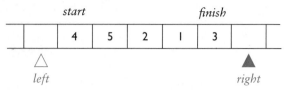

Move *left* up and *right* down, until we
find *a* [*left*] ≥*pivot* and *a* [*right*] ≤*pivot*.

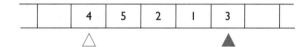

Swap the elements, and continue moving *left*
and *right* until we again find a pair to swap.

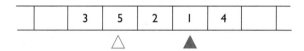

Swap the elements, and keep moving.
We stop when *left* and *right* pass each other.

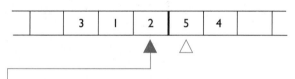

Set *split* equal to *right* and return.

As if it weren't enough for *QuickSort* to be elegant and simple, we get another benefit as well: Except for very small lists, *QuickSort* is considerably faster than *SelectionSort*. If that's still not enough for you, the advantage in speed of *QuickSort* over *SelectionSort* increases as you increase the size of the lists. Although you'll have to wait until a later course to see a proof of the speed of *QuickSort*, we'll tell you that *QuickSort*, on a typical list of size *n*, runs in time $O(n \log_2 n)$. This is a significant difference: For *n* = 512, $\log_2 n$ is 9 (since 2^9 = 512), so $n \log_2 n$ is 512 * 9 = 4,608, while n^2 is 262,144. We're ignoring any constant multiples that might appear in the real timing function, but the difference between the two sorting algorithms is significant, even so. If you don't trust the mathematics, you can run the two algorithms on the same list and time the results. We did, and found that for lists of 500 random numbers, *QuickSort* averaged 13.5 times faster than *SelectionSort*, and for lists of size 1000, *Quick-Sort* beat *SelectionSort* by a factor of better than 25.2. For lists of size 2000,

FIGURE 10.7
Procedure calls in
QuickSort

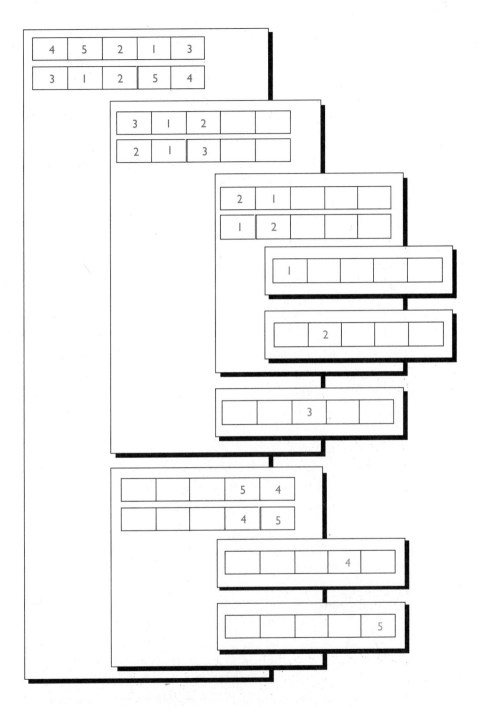

QuickSort was nearly 50 times faster than *SelectionSort*! Think of it this way: For really large lists, you might have time to go out for coffee while *QuickSort* was running, but for *SelectionSort*, you would have time to go to Colombia and pick the beans.

10.7 SUMMING UP

▶ A linear search through an array of numbers involves inspecting each element in order of position until some condition is met.

▶ A binary search finds a given element in a sorted list by looking at the middle element in the list and using the middle value to determine which half of the list to look at next. A linear search runs in time proportional to the length of the list; a binary search runs in time proportional to the logarithm of the list size and so is generally much faster.

▶ A divide-and-conquer algorithm, like binary search or *QuickSort*, breaks a problem into nearly equal pieces, solves the problem on the pieces, and uses the solutions to find a solution to the original problem.

▶ A recursive function is one that includes one or more calls to itself in its definition.

▶ A recursive function must handle two cases: the exit case, in which the problem can be solved immediately, and the recursive case, in which we solve the problem by using solutions to smaller problems.

▶ The flow of action in a recursive algorithm does not involve returning to the same function, but rather calls duplicate copies of the function, generally with different arguments.

▶ C++ cannot be relied on to check array bounds. A well-designed program will handle array bounds by checking itself.

▶ When allocating space in free store, `new` will return zero if there is no space available to fill the request. A well-designed program will verify that `new` succeeded before going any further.

▶ A copy constructor is a function that is invoked whenever an object is defined to have the value of another object of the same type, is passed to a function by value, or is returned by a function.

▶ A copy constructor must take as its argument a reference to an object of the same type.

▶ C++ will provide a copy constructor, a destructor, and a memberwise assignment operator, unless you give the class one explicitly.

▶ If a class has pointer member data, it is usually a good idea to write your own copy constructor, destructor, and assignment operator overload rather than rely on the defaults C++ will provide.

▶ The predefined *ostream* object `cerr` acts like `cout` in that it generally directs output to the screen. The object `cerr` is usually used to direct error messages.

▶ The function *exit()* forces an immediate and tidy exit from a program. It is declared in "stdlib.h" and is used to handle otherwise fatal errors, rather than trusting C++ to handle them.

▶ We can estimate the running time of an algorithm by assuming all statements take a unit amount of time and assuming the input is arranged to take the maximum number of steps.

▶ The big-O operator provides a convenient upper bound for the size of a function. It ignores constant multiples and, roughly speaking, concentrates on the fastest-growing term of the function being estimated.

▶ *SelectionSort* is a sorting algorithm that selects the smallest unsorted element after a given location and swaps the smallest element with the one in the given location. On lists of size *n*, it runs in time proportional to n^2.

▶ A logarithmic function will eventually be smaller than any polynomial function and a polynomial function will eventually be smaller than any exponential function.

▶ *QuickSort* is a sorting algorithm that first partitions a list by arranging it into two sublists in such a way that every element in the left sublist is less than or equal to every element in the right sublist. It then recursively sorts the left and right sublist. *QuickSort* on a list of size *n* will run, on the average, in time no worse than a multiple of $n\log_2(n)$. This is a huge improvement over the performance of *SelectionSort* on all but very small lists.

10.8 EXERCISES

1. Write *Find* without using a for loop. In other words, use a while or do loop with a suitable exit condition that does not require a return or break statement to exit the loop when the desired value is found. Comment on the relative comprehensibility of your version and the one in the text.

2. Change the definition of *Find* so that it starts its search at index *start*, as we did in the definition of *FindMin*.

3. In the declaration of *IntArray*, the overload of the assignment operator returned a reference to the object rather than the object itself. Why did we choose to do this? In other words, could we have declared the operator like this?

```
IntArray operator= (const IntArray& a)
```

4. In the constructor *IntArray::IntArray(int n)*, we exit the program immediately if *n* is less than or equal to zero. This seems to be a bit of an overreaction,

since we could display a warning and then go ahead and construct an array of, say, ten zeros. Modify the constructor with this in mind.

5. Augment the *IntArray* class by including overrides for the following operators.

    a.   *, which takes an integer on the left and an *IntArray* object on the right, so that if *a* = {1, 2, 3}, the expression 2 * *a* would return {2, 4, 6}.

    b.   *=, which takes an array on the left and an integer on the right, so that if *a* = {1, 2, 3}, the result of *a* *= 2 would be to set *a* to {2, 4, 6}.

    c.   ==, which takes arrays on the left and right and returns 1 if the arrays have the same size and are elementwise equal, and returns 0 otherwise.

6. Augment the *IntArray* class by including overrides for the following operators. Think carefully about whether the operations should be members or friends and what action your operators will take if the arrays are of different sizes.

    a.   +, which adds two arrays element-by-element, so that if *a* = {1, 2, 3} and *b* = {0, 5, 9}, the expression *a* + *b* would return {1, 7, 12}.

    b.   +=, which takes arrays on the left and right, adds them elementwise, and sets the left array to the sum.

7. Using a picture like Figure 10.1, show the action of *RFind* in searching for the element 25 on the sample list given in the text.

8. Trace the action of *RFind*

    a.   By searching for 212 in the list 7, 10, 39, 52, 77, 91, 178, 209, 212, 304, 456, 518, 590, 889.

    b.   By searching for 212 in the list 1, 2, . . . , 100,000.

    c.   By searching for 212 in the list 1, 2, 3, 4, 5, 6, 7, 8, 9, 10, 11, 12, 13, 212.

9. Write the binary search of *RFind* without using recursion.

10. We claimed that *RFind* will return either the position of the element sought or the position where it should be if it is not in the sorted list. For example, in searching for 25 in the list {3, 8, 12, 17, 24, 30, 39, 44, 54}, *RFind* will correctly report that 25 belongs in position 5, currently occupied by 30. That description of *RFind* is not entirely true. For what values of *x* will *RFind* not correctly return the position where *x* should be?

11. What does this function do?

```
void Puzzle(int n)
{
    if (n <= 1)
        cout << n;
    else
    {
        Puzzle(n / 2);
        cout << n % 2;
    }
}
```

12. Another way to implement *Find* is to use *InterpolationSearch*. *Interpolation-Search* is very much like the algorithm most of us use to search for a word in a dictionary. If we're looking for a data value, *d*, in the part of the array from *start* to *finish*, we first calculate how far proportionally *d* is from *a*[*start*], and then probe to that location. For example, to find "gauge" in a dictionary, we wouldn't look at "nab" (the middle of the dictionary). Instead, we'd compute that "gauge" was about 7/26 of the way along, so we'd look at the entry in the (7 / 26) * (size of dictionary) location. Show how *InterpolationSearch* would work,

   a. By searching for 212 in the list 7, 10, 39, 52, 77, 91, 178, 209, 212, 304, 456, 518, 590, 889.

   b. By searching for 212 in the list 1, 2, . . . , 100,000.

   c. By searching for 212 in the list 1, 2, 3, 4, 5, 6, 7, 8, 9, 10, 11, 12, 13, 212.

   d. Implement this version of *Find*. You should be able to conclude that in most cases *InterpolationSearch* is *very, very* fast (in fact, it can run as fast as $\log(\log(n))$, on lists of size n).

13. What is the output from the call ProcessText("alligator", 0), for the function defined below? What would happen if we reversed the order of the two statements in the if statement? What would happen if we removed the if statement and kept the two others?

```
void ProcessText(char* t, int i)
{
    if (t[i])
    {
        ProcessText(t, i + 1);
        cout << t[i];
    }
}
```

14. A *palindrome* is a string, like "DEED" or "STATS", that is the same as its reverse. Write a recursive definition of palindromes by filling in the blanks: "Any string of length _____ is automatically a palindrome. For longer strings *s*, we can say *s* is a palindrome if _____ and also _____."

15. The two following functions both compute *x* raised to the power *n*, for *n* ≥ 0. Trace the action of each for *x* = 2.0, *n* = 13. Which is more efficient, in terms of using fewer recursive calls to reach the exit case?

```
double Power1(double x, int n)
{
    if (n == 0)
        return 1;
    else
        return (x * Power1(x, n - 1));
}
```

```
double Power2(double x, int n)
{
    if (n == 0)
        return 1;
    else if (n % 2 == 1)
        return (x * Power2(x * x, n / 2));
    else
        return (Power2(x * x, n / 2));
}
```

16. Modify the two functions in Exercise 15 so that they compute x^n for any *n*, positive, negative, or zero.

17. Sometimes we can trace the action of a recursive routine by making a *tree diagram* of its calls. For instance, we can define the *Fibonacci numbers* by $Fib(0) = Fib(1) = 1$, and for $n > 1$, $Fib(n) = Fib(n - 1) + Fib(n - 2)$. In other words, the sequence of Fibonacci numbers begins with 1, 1, and continues with each term being the sum of the two preceding values, so the sequence starts 1, 1, 2, 3, 5, 8, 13, 21, 34, 55, ...

The definition of *Fib* is naturally recursive, so we could write a functional definition, as

```
int Fib(int n);
{
    if (n <= 1)
        return 1;
    else
        return (Fib(n - 1) + Fib(n - 2));
}
```

If we trace this algorithm for $n = 3$, we have the following sequence of calls:

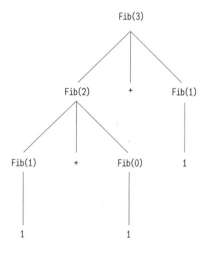

We can use such a diagram to show that the previous implementation is terribly inefficient.

a. Do a trace for $n = 6$, and use your findings to support this claim.

b. Find a nonrecursive routine that takes less computer time to compute $Fib(n)$.

c. The Fibonacci numbers have many interesting properties. For example, what can you say about $Fib(n - 1) * Fib(n + 1) - (Fib(n))^2$? What can you say about the sum $Fib(0) + Fib(1) + \cdots + Fib(n)$? Find an interesting property of your own.

18. Recursive routines can act in strange and wonderful ways. Trace the action of the following two functions on some sample input values. Try a tree diagram as in Exercise 17 to trace their action on some sample inputs. It would be instructive to code and run these routines.

a.
```
int Ackermann(int n, int m)
// This gets big very rapidly, as n and m increase.
{
    if (n == 0)
        return m + 1;
    else if (m == 0)
        return Ackermann(n - 1, 1);
    else
        return Ackermann(n - 1, Ackermann(n, m - 1));
}
```

b.
```
int Takeuchi(int p, int q, int r)
// This takes a lot of calls to produce a result.
{
    if (p < q)
        return r;
    else
        return Takeuchi(Takeuchi(p - 1, q, r),
                Takeuchi(q - 1, r, p),
                Takeuchi(r - 1, p, q));
}
```

19. Recall that $n!$, the factorial of n, is defined by $n! = n * (n - 1) * \cdots * 1$. Since $n! = (n + 1)! / (n + 1)$, why couldn't we implement a factorial function by the following recursive routine?

```
int Factorial(int n)
{
    if (n == 1)
        return 1;
    else
        return (Factorial(n + 1) / (n + 1));
}
```

20. In an attempt to discover a new secret code, a programmer thought of the following scheme: "I could divide a string into halves and interchange them. In fact, I could do this recursively, dividing each half in half and interchanging the pieces. That ought to mix things up pretty well." If you think about it for a while, you'll discover another nice feature of this scheme: The same algorithm can be used for coding and decoding. This was the algorithm that resulted:

```
void Shuffle(char* s)
{
    if (strlen(s) > 1)          //No need to shuffle a string of length 1
    {
        int half = (strlen(s) + 1) / 2;
        char leftstr[half + 1];
        char rightstr[half + 1];
        // Set leftstr to the left half of s.
        leftstr = strncpy(leftstr, s, half);
        // Set rightstr to the right half of s.
        rightstr = strcpy(rightstr, s + half);

        Shuffle(leftstr);          // Recursively shuffle the left half.
        Shuffle(rightstr);         // Recursively shuffle the right half.

        // Put the halves together in the new order.
        rightstr = strcat(rightstr, leftstr);
        s = strcpy(s, rightstr);
    }
}
```

   a. Unfortunately, this algorithm doesn't mix up the characters of a string very well at all. What does *Shuffle* do? What would be the result of applying this algorithm to the strings "ALLIGATOR" and "ABLE WAS I ERE I SAW ELBA"?
   b. Write a simpler recursive routine that does what *Shuffle* does.

21. In *InsertionSort,* we sort an array by inspecting elements from left to right, building a sorted list as we go. For each element, we place it in its correct position among the values to its left. For instance, we could sort the list {4, 5, 2, 1, 3} by the following steps. We've highlighted the element we're about to place among its neighbors to its left:

4	5	2	1	3	*The first element never needs to be moved.*
4	5	2	1	3	*5 is larger than 4, so it doesn't have to be moved.*
4	5	2	1	3	*2 will have to be inserted in its place at the start.*
2	4	5	1	3	*1 will have to be moved.*
1	2	4	5	3	*3 will have to be moved down.*
1	2	3	4	5	*We're done, and the list is sorted.*

a. Write the function void InsertionSort(IntArray& a).

b. How many times will elements have to be moved when we apply *InsertionSort* to the following three lists?

```
6  7  8
3  4  5
3  8  4
7  5  6
```

c. For which orderings of the input does *InsertionSort* have to make the fewest data moves? the most data moves?

22. a. Is *SelectionSort* sensitive to the order of the original array, in the sense that there is an arrangement of the input that requires particularly many operations to sort?

b. In the sense of part a, is *QuickSort* sensitive to the arrangement of the original array?

23. a. What condition is true if and only if a list is in sorted order, from smallest to largest?

b. Write a function, *IsSorted,* that returns *true* if and only if an array is already in sorted order, from smallest to largest.

24. a. Change *SelectionSort* so that it sorts from largest to smallest.

b. Change *QuickSort* so that it sorts from largest to smallest.

25. We could represent the action of a sorting routine graphically by letting the horizontal coordinate represent the array indices and the vertical coordinate represent the value of the element in that position. Initially, the array would be a cloud of points, as the element in a given position might have any value. For a completely sorted array, the picture would look like a diagonal line because as we increase the array indices from left to right, the elements in those positions would have increasing heights. The following two pictures represent the behaviors of *SelectionSort* and *QuickSort* at some time during their executions. Which is which?

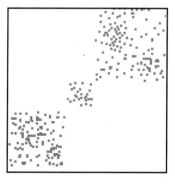
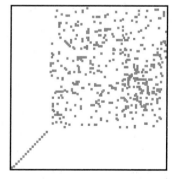

26. a. What would be the output displayed by *QuickSort* if we inserted an output statement in the function so that the statement body looked like this?

```
if (start < end)
    {
        int split = Partition(a, start, end);
        Quicksort(a, start, split);
        Quicksort(a, split + 1, end);
    }
else
        cout << a[start];
```

b. What would be the output from the modified algorithm if we also reversed the order of execution of the two recursive calls?

27. In *QuickSort*, why do we need the last call to *Swap*?

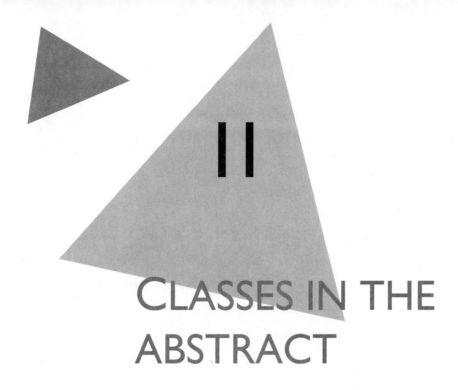

II

CLASSES IN THE ABSTRACT

While you may not consider yourself a master programmer, you have seen (with the exception of a few details we'll cover in Appendix B) all there is to C++. You've completed your apprenticeship and are ready to move on to more challenging projects. As apprentices have done for centuries in other crafts, you've learned the basic tools of your trade and have made some tools (classes, in this case) of your own to take with you when you leave us. In keeping with the tradition, we will bid you a farewell in this chapter and leave you with some words about what is ahead if you continue your progress to becoming a master yourself. In the standard computer science curriculum, the next two courses will constitute the journeyman portion of your training, in which you see that the subject matter of computer science is devoted in one way or another to the question, "What are the general principles that serve to organize our thinking about computers and their programs?"

Nicklaus Wirth can be credited with more than inventing the Pascal language. Among his other accomplishments, he also wrote a delightful book with perhaps the most felicitous title of any text on computer science, *Algorithms + Data Structures = Programs*. If you continue beyond this course, you can expect very shortly to see a course on data structures and one on algorithms. The data structures of a program are the major structural forms for the efficient representation of information, and the algorithms act on instances of these structures to process their information. Together, they should constitute an introduction to a more sophisticated view of programs and the programming process. The point of view that distinguishes an apprentice from a master is that the apprentice approaches each problem as completely unrelated to any others. The master can see that different structures or algorithms are really not as unrelated as they seem, but are rather different ways of viewing the same problem. This ability to "abstract"—to recognize and exploit common structural and procedural themes—is one (if not *the*) organizing principle of computer science.

OBJECTIVES

In this chapter, we will

▶ Introduce the notion of an abstract data type (ADT).

▶ Provide and review examples of two implementations of a list ADT.

▶ Discuss the memory and processing trade-offs between the two list implementations.

11.1 ABSTRACT DATA TYPES: BEARS, CATS, AND DOGS

If you think about it, there's no structural difference between a deck of cards and a word processing document. In both, the logical organization is the same: a collection of elements (cards or lines of text) arranged conceptually so that there is a first element, followed by a second, followed by a third, and so on, up to a last element that has no successor. This organization is common enough that it is worth studying as an abstract entity in its own right, and that's just what we'll do.

Just as biologists classify living things into categories like the *ursidae,* including black bears, brown bears, and polar bears, computer scientists group data structures into classes like the *List,* instances of which include cards in a deck, lines in a document, airplanes waiting to land at an airport, entries in a telephone book, customers in line at a bank, and so on. In an critical sense, as far as writing a program to store and manipulate a list is concerned, it is unimportant what type of information resides in the list. What matters is that the linear structure of first element, second element, . . . , last element is there, along with the operations we can perform on the structure, such as insertion or finding the number of elements in the list.

What we can do, then, is adopt an abstract approach to organization and manipulation of information. Rather than looking at each problem anew, we can take the time to look at often-used data structures in the hope that a problem we are trying to solve will be an instance of one of these structures. This approach involves the study of what is known as *abstract data types.*

▼

An abstract data type (often abbreviated ADT) is defined by describing (1) the logical structure of the information represented by an instance of the type and (2) the operations performed on the information.

Aspect I: Structures

We already have described the structure of the *List* ADT: A *List* either is empty or consists of a finite collection of elements, arranged so that each element has at most one element following it and at most one element preceding it. For nonempty lists, there is a unique first element that has no predecessor and a unique last element that has no successor. Figure 11.1 illustrates a typical list structure.

If we relax the restriction that each element have at most one successor, we have a different ADT, known as a *tree*. Trees are useful for representing information that has a hierarchical organization, like the family tree in Figure 11.2 organized by ancestry or the tree that represents the supervisory responsibility within a corporation.

We can further relax the structural requirements of an ADT and allow each element to have an arbitrary number of predecessors and successors. Doing so results in the *graph* ADT, illustrated in Figures 11.3 and 11.4. In Figure 11.3 we might imagine that the structural relation is "is involved with"; in Figure 11.4 the structure is organized by "is divisible by."

These forms of structure don't begin to exhaust all the possibilities. We might find it useful, for example, to investigate *rings*, which are like lists with the first and last elements linked; *bags*, which are collections with no structure at all (just a democratic collection of elements with no first or last elements); *tables*, where each element of one collection is associated with a single element of another collection; or any of a number of other organizations.

FIGURE 11.1
A list with five
elements

FIGURE 11.2
A (family) tree

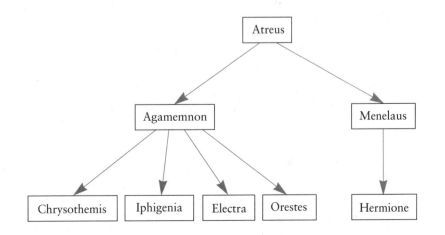

FIGURE 11.3
A graph (of personal relations)

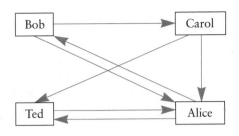

Aspect II: Operations

It is not enough, when studying abstract data types, simply to describe the logical organization of information. To be useful, an ADT must provide means by which its information may be manipulated. As changing structures can give rise to different abstract data types, so also can we make new ADTs from existing ones by keeping the underlying structure the same and changing the operations.

For an example of different ADTs with the same structure and different operations, let's first consider the *List* ADT. A reasonable collection of operations on lists might include the ability to insert a new list element at a given position, to delete the element at a given position, and to inspect an element's value without removing it. Some applications use the same linear arrangement of information that *List* does, but thay require different operations. Consider, for instance, the *Queue* abstract data type illustrated in Figure 11.5. The motivation for this ADT is a line of clients waiting for service, as we might see in a bank or in an airport where planes are backed up for takeoff.

In a queue, new elements are added at one end of the structure, and elements may be inspected and removed only at the other end. Because the first element inserted in a queue will be the first to be removed, queues are often called *first-in-first-out* (or *FIFO*) structures. Notice how a queue differs from a

FIGURE 11.4
Another graph (this time of divisors)

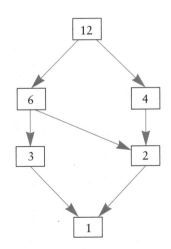

FIGURE II.5

A queue

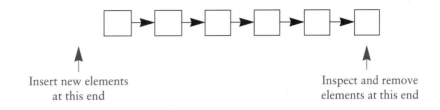

Insert new elements
at this end

Inspect and remove
elements at this end

We drew Figure 11.5 with insertion at the head of the linear structure and deletion and inspection at the tail, but we could equally well have decided to do it the other way.

list: In a list we might want to have the ability to insert and remove elements at any position, but in the *Queue* ADT, these operations may be applied only to the elements at opposite ends of the linear structure.

In a similar way, we might consider the *Vector* ADT, which also comprises a linear arrangement of numbers, this time representing coordinates of points in space. In such a structure we might not even allow insertion and deletion, but we might want operations that would be completely inappropriate for general lists and queues; for example, vector addition. Such an operation adds elements in corresponding positions so that $(2, -1, 0) + (3, 1, 8)$ would yield the vector $(5, 0, 8)$.

ADTs and OOP

One of the nice features of the abstract data type approach, from the point of view of this text, is that ADTs seem tailor-made for the object-oriented way of thinking. In fact, you might have wondered why we made such a big deal of the ADT way of looking at information, since we've been talking about describing classes by describing their member data and functions right from Chapter 1. Indeed, an abstract data type seems to be really nothing more than what we call a class. Our presentation in this text, describing classes at the beginning and introducing ADTs only at the end, is the reverse of the historical order of these ideas. The study of abstract data types began before C++ was invented, and in fact the invention of object-oriented languages was motivated in large part by the study of abstract data types.

This is not an uncommon occurrence in the history of programming languages. All programming languages are designed with some basic principles in mind. After having used and studied existing languages for some time, computer scientists discover that there are certain principles behind efficient programming practices, and these principles are then incorporated as part of new programming languages. For example, Algol and its descendants Pascal and C were developed in part as a reaction to the cumbersome, unreadable, and illogical programs that resulted from the unrestricted use of the "goto" statement. The logical flow of control in such a program tended to jump from any location to another without regard to the algorithmic structure of the program, often making such programs exceedingly difficult to understand and modify.

A number of researchers in computer science have taken note of a result in linguistics known as the *Sapir-Whorf hypothesis,* which says, roughly, that the language we use has a profound effect on the way we think, in the sense that you are more likely to come up with an idea or to use a way of thinking if the idea or way of thinking is easily expressed in the language you use. Although there is considerable criticism of the Sapir-Whorf hypothesis among linguists, there seems little doubt of its applicability in computer science. Given the usefulness of an ADT approach, for example, the argument goes that programmers will use this approach most effectively if they are writing programs in a language, like C++, that directly and easily supports the ideas behind abstract data types.

Finally, it is worth noting that an abstract data type is indeed abstract in that it makes no mention of implementation. When we consider a list, tree, or graph ADT, we look only at its structure and its operations, without concerning ourselves about how we will represent the structure or design the operations when the time comes for writing code. This high-level approach is very similar to the way we declare a class without getting bogged down in the details of how we will eventually write the definitions of the class's member functions. We will see that there are many ways to implement an ADT, and we will discover also that the choice of implementation can have profound impact on the efficiency of the ADT's operations, so that the choice of implementation often involves a trade-off between, for instance, speed and storage space, or storage space and comprehensibility.

11.2 THE *List* ADT

We'll begin by providing a precise description of the *List* abstract data type. We've already described the structure: a finite linear arrangement of elements of a given type, having a unique first and last position, and arranged in such a way that any element except the first and last has a unique predecessor and a unique successor. Notice that we are actually describing an infinite collection of lists: Depending on the element type, we could have a list of integers, a list of doubles, a list of character strings, a list of fractions, or even a list of soda machines.

If all the elements are of the same type, we say that we have a *homogeneous* list, otherwise we say the list is *heterogeneous*. We'll limit our discussion here to homogeneous lists.

We have more flexibility in defining the *List* operations than we do describing the structure. The choice of operations is not engraved in stone—we base our choice of operations on what we think would be a reasonable collection that would be useful for users of the class. We can organize our thoughts about ADT operations by grouping the operations into categories.

Some general categories of ADT operations are:

1. Construction/Initialization: used to create and set initial values for the ADT.
2. Destruction: to free the space used by instances of the ADT.
3. Modification: operations that alter some or all the information represented by the ADT.
4. Access: to allow users of the ADT to inspect the internal information.
5. Iteration: to perform the same action to all elements of the structure.

Some operations are common to most ADTs. These should be the first ones we think of when we design an abstract data type, and we'll use them in our definition of the *List* ADT. These common operations include

▶ Constructors, like a default constructor with no arguments, used to create an empty instance of an ADT and perhaps a copy constructor.

▶ A destructor. Since we'll often use pointers or arrays to represent the internal information, we'll need to free the internal information when we destroy an instance of the ADT.

▶ An assignment or copy operator.

▶ Input and output operators.

How will we gain access to the information in a list? The operations we've described so far don't allow us to inspect or modify an element, which is certainly something we'd like to be able to do. We will decide to keep track of a particular position in the list, which we'll call the *current position,* and we'll decree that all access and modification of elements will take place at the current position. For our *List* ADT, we will have the following access-related operations:

▶ Moving the current position one step up or down in the list.

▶ Moving the current position to the head or the tail of the list. Strictly speaking, we don't need these, since we could move to the head of the list by repeatedly moving the current position toward the front. Insertion and inspection are so commonly done at the head and tail of a list that we decided to include operations that move the current position directly.

▶ Retrieving a copy of the element at the current position.

▶ Returning the length of the list.

Finally, we need to be able to modify the list, by either modifying its structure or modifying the value of an element. For the *List* ADT, we will include the following modification operations:

▶ Update the element at the current position, changing it to a given value. We don't really need this operation, since we could do the same thing by deleting the element and inserting the modified element, but updating is such a common operation that we decided to include it as a single action.

▶ Insert or remove the element in the current position, as illustrated in Figure 11.6.*

---

* Look at Figure 11.6. Can you find a potential problem with inserting an element at the current position? We'll address the problem in the Exercises.

FIGURE 11.6
Inserting and removing an element in a list

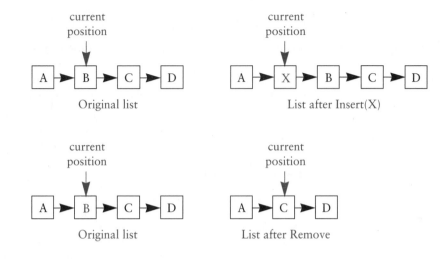

Throughout the body of the class declaration, we are free to use the type parameter, *T*, just as we would use any type name, so we can declare the *Update* function, for instance, by writing

Declaring the *List* Class

As we mentioned before, the structure and operations of a *List* ADT have very little to do with the type of elements that are stored in a list. From a practical point of view, we would rather not have to write separate classes for lists of integers, lists of doubles, lists of fractions, and so on. Fortunately for us, the newest releases of C++ have a feature that takes care of this problem.

We may describe a *parameterized class* by preceding its definition by the phrase `template<class T>`. The parameter *T* stands for any type, either a user-defined class or a predefined type like int. In the declaration part of our PIP, for instance, we declare a parameterized class, *TList,* by writing

```
template<class T>
class TList
{
    // Declarations of member functions, friends, and member
    // data, as usual.
};
```

Throughout the body of the class declaration, we are free to use the type parameter, *T*, just as we would use any type name, so we can declare the *Update* function, for instance, by writing

```
void Update(T x);
```

just as we would write void *Update(int x)* in an ordinary class declaration. Such a declaration serves as a template for an infinite collection of class declarations. In a program that uses a list of integers we would refer to the type name *TList<int>,* and similarly *TList<Fraction>* would be the name of a type representing a list of fractions. There's nothing special about our use of the name *T* for the type parameter. We could have called it ELEMENT_TYPE, if we'd wanted, or used any other legal C++ identifier. Similarly, there's no special importance attached to the class name *TList*. We could have called it *PList* or *Foo* if we had so desired.*

Having defined a class template, we can use the angle bracket notation to refer to the type name, as we do when we declare the overload of the assignment operator:

```
TList<T>& operator= (const TList<T>& lst);
```

This notation is a bit intimidating at first glance, we'll admit. Just keep in mind that TList<T> refers to "a list of elements of type *T*," so the operator declaration would be read as "The operator = returns a reference to an object of type TList<T>. It takes as its argument a reference to a constant TList<T> object, here named *1st*."

The listing below is the declaration of our parameterized class *TList*. The declarations of the public member functions and the friend operator << should be easy enough to understand. Note that we decided to overload the postfix forms of ++ and -- to increment and decrement the current position, moving it one place closer to the tail or the head of the list, respectively.

```
//---------- ALISTS.H ----------

#ifndef ALISTS_H
#define ALISTS_H
#include <iostream.h>

//------------------------ TList

// Declaration of an array implementation of list of values of parameterized type.
// All insertion and deletion is done at the current position in the list.

template <class T>
class TList
{
    friend ostream& operator<< (ostream& os, TList<T> l);

public:
    TList();                        // Construct an empty list.
    TList(const TList<T>& l);       // copy constructor
    ~TList();                       // destructor

    TList<T>& operator= (const TList<T>& l);// assignment overload
```

---

* We could have made the obvious choice of calling it *List*, except that some C++ implementations come with a *List* class built in, whose definition would conflict with ours.

```
    void Insert(T x);        // Insert x at current position.
    void Remove();               // Delete the node at the current position.

    void Head();                 // Move current location to the head.
    void Tail();                 // Move current location to the tail.
    TList<T>& operator++ (int);  // Move current to next position (postfix)
    TList<T>& operator-- (int);  // Move current to prior position (postfix)

    T Retrieve() const;          // Return the element at the current position.
    void Update(T x);            // Store x in current location.

    int Length();                // Return the size of the list.
private:
    T   *value;                  // pointer to the array
    int size,                    // number of elements in the list (=< max)
        max,                     // size of the array
        current;             // current index in the array (0 =< current < size)
    void Grow();             // Grow the array to twice its size.
};
#endif
```

In the private part of the class declaration we see the choice of implementation. In this version of the *TList* class we represent the list itself by an array in free store, accessed by a pointer named *value*. In addition, we keep integer member data items representing the size of the list, the maximum number of elements possible in the array, and the index of the current position in the array. In addition, if we think about how we'll use this implementation, we see that there might be times when insertion would fail because the array is full. In that case, we'll call the function *Grow* to double the size of the array. Figure 11.7 illustrates this implementation of the structure of a *List* object.

Defining the *List* Class

Much of what we do in the definition part of the *List* class should hold few surprises, since we defined most of the member functions in the last chapter. You

FIGURE 11.7

An implementation of the *List* ADT using arrays

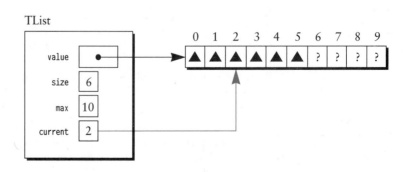

should recognize the default and copy constructors, the assignment operator, and the insertion overload; and the *Head*, *Tail*, *Update*, and *Retrieve* functions should be simple enough to understand at first glance.

One thing that is new is that the member functions, like the *TList* class itself, are parameterized so that they serve as templates for functions that use arbitrary types in their definitions. We parameterize functions in much the same way that we did for classes: We precede the definition by the phrase `template<class T>` and then define the function as expected, using the type parameter *T* as we would any other type name. Consider, for example, the header of the definition of the assignment overload:

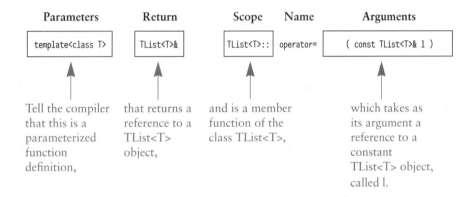

Again, this is rather verbose, but it's not hard to understand if you keep in mind that except for the parameters, it's just like the header of every function definition we've seen so far. We describe the return type, the owner of the function (if any), its name, and its argument list. If you look back at the header file for this class you'll notice that we didn't include the phrase `template<class T>` in the function declarations. We didn't need it because the entire class was parameterized, so it was assumed that all member functions and friends mentioned in the declaration were also.

By the way, parameterized functions are not limited to member functions and friends. We could, for instance, define a generic swapping function that could be used by many classes, parameterized or not, by writing

```
template<class SWAP_TYPE> void Swap(SWAP_TYPE& a, SWAP_TYPE& b)
{
    SWAP_TYPE temp;
    temp = a;
    a = b;
    b = temp;
}
```

Take a moment to read the definitions of the *TList* member functions that follow. After the listing, we'll delve more deeply into an explanation of the insertion and deletion functions.

```
//---------- ALISTS.CPP ----------


#include <stdlib.h>              // for exit
#include "ALISTS.H"


//----------------- Definition of TList member functions and friends

template<class T> ostream& operator<< (ostream& os, TList<T> l)
// Display an entire TList, from first position to last.
{
    for (int i = 0; i < size; i++)
        os << l.value[i] << '\t';
    return os;
}


template<class T> TList<T>::TList()
// Default constructor.  Builds an empty list, using an array of 10 elements.
{
    size = 0;
    max = 10;
    current = 0;
    value = new T[max];
}


template<class T> TList<T>::TList(const TList<T>& l)
// copy constructor
{
    size = l.size;
    max = l.max;
    current = l.current;

    value = new T[max];
    for (int i = 0; i < size; i++)
        value[i] = l.value[i];
}


template<class T> TList<T>::~TList()
// Delete all nodes in the List.
{
    delete []value;// We need the brackets because T might have its own destructor.
    size = 0;
    max = 0;
    current = 0;
}
```

```
template<class T> TList<T>& TList<T>::operator= (const TList<T>& l)
// assignment overload
{
    size = l.size;
    max = l.max;
    current = l.current;

    // Kill the old array and construct a new one, filling it with l's values
    delete []value;
    value = new T[max];
    for (int i = 0; i < size; i++)
        value[i] = l.value[i];

    return *this;
}


template<class T> void TList<T>::Insert(T x)
// Insert x at the current position.
{
    if (size == max)        // No room in the array, so make it larger.
        Grow();

    for (int i = size - 1; i >= current; i--)
        value[i + 1] = value[i];
    value[current] = x;
    size++;
}


template<class T> void TList<T>::Remove()
// Delete the node at the current position.
// If the list is empty, display a warning, but continue working.
{
    if (size > 0)
    {
        for (int i = current; i < size - 1; i++)
            value[i] = value[i + 1];
        size--;
    }
    else
        cerr << "Attempt to Remove an element from an empty list" << endl;
}


template<class T> void TList<T>::Head()
// Move current location to the head.
{ current = 0;}
```

```
template<class T> void TList<T>::Tail()
// Move current location to the tail.
{
    if (size > 0)        // We don't have to do anything if the list is empty.
        current = size - 1;
}


template<class T> TList<T>& TList<T>::operator++ (int)
// Move current location to next node (postfix operator).
// Do nothing if current is at the tail of the list.
{
    if (current < size - 1)
        current++;
    return *this;
}


template<class T> TList<T>& TList<T>::operator-- (int)
// Move current location to previous node (postfix operator).
// Do nothing if current is at the head of the list
{
    if (current > 0)
        current--;
    return *this;
}


template<class T> T TList<T>::Retrieve() const
// Return the element at the current position.
// Quit the program if the list is empty, since we can't return anything.
{
    if (size > 0)
        return value[current];
    else
    {
        cerr << "Cannot Return an element from an empty list";
        exit(1);
    }
}


template<class T> void TList<T>::Update(T x)
// Store x in current location.
// Quit the program if the list is empty.
{
    if (size > 0)
        value[current] = x;
    else
    {
```

```
            cerr << "Cannot Update an element in an empty list";
            exit(1);
        }
}
 template<class T> int TList<T>::Length()
// Return the number of elements in the list.
{ return size;}

template<class T> void TList<T>::Grow()
// PRIVATE.  Double the size of the array
{
    max *= 2;
    T* newValue = new T[max];
    for (int i = 0; i < size; i++)
        newValue[i] = value[i];
    delete []value;
    value = newValue;
}
```

To insert an element in an array, we have to move all the elements after the location of the new element up by one, to make room for the element to be inserted, as we illustrate in Figure 11.8.

The code for the insertion function is simple enough:

```
template<class T> void TList<T>::Insert(T x)
// Insert x at the current position.
{
    if (size == max)
    // No room in the array, so make it larger.
        Grow();

    for (int i = size - 1; i >= current; i--)
        value[i + 1] = value[i];

    value[current] = x;
    size++;
}
```

FIGURE 11.8
Inserting an element
into an array

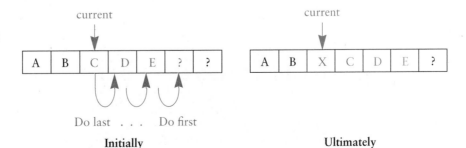

FIGURE 11.9
Removing an element from an array

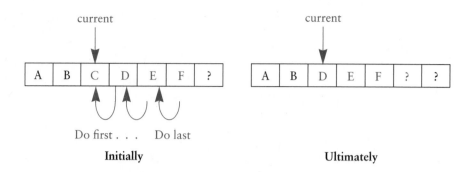

Do first . . .   Do last

Initially   **Ultimately**

Before moving the elements, we first check that there's room in the array for the new element and grow the array if not, and after performing the insertion we make sure that we update the *size* member datum to reflect the new size of the list. To check your understanding of this function, you should make sure you understand why we moved the elements from highest index to lowest and not the other way around.

Deletion, shown in Figure 11.9, is similar to insertion, but even simpler:

```
template<class T> void TList<T>::Remove()
// Delete the node at the current position.
// If the list is empty, display a warning, but continue working.
{
    if (size > 0)
    {
        for (int i = current; i < size - 1; i++)
            value[i] = value[i + 1];
        size--;
    }
    else
        cerr << "Attempt to Remove an element from an empty list"
                << endl;
}
```

You can see that we have to check the size to make sure we're not trying to delete an element from an empty list and that we shift the array elements down, rather than up, to "close up" the hole where the element to be deleted is located.

11.3 *List* (II): LINKED LIST IMPLEMENTATION

One drawback to the array implementation of the *List* ADT is that arrays are contiguous (i.e., adjacent in memory), so there's a chance that a call to new won't be handled successfully, even though there's room in free store. The problem is analogous to what might happen when you and your friends go to the movies. A call to make a new array is similar to demanding that you and your friends sit in adjacent seats. In a half-full theater, there might be 200 empty seats, but there might not be ten adjacent empty ones, so your request may be denied, even though there was plenty of noncontiguous room available. We don't have this problem with a collection of nodes linked by pointers, but you'll see that we pay the price of producing a somewhat more complicated implementation.

We don't have to provide the declarations in the header file for the pointer version of *TList* because the declarations are in all respects identical to those of the array-based declaration. That's a big advantage of our object-oriented approach: By separating the interface from the implementation, we have to change only the definition for the new implementation and not any other part of the program.

To represent a list using pointers, we define a new parameterized class, *Node,* that contains a data element and a pointer to another node:

```
template <class T>
class Node
{ public:
    Node() { next = NULL;}              // default constructor

    T value;                            // data stored in a node
    Node<T>* next;                      // pointer to next node
};
```

As you can see, there is only one simple member function, and that function and the two member data items are all public. Having done that, we define *TList* to be a linked collection of nodes by defining the (private) member data to be pointers to the first, current, and last nodes, along with an integer representing the current size of the list. See Figure 11.10 for a picture of this version of the *TList* class. Notice that the last node in the list has a zero pointer (or NULL,

FIGURE 11.10

Implementing a *List* with pointers

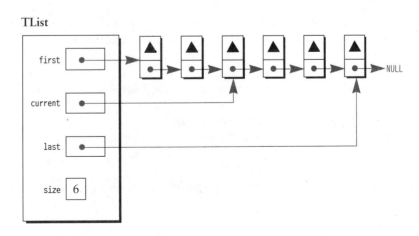

which C++ recognizes as a synonym for zero) as its next member datum. This special pointer will come in handy when we need to track our way through the list, as it provides an easy way to tell when there are no further elements, as you'll see.

```cpp
//---------- LLISTS.CPP ----------

#include <stdlib.h>              // for exit
#include "LLISTS.H"

//----------------- Definition of TList member functions and friends

template<class T> ostream& operator<< (ostream& os, TList<T> l)
// Display an entire TList, from first position to last.
{
    Node<T>* p = l.first;
    while (p)
    {
        os << p->value << '\t';
        p = p->next;
    }
    return os;
}

template<class T> TList<T>::TList()
// Default constructor.  Builds an empty list.
{   first = current = last = NULL; size = 0; }

template<class T> TList<T>::TList(const TList<T>& l)
// copy constructor
{
    Node<T>  *lptr = l.first, // tracks through the argument list
             *nptr;           // tracks through this list

    if (lptr == NULL)
    {   current = first = last = NULL; size = 0;}
    else
    {
        //---- Construct the first node in the list.
        nptr = new Node<T>;
        nptr->value = lptr->value;
        if (lptr == l.current)
            current = nptr;
        first = nptr;
        lptr = lptr->next;
```

```
                //---- Track through the remainder of the list, copying nodes.
                while (lptr)
                {
                    nptr->next = new Node<T>;
                    nptr = nptr->next;
                    if (lptr == l.current)
                        current = nptr;
                    nptr->value = lptr->value;
                    lptr = lptr->next;
                }
                nptr->next = NULL;
                last = nptr;
                size = l.size;
        }
}


template<class T> TList<T>::~TList()
// Delete all nodes in the List.
{
    Node<T>* nptr = first;
    current = first;
    while (current)
    {
        current = current->next;
        delete nptr;
        nptr = current;
    }
    first = current = last = NULL;
    size = 0;
}


template<class T> TList<T>& TList<T>::operator= (const TList<T>& l)
// assignment overload
{
    //--------- First, destroy the existing list.
    Node<T>* nptr = first;
    current = first;
    while (current)
    {
        current = current->next;
        delete nptr;
        nptr = current;
    }
```

```
//--------- Now build the new list
Node<T> *lptr = l.first;        // tracks through the argument list

if (lptr == NULL)
{   current = first = last = NULL; size = 0;}
else
{
    //---- Construct the first node in the list.
    nptr = new Node<T>;
    nptr->value = lptr->value;
    if (lptr == l.current)
        current = nptr;
    first = nptr;
    lptr = lptr->next;

    //---- Track through the remainder of the list, copying nodes.
    while (lptr)
    {
        nptr->next = new Node<T>;
        nptr = nptr->next;
        if (lptr == l.current)
            current = nptr;
        nptr->value = lptr->value;
        lptr = lptr->next;
    }
    nptr->next = NULL;
    last = nptr;
    size = l.size;
}
return *this;
}


template<class T> void TList<T>::Insert(T x)
// Insert x at the current position.
{
    Node<T>* nptr = new Node<T>;
    if (current == NULL)      // List is empty.
    {
        nptr->value = x;
        nptr->next = NULL;
        current = first = last = nptr;
    }
    else                            // List is nonempty.
    {
        nptr->value = current->value;
        nptr->next = current->next;
```

```
            current->value = x;
            current->next = nptr;
            if (current == last)
                last = nptr;
        }
        size++;
}


template<class T> void TList<T>::Remove()
// Delete the node at the current position.
{
    //You fill it in!!!
}


template<class T> void TList<T>::Head()
// Move current location to the head.
{ current = first;}


template<class T> void TList<T>::Tail()
// Move current location to the tail.
{ current = last;}


template<class T> TList<T>& TList<T>::operator++ (int)
// Move current location to next node (postfix operator).
// Do nothing if current is at the tail of the list.
{
    if (current != last)
        current = current->next;
    return *this;
}


template<class T> TList<T>& TList<T>::operator-- (int)
// Move current location to previous node (postfix operator).
// Do nothing if current is at the head of the list
{
    if (current != first)
    {
        Node<T>* nptr = first;
        while (nptr->next != current)
            nptr = nptr->next;
        current = nptr;
    }
    return *this;
}


template<class T> T TList<T>::Retrieve() const
```

```
// Return the element at the current position.
{
    if (current)
        return current->value;
    else
    {
        cerr << "Attempted to Return an element from an empty list";
        exit(1);
    }
}


template<class T> void TList<T>::Update(T x)
// Store x in current location.
{
    if (current)
        current->value = x;
    else
    {
        cerr << "Attempted to Update an element in an empty list";
        exit(1);
    }
}


template<class T> int TList<T>::Length()
// Return the number of nodes in the list.
{ return size;}
```

Exploring Linked Lists

The insertion operator << is a useful place to start our exploration, since it embodies in a simple form the linked list version of a common action we perform on lists— traversing a list in order, from first element to last:

```
template<class T> ostream& operator<< (ostream& os, TList<T> l)
// Display an entire TList, from first position to last.
{
    Node<T>* p = l.first;
    while (p)
    {
        os << p->value << '\t';
        p = p->next;
    }
    return os;
}
```

There are two key features here. First, we use a loop to display an element in a node at position *p* and, second, within the loop we repeatedly move *p* to the next node following it. The loop is controlled by the value of the pointer *p*; when that pointer is zero, we know that we have reached the end of the list. In the context of a while statement, any nonzero value for p will be interpreted as *true*, so the loop will continue until *p* becomes zero, at which point the expression (*p*) will evaluate as *false*, terminating the loop.

We advance the pointer *p* to the next node by writing

```
p = p->next;
```

We can traverse a NULL-terminated linked list of nodes (where each node has a pointer member datum named *next*) by using a loop like this:

```
p = some pointer to the head of the list;
while (p)
{
    do whatever processing is necessary at location p
    p = p->next;
}
```

The following diagram illustrates how we can point our way through a linked list of nodes, using the pointer equivalent of incrementing an index in an array.

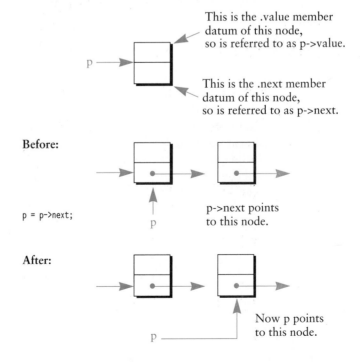

This is the .value member
datum of this node,
so is referred to as p->value.

This is the .next member
datum of this node,
so is referred to as p->next.

Before:

p = p->next;

p

p->next points
to this node.

After:

p

Now p points
to this node.

If you look at the definitions of the copy constructor and the assignment operator, you'll see that both do the same thing: While pointing their way through the argument list they build the list by constructing new nodes, linking them to existing nodes, and filling their value data with copies of the values in the argument lists.

We've seen that the array version of *Insert* is quite simple conceptually: To insert a new element into an array, all we have to do is shift the elements above the insertion point up by one to make room for the new element. Insertion in a linked list takes a few more lines of code, but the underlying idea is just about as simple as array insertion. To insert a new element in a nonempty list we begin with a pointer, *current*, to the position where the new element will go. Having done that, Figure 11.11 shows that there are only five basic steps required:

```
Node<T> *nptr = new Node<T>;          // Construct a new node.
nptr->value = current->value;         // Copy the current node's value
                                      // into it.
nptr->next = current->next;           // Link it to the node after
                                      // current.
current->value = x;                   // Put the new value into the
                                      // current node.
current->next = nptr;                 // Link the current node to the
                                      // new node.
```

The full definition of *Insert* is only a little more complicated than this. The only other things we have to do are (1) handle the special case where we are inserting into an empty list, since then *current* is a NULL pointer, so it makes no sense to refer to the node pointed to by *current*; (2) remember that if we happen to insert a node at the last position in the list we have to move the last member pointer up by one position; and (3) increment the *size* member datum to reflect the new size of the list.

As with array deletion, linked list deletion is more or less the opposite of insertion. To delete an element in a linked list, we can copy the next node's value into the current node, make a pointer to the next node (so we don't lose it in the next step), move the current node's *next* pointer around the cell to be deleted, and delete the cell after the current cell, as we do in Figure 11.12.

Take a closer look at Figure 11.12. Pictures don't lie, but they do sometimes mislead. Every picture carries with it a set of assumptions. What assumptions are we making in the figure that may not be true in all possible cases? Take a minute before you go on—there are at least three assumptions implicit in the picture that are not necessarily true in general. Hint: There are some features of the linked list version of *TList* that we omitted for clarity.

*   *   *

FIGURE 11.11
Inserting a new element at the current position

Initially:

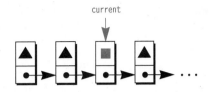

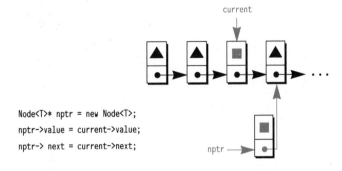

```
Node<T>* nptr = new Node<T>;
nptr->value = current->value;
nptr-> next = current->next;
```

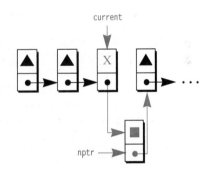

```
current->value = x;
current->next = nptr;
```

Ultimately:

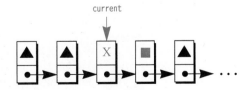

FIGURE 11.12
Deleting the element at the current position

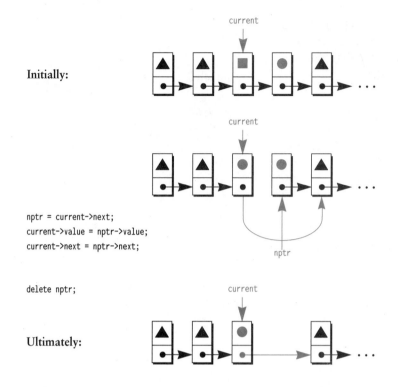

Initially:

current

Ultimately:

current

```
nptr = current->next;
current->value = nptr->value;
current->next = nptr->next;
```

nptr

```
delete nptr;
```

Did you get all three? Here's how the picture lied:

1. It showed *current* pointing to a node. The list may be empty, so we have to take some special action in that case, such as warning the user.
2. It omitted the first and last pointers, which are essential pieces of information about the list. What if the list had only one element? Deleting that element would require us to reset the values of first and last to NULL.
3. It assumed that there was a next node after the current one. We may, though, want to delete the last element in a list. The algorithm in the picture would not work correctly in this case, so we have to find a different way to delete the last node in the list.

There are, then, four cases we have to deal with when we delete an element from a linked list: the one in which our picture told the truth and the three that were not covered. We'll leave the details of deletion to you in the lab, now that we've given you the necessary hints.

> It's important to realize the difference between linked lists and arrays: An array can have only one form, but linked structures may come in several logically distinct forms. When we deal with linked structures, we ignore the special cases at our peril.

11.4 COMPARING IMPLEMENTATIONS

You've just seen two entirely different ways of programming the *List* ADT. A bright but contentious apprentice might ask why we bothered to do the same thing in two different ways: "Why learn another way, since the first one worked just fine?" The glib answer to that would be "for the experience." A journeyman might pose the better question: "You're evidently making me do the same job in two ways to teach me a lesson. What should I be learning here?" That question deserves a more complete answer, which is what we'll do in this section. You've seen that there are always many ways of solving a programming problem; some are better than others in some respects and worse than others in other respects. It's worth our while to consider the criteria we can use to compare different solutions to a problem.

Space

Our expressed motivation for considering a pointer-based implementation of the *List* ADT was that there were space considerations that gave an edge to a linked collection of many nodes over one large monolithic array. Recall that C++ arrays, like arrays in many other languages, must occupy adjacent locations in memory, whether they are allocated in free store or not. A request to set aside space for an array, as in the statement *p = new int[10000],* might be denied by the system even if there were forty thousand integer-sized locations available, simply because there was no single free block large enough to fill the request. On the other hand, a single node takes up very little space by comparison, and a collection of ten thousand such nodes, linked by pointers, can be scattered around in memory wherever there is room for them.

There's more to the space requirements of the two implementations than simply avoiding asking for large chunks of memory. If our lists are large enough, we might need nearly the entire available amount of memory in our computer, regardless of implementation. In that case, we would be wise to consider the total amount of memory needed to store a list.

Suppose, for example, that we are going to use a computer/compiler combination in which pointers are four bytes long and integers are two bytes long. The data type of the elements in the list requires d bytes (d might be 2 for lists of integers, 16 for a rather improbable list of soda machines, or 60 for the far more reasonable list of phone book entries). Let's compute the total amount of memory needed to store N entries of size d.

The array implementation requires 6 bytes for the size, max, and current member data, plus d times the average size of the array. Since we double the size of the array when we run out of room to insert an element, we rather arbitrarily decide that the average size of an array holding N elements is $(3/2)N$. This means that the array implementation will require $6 + (3/2)Nd$ bytes to store an N element list, on the average. The linked list will require 14 bytes for the first, current, and last pointers and the size member datum, along with N nodes, each requiring d bytes for the element plus 4 for the pointer in each node. Therefore, the linked list implementation will use $14 + N(d + 4)$ bytes to store a list of N elements. This means that the array implementation will require less memory space as long as

$$6 + (3/2)Nd < 14 + N(d + 4)$$

which is equivalent to saying

$$d/2 - 4 < 8/N$$

If you try some values for d, you'll see that the array implementation uses less memory, on average, if $d \leq 8$, and that the linked list implementation uses less space when $d \geq 24$. The behavior between $d = 8$ and $d = 24$ depends on N, but we can conclude, as a rule of thumb, that if space is our main criterion, we are better off using arrays if the list elements are small and linked lists if the elements are large.

Time

The choice of implementation affects not only the space needed to store an ADT object. It also may have a profound effect on the running times of the operations. Consider the *List* insertion operation, for instance. If we represent a list by an array, we must shift the list elements toward the tail of the list to make room for the new element. In the worst case, when we are inserting a new element at the head of the list, this could require us to shift the entire array element by element. In big-O terminology, we would say that insertion runs in time $O(n)$ for arrays, where n is the size of the list. On the other hand, in the pointer version of *List*, insertion runs in constant time so that the steps required to insert a new element are independent of the size of the list. Deletion behaves similarly; it can be written to run in time proportional to the length of the list for arrays and in constant time for linked lists. If we were writing a program that used a list, then, and we knew that the program would make a large number of insertions or deletions, we might decide to choose a pointer implementation, even if it meant giving away some space in memory.

In a similar way, we can compare the rest of the *List* operations in terms of their running times. Table 11.1 shows that arrays have a time advantage for the destructor (unless the elements had their own destructors, in which case the time taken by the destructor would be $O(n)$) and the -- operator, and linked lists have the edge in insertion and deletion.

Comprehensibility

Programs are written and maintained by people. Therefore, if we have several possible ways to write a program and there are no compelling space or time reasons for picking one implementation over the other, the smart choice would

TABLE 11.1

Comparison of worst-case running times of *List* operations

Operation	Arrays	Pointers
Default constructor	1	1
Copy constructor	n	n
Destructor	1	n
operator=	n	n
Insert	n	1
Remove	n	1 (*n*, if removing tail)
Head	1	1
Tail	1	1
operator++	1	1
operator--	1	n
Retrieve	1	1
Update	1	1
Length	1	1

be to use the one that is easiest to understand and modify. For our *List* example, you would probably agree that the array version is the hands-down winner in terms of readability. Part of this choice is due to the fact that you've had far more experience with arrays than you have with linked structures. The choice will be much less compelling once you become comfortable with pointers, but even an experienced programmer would probably agree with you that the array implementation is the easiest to understand at first glance.

This criterion is at least as important as the other two. After all, there's no benefit to be gained from using a fast, small implementation if it is so complicated and abstruse that it never gets successfully completed or is impossible to modify.

Trade-Offs

After all our comparison, which is the better implementation for the *List* ADT? As stated, there's no answer to this question except perhaps to respond with another question: "What do you mean by 'best'?" The question of which way to solve a programming problem illustrates the engineering flavor of computer science.

The two-fold nature of computer science is reflected in its placement in the curriculum. In some schools, computer science is grouped with mathematics, and at others finds itself in the School of Engineering.

We can look at computer science as the marriage of mathematics and engineering. The mathematical aspect is seen in questions such as "How fast can we sort a list?" and "Is this algorithm correct?" These are questions to which there is one and only one right answer. Engineering, on the other hand, devotes a considerable amount of attention to choosing among alternative designs, based on an often complicated web of interdependent considerations. There are many ways to build a bridge, for instance; the decision of how to do the job depends on the factors that are considered important for the particular problem. If the only consideration was ease of maintenance, it might make sense to build the bridge out of gold, since gold never rusts or needs painting. On the other hand, gold is hideously expensive compared to steel and is much weaker and heavier.

To decide which *List* implementation we should use, then, we must answer questions such as "Is space important, or are we dealing with small lists?", "Are we going to be doing a lot of insertions and deletions into large lists?", and "Is our list package going to be maintained by novices or experienced programmers?" As is so often the case, there may not be any clear-cut preference. Instead, we are often faced with trade-offs, having to give up comprehensibility for a gain in speed, or picking an implementation that is space-efficient but not as fast as it could be.

11.5 SUMMING UP

▶ An abstract data type is defined by describing the logical structure of the information represented by an instance of the type and the operations performed on the information.

▶ Put another way, in C++ an ADT is almost the same thing as the declaration of a class.

▶ The *List* ADT has a structure in which each element has at most one successor and at most one predecessor. There are two special locations in a list: the head of the list, having no predecessor position, and the tail, which has no successor. Except for those, all elements have a unique predecessor and successor.

▶ In a *Tree* ADT, each element (except for a special one, called the *root*) has a unique predecessor, but may have arbitrarily many successors. Trees are used to express hierarchical organizations of information.

▶ In a *Graph* ADT, each element may have arbitrarily many predecessors and successors.

▶ Some general categories of ADT operations are:

1. Construction/Initialization: used to create and set initial values for the ADT.
2. Destruction: to free the space used by instances of the ADT.
3. Modification: operations that alter some or all of the information represented by the ADT.
4. Access: to allow users of the ADT to inspect the internal information.
5. Iteration: to perform the same action on all elements of the structure.

▶ Most ADTs include the following operations:

• Constructors, like a default constructor with no arguments, used to create an empty instance of an ADT, and perhaps a copy constructor.

- A destructor. Since we'll often use pointers or arrays to represent the internal information, we'll need to free the internal information when we destroy an instance of the ADT.

- An assignment or copy operator.

- Input and output operators.

▶ We may describe a *parameterized class* by preceding its definition by the phrase `template<class T>`. The parameter T stands for any type, either a user-defined class or a predefined type like `int`. A parameterized class declaration looks like this:

```
template<class T>
class TList
{
    // Declarations of member functions, friends, and
    // member data, as usual.
};
```

▶ In a parameterized class definition, we may use the type parameter just as if it were a predefined type name.

▶ We can parameterize functions in much the same way that we did for classes: We precede the definition by the phrase `template<class T>`, and then define the function as expected, using the type parameter T as we would any other type name.

▶ Arrays are a natural choice for implementing linear ADTs like lists or stacks. Arrays, though, require contiguous space in memory. Implementing a linear structure by a linked collection of cells removes the restriction of contiguity by allowing elements to be scattered in memory.

▶ If a linked structure is connected by pointers named *next*, a common way to traverse such a structure is by using a pointer p to an element and repeatedly performing the assignment $p = p$->*next*;.

▶ When thinking about a linked structure, be aware that such structures often occur in logically different forms, depending, usually, on whether the structure is empty, has a single element, or has more than one element. An operation that works correctly on one form should not be assumed to work correctly on the others.

▶ A useful feature of C++ is that we can often completely change the implementation of a class representing an ADT merely by changing the private part of the declaration and then suitably modifying the class definition. Doing so requires no modification on the part of the program that uses the class.

▶ It is worthwhile to study different implementations of a class, since different implementations may have quite different time, space, and comprehensibility measurements.

▶ There is no "best" implementation of an ADT, in general. The choice is often based on the requirements of the client program.

11.6 EXERCISES

1. Describe the structure (using pictures as necessary) and a reasonable collection of operations for the following ADTs:
   a. *Ring*, as described in Section 11.1
   b. *SortedList*, in which the underlying set of elements is such as to permit the elements to be arranged in sorted order, from smallest to largest

2. Do Exercise 1 for the following ADTs:
   a. *Vector*, as described in Section 11.1
   b. *Sets* of (for instance) integers

3. Invent appropriate implementations of the ADTs in Exercise 1.

4. Invent appropriate implementations of the ADTs in Exercise 2.

5. Rewrite the linked list versions of << and = using for loops.

6. The array implementation of *TList* isn't safe, since it doesn't check that new succeeded. What would it take to make the array version safe in that sense?

7. Why didn't we use the natural choice *Delete* for the name of the *List* operation that removes the element at the current position?

8. If you think about it, you'll see that *Insert* has a major deficiency: It is impossible to insert a new element after the last element in the list. Write the function *Append* to do that.
   a. Write *Append* for the array implementation of *List*.
   b. Write *Append* for linked lists.
   c. Compare the running times of the function in the two implementations. Is *Append* more efficient or easier to understand in one implementation than in another? Explain.

9. In inserting an element into an array, what would happen if we shifted the elements in the opposite order, starting with position *current* + 1? In other words, would there be anything wrong with reversing the directions "Do first" and "Do last" in Figure 11.8? In a similar vein, could we delete an element by shifting the elements starting at the right?

10. Would there be any advantage in comprehensibility or efficiency from inserting an element in a linked list *after* the current position or removing the element after the current position? Let's see.

a. Write this new version of *Insert* and compare it with the old version.

b. Write this new version of *Remove* and compare it with the old version.

11. Could we remedy the deficiency in *Insert* by redefining it to insert an element after the current position? Explain.

12. Consider the function with header

```
template<class T> void TList<T>::Find(T x)
```

that sets the current position to the location of the node containing the value *x*, if there is one, and does nothing if *x* is not in the list.

a. Define this function for the array implementation of lists.

b. Define this function for linked lists.

c. Compare the running times of your two definitions in parts a and b.

d. It might be a better idea to have *Find* return an int, indicating whether or not the sought-for element was in the list. Rewrite your definitions in parts a and b for this new function.

e. Even better might be to combine the action in part d with a definition that also sets the current position to the location where *x* would belong, if it is not in the list. Write this version.

13. Write an overload of the + operator that would concatenate two lists, producing a new list by appending the contents of one list at the end of the other. For example, if *a* and *b* were of type TList<int>, with *a* = [3, 5, –1] and *b* = [0, 6, 6, 3], then *a* + *b* would be the list [3, 5, –1, 0, 6, 6, 3].

14. The function *Find* requires the ability to compare *x* with the value member datum in a node. It may be the case, though, that a node has a key value that is used for comparison, along with a number of other member data, as in the following example:

```
struct PersonnelData
{   int ID;           // This is the key value used for searching.
    char    *name,    // These are not used by Find.
            *address;}
```

Suppose we wanted *Find* to take just an int argument representing a possible key value, as might be the case in a database program in which we would get information about a person by using his or her ID number. How would you augment this structure to allow a *PersonnelData* object to be compared with an integer?

15. Show that we don't really need the *last* member datum in the pointer implementation of *List* by writing *Tail* without referring to *last*. How does this affect the running times of the *List* operations in Table 11.1?

16. Assume that *T* was a type for which the operators ==, !=, <, <=, >, >= were defined. We could then declare a derived type of *TList<T>*, named

TSortedList<T>, in which the list elements were stored in sorted order, from smallest to largest.

a. How would the member functions of *TSortedList<T>* differ from the member functions of the base class *TList<T>*? In other words, which of the base class functions would be inappropriate for the derived class? Which of the base class functions would need to be redefined in the derived class? Would you want to define any functions for sorted lists that would not be appropriate in the base class?

b. Should *TList<T>* be a public or private base class for *TSortedList<T>*? Why?

c. Write a declaration of the class *TSortedList<T>*.

d. Write definitions of the member functions of *TSortedList<T>*. Try to make your definitions implementation independent by defining them in terms of the base class member functions.

17. If we had written the array and pointer versions of *List* without using the member datum *size*, how would the timings in Table 11.1 be changed? Caution: There are some hidden consequences in the array implementation.

18. A *dequeue* (pronounced "deck" in this context*) is a double-ended queue, where insertion, deletion, and inspection are defined only at the head and the tail of the underlying linear structure.

a. Write a declaration of *TDequeue<T>* as a derived class of *TList<T>*.

b. Give declarations of *TStack<T>* and *TQueue<T>* as derived classes of *TDequeue<T>*.

---

* The queue operation that removes the element at the head of the queue is also written "dequeue," but in that context the name is pronounced "D-Q."

A PASCAL-C++ DICTIONARY

There are two good reasons to be able to translate from Pascal to C++ and back again. Both reasons have to do with the fact that, for the time being at least, Pascal is far more popular in academic circles than C++. First, there are a number of people who will come to this course as more or less fluent speakers of Pascal. If you fall into this category, you have probably taken an introductory programming course in Pascal and would profit from the knowledge that there is a fairly simple collection of mappings you need to know to translate from thinking in Pascal to thinking in (non-object-oriented) C++. Second, you might find that subsequent courses or examinations (like the Graduate Record Examinations) assume that you speak Pascal. In that case, you'll need this dictionary after this course, rather than before, but you' ll still benefit from knowing that the two languages are similar enough that going from one to the other isn't difficult. In terms of both syntax and semantics, the two languages are close cousins, at least as long as you don't worry about trying to do object-oriented programming in Pascal, and if you treat C++ as just a Pascal relative.

If you are serious about learning one language and you know the other already, the best way to proceed is get your hands on an appropriate compiler and translate some of your simpler programs into the other language (it's easier to do this from Pascal to C++ than the other way around, especially if your C++ program makes heavy use of classes).

In this appendix, we will spend most of our time on the features that are more or less common to the two languages. We will concentrate as much as possible on the standard features of these two languages and will make only passing mention of extensions that exist in some compilers but not in others. In what follows, we assume that you know either Pascal or C++, so we will skimp on the details of what an if statement or a pointer is, for instance. To indicate constructions in the two languages,

`we will use this typeface for C++`

and

`we'll use this one for Pascal`

and

we'll italicize words that are the same in both.

A.1 INFORMATION

Both languages have integer and real numeric types. C++ has a richer assortment of numeric types. In C++ the integer types are, in order of the amount of space they take in memory, `short`, `int`, and `long`. Standard Pascal has only the type `integer`. The floating-point types in C++ are (again, in order of size, which translates roughly to number of digits of precision) `float`, `double`, and `long double`; Pascal has the type `real`. The rules for representing literal numbers, like -32 and $0.4e8$, are nearly identical in the two languages.

Both languages have arithmetic and comparison operators. The correspondences are

C++	Pascal
+, −	+, −
/ (for real types)	/ (for real types)
/ (for integral types)	**div** (for integral types)
%	**mod**
++	(no Pascal equivalent)
--	(no Pascal equivalent)
<, <=, >, >=	<, <=, >, >=
==	=
!=	<>

The operators ++ and --, when applied to a variable, cause the value of the variable to be increased or decreased by one, respectively. In other words, the C++ expression a++ is equivalent in effect to the Pascal statement a := a + 1. C++ has many more precedence levels than Pascal. The best advice in either language is to make liberal use of parentheses (which are the same in both languages) in any arithmetic or logical expression.

Both languages support characters as a type. The typename is *char* in both. In both languages, character literals consist of a single character enclosed within single quotes. Both languages support character string literals: A C++ string is enclosed in double quotes and a Pascal string is enclosed in single quotes:

"A C++ string"   'A Pascal string'

Pascal has a boolean type consisting of two values, written true and false. There is no separate boolean type in C++. Instead, the integer 0 represents *false* and any non-zero integer evaluates as *true* in a context where boolean values are expected. This means that the Pascal expression (n <> 0) may be written (n) in C++.

C++	Pascal
int	boolean
0	false
(non-zero)	true
&&	**and**
||	**or**
!	**not**

Unlike Pascal, C++ uses the convention of short-circuit evaluation: A sequence of expressions combined by the && operator is evaluated from the left and evaluation stops as soon as a *false* value (zero) is found, and a collection of expressions using the || operator is evaluated from the left and evaluation stops as soon as a *true* value (non-zero) is found.

Both languages support enumerated types, which are types in which the programmer specifies the literal names. In both languages, the names are represented internally by integers, so the comparison operators <, <=, and so on may be used with enumerated types. These types are specified as follows:

```
                              type
enum State = {error, warn, ok};   State = {error, warn, ok};
```

Pascal supports subrange types of integers, characters, and enumerated types, specifying the range by using the lower and upper limits separated by two periods (..), as in the specification 0 .. 99. This is not a feature of C++.

Declaring Information

Both C++ and Pascal are *strongly typed,* in the sense that any variable or constant has an associated type. In both languages, variables must be declared before they may be used. The declarations have different forms, as you can see from the following table. In C++ a variable may be defined to have an initial value, which cannot be done in Pascal. In both languages, identifiers may be declared to be *constants,* meaning their value may not be modified. In C++, variables may be declared anywhere in a program. In Pascal, variables must be declared at the beginning of the program, procedure, or function, after constant and type declarations. The section of variable declarations in Pascal is headed by the word **var.** In Pascal, all constant definitions are made at once, in a section of the program, function, or procedure headed by the word **const.** In C++, constants may be computed, but in Pascal the only allowable constant computations are negation.

C++	Pascal
	const
`const double PI = 3.1416;`	PI = 3.1416;
`const char BLANK = ' ';`	BLANK = ' ';
`const double NEG_PI = -PI;`	NEG_PI = –PI;
`const double TWO_PI = 2 * PI;`	(no Pascal equivalent)
	type
`typedef int IntArray[100];`	IntArray = **array**[0 .. 99] **of** integer;
	var
`int a, b;`	a, b : integer;
`double x;`	x : real;
`char c;`	c : char;
`char dollar = '$';`	(no Pascal equivalent)
`int sum = a + b;`	(no Pascal equivalent)

In both languages, it is possible for the programmer to give names to types that are defined in the program. In Pascal, one makes a **type** declaration, with the typename followed by = and the specification of the type. The corresponding form in C++ is the `typedef` specification.

A.2   PROGRAM STRUCTURE

C++ programs generally are spread over many files; this is less true for Pascal. In standard Pascal, all definitions and declarations occur in the main program, and they must be placed immediately after the program header. Here are what programs look like in the two languages:

```
void main()
// C++ Comment




{
    statements
}
```

```
program AnyName;
{Pascal comment}
        constant, type, variable,
        function and procedure
        definitions
begin
    statements
end. {note period at end}
```

As you can see, { and } in C++ correspond to **begin** and **end** in Pascal: They both group statements into blocks, which lead to basically the same scope rules in both languages. The rules for identifiers are also the same in both languages, but Pascal makes no distinction between upper- and lowercase letters, while C++ does. Comments in C++ begin with // and continue to the end of the line, while comments in Pascal are enclosed in { and } braces.

Functions

C++ and Pascal both use functions as a fundamental structure for encapsulating algorithms. In both languages, a function header consists of the function name, its return type, and a description of the information passed to the function. The order in which these are written is quite different in the two languages:

```
int F(double x, int n)
{

    Local declarations
    and statements

}
```

```
function F(x : real; n : integer) : integer;
            Local declarations
    begin
            statements
    end; {note semicolon at end}
```

These forms parallel the way programs are written: In Pascal, declarations of local constants, types, and variables are made outside the statement body; in C++ they are part of the body. Notice that a C++ argument list is separated by commas, while in Pascal semicolons are used as the separators. Functions are called in the same way in both languages: The function call invokes the function, and its return value is used in the expression just like any ordinary value of the appropriate type.

In C++, a function that returns no value is given a void return type. Calls to such functions are written as single statements in either language. The corresponding entity in Pascal is called a procedure, and its definition begins with the keyword **procedure**.

```
void Print(int x)
{
    cout << "***";
    cout << x << endl;
}

    . . .
```

```
procedure Print(x : integer);
begin
    write('***');
    writeln(x)
end;

    . . .
```

```
// Later we make the call
Print(3);
```

```
{ Later we make the call }
Print(3);
```

In the example above, notice that C++ output is performed by using the << operator to send information to the standard output stream cout. In Pascal we use a predefined procedure write (which doesn't move down to the next line) or writeln (which does). The input operator in C++ uses >> to get information from the standard input stream cin, while in Pascal a readln procedure is used for input.

```
int GetNum()                    function GetNum: integer;
{                                       var x : integer;
    int x;                      begin
    cout << "Number? ";                 write('Number? ');
    cin >> x;                           readln(x);
    return x;                           GetNum := x
}                               end;
```

Notice that value of a C++ function is sent back by a `return` statement; in Pascal, the return is indicated by a statement that looks very much like an assignment with the function name on the left. In C++ a `return` forces an immediate exit from the function, but in Pascal an assignment with the function name on the left merely sets the value to be returned, without leaving the function (which happens when execution passes out of the statement body). Notice also that a C++ function with no arguments must still have parentheses for the argument list; in Pascal an empty parameter list (arguments are called parameters in Pascal) must be omitted.

Pascal programmers often nest function and procedure definitions in other function definitions; this is not allowed in C++.

A.3 STATEMENTS

While most statements in C++ correspond closely to their counterparts in Pascal and vice versa, there is a significant difference in the most common statement in the two languages. Another minor, but important, difference between the two languages is the role of the semicolon punctuator.

The Semicolon

In C++, a semicolon is a statement terminator. Pascal uses the semicolon as a statement separator. The consequence of this difference is that a semicolon in Pascal is not needed before the keyword **end** and is forbidden before the **else** part of an **if** statement. In C++, both of these cases require a semicolon. A simple rule to follow is to place semicolons at the end of every statement. In almost all cases, that will be acceptable in either language. The exception to remember is that in Pascal there cannot be a semicolon before the word **else**.

Assignment

In C++, assignment is an operator that sets its left argument to the value of its right and then returns the value, while in Pascal assignment is a statement. For most purposes, you can simply ignore the subtleties of the difference, but one important consequence is that in C++ you can write a = b = 3, setting the value of both a and b to 3. In Pascal, such multiple assignments are illegal. The assignment operator in C++ is written =, while its Pascal counterpart is written :=. This difference, when combined with the differences between the equality operators in the two languages, is a frequent source of confusion to beginners.

C++	Pascal
a = b; // assignment	a := b; {assignment}
a = b = c;	(no Pascal equivalent)
if (a == b) // equality	**if** a = b **then** {equality}
cout << a;	write(a);

C++ has a number of assignments that combine assignment with arithmetic operations. These operators have no direct counterparts in Pascal.

C++	Pascal
a += b;	a := a + b;
a -= b;	a := a − b;
a *= b;	a := a * b;
a /= b;	a := a / b; or a := a **div** b;
a %= b;	a := a **mod** b;

Selection

Both languages support one- and two-way selection, using the *if* or *if-else* statement. There is very little difference between the two versions, except that in C++ the controlling logical expression must be parenthesized while parentheses are optional in Pascal. In addition, a Pascal **if** statement requires the keyword **then**. Both allow multiple statements to be grouped into clauses with the respective block delimiters, { and } in C++ and **begin** .. **end** in Pascal.

```
if (a < 0)                    if a < 0 then
    negs++;                       negs := negs + 1;

if (x * y < 0)                if x * y < 0 then
{                                 begin
    x = -x;                           x := − x;
    y = -y;                           y := −y
}                                 end;

if (t == 0)                   if t = 0 then
    cout << "Zero";               write('Zero')
else                          else
    cout << "Non-zero";           write('Non-zero');
```

To do multiway selection in C++, one uses the switch statement, and the Pascal equivalent is the **case** statement. The two have similar forms, but act in quite different ways:

```
switch (ch)                 case ch of
{
    case 'Y':                   'Y':
        yesSum++;               yesSum := yesSum + 1;
        break;
    case 'N':                   'N':
        noSum++;                noSum := noSum + 1;
        break;
    case '?':                   '?':
        maybeSum++;             maybeSum := maybeSum + 1;
}                           end;
```

First, observe the punctuation: C++ requires braces and the Pascal **case** statement ends with the word **end** (without a matching **begin**). Notice the break statement in the C++ version. This statement forces an immediate exit from the nearest enclosing switch statement (it also can be used to force exit from a loop) and is needed because without it, execution would continue through all the statements in the switch. This is not true in the Pascal version, where execution is terminated as soon as control is about to pass to the next label. For example, if *ch* has the value 'Y', both statements will increment *yesSum*; in the Pascal version, control would then pass out of the **case** statement. In C++, however, execution continues through the rest of the statements in the list, so we require a break statement to ensure that *noSum* and *maybeSum* will not also be incremented.

Pascal allows multiple case labels; C++ does not, although one can get around that by using the "fall-through" property:

```
switch (ch)                 case ch of
{
    case 'Y':                   'Y', 'y':
    case 'y':                       yesSum++;
    yesSum := yesSum + 1;       break;
    . . .                           . . .
}                           end:
```

Finally, C++ allows a default: label to take care of instances not handled by the case labels. Standard Pascal has no such feature, although a common Pascal extension is to allow an **otherwise** clause as the last part of the statement.

Indexed Iteration

Both languages have *for* statements, although the C++ version is more powerful (and more complicated) than its Pascal counterpart. The most common

C++ use of the *for* statement, though, is almost an exact parallel of the Pascal version.

```
for (int i = 0; i < n; i++)        for i := 0 to n – 1 do
{                                     begin
    statements                            statements
}                                     end:
```

Pascal *for* loops can only increase or decrease the loop control variable by one at each iteration. To decrease the variable, one uses **downto** in place of **to**.

```
for (int i = 20; i >= 5; i--)      for i := 20 downto 5 do
{                                     begin
    statements                            statements
}                                     end:
```

Controlled-Exit Iteration

There are two other forms of Pascal and C++ loops, distinguished by whether the test for the loop exit is made at the start of the statement body or at the end. The *while* loop makes its test at the beginning and looks very much the same in both languages. The only important differences are that the Pascal version uses the additional keyword **do** and the C++ version requires parentheses (optional in Pascal) around the boolean expression that controls iteration.

```
while (a != 0)            while a <> 0 do
{                           begin
    cin >> a;                 readln(a);
    sum += a;                 sum := sum + a
}                           end:
```

The loop form where the test is made at the end, however, is expressed quite differently in C++ and Pascal:

```
do                        repeat
{
    cin >> a;                 readln(a);
    sum += a;                 sum := sum + a
} while (a != 0);         until a = 0;
```

The C++ version begins with the word do and ends with a while clause (note the required semicolon at the end—this differs from all other C++ iteration and selection statements). If the loop body is a compound statement, it is enclosed in braces. The Pascal version begins with **repeat** and ends with **until**, and these words take the place of the usual **begin .. end** pair.

The most important difference between these is not syntactic, though. In the C++ version, the expression in the while clause causes execution to stay in the loop when it is *true,* whereas the expression in the **until** clause, when *true,* causes exit from the loop.

A.4 COMPOUND DATA TYPES

C++ and Pascal both support compound types, data structures that are declared to be a collection of simpler types, either predefined or defined in the program. As you might expect by now, the versions in the two languages are similar enough to be recognizable at a glance and different enough to cause headaches for a novice.

Arrays

The *array* type in both languages is an indexed collection of elements of the same type. The declarations mirror the form of declaration of simple types in the languages: They may be made "on the fly" as part of variable declarations or they may be used to define type names to be used later.

	type
`typedef int Nums[20];`	Nums = **array**[0 .. 19] **of** integer;
	var
`char c[10];`	c : **array**[0 .. 9] **of** char;
`Nums p, q;`	p, q : Nums;

Pascal is more flexible here, since C++ arrays always begin with index 0 while Pascal arrays may have any starting and ending indices. Pascal also checks array bounds to make sure that an array element has a legal index. C++ does not, in general. On the other hand, since C++ regards an array name as a pointer to the first element in the array, arrays in C++ may have their sizes changed during the execution of a program. In Pascal an array maintains the same size throughout the life of its program.

Access to arrays is similar in both languages: The element with index i in the array a is referred to by $a[i]$ in both. Neither language allows arrays to be the return values of functions, although both allow arrays to be passed as arguments to functions or procedures. In Pascal, it is legal to perform assignment between arrays of the same type. This is not allowed in C++: To copy an array, the programmer must write a routine that copies the array element by element.

Both languages support multidimensional arrays, although the syntax is slightly different:

`int table[2][3];`	table: **array**[0 .. 1, 0 .. 2] **of** integer;
`table[0][2] = 16;`	table[0, 2] = 16;

Structures and Records

Heterogeneous compound types, where the elements may be of different types, are parts of both Pascal and C++. The C++ version is called a struct (short for "structure") and the Pascal version is called a **record.** The elements of each are declared as they normally would be if they weren't part of the type:

```
                              type
struct MachineState           MachineState = record
{
    int level;                    level: integer;
    double temp, press;           temp, press : real;
    int lights[5];                lights: array[0 .. 4] of integer;
}                             end;
                              var
MachineState m1, m2;          m1, m2 : MachineState;
```

In both, the elements of the object are accessed through the dot operator:

```
cout << m1.level;             write(m1.level);
m2.temp += 22.3;              m2.temp := m2.temp + 22.3;
m1.lights[2] = 0;            m1.lights[2] := 0;
```

Structures and records have different properties with regard to assignment and their behavior as function (or procedure) arguments and function returns. They also differ from arrays in their respective languages, as we illustrate here:

	C++ arrays	Pascal arrays	C++ structs	Pascal records
Assign to each other?	No	Yes	Yes	Yes
Be function arguments?	Yes	Yes	Yes	Yes
Be returned by functions?	No	No	Yes	No

A.5 POINTERS AND REFERENCES

Both pointers and references deal with the address of an object in memory. You will see that these types represent both a significant similarity and a significant difference between C++ and Pascal.

Pointers

Both languages support pointers. In fact, except for minor syntactic differences, Pascal and C++ treat pointers in virtually the same ways. A C++ pointer is declared and then used by using the * symbol. In Pascal, one uses either the up-arrow, ↑, or the caret, ^. Since the caret is by far the more common symbol, we will use it in our Pascal samples.

```
int* a; // declaration              a : ^integer; {declaration}
char *b, *c;                        b, c : ^char;
    . . .                               . . .
*a = 3; // use                      a^ := 3;   {use}
b = NULL;                           b := nil;
```

In C++, the pointer operator, *, binds to the variable, whether we write it next to the variable or the type. This means that, unlike in Pascal, we must use the * twice to declare two pointers. Notice that the special pointer constant NULL corresponds to the Pascal form **nil**, and the two have the same properties. In C++, NULL is defined to be a synonym for 0, and the two forms may be used interchangeably.

If we have a pointer to a record or a structure, Pascal uses the caret to access the record and then uses the dot to access an element in the record. In C++ we can do much the same thing, but we have to use parentheses because the precedence of the dot is higher than that of *. Because of this, C++ provides a shorthand notation, using the dash and the > symbol to make an operator that looks like a right-pointing arrow.

```
                                    var
MachineState* mp;                   mp : ^MachineState;
    . . .                               . . .
(*mp).level = 0;                    mp^.level := 0;
mp->level = 0; // equivalent
```

Both languages use the operator *new* to allocate space in memory for a pointer to point to. In Pascal, **new** is a procedure that takes a pointer argument. On the other hand, the C++ **new** operator returns a pointer and is (usually) given a type name on its right. To free a memory location that was allocated by *new*, C++ provides the delete operator and Pascal uses the dispose procedure.

```
mp = new MachineState;      new(mp);
    . . .                       . . .
delete mp;                  dispose(mp);
```

References

In C++, a reference is the address of an object. There is no similar entity available in standard Pascal (although some extensions to Pascal provide the @ operator, which does some of the things that references do in C++). Because of this difference, we wouldn't discuss references except for the fact they provide a way to do what **var** parameters do in Pascal.

A C++ variable is declared to be a reference type by using the & operator in its definition. The definition

```
int& a = b;
```

gives the variable *a* the same address as the (previously declared) variable *b*. In other words, after the definition, *a* and *b* are two names for the same location in memory. Thus, modifying *a* will also modify *b* (and vice versa), since they are just aliases for the same object.

Reference types allow us to circumvent a feature we haven't mentioned explicitly about C++ functions: They cannot modify the values of their arguments. When a C++ function is called, the actual argument is used to set the initial value of the formal argument, so any changes made to the argument in the function are made only to the local copy. By using a reference type as a function argument, we use the alias property to assure that any changes made to the local argument will also be made to the actual argument used in the function call. This corresponds to variable (**var**) parameters in Pascal, so the following two definitions will act in the same way:

```
void X(int& n, double z)          procedure X(var n : integer; z : real)
{                                 begin
    n++;                              n := n + 1;
    z *= 2.0;                         z := z * 2.0
}                                 end;


    . . .                             . . .


m = 3;                            m := 3;
w = 9.2;                          w := 9.2;
X(m, w);                          X(m, w);
```

In both versions above, *m* will have the value 4 after the call, but *w* will still have its original value 9.2, since it wasn't modified by the function (only its local copy was doubled).

A.6 TWO SAMPLE PROGRAMS

We present for your inspection two programs that do the same thing, the first in Pascal and the second in C++. They compute an interesting sequence: Starting with a positive integer entered by the user (say, 376), they repeatedly perform the following steps:

1. Reverse the number (yielding 673, in our example).
2. Add the reverse to the original number (giving 1049).
3. Display the result.

This process continues until the resulting number is a *palindrome*, or the number is equal to its reverse. In our example, this process terminates after three steps, producing 1049, 10450, and finally 15851, which is a palindrome.

The Pascal Program

```pascal
program ReverseGame;

    const
        MAX_SIZE = 399;
    type
        Num = record
            size: integer;
            digit: array[0..MAX_SIZE] of integer
        end;
    var
        n, r, s: Num;

    procedure Get (var n: Num);
    { Gets a Num from input.}
    var
        m, i: integer;
    begin
        write('> ');
        readln(m);
         i := 0;
        while m > 0 do
        begin
            n.digit[i] := m mod 10;
            m := m div 10;
            i := i + 1
        end;
        n.size := i - 1
    end;

    procedure Show (n: Num);
    { Displays a Num.}
    var
        i: integer;
    begin
        for i := n.size downto 0 do
            write(n.digit[i] : 1);
        writeln
    end;

    procedure Reverse (nIn: Num; var nOut: Num);
    { Reverses the digits in a Num.}
    var
        i: integer;
```

```
procedure Swap (var a, b: integer);
    var
        temp: integer;
    begin
        temp := a;
        a := b;
        b := temp
    end;


begin { Reverse}
    for i := 0 to nIn.size do
        nOut.digit[i] := nIn.digit[i];
    nOut.size := nIn.size;

    for i := 0 to nOut.size div 2 do
        Swap(nOut.digit[i], nOut.digit[nOut.size - i])
end;

procedure Add (n1, n2: Num; var sum: Num);
{ Adds two Nums of the same size.}
var
    i, carry, s: integer;
begin
    carry := 0;
    for i := 0 to n1.size do
    begin
        s := n1.digit[i] + n2.digit[i] + carry;
        sum.digit[i] := s mod 10;
        carry := s div 10
    end;
    sum.size := n1.size;
    if carry <> 0 then
    begin
        sum.size := sum.size + 1;
        sum.digit[sum.size] := carry
    end
end;

function IsPalindrome (n: Num): boolean;
{ Returns true if and only if n is the same as its reverse.}
    var
        i: integer;
        result: boolean;
begin
    i := 0;
```

```
          result := true;
          while result and (i <= n.size div 2) do
          begin
              result := result and (n.digit[i] = n.digit[n.size - i]);
              i := i + 1
          end;
          IsPalindrome := result
      end;

begin { Main}
    Get(n);
    repeat
      Reverse(n, r);
      Add(r, n, s);
      n := s;
      Show(n)
    until (IsPalindrome(n)) or (n.size >= MAX_SIZE)
end.
```

The C++ Program

```cpp
//----------- program ReverseGame;

#include <iostream.h>

const int MAX_SIZE = 399;
struct Num
{
    int size;
    int digit[MAX_SIZE + 1];
};

void Get(Num& n)
// Gets a Num from input.
{
    int m, i = 0;
    cout << "> ";
    cin >> m;
    while (m > 0)
    {
        n.digit[i] = m % 10;
        m /= 10;
        i++;
    }
    n.size = i - 1;
}
```

```
void Show(Num n)
// Displays a Num.
{
    for (int i = n.size; i >= 0; i--)
        cout << n.digit[i];
    cout << endl;
}

void Swap(int& a, int& b)
{
  int temp = a;
  a = b;
  b = temp;
}

Num Reverse(Num nIn)
// Reverses the digits in a Num.
{
    Num nOut;
    int i;
    for (i = 0; i <= nIn.size; i++)
        nOut.digit[i] = nIn.digit[i];
    nOut.size = nIn.size;

    for (i = 0; i <= nOut.size / 2; i++)
        Swap(nOut.digit[i], nOut.digit[nOut.size - i]);
    return nOut;
}

Num Add(Num n1, Num n2)
// Adds two Nums of the same size.
{
    Num sum;
    int carry = 0, s;
    for (int i = 0; i <= n1.size; i++)
    {
        s = n1.digit[i] + n2.digit[i] + carry;
        sum.digit[i] = s % 10;
        carry = s / 10;
    }
    sum.size = n1.size;
    if (carry)
    {
        sum.size = sum.size + 1;
        sum.digit[sum.size] = carry;
    }
```

```
        return sum;
}


int IsPalindrome(Num n)
// Returns true if and only if n is the same as its reverse.
{
    int i = 0, result = 1;
    while (result && (i <= n.size / 2))
    {
        result = result && (n.digit[i] == n.digit[n.size - i]);
        i++;
    }
    return result;
}


void main()
{
    Num n, r, s;
    Get(n);
    do
    {
        r = Reverse(n);
        n = Add(r, n);
        Show(n);
    }
    while ((!IsPalindrome(n)) && (n.size < MAX_SIZE));
}
```

If we look at the source code of our programs, we find the Pascal version is slightly larger than the C++ one in terms of lines of code and number of characters. If you have access to both a Pascal and a C++ compiler, it is informative to compare their efficiencies by compiling both programs and looking at the size of the object code generated. We did and discovered, somewhat to our surprise, that the C++ version compiled to a file that was just a bit over half the size of its Pascal counterpart. Counting the total compiled program size, including all the necessary libraries, though, the C++ version was about half again as large as the Pascal one, which is to be expected, given the relative complexities of the two languages. For the curious, we present our figures (your results may vary, as the car ads say).

	Pascal	*C++*	*C++/Pascal*
Source characters	2,003	1,439	0.72
Source lines	96	87	0.90
Object file bytes	1,386	784	0.57
Program bytes	37,018	59,234	1.60

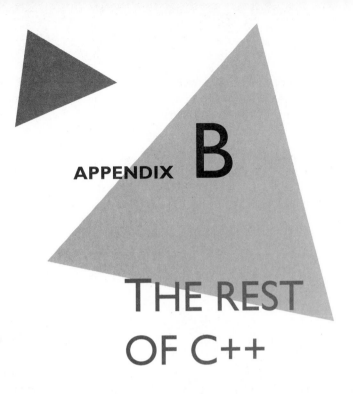

APPENDIX B

THE REST
OF C++

We have in the body of the text described those features of C++ that we believe are essential, useful, and accessible to novice programmers. In our presentation we frequently alluded to other features of C++ that we would not be covering for a variety of reasons (foremost among them that we didn't need them to write our PIPs). The fact is that, due in large part to its derivation from and compatibility with the language C, there are many details of C++ that we have quite intentionally avoided discussing until now.

In this appendix we will briefly describe some of the more common of these details. We do so in the interest of avoiding surprises. That is, we don't want you to be shocked when you read a C++ program and come across some use of the language that you have never seen before (although this is almost unavoidable). Neither do we want you to leave this course thinking that you have seen all there is to programming in C++. You haven't, but we'll present a few more pieces of the language here.

Structures

A structure is a compound data type identical to a class, except: (1) its member data and functions default to public, rather than private, and (2) it is declared by using the word struct rather than class. The struct was the notation for representing heterogeneous compound data in C. It has since been expanded to al-

415

low for the encapsulation of functions as well as data. It remains part of C++ in the interest of keeping C++ programs compatible with C, and despite the fact that it is naturally subsumed by the class construct.

Example 1

```
class Point                          struct Point
{                                    {
//defaults to private               //defaults to public
 int x, y;                                  Point Get(int x, int y);
public://public part must be
        //made explicit                     Point(int x, int y);
    Point Get(int x, int y);                double Magnitude();
    Point(int x, int y);         private:      //private part must be
                                               //made explicit
    double Magnitude();                  int x,y;
};                                   };
```

The this **Pointer**

The C++ keyword this is a pointer that refers to the address of the current object. It can be used only by member functions of that object. In computer jargon, this is an "implicitly declared self-referential pointer." The statement *this returns the current object. In Example 2, the *Complement* function returns the current object, with its *imagPart* member changed. Function *Current_Address* returns the address of the current object. If we had declared a *Complex* variable *c* and then said *c.Current_Address*, the function would return the address of the variable *c*.

Example 2

```
class Complex
{
public:
    Complex Complement () {imagPart = - imagPart; return (*this); };
    unsigned Current_Address () { return(unsigned(this)); };
private:
    int realPart, imagPart;
}
```

The ',' (comma) Operator

The comma operator evaluates a list of expressions in order and returns the value of the last expression. For example, the expression *expression1, expression2* evaluates both expressions and then returns *expression2*. This is most commonly used to collapse the body of a for loop into the for statement itself, as in Example 3, where we print out the integers from 0 to 10 without a loop body.

Example 3

```
for (int i=0; i<=10; cout<<i , i++);
```

Precedence Rules

We discussed mixed-mode expressions in Chapter 2 and made the point there that one should make liberal use of parentheses to clarify how expressions involving more than one operator should be evaluated. The following table lists the C++ operators in decreasing order of precedence (level 1 is the highest precedence, level 17 the lowest). When there is a conflict (that is, two operators with the same precedence in a given expression), C++ uses its associativity rules to resolve it.

Level	Operator	Associativity
1.	:: (global scope & class scope)	left to right
2.	() [] -> .	left to right
3.	! ~ ++ -- +(unary) - (unary) sizeof	
	*(indirection) & (address) new delete	right to left
4.	.* ->*	left to right
5.	* / %	left to right
6.	+ -	left to right
7.	<< >>	left to right
8.	< <= > >=	left to right
9.	== !=	left to right
10.	&	left to right
11.	^	left to right
12.	|	left to right
13.	&&	left to right
14.	||	left to right
15.	?=	left to right
16.	= += -= *= /= %= &=	
	^= <<= >>=	right to left
17.	, (comma) operator	left to right

Bit-shift Operators

C++ has a set of operators leftover from C that work on the binary representations of integers (note that this may be machine dependent). The left shift and right shift operators have been overridden in C++ to stand for stream insertion and extraction. These "bitwise" operators are:

Operator		Example	
~	unary complement	~x	bitwise complement of x
<<	left shift	x<<n	left shift by n
>>	right shift	x>>n	right shift by n
&	AND	x & y	bitwise AND
^	XOR (exclusive or)	x ^ y	bitwise XOR
|	OR	x | y	bitwise OR

Example 4   If *x* has value 3, then the 8-bit binary representation of *x* is 00000011. The command x<<2 changes it to 00001100 (left shift 2 places), which is the decimal 12. When *x* is decimal 12, both x<<2 and x*4 have the same value, 48.   ◁

The sizeof Operator

sizeof is a C++ operator that takes a type or variable as argument and returns the storage size of the type (or variable) in bytes. Note that the amount of storage reserved for different types is implementation dependent. Usually, a character is the fundamental unit of storage in C++ (using 1 byte of storage) so that the expression sizeof(char) will return 1.

Pointer Arithmetic

Since pointers are numbers (addresses), they can be manipulated by the arithmetic operators. This notation, examples of which we saw in Chapter 6 when we described C++ strings, is most often used in manipulating arrays. When performing pointer arithmetic, C++ takes into account the size of the object being pointed to. In Example 5, the last expression statement (*p++*) actually increments *p* by sizeof(char), and so *p* points to the next character in the array. We can add and subtract pointers in the same way.

Example 5
```
char* p;        //a variable p that contains the address of a character
char a[10];     //an array of ten characters
p=&a[0];        //p points to the first element in the array
p++;            //p now points to the second element in the array
```
        ◁

Inline Functions

If a function declaration is preceded by the keyword inline, the compiler replaces each call to the function with the code that implements the function. This eliminates function call overheads, potentially making programs run more efficiently. It is most often used when defining very short, straightforward functions, as that is where one stands to gain processing speed by eliminating function calls.

Example 6
```
inline int Max(int a, int b)
{
    if (a>b) return a;
    return b;
}


main()
{
```

```
        int x=5, y=4;
        int z=Max(x,y);              //no function call here - call to Max
                                     //replaced directly by the code for Max

}                                                                            ◁
```

goto

The goto statement, mentioned as an historical aside in Chapter 4, transfers program control unconditionally to a labeled statement. A statement is labeled by prefixing it with a label (an identifier followed by a colon). Both the goto statement and the labeled statement must be in the same function body.

Example 7

```
void EvenOdd(int i)
{
    if (i mod 2) == 0
        goto even; //go to the statement labeled "even"

    cout<<"odd number"; return;

    // this is the labeled statement
    even: cout<<"even number"; return;
}                                                                            ◁
```

Local Classes

Even though C++ does not allow functions to be nested inside one another, it does allow a class to be nested (that is, declared locally) within a function definition. The class and its members are considered local to the block in which they are defined. Below, class *X* is local to function *Y*. The usual scope rules apply.

Example 8

```
void Y(int i)
{
    char c;
    class X { ...class declarations... }
}                                                                            ◁
```

Assertions

We have referred to the notion of assertions at various points, particularly in our discussions of class actions and algorithms. An assertion is simply a logical condition that must always be true at some particular point in the program. The three most common types of assertions are:

Preconditions: a condition that must be true upon entry into a function

Postconditions: an assertion that must be true just before exit from a function

Class invariants: an assertion that must be true for the class as a whole

Class invariants are called after a constructor call and at entrance and exit from the public functions of the class.

Example 9

If we have a function that adds an element to an array, a good precondition might be to make sure the array is not full, and a postconditon could be to confirm that the array is not empty after the addition. In the example below, if the assertion *(!full())* is not satisfied (that is, the array *is* full), the program signals an error. To use assertions, your program must include file "assert.h."

```
void AddElement(int i)
{
    assert(!full());  //full() returns true if the array is full
    items[++current_position] = i;
    assert(!empty()); //empty() returns true if the array is empty.
}
```

Private Base Classes

In all the instances of inheritance presented in the text, the base class was public in the derived class. We could also declare a base class to be private, as follows. In the class header in Example 10, the functions and data of *Geometric_Object* would be private to Two_D_Object. This is usually done when we want to use the base class in the definition of the derived class, but we don't want the base class members to be used by clients of the derived class.

Example 10

```
class Two_D_Object : private Geometric_Object
```

malloc

The `malloc` function allocates memory to an object. This allows a program to allocate memory explicitly. It is very similar to the C++ construct new. The following statement allocates and returns a pointer to a block of *size* bytes from the storage heap.

Example 11

```
char * malloc (size)
```

Format State Flags

The class ios (which is usually declared in the library header file "iostream.h"), provides a variety of functions that can be used to control the flow of data in a stream. Some of these functions deal with describing and setting the format properties of the stream. Every ios stream has two member functions, setf and unsetf, which can be used to set or clear any or all of the format state "flags." For example, if you wanted to make sure that numbers in an output stream are displayed in fixed decimal rather than, say, scientific notation, you can invoke the setf command as:

Example 12

```
cout.setf (ios:: fixed, ios:: decimal);
```

Some other state flags that can be accessed using `setf` and `unsetf` are listed here:

Flag Name	Effect
skipws	skips white space on input (set by default)
left	left adjust fields on output
right	right adjust fields on output (set by default)
internal	fill fields on output
dec	assumes numbers in decimal notation (for input and output)
oct	assumes numbers in octal notation (for input and output)
hex	assumes numbers in hexadecimal notation (for input and output)
showbase	display base indicator on output
showpoint	display decimal point on output
uppercase	use uppercase for hexadecimal output
showpos	show '+' for positive integers on output
scientific	use scientific notation for float output
fixed	use fixed decimal notation for float output
unitbuf	flush all streams after insertions (output)
stdio	flush standard output and error streams after insertion (output)

There are some other components of a stream's format state that are not binary in nature (that is, they are not switches to be set to true or false), but require parameters to describe how they should be set. For example, to set the width of the fields to be used for displaying numeric output we use the `width` function as follows :

```
int w = cout.width(8);
```

Similarly, we can set the precision of floating point numbers as follows:

```
int p = cout.precision(3);
```

Storage-class Specifiers

Objects can be declared in four different ways:

`automatic`: most objects are automatic by default. This means that storage for the object is allocated when its identifier is declared, and is destroyed when execution passes out of the scope of its identifier.

`static`: An object can be declared as static by preceding its declaration with the keyword `static`. Static variables preserve their storage allocation and values even after program execution leaves the block. Scope rules still apply, so it is an error to refer to a static variable outside its scope. If control returns to the block at a later time, however, the old values of the static variable can be accessed.

Example 13   `static int i =0;`   ◁

register: Register objects behave just like automatic objects in that they are local to their scope. Declaring an object as a register object means that a request has been made to the compiler to store the object in one of the computer's registers, if one is available. Register objects can be declared by preceding the object declaration by the keyword register. This improves program efficiency, as computations performed on registers are extremely fast.

Example 14   register int a;   ◁

external: Objects declared as external objects are globally available to all of the functions within the same file, as long as the object is declared outside the scope of any function. An external object can be declared by preceding the declaration with the keyword extern.

Example 15   extern int a = 1;   ◁

Some Popular Libraries

Most modern implementations of C++ include an extensive collection of class libraries. Although there is no single standardized list of such libraries, the following are among the most common header files for these libraries:

"alloc.h": declares the memory allocation functions
    Sample functions: *malloc, free*

"ctype.h": declares functions for manipulating characters
    Sample functions: *isalpha, isdigit, toupper, tolower*

"graph.h": provides graphics and color support
    Sample functions: *bar, circle, drawpoly, getcolor*

"iostream.h": declares the basic C++ streams

"stdio.h": the older (C) version of "iostream.h"; it deals with input and output
    Sample functions: *scaf, printf, getc*

"complex.h": declares the complex math functions
    Sample functions: *acos, atan, sqrt, real*

"string.h": declares and provides support for the string type
    Sample functions: *strcpy, strlen, strcat, strset*

"iomanip.h": declares the C++ stream input/output manipulators

"stdlib.h": declares some standard utility functions
    Sample functions: *max, qsort, min, randomize*

argc **and** argv

argc is a global variable that keeps track of the number of arguments being sent to main. argv is a global variable that contains pointers to each of the arguments being sent to main. The size of argv is determined by the value of argc.

The *printf* Functions

The *printf* functions are declared in "stdio.h," except *cfprintf*, which is declared in "conio.h." These functions accept a series of arguments and a format string. They apply the first format specifier in the string to the first argument, the second format specifier to the second argument, and so on, to produce formatted output. The functions are:

1. *cprintf*: sends formatted output to the text window on the screen
2. *fprintf*: sends formatted output to a stream
3. *printf*: sends formatted output to *stdin*
4. *sprintf*: sends formatted output to a string
5. *vfprintf, vprintf, vsprintf*: exactly like *fprintf, printf,* and *sprintf*, respectively, except that they accept a pointer to a list of arguments and not the actual arguments themselves.

Example 16

```
int i1;
long lg1;
cout << i1 << " "<< lg1;
printf("%d %ld", i1, lg1);
```
◁

ANSWERS TO SELECTED EXERCISES

CHAPTER 1

3. a. 1, 10, 100, 1000, 10000, 100000, 1000000
   b. 110, 10111, 11111010001
   c. 6, 12, 45, 127

7. a. A high-level language is one that must be translated into machine language so that it can be executed. We invent high-level languages because programming in machine language is so unpleasant that nobody who's ever done it would do it again except under duress.
   b. The files are compiled into object code, then linked into a program that can be executed.

9. a. Legal.
   b. Illegal. An object name must begin with a letter.
   c. Illegal. The name "class" has a special meaning in C++ and so can't be used as an object name.
   d. Illegal. A name cannot include a space character.
   e. Illegal. A name cannot include periods.
   f. Legal.
   g. Legal.

13. a. First, keeping logically related classes and operations together in a file makes it much easier for the reader to make sense of a program. Second, from the point of view of efficiency, allowing separate files to be compiled separately means that a change in one file doesn't require the entire file to be recompiled.

b. A header file, containing declarations of classes, functions, and so on, separates the interface needed to use the information from the definitions of how these entities do what it is they do, thereby simplifying the job of the reader.

15. No change would have to be made to the *Display* class. The *Timer* class would need another member data item of type *Display* called, perhaps, *seconds*. Minor changes would have to be made in the definition to the member functions *Timer*, *Set*, and *Show*. The function *Increment* would have to be changed to reflect the possibility that incrementing *seconds* would have to be "carried" to the other displays, as would happen when we incremented 10:59:59.

17. Since everything from the // to the end of the line is ignored, the compiler would never "see" the semicolon and would read the line as missing a needed punctuation.

CHAPTER 2

1. 2^{24} = 16,777,216, so unsigned int would represent integers in the range 0 . . . 16,777,215. The values of int (that is, signed integers) would depend on the way the computer represented negative integers, but usually the range would be −8,388,608 . . . 8,388,607.

3. Trick question. The output would be the string 2 * p + r.

5. a. ((1 − (2 * 3)) + (4 % 5)) We can't say which of 2 * 3 or 4 % 5 would be done before the other.
   b. (((--x) * p) − (−(y + 3))) The first − is subtraction; the second is unary minus.

7. a. 0, int
   b. 3, int
   c. 1.0, double
   d. 4.0, double

9. We could check that the remainder of *n*, when divided by 17, is zero by testing the value of *n* % 17.

11. No. They're equal in all cases except when *x* = *y*. In that case, the first expression yields a division-by-zero error while the second is equal to zero.

13. a. (3 * p + q) * (p − 2 * q) Remember, C++ doesn't permit implicit multiplication, so we need the * operators.
   b. 1 / (x + y) + 1 / (x − y) This is correct, though it might be easier to read if we parenthesized it as (1 / (x + y)) + (1 / (x − y)).
   c. The obvious way is x * x * x * x − x * x * x + x * x − x + 1. A more efficient, but less obvious way is to use *Horner's rule* and write 1 + x * (−1 + x * (1 + x * (−1 + x))). This uses three multiplications, while the obvious way needs six.
   d. 1 + (1 / (1 + 1 / (1 + x)))

15. a. Incorrect. The square brackets can't be used as parentheses. They have an entirely different meaning, as we'll see in Chapter 5.
   b. Incorrect. This would be parenthesized as (x + y) = z, and x + y isn't the name of a storage location.

   c.   Incorrect. Order matters: =/ isn't a C++ operator, but /= is.

   d.   Correct. Because of precedence, this expression would be evaluated p = (p = p).

17. a.   Incorrect. A `return` statement must have a semicolon punctuator.

   b.   Correct.

   c.   Incorrect. ":=" is not a C++ operator.

   d.   Almost correct, but close counts only in horseshoes and hand grenades. The inner statement int x = 2 needs a semicolon. Congratulations if you understand that the value 1 would be displayed by cout << x; (since the inner declaration of *x* has no effect on the outermost uses of the variable with that name).

19. a.   If you thought this was correct, you may have some Pascal training. The argument list of a C++ function is separated by commas, not by semicolons.

   b.   Incorrect. Function declarations don't require argument names, just types. The problem is that we're missing a semicolon at the end.

   c.   Incorrect. Default arguments must occur at the end of the argument list.

   d.   Incorrect. It's impossible to decipher the programmer's intent here: Either the function name is missing, or the programmer tried to name a function float and omitted the return type. Either way, the declaration is incorrect.

   e.   Just fine.

21. If the left subexpression, *i*, was evaluated first, the whole expression would evaluate to 3 * (2 + 3) = 15. On the other hand, if the right subexpression, (2 + *i* ++), was evaluated first, the expression would have the value 4 * (2 + 3) = 20. In either case, of course, *i* would eventually be incremented to 4.

23. A constructor's declaration cannot have a return type, and the constructor must have the same name as the class. A call to a constructor begins with the class name, followed by the name of the object being constructed, followed by the actual argument list, if any. A non-constructor member function is called by writing the object name, a dot, the function name, and the argument list:

```
ItsClass theObject(3, 2);        // constructor
theObject.ItsFunction(3, 2);     // non-constructor
```

25. Nothing unusual would happen: the *divsign* variable would cheerfully consume any character you put between the two numbers. We use the descriptive name *divsign* for our assistance; the computer has no way of knowing our intent.

27.
```
class Change
// This is one way to declare this class. It's certainly
// not the only possible solution.
{
    //-------- Overloaded operators --------
    friend Change operator+ (Change c1, Change c2);  // add money
    friend Change operator* (int n, Change c);       // multiply


public:
    //-------- Constructors --------
    Change();                              // set all amounts to zero
    Change(int amt);                       // set the change to equal amt cents
    Change(int p, int n, int d, int q, int h);
                                           // set individual numbers
```

```
//-------- Access and display --------
void Set(int p, int n, int d, int q, int h);
                                    // set individual numbers
void Set(int amt);                  // set the change to equal amt cents
void Show();                        // display the member data
int Value();                        // return the worth in cents
private:
    int pennies,                    // number of pennies
        nickels,                    // number of nickels
        dimes,                      // number of dimes
        quarters,                   // number of quarters
        halves;                     // number of half dollars
    void MakeChange(int amt);       // given amt, set members
                                    // (helper for other functions)

};
```

It's worth noting, by the way, that we don't have to declare the overloaded operators as friends. Do you see why?

29. a.
```
class Account
// Note that for exactness, we've chosen to keep
// the current balance in cents
{
public:
    //-------- Constructor --------
    Account(double amt = 0.0);                  // set starting balance
    //-------- Access, display --------
    void Deposit(double amt);                   // deposit an amount
    void Withdraw(double amt);                  // attempt a withdrawal
    void Interest(double rate);                 // update account
    //-------- Access --------
    double Current();                           // return current balance
    void ShowBalance();                         // display current balance
private:
    long balance;                               // current balance, in
                                                cents

    //-------- Private utilities --------
    long ConvertToCents(double amt);
    double ConvertToDollars(long amt);
};
```

b. We assume that these definitions will be in another file, so we need the scope resolution operator here. We've left out all error checking, such as handling negative withdrawls, handling withdrawls of more than the current balance, and checking for unreasonable interest rates, because such checking is better done with the `if` statement, which we won't discuss until the next chapter.

```
Account::Account(double amt = 0.0)
    // Set starting deposit.
    {    balance = ConvertToCents(amt);}

    void Account::Deposit(double amt)
```

```
// Record a deposit.
{    balance += ConvertToCents(amt);}
void Account::Withdraw(double amt)
// Perform a withdrawal.
{    balance -= ConvertToCents(amt);}
void Account::Interest(double rate)
// Update the balance by adding in the amount of interest.
{
    long amount = ConvertToCents(balance * rate / 100.0);
    balance += amount;
}

double Account::Current()
// Return the current balance, in dollars.
{    return ConvertToDollars(balance); }

void Account::ShowBalance()
// Display the current balance, in dollars.
{
    cout << "Current balance = $";
    cout << ConvertToDollars(balance) << '\n';
}

long Account::ConvertToCents(double amt)
// Convert a (double) dollars-and-cents amount to
// a (long) amount of cents.
{    return long(100.0 * amt);}

double Account::ConvertToDollars(long amt)
// Convert a (long) amount of cents to
// a (double) dollars-and-cents amount.
{    return double(amt / 100);}
```

CHAPTER 3

1. a. x > 10
    b. (3.7 < temp) && (temp < 3.8)
    c. (j % 2 == 1) || (k % 2 == 1) || (l % 2 == 1)
        A simpler, but less obvious way is (j % 2) || (k % 2) || (l % 2)
    d. (j % 2 == 1) && (k % 2 == 1) && (l % 2 == 1)
        We could (but wouldn't, in consideration of the reader) also write the cryptic
        j * k * l % 2
    e. (newChar < '0') && (newChar > '9')
    f. (found >= 2 * given) || ((found == 0) && (given < 0))

3. if (a > 1)
    if (m <= 0)

This is executed when   <u>a > 1 and m =< 0</u>
else
This is executed when   <u>a > 1 and m > 0</u>
else
This is executed when   <u>a =< 1</u>

5. In the following statements, we use *E* to indicate an erroneous place for a semicolon, *U* for unlikely (but legal), and *R* for a required place.

   a. if *E* (x != 0 *E*) *U*
          a = a / x *R*

   b. if *E* (n % 2) *E*
          n = 3 * n + 1 *R*
      else *U*
          n = n / 2 *R*

7.
```
int Ordered(int p, int q, int r)
{ return (p <= q) && (q <= r); }
```

9.
```
int TestEligibility(double income, int minorChildren)
{
    int error = 0;            // no errors seen yet
                              // We declare this here, since it's used
                              // in two separate blocks below, as well
                              // as in this level
    if ((income < 0.0) || (income > 1e7))
    {   error = 1;
        cout << "Probable income error\n";
    }
    if ((minorChildren < 0) || (minorChildren > 20))
    (   error = 1;
        cout << "Probable error in number of children\n";
    }
    if (error)                // We only continue if no errors.
        return -1;            // Here's where we dump out in error.
    // no errors, so we decide on eligibility
    return (income - 2500.0 * minorChildren < 30000);
}
```

11. a.
```
int Divides(int n, int m)
{ return !(n % m); }
```
    b.
```
int Divides(int n, int m)
{   if (m == 0)
    {   cout << "Attempted division by zero\n";
        return 0;
    }
    else
    return !(n % m);
}
```

13.
```
if (height > 75)
    cout << "This is a tall person.\n";
```

14. a. `double TaxPayment(double income)`

```
    {
        if (income < 0.0) || (income > 97620.0))
        {
            cout << "Income must be between 0 and 97,620\n";
            return -1.0;
        }
        else if (income < 19450.0)
            return 0.15 * income;
        else if (income < 47050.0)
            return 2917.5 + 0.28 * (income - 19450.0);
        else
            return 10645.5 + 0.33 * (income - 47050.0);
    }
```

b. Yes. 0.15 * 19450.0 = 2917.5, so the top of the first bracket has the same tax as the bottom of the next. Similarly, 2917.5 + 0.28 * (47050.0 – 19450.0) = 10645.5, so the top of the second bracket has the same tax as the bottom of the third.

CHAPTER 4

2. a. Nothing's wrong here.
   b. There's a missing semicolon. A do statement requires a semicolon punctuator.
   c. There are two missing semicolons in the header. Change the commas to semicolons to fix it.

4. a. The intent is probably to add the numbers entered, until a –1 sentinel is encountered. The problem is that the test should then be (n != –1), rather than the assignment (n = –1). The way it's written, the loop would never terminate, since n = –1 would always return –1 (which would be considered to be true). Also, the loop body needs to be enclosed in brackets; otherwise, only the first statement would be part of the loop.
   b. The intent here is probably the same as in part a. This loop would incorrectly add the sentinel –1 to the sum, since the test is performed after the loop body. It would be better to use a while loop for this.
   c. This seems to find the sum, $1 + 2 + 4 + \cdots$, of the powers of 2 that are less than n. There's nothing wrong, once we fix the syntax.

7. a. Five times in the inner loop for each iteration of the outer loop, for a total of 25.
   b. As i goes from 0 to 4, the inner loop iterates 5, 4, 3, 2, and 1 times, for a total of 15.
   c. 9 times. The inner loop iterates 5, 3, 1, 0, and 0 times, since for $i = 3$ and 4 the test condition is false at the start of the inner loop. By the way, if we replace 5 by n wherever it appears, statement S will be performed $(n - 2)^2$ times.

9. The first three lines of output are

$n = 2$ sum = 1   *(which is correct)*
$n = 3$ sum = 0   *(which is wrong)*
$n = 4$ sum = 0   *(which is also wrong)*

The problem is that the variables *trialDivisor* and *sumOfDivisors* aren't initialized where they should be. Since both of these need to be reset for each iteration of the outer loop, they should be initialized inside the outer loop, but outside the inner loop, like this:

```
for (int n = 2; n <= 1000; n++)
{
    int trialDivisor = 1;
    int sumOfDivisors = 0;
    while (trialDivisor < n)
    {
        if (n % trialDivisor == 0)
            sumOfDivisors += trialDivisor;
        trialDivisor++;
    }
    cout << "\nn = " << n << "\tsum = " << sumOfDivisors;
}
```

11. $n \mathrel{!=} 0$. We stop when we've consumed all the digits of n.

13. a.
```
int Reverse(int n)
{   int r = 0;                      // The reversed number to be returned.
    while (n != 0)
    {   int digit = n % 10;         // Get the rightmost digit,
        n = n / 10;                 // strip it from n,
        r *= 10;
        r += digit;                 // add it to the reverse,
    }
    return r;
}
```

b.
```
int Palindrome(int n)
{   return (n == Reverse(n)); }
```

15.
```
const int WIDTH = 41;                   // width of print area; should be odd

void DisplayStars(int n)
// Display an odd number of stars, centered in print area.
// If we're displaying n stars, there must be at least
// (WIDTH - n) / 2 spaces on each side, particularly the left
{   for (int i = 1; i <= (WIDTH - n) / 2; i++)
        cout << ' ';
    for (int i = 1; i <= n; i++)
        cout << '*';
    cout << '\n';
}

void DisplayTree()
{
    // Display the foliage
    for (i = 0; i < 6; i++)
        DisplayStars(2 * i + 1);
```

```
                    // Display the trunk
                    for (i = 0; i < 3; i++)
                        DisplayStars(3);
             }
17. a.   int IsPrime(int n)
             { if ((n==1) || (n==2))
                        return 1;
                     else{ int divisor = 2;
                     {
                        int divisor = 2;
                        while ((n % divisor != 0) && (divisor < sqrt(n))
                            divisor++;
                        return !(n % divisor);
                     }
             }
```

There's a fairly simple way to speed this function up by a factor of 2. *Hint:* if 2 doesn't divide *n*, we don't need to check any other even divisors.

b.
```
    int IsPrime(int n)
    {    int prod = 1;       // This will be n - 1 factorial mod n
         for (i = 1; i < n; i++)
              prod = (prod * i) % n;
         return ((prod + 1) % n == 0);
    }
```

19. Here are the sequences of *a* values we got:

100.00000000	10000.00000000
50.50000000	5000.50000000
26.24009859	2501.25000000
15.02552986	630.30364990
10.84043503	323.08450317
10.03257847	177.01808167
10.00005245	101.20218658
10.00000000	100.00714111
	100.00000000

Notice particularly that it takes only one more iteration to find the square root of 10,000 than it did to find the square root of 100.

CHAPTER 5

1. a.   Illegal, for two reasons. First, there's a missing dot selector. *thisPage* is a class object, so we can gain access to its member data *theLine* only by using *this-Page.theLine*. Second, the array selectors are reversed. *thisPage.theLine[i]* is

one of 50 arrays of characters, so to access the *i*-th character in the third line we would use *thisPage.theline*[3][*i*].

b. Legal.

c. Illegal. Both sides are the same type, but they are both arrays, and we cannot assign arrays.

d. Illegal. *CharArray* is a type name, not a member name. This would be legal if we had written *thisPage.theLine*[3][1] = *thisLine*[2];

e. Legal. A function may return class objects.

3. a. 64 characters

   b. An integer and $50 \times 64 = 3200$ characters

5. a.
```
enum SquareState {EMPTY, BLACK, RED, BLACK_KING, RED_KING}; typedef Square-State-
Board[8][8];
// Note that this is less efficient than it could be, since
// only half the squares are used to play a game of checkers.
```

   b.
```
class Items
{    char name[30];
     double price;
     int numberOnHand;
};
```

   c.
```
typedef Items Inventory[1000];
```

7. a. The two data types look like this:

Data1

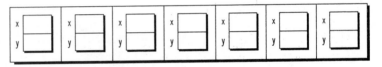

Data2

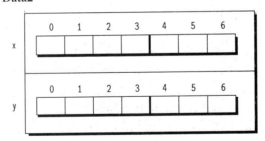

   b. 14

   c. *d*[3].*x* refers to the member *x* of a structure that is an array element, so *d* must be of type *Data1*. For similar reasons, *e* must be of type *Data2*.

   d. For seven points in the plane, the smallest logical unit is a pair of numbers, and we then group those into a collection of seven, so *Data1* would be the better choice. For a week's worth of high temperatures in two cities, the most reasonable organization would be to collect the temperatures into a single unit and have two such collections, so *Data2* would be preferable.

e. *double temps[2][7];*, or *double temps[7][2];*.

9. a. This is one way to do it. It's certainly not the only way.

```
typedef char NameString[30];
class Students
{    NameString name;
     int quiz[10];
};
class Course
{    double weight[10];
     Students student[20];
};
```

b. In this part, assume that *cs241* is of type *Course*.

i. `cs241.student[n].name`

ii.
```
double sum = 0.0, weightSum = 0.0;
for (int i = 0; i < 10; i++)
{
sum += cs241.weight[i] * cs241.student[n].quiz[i];
weightSum += cs241.weight[i];
}
double studentAverage = sum / weightSum;
```

iii.
```
for (int i = 0, int sum = 0.0; i < 20; i++)
    sum += cs241.student[i].quiz[n];
double quizAverage = double(sum) / 20.0;
```

iv.
```
double sum = 0.0, weightSum = 0.0;
for (int i = 0; i < 20; i++)// For each student,
{    weightSum += cs241.weight[i];
    for (int j = 0; j < 10; j++)
    // add weighted sum.
        sum += cs241.weight[i] * cs241.student[i].quiz[j];
}
double classAverage = double(sum) / (20.0 * weightSum);
```

v. We would first compute the class average and *weightSum* as we did in part iv and then do the following:

```
for (int i = 0; i < 20; i++)
{
// Compute weighted average of i-th student
for (int j = 0, double sum = 0.0; j < 10; j++)
    sum += cs241.weight[j] * cs241.student[i].quiz[j];
double average = sum / weightSum;


// Now compare with classAverage
if (average < classAverage)
{
```

```
        // Display the student's name
            for (int k = 0; k < 30; k++)
                cout << cs241.student[i].name[k];
            cout << "\tHas average " << average << '\n';
        }
```

11. ```
    void Copy(int n, int sourceStart, int destStart, NumArray a)
    {   for (int i = 0; i < n; i++)
            a[destStart + i] = a[sourceStart + i];
    }
    ```

13. ```
    void Reverse(NumArray a)
    {   for (int i = 0; i < SIZE / 2; i++)
        {   int temp = a[i];
            a[i] = a[SIZE - i - 1];
            a[SIZE - i - 1] = temp;
        }
    }
    ```

15. It sorts the array in increasing order, so the *postcondition* of the function—the condition that is true after the function returns—is that $a[0] \le a[1] \le \ldots a[SIZE - 1]$. This is one of many sorting algorithms and is called *Insertion Sort*. You'll see many more sorting algorithms in the course that follows this one.

17. Yes.

19. They both compute the sum $a[1] + a[2] + a[3] + a[4] + a[5]$, since i is incremented and $a[i]$ is added to the sum *before* the loop test.

21. It sets $a[i] = b[i]$, for $i = 0, 1, 2, 3$ (since i is incremented *before* it is tested against 4). All we gain by eliminating the iteration part of the header is an increase in incomprehensibility.

23. a. ```
       void WriteDay(Days d)
       {   switch d
           {   case SUN: cout << "SUN"; return;
               case MON: cout << "MON"; return;
               case TUE: cout << "TUE"; return;
               case WED: cout << "WED"; return;
               case THU: cout << "THU"; return;
               case FRI: cout << "FRI"; return;
               case SAT: cout << "SAT"; return;
           }
       }
       ```
    b. ```
       Days ReadDay()
       {   char c1, c2, c3;
           cin >> c1 >> c2 >> c3;
           if ((c1 == 'S') && (c2 == 'U') && (c3 = 'N'))
               return SUN;
           else if ((c1 == 'M') && (c2 == 'O') && (c3 = 'N'))
               return MON;
                   . . . and so on . . .
       }
       ```

25. a.
```cpp
void DynamicArray::Append(int score)
{    if (num == 10)
         cout << "\nNo room for the new score";
     else
     {   quiz[num] = score;                    // Put new score into array,
         num++;              // and increase current number of scores.
     }
}
```
b.
```cpp
void DynamicArray::Update(int k, int score)
// NOTE: the k-th score is stored in quiz[k - 1].
{    if ((k < 1) || (k > num))
     {   cout << "\nInvalid quiz number"; return; }
     else
         quiz[k - 1] = score;
}
```
c.
```cpp
void DynamicArray::Display()
{    for (int i = 0; i < num; i++)
         cout << '\t' << quiz[i];
     cout << '\n';
}
```
d.
```cpp
double DynamicArray::Average()
{    if (num == 0)
         cout << "\nNo scores, so can't compute average";
         return 0.0;
     else
     {   int sum = 0;
         for (int i = 0; i < n; i++)
             sum += quiz[i];
         return double(sum) / num;
     }
}
```

27.
```cpp
void Delete(CharArray a, int n)
{    if ((n < 0) || (n > 63))
     // Bad position, so return immediately.
     {   cout << "\nIllegal position in Delete";
         return;
     }
     else
     // Shift the contents of the array to fill the "hole".
     {   for (int i = n; i < 63; i++)
             a[i] = a[i + 1];
         a[63] = '\0';                      // Fill in the last element,
     }
}
```

CHAPTER 6

1.

```
p = new SomeObject;
```

p → *p

q

```
q = new SomeObject;
```

p → *p

q → *q

```
q = p;
```

p → *This is both*
*p and *q.

q → *This is lost forever!*

```
delete p;
```

p

q → *Still lost*

3.
`i = 100;`	*OK*
`pi = 1024;`	*No. We can't assign a numeric value to a pointer,*
`pj = 0;`	*except for the NULL value, zero.*
`*pi = i;`	*No. pi is a pointer but has no declared storage.*
`px = pi;`	*No. The two pointers have different type targets.*
`pi = 2 * pi;`	*No. We can only add and subtract.*
`cout << pj;`	*OK*
`if (pi < pj)`	*OK*
`    cout << "pi's target is before pj's in memory";`	

5. ```
   // As long as q doesn't point to the zero character,
   while (*q)
   // copy the target of q to the target of p
   // and increment both p and q to point to the
   // next characters in their respective strings.
   *p++ = *q++;
   ```

7. ```
   int *x[10];
   int (*x)[10];
   ```
   x is an array of 10 pointer-to-ints
   x is a pointer to an array of 10 ints

   This is confusing, we'll admit. Even Bjarne Stroustrup, the inventor of C++, says "Most people simply remember how the most common types look."

9. 19, the index-1 entry of *a*.

11. Remember, functions only modify local copies of their arguments. We do move *str* down the array, but we're moving only a local copy and not the actual argument itself.

13. *p* (and *u*, for that matter) would point to the string "dogbone".

15. ```
    int strlen(char* str)
    {   int i = 0;
        while (str[i] != '\0')
            i++;
        return i;
    }
    ```

    A less-obvious way to do this is to use pointer arithmetic, which we're allowed to do in arrays, you may recall.

    ```
    int strlen(char* str)
    {   int i = 0;
        while (*str++)
            i++;
        return i;
    }
    ```

17. a. We need *index* ≥ 0, *n* > 0, and *index* + *n* ≤ *length of src*, as we see below.

    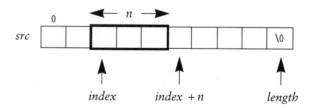

    b. ```
        char* Remove(char* src, int index, int n)
        // Removes n characters from src, starting at index.
        // This works by shifting the characters after the part to be
        // deleted down n positions.
            {
                int toIndex = index;   // where shifted chars will go
                int fromIndex = index + n; // where we'll get the chars
        ```

```
        // We loop until we find the zero terminator.
        while (src[fromIndex] != 0)
            src[toIndex++] = src[fromIndex++];

        src[toIndex] = '\0';                    // Put the terminator back in.
        return src;
    }
```

   c.   You're on your own for this one.

19. This would first set *entryList*[*currentSize* – 1] to *entryList*[*currentSize*], then set *entryList*[*currentSize* – 2] to the new value of *entryList*[*currentSize* – 1], making the last three elements the same as the last one. Continuing this process would make all the elements from *thisEntry* on up equal to the last entry, which is clearly not what we want to happen.

CHAPTER

3. The DDU approach is coupled directly with C++ because the methodology exploits and depends on many features of the language. For example, in order to use the DDU approach effectively we need the equivalent of classes to describe the agents in our program. Similarly, the methodology depends to varying degrees on the ability to distinguish header files from implementation files, the availability of extensible program libraries, and the ease with which driver programs can be created and used in testing class definitions.

4. A working program produces correct output. A workable program does that and also lends itself readily to manipulation—debugging, testing, extending—by humans. The DDU supports the development of workable programs in many ways. It makes it easy to debug and test programs because they are developed incrementally, class by class. It also encourages complete program documentation and provides regular opportunities for revising previous code and for integrating it with new code.

5. The most glaring question is: What exactly counts as a word? For example, do abbreviations count? How about punctuation? Numbers? If a word is any string surrounded by blanks, is a string of three consecutive blanks a word? What about hyphenated words—do they count as one word or two? By the way, how long should the program keep reading? And where is the text to be processed stored?

7. a.   Every automobile (or, at least every working one) has an engine, so we would need the definition of an engine in order to define an auto.

   b.   This one could go either way, and the choice may come down to which of the two classes was to be the focus of the program. If, for example, we were concerned more with modeling and tracking customers, it may help to have the *Salesperson* class defined before describing a *Customer*. You could make the reverse argument if the program was intended primarily to simulate the performance of the sales staff.

   c.   This is a pretty clear case of classes being dependent on one another. We can describe a line in terms of two points, and a triangle in terms of the lines (two of them are all you'd really need) that form it.

d. *Airplane* should be defined before *Flight*, since every flight requires an airplane. We'd probably define *Passenger* last because we are interested in a passenger only so far as he/she interacts with flights (much as was the case with our elevator riders).

9. Here's a partial first crack at a class, *Rational*:

```
class Rational
{
friend istream& operator >> (istream& i, Rational& r);
friend Rational& operator + (Rational r1, Rational r2);
... overload other operators in similar fashion
public:
        // a few constructors are probably in order
        Rational();                  //create 0/1
        Rational(int);               //create int/1
        Rational(int int)            //create int1/int2

        void Display();
        float Evaluate();

        // how about access to the private data
        void SetNumerator(int);
        int GetNumerator();
        void SetDenominator(int);
        int GetDenominator();

private:
        int numerator;        // the floor from which service was requested
        int denominator;      // the rider's destination
};
```

CHAPTER 8

3. None of the classes derived from *GeometricObject* would have direct access to the variables *top*, *left*, *bottom*, or *right* if these were declared as private. We could get around this restriction, as usual, by providing public access functions in class *GeometricObject*.

5. The following program would animate a simple scene composed of three GeometricObjects.

```
main()
{
    GeometricObject* GO[3];
    // this array will hold (pointers to) our objects

    // First, we create three figures for a drawing
    Rectangle r;
    Circle c;
    Line l;
```

```
// Then, we load the figure addresses into our array
GO[0] = &r;
GO[1] = &c;
GO[2] = &l;

// Animate each figure 10 times
for(int moves = 0; moves < 10; moves++)
{
    // draw each figure
    for(i = 0; i < 3; i++)
        GO[i]->Draw();

    //   erase each figure
    for(i = 0; i < 3; i++)
        GO[i]->Erase();

    // and move each figure horizontally
    for(i = 0; i < 3; i++)
        GO[i]->Move(5, 0);
};
Terminate();
};
```

7. A derived class contains more information (member data and functions) than does its base class, and so instances of the derived class occupy more memory than do instances of the base.

11. The output would be:

```
First base f1
First base f2

Lou f1

First base f6

Lou f6

First base f6

Lou f4
```

CHAPTER 9

1. a. xr7   *Bad—unless our program is describing some domain in which this name means something (a cleaning fluid? an old Mercury convertible?)*

   b. thisLine   *Good, as long as the notion of a line makes sense in the context of the program*

   c. charPointer *Good*

   d. fileName   *Good*

e.   this   *Bad—and dangerous! First, the term*
                             "this" is vague and context dependent.
                             Worse, it is a C++ keyword (the meaning
                             of which is explained in Appendix B).

3. You can think of the file as the computer does: as a long, single string of characters
   with two distinguishing properties. All comments are ignored (effectively not there).
   Each collection of white space (space characters, tabs, carriage returns, line feeds),
   except those appearing within string literals, is replaced by a single-space character.
   If the file had used any #include directives, they would have been replaced by the files
   they referenced, similarly edited.

5. a.   ```
        void DisplayFindings(int s, float d, int t)
        {
            cout << "The car traveled at a speed of "
                    << d << "mph\n"   //missing ';' here
            cout << "The car traveled a distance of "
                    << s << "miles\n;   //missing "here
            cout << 'The car traveled at a speed for "
                    << t << "minutes\n";
                    //should be a ", not a ', before "The"
        }
        ```

7. Logical runtime errors are often the toughest to detect because as far as the computer is concerned there was no error. As a result, we get no error messages and
   must rely on the program's output for any clues as to what caused the incorrect
   behavior.

9. "Backward" in the context of compiler errors means earlier in the file in which
   the error was signaled. That is, it means "physically before." "Backward" in the
   run-time sense means "logically before." In tracking down run-time errors we
   must retrace the computer's steps in executing your program, following the flow
   of control from one function to the next up to the point at which the error was
   reported.

**CHAPTER 10**

1. ```
   int Find(IntArray a, int x, int end)
   {   int i = 0;
       while ((i <= end) && (a[i] != x))
            i++;
       if (i > end)
            return -1;
       else
            return i;
   }
   ```

It's a close call in comprehensibility between this version and the for loop version.
We'd give the nod to the for loop, because this one uses short-circuit evaluation of
&& and requires a separate test at the end to determine whether the function succeeded or failed to find *x*.

3. We could have returned an *IntArray*, rather than a reference to the array, although doing so would be less efficient than returning a reference. This is in sharp contrast with the overload of <<, where we must return a reference, because << groups from the left and = groups from the right. In particular, the multiple assignment *a* = *b* = *c* would be performed in order *a* = (*b* = *c*), which would work correctly whether = returned an array or a reference to an array.

5. a.
```
IntArray operator* (int n, const IntArray& a)
    // This would be declared as a friend, rather than a member
    // function, since the first argument of a member function
    // is implicit and is the object itself (which can't be
    // an int, of course). It returns an IntArray, rather than a
    // reference to an array, because the return is a local value
    // and we can't return pointers or references to local values.
    {   IntArray r(a.Length());          // the return value
        for (int i = 0; i <= a.upper; i++)
            r.data[i] = n * a.data[i];
        return r;
    }
```
  b.
```
IntArray& IntArray::operator*= (int n)
    // This can be a member function, since in a *= b, the
    // first argument is the object itself (a, here).
    // Because the first argument is not local, but is rather
    // the object itself, we can return a reference to it, rather
    // than returning a copy (which would be less efficient).
    {   for (int i = 0; i <= upper; i++)
            data[i] *= n;
        return *this;
    }
```
  c.
```
int operator== (const IntArray& a, const IntArray& b)
    // This is better as a friend, since it takes in two IntArrays
    // and returns a result, rather than sending a message to
    // an IntArray to inspect or modify itself.
    {   if (a.upper != b.upper)
            return 0;
        else
        {   int i = 0;
            while ((i <= a.upper) && (a.data[i] == b.data[i]))
                i++;
            if (i > a.upper)            // We went past the end of the arrays,
                return 1;               // so they're equal.
            else                        // We found a mismatch.
                return 0;
        }
    }
```

7. The probes will be:

Index	Element	Sublist
4	24	30, 39, 44, 54
6	39	30, 39
5	30	30 (We've found where 25 belongs.)

9. ```
int RFind(SortedArray a, int x, int start, int end)
{   while (start < end)
    {   int middle = (start + end) / 2;
        if (x < a[middle])
            end = middle;
        else if (x > a[middle])
            start = middle + 1;
        else
            return middle;   // We found x.
    }
    return start;
}
```

11. It displays the binary expression of $n$.

13. ProcessText("alligator", 0) would display the string "rotagilla." If we reversed the order of the two statements in the if statement, it would display the string "alligator." If we removed the if statement (which serves as the exit case), the function would continue recursively beyond the end of the string and would crash eventually.

15. *Power1* will use $n$ function calls to compute $x^n$. *Power2* will use only about $\log_2 n$ calls. *Power2* is a big winner.

17. a. It would take 25 calls to compute *Fib*(6). In fact, the number of calls it takes to compute *Fib*($n$) this way is $2Fib(n) - 1$.

   b. ```
int Fib(int n)
// This takes O(n) steps to compute Fib(n).
{   int recent = 1, prior = 0, old;
    for (int i = 0; i < n; i++)
    {   old = prior;
        prior = recent;
        recent = prior + old;
    }
    return recent;
}
```

19. The only exit from this function is when n is 1. The problem is that unless this function is called with n equal to 0, it will never reach the exit case, and so will run forever (or until it has used up all available memory storing information for the pending function calls).

21. a. ```
void InsertionSort(IntArray& a)
{   for (int i = 1; i < a.Length(); i++)
    {   element = a[i];
        testIndex = i - 1;
        while ((testIndex >= 0) && (a[testIndex] > element))
        {   a[testIndex + 1] = a[testIndex];
            testIndex--;
        }
        a[testIndex + 1] = element;
    }
}
```
```

b. 6 7 8   *0 moves*
    3 4 5   *0 moves*
    3 8 4   *1 move*
    7 6 5   *3 moves*

c. *InsertionSort* makes the fewest data moves when the input array is already sorted from smallest to largest. It makes the most data moves when the data is in reverse sorted order.

23. a. $a[i] \leq a[i + 1]$, for all $i = 0, 1, \ldots, upper - 1$.
    b.
```
void IsSorted(const IntArray& a)
{   int i = 0;
    while ((i < a.Length() - 1) && (a[i] <= a[i + 1]))
        i++;
    return (i = a.Length() - 1);
}
```

25. The picture on the left represents *QuickSort*; the one on the right represents *SelectionSort*.

CHAPTER 11

1. a. A *Ring* consists of a collection of elements arranged as follows, along with a special *current* position, where all insertion, deletion, and inspection take place.

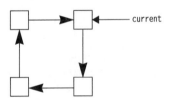

It seems that a reasonable collection of operations would be the same as those for *List*. It's worth noting, by the way, that such structures do crop up in practice. For example, rings are useful for storing requests for time on a computer. In such *time-sharing* environments, a small slice of computer time is given to each user in turn. Since computers work much faster than people type, every user has the illusion that he or she has sole use of the machine.

   b. A *SortedList* has exactly the same structure as a list, but with the additional condition that the elements in the list are arranged in order of their size. We can dispense with the *current* location in this ADT because we don't want the user of our class to be able to insert a new element in an arbitrary location. A reasonable collection of operations might be

   ▶ Construct an empty sorted list.

   ▶ A copy constructor

   ▶ A destructor

▶ An assignment operator

▶ *Insert* an element in its correct place.

▶ *Remove* a given element.

▶ *Retrieve* an element. This would be useful if the elements were compound types, sorted by one part of the element (for example, a list of employee records sorted by ID number). In such a case, we would give the ID as an argument and the function would return the entire element.

3. a. Rings would naturally be represented by a linked collection of nodes, although that wouldn't be the only possible implementation.

   b. Since we can find an element in a sorted array very quickly (see Chapter 10 for binary search), it would make sense to make *SortedList* a derived class of the private base class TList<T>, where we would choose the array implementation of TList<T>.

5.
```
template<class T> ostream& operator<<
                              (ostream& os, TList<T> lst)
{    for (Node<T>* p = lst.first; p; p = p->next)
          os << p->value << '\t';
     return os;
}
```

We save a few statements by folding much of the routine into the loop header; otherwise there's very little change, except perhaps that we've made the routine a bit harder to understand. The assignment operator would be defined in much the same way.

7. The function name *Delete* would be too similar to the predefined C++ operator delete. It would be too easy to confuse the two, making the class too difficult to understand and use.

9. Making room for the new element by shifting the elements up from left to right would result in every element from *current* + 1 to the end having the same value—and we'd lose all of the tail of the list. A similar problem would happen with *Remove* if we shifted the elements from right to left.

11. Unfortunately, no. The problem would be that redefining *Insert* to insert an element after the current position, although easier to implement, would then make it inpossible to insert an element at the head of a list.

13. Because of the symmetric role of the two arguments to +, it makes most sense to declare our overload as a friend of the class TList<T>. In the linked list implementation, this overload could be declared this way:

```
template<class T> TList<T> operator+
                         (TList<T> left, TList<T> right)
{
     TList<T> r,s;                    // the return list
     if (left.size == 0)             // Left list is empty,
          r = right;                 // so return a copy of the right.
     else if (right.size == 0)
          r = left;
     else
     {    // Both lists are nonempty, so copy the lists and link
```

```
        // the end of the left copy to the start of the right.
        r = left;                           // Copy the left list.
        s = right;                          // Copy the right list.
        r.last->next = s.first;             // Hook them together
        r.last = s.last;                    // Point to the new last node.
        r.current = r.first;                // Set the current pointer.
        r.size = left.size + right.size;    // Fix the new size
    }
    return r;                               // Return the new list in any case.
}
```

Try doing this with the array implementation. It's a trifle more complicated, since we need to set the size of the returned array so that it's big enough to hold the result.

15.
```
template<class T> void TList<T>::Tail()
{   current = first;                    // Move current to the head.
    if (first)                          // If the list is nonempty,
        while (current->next)           // track our way to the end.
            current = current->next;
}
```

This changes the running time of *Tail* from $O(1)$ to $O(n)$, where n is the size of the list. If we eliminated *last* entirely, we would have to rewrite all the member functions except *Head* and the operator overloads << and —, although all of our rewrites could be done without changing the running times of the functions involved.

17. To find the size of a list, we would have to track our way through the list, counting as we went, until we came to the end (a NULL pointer in the linked list, and some sentinel value we would have to include in the array version). This would change the running time of *Length* in both implementations and would double the running times of *Insert* and *Remove* in the array version (though the big-O running time would stay $O(n)$). It would also change the running time of *Tail* in the array implementation from $O(1)$ to $O(n)$.

INDEX